The Language Teacher Toolkit

Second edition

Steve Smith and Gianfranco Conti

Independently Published

Edited by Elspeth Jones

Dedicated to

Dr Joel Smith, Dr Amy Howard and Catrina Jade Conti

Acknowledgements

We thank the many colleagues who have inspired or supported us over the years. Particular thanks to Professor Elspeth Jones for formatting and editing the text.

About the authors

Steve Smith taught French for over 30 years in British high schools, including 24 years as Head of Department at Ripon Grammar School in England. His Master's degree focused on second language acquisition and Stephen Krashen's Monitor Theory. He publishes classroom resources for his website *frenchteacher.net*, writes a blog on language teaching, Language Teacher Toolkit, and has a YouTube channel with professional development screencasts. He curates the website informedlanguageteacher.com with links to readings and videos about language learning and teaching. Steve is an occasional professional development provider, was PGCE Lead Subject Tutor at the University of Buckingham for several years and has written and presented for the AQA examination board. His solo publications are *Becoming an Outstanding Languages Teacher* (2nd Edition) (2023) and *50 Lesson Plans for French Teachers* (2020).

Dr Gianfranco Conti taught languages for over 20 years in schools in England and Malaysia, most recently at Garden International School, Kuala Lumpur. He is the founder of the interactive website The Language Gym and the co-author of numerous workbooks based on his EPI (Extensive Processing Instruction) approach to language teaching. He is the author of the best-selling Sentence Builders book series. He is a visiting fellow at Reading University. Gianfranco holds a Master's degree in applied linguistics and a PhD in metacognitive strategies as applied to second language writing. He won the TES Resource Author of the Year Award in 2015. He writes a blog on instructed second language acquisition and is a popular professional development presenter in the UK, Australia and elsewhere, focusing on topics including EPI and curriculum planning.

By the same authors

Memory: What Every Language Teacher Should Know (Smith & Conti, 2021)
Breaking the Sound Barrier: Teaching Language Learners How to Listen (Conti & Smith, 2019)
The Language Teacher Toolkit (1st Edition) (Smith & Conti, 2016)

Steve	**Gianfranco**
frenchteacher.net	language-gym.com
frenchteachernet.blogspot.com	gianfrancoconti.com
@spsmith45	@gianfrancocont9
YouTube: Steve Smith Languages	YouTube: The Language Gym

Contents

LIST OF TABLES

LIST OF FIGURES

STEVE AND GIANFRANCO'S BOXES OF TRICKS

Introduction to the Second Edition

Language teaching is both an exciting and challenging endeavour. We have quite a responsibility helping learners develop not just their linguistic skill, but their attitudes to language learning, new cultures and ways of thinking. This book is written to help navigate the research in our field and to develop a wide range of practical classroom ideas and techniques. It is both for teachers who are learning the craft and for practising teachers who wish to improve their understanding and skills. In either case the book should help develop what has been called **reflective practice**, defined by one writer as the "mental activity that teachers do as they think in teaching situations" (Freeman, 2016 p. 207).

Many ways to teach languages have been advocated over the centuries. These include grammar-translation, so-called direct methods, the audiolingual method and the communicative movement, not to mention a whole host of other approaches, some based on 'natural' methods which tend to equate learning a new language with learning one's first language(s). Others place greater emphasis on formal learning, grammar explanation and the building of linguistic skill through repetitive practice. Given the range of possible approaches, it is easy to feel confused.

Questions which might be asked include:
- Are some methods better than others?
- What principles of learning should I apply to my lessons?
- What does a good lesson look like?
- How do I know I am doing things right?
- What can I realistically expect my students to achieve?
- How can my students make progress in so little time?
- How much target language should I use?
- How should I teach grammar? Should I teach it at all?
- How do I get my students to speak fluently and spontaneously?
- How do I create enjoyable and effective language lessons?

To start with, there is no consensus about what works best in every language classroom. As we shall see, there is no 'best method' (Prabhu, 1990) because there are so many variables involved in the process of language learning: the teacher, the setting, the students' background and aims, and the cultural context, to name just a few. There is the danger, however, of choosing to adopt an 'anything goes' approach. This would be unwise since we can identify, with the aid of research and experience, which specific strategies, procedures and curriculum design tend to work better than others. This book tries to throw some light on the craft of language teaching, partly by exploring the **research evidence**, but above all by providing **practical ideas** for the classroom. Each is clearly marked throughout the text with the following symbols.

Research

Practice

So, just like the first edition, this much revised book is for teachers, written by teachers. We make use of our knowledge of research and, between us, over fifty years of experience teaching languages to students aged 6-18 to help describe principles and practice. 'Scientific' research in this field is actually only several decades old but is growing all the time. It offers some very useful pointers but, as in all areas of education, it cannot tell us what works in every classroom, with every teacher and with every class. Language teaching is a craft, not a science.

The book does not advocate one method over others. On the one hand, the view is taken that language learning has much in common with all types of learning, such as learning to ride a bike or play the guitar; on the other, that it shares similarities with how humans learn their first language(s), through exposure and communication. We believe a teacher can build up students' skills and knowledge through presentation of language input (listening and reading), practice, explanation and what scholars call 'focus on form' (explaining and practising grammar). But it is also recognised that language acquisition happens subconsciously or *implicitly*, just as when a child picks up their first language(s). This reflects an assumption shared by most language teachers: we need to provide students with as much exposure to meaningful language as possible while ensuring they get the opportunity to think about how the language works and to do repeated practice in an ordered, structured way.

More than this, we recognise that good language lessons depend on some key generic teacher skills.

- Helping students to feel motivated and persistent.
- Teaching 'responsively' by using effective formative assessment techniques.
- Ensuring students value the subject.
- Empathising both emotionally and cognitively with students.
- Building effective relationships.
- Ensuring good classroom behaviour.

A wide range of areas are covered in this book, with many lesson ideas shared along the way. The book begins with an overview of **language teaching methods**. For the four interconnected skills of **listening, speaking, reading** and **writing** we examine what the research says, what activities might ensue from the research, **how these activities can be sequenced and managed effectively**, and **how we know students have learned** from them. We discuss **motivation**, how to **manage**

classroom speaking, the use of **pictures** and making the **best use of written texts**. Guidance is provided on **pair** and **group work, songs** and **drama, phonics, intercultural understanding** and **teaching students with varying needs**.

The chapters on teaching **grammar and vocabulary** offer numerous examples of practical classroom techniques. Examples are also included of **'zero-preparation tasks'**, given how pressed teachers are for time and how the photocopier and computer do not always work when needed. Ideas are shared on how to help students develop the toughest of skills, **spontaneous, fluent speech**. We also explore the use of **teacher questioning, target language** and **translation** as well as the **importance of subject knowledge** and how to improve it.

Many examples are in English on the assumption that readers will be teachers of various world languages. For the sake of convenience, and to recognise that the reader's and students' first language may not be English, we **use L1 for first language(s) and L2 for second (or additional) language(s)**. We have also done our best to choose terminology understandable to readers around the world.

To help write this new edition we have drawn on a rich variety of resources, some from the academic fields of **second language acquisition** and **cognitive psychology**, others from practical handbooks, websites and blogs, including our own. This includes the latest research as well as some of the best wisdom from the past.

Changes from the first edition

- The chapters on behaviour management, games and technology have been removed, as well as the final section with example lessons. This has enabled us to devote more space to recent research findings and to take account of new trends in language teaching. In particular, we wanted to give more attention to **lexicogrammar**, research from **cognitive science** and **intercultural understanding**.

- There is also much more guidance on the teaching of listening and fluency, both spoken fluency in the traditional sense, and the notion of **cognitive fluency**. We have added new chapters on **lesson** and **curriculum planning** with a focus on **communication**.

- Finally, reflecting our own evolving understanding, new **lesson ideas** have been added and extensive changes made to the original text, each chapter and the structure of the book.

1

Language teaching methods

Introduction

A leading scholar in the field of second language acquisition research, Jack Richards (1990), described language teaching methodology as "the activities, tasks and learning experiences used by the teacher within the (language) learning and teaching process". A methodology usually has a theoretical basis which should bring coherence and consistency to the choice of classroom teaching procedures.

Why learn about methods at all? Diane Larsen-Freeman and Marti Anderson (2011) believe there are five reasons why a study of methods is invaluable for teachers.

- Methods help bring a conscious awareness of what underlies our classroom practice; we become clearer about why we do what we do.
- Given that we may be hugely influenced by the way we were taught ourselves, by learning about where we stand methodologically, we can teach differently; we become aware of alternative tools of the trade.
- Learning about methods allows us to communicate professionally with others, to create a 'discourse community'.
- Interacting with others' conceptions of practice, helps to stop teaching become stale.
- A knowledge of methods helps expand our repertoire of techniques and thus furthers professional growth. It has been claimed that expert and experienced teachers have a larger and more diverse repertoire of best practices which enable them to cope with the idiosyncrasies of their students.

In light of this, a selective summary of some influential methods in language teaching are presented here. Scholars categorise methods in different ways, but this chapter keeps it basic and focuses on the mainstream approaches which have tended to dominate in high schools. This means approaches with tantalising names such as The Silent Way, Dogme or Desuggestopedia are not included, but further information is available elsewhere.

It should be stressed at the outset that few teachers apply one method to the exclusion of others and that most do not think too deeply, if at all, about how their own general approach fits within any theoretical framework. Research shows that the main influence on teachers' chosen methodology is the way they were taught themselves. Many effective teachers then instinctively pick out the best aspects of a range of methods, depending on their teaching context and how classes respond. This may be beneficial in addressing the needs of different groups of students.

So which methods have dominated over the decades? Which approach resembles your own ideal most closely? Are some methods better than others? The chapter considers the following:

- ✓ Grammar-Translation (GT)
- ✓ The Audiolingual Method
- ✓ Direct Method
- ✓ Task-Based Language Teaching (TBLT)
- ✓ Natural or 'comprehension' approaches
- ✓ Communicative Language Teaching (CLT)
- ✓ Natural or 'comprehension' approaches
- ✓ Lexicogrammatical approaches
- ✓ Is there a best method?
- ✓ 10 principles of language teaching

Grammar-Translation (GT)

An offspring of German scholarship, first known as the Prussian method in the USA, the main aims of this method, were to develop mental discipline and intellectual development through language study, and to produce students who could read literary texts. Grammar rules are studied in detail and used to translate from L1 to L2 and vice versa. Reading and writing are the goals, not communication (speaking and listening). Classes are usually teacher-led, students analyse the grammar, memorise vocabulary and verb forms, translate and do comprehension questions. Grammar is taught 'deductively', meaning that students are presented with a rule and then apply it, principally through comprehension and translation tasks. It is assumed that you can learn the language *synthetically*, i.e. by piecing together and building up its constituent parts into a whole. Language is seen as a body of knowledge to acquire. There is little interest in authentic texts or real-life language use here!

This method, common up to the 1960s, is still used by many teachers and by advanced students who need to learn a language for a specific purpose, such as studying literary texts. However, it is generally discredited as a way of learning a language. Only a minority of high-achieving students enjoy it or learn much from it, and even they usually fail to develop good spoken proficiency. In its favour is the way it develops careful readers and accurate users of the written language and the fact that it can be applied by teachers who have little oral and aural skill themselves. Indeed, the second point is a major reason why it persisted for so long.

Early scholars associated with this method include Johann Seidenstücker and Karl Plötz.

The Audiolingual Method

In 1942 the Army Specialized Training Programme (ASTP or 'Army method') was devised by the American military for rapidly acquiring languages for conversational use in the field. It was inspired by linguists such as Leonard Bloomfield who learned about languages by interviewing speakers of Native American and other languages. At that time conversation had not been a goal of language learning in the USA. ASTP lessons involved 15 hours of oral drilling with native speakers, together with 20-30 hours of private study. Students studied for 10 hours each day, six days a week. Results were often impressive, largely because of intensive immersion in the language. The result was that prominent linguists encouraged an oral approach to language learning. By the mid-1950s influenced by findings from behaviourist psychology, the American method of audiolingualism was established. By the mid-1960s it was losing momentum.

In this method, learning is viewed as a process of habit formation through stimulus and response. Language habits are 'stamped in' by repeated repetition and oral drilling ('pattern practice') with little reference to L1. Dialogues are the main source of text with the teacher or an audio source providing the models. Every effort is made to avoid L1 interfering with L2. The input language is tightly controlled and selected, with grammar taking precedence over vocabulary and meaning. Errors must be avoided so they do not persist and become 'fossilised'. The aim of the method is ultimately to allow students to build their grammatical system, allowing them to communicate, so speaking and listening take priority. From the late 1960s the audiovisual approach, combining habit forming with images, featured in many school classrooms. The invention of the reel-to-reel tape recorder added impetus to the method.

The approach is usually criticised for neglecting vocabulary, meaningful communication and grammatical analysis, while ignoring the creative nature of language learning and use. However, the importance of repetition and focus on good pronunciation may be its strongest legacies. Psychologists are beginning to understand what 'stamping in' might mean in terms of how the brain functions.

Scholars associated with this method include Charles Fries and Charles Hockett who wrote that the patterns to be learned required "drill, drill, and more drill, and only enough vocabulary to make such drills possible" (cited in Richards and Rodgers, 2014).

Direct Method

Direct Method developed late in the 19th century, as result of the Reform Movement which was highly critical of traditional grammar-translation. In its early years it was sometimes called the Natural Method or Gouin Method, after François Gouin. At this time there was a growing interest in the new science of phonetics, which emphasised the perception and production of the spoken word.

In the Direct Method listening and speech take precedence over reading and writing, notably during the early stages of learning. In the purest form of Direct Method, classes are entirely conducted in L2, with the teacher taking the lead and making great use of repetition and question-answer sequences. Classroom objects, pictures and gesture are used as aids to meaning. Explanation and translation are avoided, as is comparison with L1. Grammar is taught inductively, with students picking up the rules from examples they hear. The main aim ultimately is communication, but the language is still seen as something to be gradually built up through exposure and practice. The teacher generally provides the input, with relatively little time given to pair or group work.

The syllabus is often based on topics and situations, as well as a grammatical sequence – skills are built up slowly, with selection of language by assumed difficulty playing an important role. Vocabulary choice is largely dictated by frequency counts. Accuracy is encouraged and grammar may be explained, even in L1. Many teachers combine aspects of the Direct Method with elements of audiolingualism, communicative approaches and even grammar-translation. One particular strand of Direct Method, influential in Britain in the second half of the twentieth century, was the **Oral Approach**, sometimes called the Oral-Situational Approach, wryly known by some as 'death by question and answer'.

In many countries some form of adapted Direct Method still dominates classrooms. In its favour is the central importance accorded to the use of L2. One criticism is that L2 may be used in too doctrinaire a fashion. A second is whether the approach aligns with what research suggests about second language learning, namely that we do not acquire a new language based on the gradual building of skill with grammatical structures, one at a time.

Scholars associated with this approach include Gouin, Harold Palmer, Henry Sweet and Maximilian Berlitz (famous for the Berlitz language schools).

Communicative Language Teaching (CLT)

According to Richards and Rodgers (2014), the origins of CLT can be traced to changes to the British language teaching methods of the 1960s, when grammar-translation and versions of direct method teaching held sway. Becoming established as an antidote to grammar analysis and audiolingualism, the communicative approach is hard to define, but was essentially a move away from teaching structures, towards teaching communicative proficiency.

In its 'strong' form CLT claims that language is acquired just through communication; it is not just about using communicative activities to activate knowledge of the language that has been taught structurally at an earlier stage. The belief is that communicative confidence only develops if students are required to do activities which require real-life communication. Since many teachers have difficulty seeing the learning value of communicative activities, a so-called weak form of the approach has evolved where teachers include opportunities to do communicative tasks within a traditional grammar or topic-based curriculum.

Whenever possible, authentic language is used in classroom activities which resemble real-life situations. The social functions of language are stressed more than grammar and vocabulary (although the balance varies from teacher to teacher). As with direct methods, L2 is the means of communication. Great use is made of paired and group tasks, with a focus on information gaps (where one student needs to find information from another), role-plays, games and tasks to complete. The teacher becomes a facilitator as much as a provider of information. Students are given the freedom to 'negotiate meaning', as the jargon has it. There is emphasis on ideas and opinions, authentic resources and real-life needs. Errors are tolerated, even welcomed, since the stress is on communication, not accuracy.

CLT provides opportunities for students to focus not only on the language, but also on the learning process itself: an enhancement of their own personal experiences, viewed as an important contribution to classroom learning. The claim is that L2 is learned best when the students try to communicate, i.e. to say something that they really want or need to say. CLT still dominates many EFL (English as a Foreign Language) classes because EFL students may have a stronger focus on the practical, communicative purpose of language.

Scholars associated with this methodology include Henry Widdowson, Dell Hymes (who coined the term 'communicative competence', redefining what it meant to 'know' a language), and David Wilkins (who defined language using 'notions' and 'functions', rather than more traditional categories of grammar and vocabulary).

Task-Based Language Teaching (TBLT)

Task-Based Language Teaching can be viewed as an extension of CLT, with an extra emphasis on the 'real-life', goal-oriented nature of activities which are called 'tasks'. The origins of the method can be traced back to the 1970s. Real-life tasks can include visiting a doctor, conducting an interview, or calling customer service for help. Classroom tasks could include carrying out a survey, filling in a map of a town based on an aural description or planning a holiday with the help of online comments on destinations. You can see the clear overlap with CLT.

According to Rod Ellis (2003) a task:
1. involves a primary focus on meaning;
2. has some kind of 'gap'. N.S. Prabhu identified the three main types as information gap, reasoning gap, and opinion gap;
3. requires students to choose the linguistic resources needed to complete the task;
4. has a clearly defined, non-linguistic outcome.

N.S. Prabhu (1987) proposed that a communicative task should require a 'gap'. He identified the three main types as information gap, reasoning gap, and opinion gap.

Critics of the approach argue that it is not sufficiently structured, especially for novices in high schools working towards a defined assessment regime. To carry out 'tasks' often requires a level of knowledge and skill beginners do not possess. In response, proponents of TBLT argue that tasks can be designed with an emphasis on input language, with students not having to produce much language of their own.

Scholars associated with TBLT include N.S. Prabhu, Teresa Pica, David Nunan, Rod Ellis and Michael Long. Prabhu pioneered a task-based English programme in the 1980s, working for the British Council in Indian state primary schools.

Natural or 'comprehension' approaches

These come in various forms, but see L2 learning as the same, in principle, as child language acquisition. Such 'comprehensible input' (CI) approaches have much in common with direct methods and communicative approaches, but with a greater emphasis on listening and reading, since the belief is that languages are picked up by understanding messages, no more. Storytelling plays a strong role, as does oral communication, but the latter is given time to develop from the receptive to the productive, as with infants.

It was in 1977 that Californian Spanish teacher Tracy Terrell outlined his proposal for this philosophy of language teaching, which, while not really new, did seem revolutionary at the time. In reality, it was a modern version of the Direct Method, with differences. Terrell joined forces with researcher Stephen Krashen to share their approach (Krashen and Terrell, 1983).

There is less focus on grammatical form than with other methods, but it would be wrong to assume that there is no selection of language material by difficulty. Selection is, however, loosely based on the students' current level, focused on meaning, whereas in earlier direct methods and audiolingual methods selection of language is 'finely tuned' and based to a greater degree on grammatical structures.

Translation is often accepted in so far as it acts as an aid to meaning. Content and meaning take precedence over language form. In this respect natural approaches sit comfortably with content-based instruction. Proponents of natural ('comprehensible input') approaches, such as those who use the Teaching Proficiency through Reading and Storytelling (TPRS) approach, argue that they work well for students of all abilities, that they make languages seem easier and that all students can pick up a language with the right input, whereas, they claim, grammatical, analytical approaches favour the highest achievers, or else just fail.

Natural, 'comprehension' approaches have the great merit of supplying students with interesting L2 input but are criticised for neglecting grammatical explanation and structured grammar practice. Within natural approaches, it is sometimes argued that knowing the rules of grammar can help students monitor their accuracy as they speak and write.

Scholars often associated with natural methods and comprehensible input include Stephen Krashen and Bill VanPatten.

Lexicogrammatical approaches

We usually think of a language as having a grammar and a vocabulary, and that we produce sentences by putting words from the vocabulary into appropriate grammatical structures. While this might explain how we can be creative with language, it does not easily explain fluency. In recent years there has been a growing dissatisfaction with the idea that to learn a language we need to combine knowledge of words with grammatical rules. Some researchers argue that the distinction between vocabulary and grammar is artificial and that students will learn a language most effectively when there is a large emphasis on what are called collocations – common combinations of words which students can hear, read and use to create connected utterances. These are often called formulaic language or chunks.

One lexicogrammatical method which has become popular in the last few years is called Extensive Processing Instruction (EPI). Devised by Gianfranco Conti, and used by many teachers, notably in the UK and Australia, this way of teaching draws on research from both second language acquisition and cognitive science. Like natural methods, it assumes that students learn language largely unconsciously ('implicitly'), through intensive repeated exposure to and use of language chunks. The focus on chunking makes more efficient use of short-term memory and facilitates the creation of utterances through a 'chunk and chain' process.

Grammatical rules are explained during the teaching cycle so that students should develop both explicit and implicit knowledge. Listening and speaking are prioritised. Translation of language is welcomed, e.g. through the use of 'sentence builders' – frames resembling traditional substitution tables, and which contain the key language to be learned.

Lessons typically involve working with sentence builders and short written and aural texts containing multiple repetitions of chunks. In addition, gamified activities of many types involve a focus on phonology, phonics (sound-spelling correspondences), lexical retrieval, dictation and fluency building.

Critics of lexicogrammatical approaches in general sometimes argue that there is too much emphasis on learning formulaic language and that students may not acquire the ability to create novel utterances. As one scholar, Scott Thornbury (2010) famously put it, the approach may be 'all chunks, no pineapple'. In reality, this criticism may not apply to all versions of lexicogrammatical teaching.

Scholars associated with the burgeoning area of lexicogrammar include Frank Boers, Michael Lewis, Norbert Schmitt and Michael Hoey.

We explore the lexicogrammatical approach further in Chapter 12. If you wish to know more about different methodologies, we recommend the book *Approaches and Methods in Language Teaching* (Richards and Rogers, 2014).

Is there a best method?

To return to this question, few teachers stick religiously to one method and, as can be seen, those described above have some things in common. Long and Doughty (2011) note that teachers do many of the same sorts of activities in language classrooms. Even so, some teachers passionately defend their chosen method, claiming it works best for them. Our advice would be to treat claims of unique efficacy with a little scepticism. Just like the golfer who would not play with just one club in their bag, we need to make best use of all the tools at our disposal.

Many teachers would agree with an idea that has been called **principled eclecticism** - picking and choosing aspects from the various methods described above. By doing this their own principled, hybrid method can be created and adapted to classes depending on a range of factors, a key one being the nature of the assessment regime. But principled eclecticism has to be principled. It is not a random pick 'n mix. As Larsen-Freeman and Anderson put it, the teacher "should be able to give a particular reason for why they do what they do" (2011 p. 229).

The same authors go on to say that another reason for not supporting one method over others is that research into the effectiveness of methods is so fraught with difficulty. If you compare two methods over time with the same teacher, they may not invest the same enthusiasm into each one, so any claim to scientific validity goes up in smoke. (Not to mention all the other variables involved in comparative studies: students, timing of lessons, school culture and so on.) So beware the teacher who claims that research uniquely supports their preferred method.

Keep in mind also that language teaching is subject to the bandwagon effect, not surprising given our thirst to find easy solutions when our efforts meet with mixed success. Several researchers have written about a 'post-method condition' (Kumaravadivelu, 1994) and recommend what has been called 'context-sensitive pedagogy' (Sun, 2021). We do not need some one-size-fits-all solution, but rather pedagogical practices which relate to local contexts, needs and objectives. In high schools one of these is simply the nature of high-stakes assessment.

The approach a teacher adopts is also heavily dependent on the learning context. Working with youngsters in a high school is not the same as working with adults in a work setting or immigrants learning a language in their new country. As authors, because of our own teaching backgrounds and experience, the ideas presented are of most relevance to high school settings, but general principles are the same.

Even if there is no best method, studying them, as we have seen, gives a better idea of why we do what we do and can widen our repertoire of techniques. The process is also interesting in itself! N.S. Prabhu (1992), who argues against the idea of a panacea method, writes:

> *...if the teacher engages in classroom activity with a sense of intellectual excitement, there is at least a fair probability that learners will begin to participate in the excitement and to perceive classroom lessons mainly as learning events - as experiences of growth for themselves.* (Prabhu, 1992 p. 239)

A particular conundrum for teachers in training, and teacher educators, is whether to prepare thoroughly for one particular method, or to use a set of principles on which to build a methodology. Second or additional language learning is a broad and complex area. There is a lot to take in. On balance, we believe that pre-service teachers should have a sound knowledge of the principles of instructed language acquisition, alongside experience with a range of methods and procedures. In this way they can start to become critically reflective practitioners (Christie and Conlon, 2016).

So while a single overall method for all settings cannot be recommended, the growing body of research now available points to certain provisional, broad principles which can act as a guide. To prepare for the rest of the book our own methodological principles are listed here. These are explored in more detail in the book with explanations of how they can be put into practice.

10 principles of language teaching

1. **Comprehensible input.** Comprehension of meaningful language is the foundation of language acquisition. When listening and reading input are understood by students, implicit (unconscious) learning mechanisms come into play and the input contributes to long-term acquisition. Language is comprehensible when students already know the words and grammar, and can work out the meaning in other ways, e.g. by inferring meaning, through images, gesture or translation.

2. **Communication**. Comprehension alone is not enough. Promote interaction with input in a structured and less controlled fashion, led by the teacher and via communication between students. Through interaction with the input and opportunities to produce output language (speech and witing), students can further develop their proficiency and communicative skill.

3. **Multi-mode teaching**. Use an integrated combination of the four skills of listening, speaking, reading and writing, but with a greater emphasis on listening and speaking. By exploiting all the skills, students gain a deeper understanding of vocabulary, grammar and phonology. Activities in each skill reinforce each other.

4. **Receptive to productive**. Proceed from modelling receptive listening and reading input, via controlled practice towards spontaneous production. Allow students to hear and see plenty of examples of input language before they are asked to produce language themselves. Tightly controlled output activities should usually precede free tasks requiring unrehearsed, spontaneous language. Fluency is developed in all the skills along the way.

5. **Meaning and form**. Acquisition involves associating meanings with linguistic forms (words, sounds, grammar). The main focus should be on meaningful communication, but time needs to be spent on making students aware of the formal properties of the language (grammar, morphology, phonics), especially aspects they may not naturally notice.

6. **Grammar**. Select the grammar students encounter and practise, while keeping in mind what is learnable and whether they are developmentally ready to acquire it. Anticipate which areas

are most likely to cause confusion. This means being selective about what is taught. It may not mean basing a curriculum on a step-by-step grammatical sequence, but focusing on the grammar which is most useful for students' communicative goals.

7. **Vocabulary**. Select vocabulary based on frequency and relevance to students' needs, including the requirements of the assessment regime. Focus both on words and multi-word units. Remember that 'knowing a word' is complex and involves sounds, spellings, meanings, the different grammatical forms of words and how words function with other words.

8. **Implicit and explicit learning**. Prioritise implicit (unconscious) learning and communication, supported by explicit teaching of vocabulary, grammar and phonics. Implicit learning is 'unconscious' and is more likely to occur when meaningful language is recycled and memorable. Explicit learning occurs when students are consciously thinking about the form of the language. It can support implicit learning.

9. **Self-efficacy**. Place a strong emphasis on developing students' self-efficacy or feeling of competence – their sense that they can be successful at learning the language. When they can understand language at every stage and have opportunities to enjoy using it, they are more likely to feel confident and thus be more highly motivated.

10. **Intercultural understanding**. One of the unique aspects of a languages curriculum is the opportunity it affords for students to better understand other cultures and their own. Incorporating strong elements of intercultural understanding is both valuable in its own right and motivational. A language teacher has a duty to foster positive attitudes to difference and diversity.

2

Listening: it all starts here

Introduction

It is not by chance that we begin with listening, as it is fundamental to language acquisition. It provides the input needed to acquire both our first and additional language(s). Supplying aural input students understand, enables nature to take its course and language acquisition to happen. There is more to it than that, of course! But by doing regular listening-focused activities in nearly every lesson, the long-term goal of helping students learn a language to whatever level they aspire can be achieved.

But how do we actually 'teach listening'? In recent years, perspectives from second language acquisition and cognitive science research have provided new frameworks for analysing listening and improving how we teach it.

This chapter considers:

Research evidence
- ✓ Bottom-up and top-down processing
- ✓ A process approach
- ✓ Phonology and phonics
- ✓ Paying attention
- ✓ Metacognitive strategies

Classroom practice
- ✓ Listening-as-Modelling
- ✓ Dictation tasks
- ✓ Using metacognitive strategies
- ✓ Sources of listening
- ✓ Narrow listening
- ✓ Interpersonal listening
- ✓ Independent listening
- ✓ Immersion
- ✓ Task-based listening
- ✓ Working with listening texts
- ✓ Assessing listening

Research evidence

Bottom-up and top-down processing

Think of a student listening to a text about the environment. To understand the message, they need to use their knowledge of the linguistic system together with their background knowledge of the topic. They first have to decode the linguistic features, recognising words, word boundaries, intonation, grammar and so on. Then they make greater sense of the message by applying what they know about the environment.

Decoding the linguistic content is called **bottom-up processing**. L1 speakers do this automatically, but L2 students must rely on slower, controlled processing of the language they hear. Using background knowledge is called **top-down processing**. The more background knowledge you already have, the easier it is to compensate for any decoding deficiencies when working out meaning. Sometimes students are so focused on trying to decipher the code that they forget to apply their general knowledge.

Beginners come with some decoding knowledge, based on their L1 experience, but have a lot to learn about the sounds, vocabulary and grammar of the new language. Younger beginners also have less background knowledge The key priority, however, is to teach students how to decode the message from the language. It is a challenging task! Processing listening input depends on quick reactions under time pressure. Research has shown that the brain has a two-second window to process all types of input. If one piece of input is not processed in these two seconds, it interferes with the next, and so on. This is the main reason why students often say they find listening tests hard and stressful. The best listeners are able to combine bottom-up and top-down processing, along with non-linguistic metacognitive strategies (see below) which direct their attention, monitor their performance and problem-solve.

A process approach

With decoding a priority, in our book *Breaking the Sound Barrier: Teaching Language Learners How to Listen* (Conti and Smith, 2019) we examine in great detail the principles of what is called a **process approach** and describe a large number of classroom activities which support it. One of the starting points is the work of researcher John Field in his book *Listening in the Language Classroom* (Field, 2009). His main idea is that to teach listening we need to do a lot more than just comprehension exercises and tests. He contrasts this sort of **product approach** with the process approach. In Conti and Smith (2019) we call it **Listening-as-Modelling** (LAM) (as opposed to Listening-as-Testing).

To teach listening, Field proposes that we break down the processes, or **micro-skills**, involved in listening, then target specific classroom activities to develop them. The LAM approach is partly rooted in the **skill theory** model of classroom L2 acquisition, the key premise of which is that any language skill, including listening, can be acquired in much the same way as any other set of human skills (e.g. playing football or driving a car). The task is broken down into sub-skills, then each is practised in the same way, for example, that a footballer practises passing, dribbling and heading.

Within skill theory the goal of listening instruction is the **automatisation** of the micro-skills our brain needs to listen, in real time, in order to extract meaning from any utterance we hear. Table 2.1 shows Field's bottom-up processes and micro- skills.

Table 2.1 Bottom-up processing skills (adapted from Field, 2009)

Process level	Processes involved
Phoneme	• Identifying consonants and vowels • Adjusting to speakers' voices
Syllable	• Recognising syllable structure • Matching weak syllables and function words
Word	• Working out where words begin and end in connected speech (segmenting) • Matching sequences of sounds to words • Identifying words which are not in their standard forms • Dealing with unknown words
Syntax	• Recognising where clauses and phrases end • Anticipating syntactic patterns • Checking hypotheses
Intonation group	• Making use of sentence stress • Recognising chunks of language • Using intonation to support syntax • Reviewing the decoding process

As students become more proficient at decoding, they can extract meaning by using their top-down knowledge. Table 2.2 shows how Field summarises top-down processes.

Classroom activities can be designed which develop each of the micro-processes. For example, to develop bottom-up skills we can produce tasks with the focus on phonemes and syllables (phonological awareness and phonics), lexical retrieval, syntax and intonation. For top-down skills, particularly with more proficient learners, we can target these processes.

Table 2.2 Top-down processing skills (adapted from Field, 2009)

Process	Examples of micro-skills
Context: using knowledge sources	• Drawing on world knowledge, topic knowledge, cultural knowledge
Deriving meaning	• Storing the literal meaning of an utterance • Accepting an approximate meaning • Checking understanding
Adding to the meaning	• Making inferences • Dealing with pronouns • Dealing with ambiguity
Selecting information	• Selecting what is relevant or important • Recognising redundant information
Integrating information	• Carrying forward what has been said so far • Connecting ideas • Self-monitoring for consistent interpretation of the message
Recognising the overall argument structure	• Noticing connecting words used by the speaker (e.g. *on the other hand*)

Phonology and phonics

Phonology refers to the sound system of a language – its sounds (phonemes) and prosodic features (intonation, pitch, stress). Phonics refers to the relationship between sounds and spelling (with alphabetic languages). As far as phonics is concerned, some languages have a very 'transparent' sound-spelling relationship, e.g. Spanish and German. In other words, we can work out the sound of words easily from the spelling. What you see is what you get. Other languages, such as English and French are described as 'opaque', meaning it is not always clear how sound relates to spelling.

Research (Erler, 2003) and experience shows that many student learners of French in particular find it hard to read aloud words and phrases, even after a few years of learning. They are unable to decode and sound out words when reading without explicit help from the teacher. This is also a handicap when listening, since students cannot visualise vocabulary they hear. Furthermore, when they cannot read aloud accurately it affects their feelings of competence as language learners (Erler and Macaro, 2011).

Robert Woore (2022) cites emerging research which suggests that phonics knowledge may impact positively on various other aspects of L2 learning, such as spelling, vocabulary learning and oral communication. But in the same paper Woore acknowledges that, to date, there is little evidence that focusing explicitly on phonics improves overall proficiency outcomes. His conclusion is:

There are… good reasons to suppose that mastery of the L2 orthographic code is a foundation skill which facilitates many other aspects of classroom-based L2 learning. Further, the evidence suggests that many students will not achieve such mastery simply through exposure to the language, even after several years of study – at least, not in French (Woore, 2022).

Paying attention

For students to become good listeners, we must help them pay attention. Cognitive psychologists say there are three key aspects of attention to keep in mind:

- It is limited, because our short-term memory (also known as working memory) is limited. Think of attention like a bottleneck – only so much can get through.
- It is selective. We usually fail to learn what we do not pay attention to.
- It is biased towards novelty – we instinctively pay attention to what is new or unexpected.

Listening is particularly demanding with regard to attention. Unlike with reading, we do not have the opportunity to go back and recap what we heard. The so-called phonological loop (Baddeley and Hitch, 1974) is divided into a phonological store (an 'inner voice' which holds information in a speech-based form) and an articulatory process (like an 'inner voice' which allows us to repeat verbal information in a loop).

1. **Phonological Store:** processes speech perception and stores spoken words we hear for 1-2 seconds.
2. **Articulatory control process**: handles speech production, and rehearses and stores verbal information from the phonological store.

Thus, to maintain what we hear in working memory we need to use **rehearsal**, i.e. saying things out loud or in our heads to keep them alive. Think of repeating a phone number to help remember it. If students rehearse language in their heads or out loud repeatedly, there is more chance of it being retained for future use. Some ideas for generating rehearsal appear later in the chapter.

Metacognitive strategies

Researchers have suggested that to improve listening skills, students need to be taught how to do it. This is not just about the process approach described earlier, but also involves helping them develop strategies for dealing with listening input. It is about what Rost (2002) calls 'conscious plans to manage incoming speech'. Metacognition is often described as 'thinking about thinking' or 'thinking about learning'. According to Goh (2008), "Metacognitive learning activities should aim at deepening learners' understanding of themselves as L2 listeners and the demands and process of L2 listening, as well as teaching learners how to manage their comprehension and learning" (p.192). Students who have appropriate knowledge about listening and what a task requires can plan, monitor and evaluate what they do, compared with those who approach listening in a random manner.

Specific metacognitive strategies include:

- Discussing problems when listening with the teacher or a partner.
- Using the context of the listening text to help with comprehension, e.g. who is talking? What would they be expected to say?
- Using background knowledge, e.g. what is known about this topic already.
- Using knowledge of L1 to help, e.g. cognates.
- Anticipating what language will be used for the topic at hand.
- Using the questions to help work out what will be said.
- Using the meanings of known vocabulary to figure out the meaning of the text as a whole.

While we should not overestimate the value of metacognitive strategies, some studies have suggested the following (Goh, 2008).

- They have a positive effect on listening performance.
- They help students feel less anxious and more confident about doing listening tasks.
- They may be most useful with the weakest listeners.

Graham (2017) cites other studies which show benefits from teaching metacognitive strategies and awareness. We suggest some practical strategies later in the chapter.

Classroom practice

Listening-as-Modelling

A lot of classroom time needs to be devoted to listening in general (through the types of interactions described in Chapters 3 and 4) as well as teaching students *how* to listen. This implies spending less time on *testing* and producing right or wrong answers, and more time helping students interpret the stream of sound and developing strategies for successful listening. This helps give them confidence and takes the fear factor out of listening.

Students who struggle with listening often say they are just hearing a meaningless stream of sound, with just the occasional word or phrase popping out. So a key aim is to help them develop the ability to decode the message, in particular to break it down into words and multi-word units (chunks). Below are examples of classroom tasks which operate at the different processing levels Field (2009) described.

Phonemes and sound-spelling correspondences (phonics)

- **Spot the foreign sounds**: provide students with a list of words or a sentence. As they hear you or a recording, they highlight any sound that does not exist in L1, by underlining/circling the relevant part of the word. This activity is very useful for enhancing awareness of how the L2 written and sound systems relate to each other.

  e.g. (French) *sœur ; père; famille; grands-parents; moins.*

- **Spot the silent letters**: give students a list of sentences like the one below and read them aloud. The task is to highlight the letters that have not been pronounced by the teacher because they are silent in the L2.

  e.g. (French) *Manon et Jacques sont employés à Paris*

- **Minimal pairs**: pronounce two words containing very similar sounds, or which students may mistake for homophones, and they need to spot the correct spelling.

  e.g. (French) *moi / moins; bon / bonne; achète / acheté.*

- **Spot the mistake**: provide students with a series of words. Pronounce all the words correctly but one. They spot the mistake in each word series.

Syllables

Remember that syllables are basic building blocks of language. They fall between phonemes and morphemes or words in language structure.

- **Broken words**: give students a list of words with missing letter clusters. The missing parts may be provided separately.) The words chosen could belong to the same semantic field. You could even dictate the words.

  French: *man___ ; ch___ ; ___mpignon; b___re; v___*
  Options: *oux cha oi in ger eu ie eux.*

  German: *Mäd____, Möglich_____, geh___, ___gangen, Fussballspiel_;*
  Options: *en chen keit s ge schaft er*

- **Syllables bingo**: give students a list of 10 syllables and ask them to copy six of them in random order, e.g. into a grid with two rows and six cells in total. Play bingo, calling out words which contain the syllables. The first to get three in a row wins the first round. The first to get two rows wins the second round. Look at the example below for Spanish with six syllables and a set of names to read aloud.

Syllables	*ge*	*ja*	*jo*
	go	*gu*	*ga*
Names	Juan, Gustavo, Jaime, Gertrude, José, Gabriela, Gulta, Corina, Gonzalo, Jorrin		

Words

- **Listen and re-arrange:** (for complete beginners). Provide a series of four or five words or short sentences. Read the words in a different order to the one given to the students, who rearrange the words accordingly.

  e.g. (French)   Students' series: *chambre, lit, armoire, tapis, mur;*

  Teachers' series: *mur, armoire, chambre, tapis, lit.*

- **Gapped sentences with multiple choice**: a classic word recognition task. Read out sentences and students fill gaps selecting the correct word from a choice of three or four provided alongside. Using tongue twisters and songs for this kind of activity can make it more fun.

- **Listening slalom**: Give students a grid like the one in Table 2.3. As you read aloud a series of L2 sentences or short paragraphs, they select an item from each column. The columns can contain distractors which will never be heard. Students use the coordinates or draw a line between each word or chunk to record what they hear. This is suitable for near-beginners, but can be made much more challenging if they have to transcribe what they hear.

Table 2.3 Listening slalom game for lexical retrieval

	1	2	3	4
a	I go	I play	I never do	I never play
b	tennis	to the beach	football	pilates
c	rarely	occasionally	quite often	every week
d	because	even though	because it is	but
e	very hard	relaxing	it is boring	it's fun
f	I often play	I often go	I play cards	I never swim
g	healthy	exhausting	it's tiring	and fun
h	I often	I never	play netball	as it's fun
i	and fun	and tiring	and competitive	and boring

Syntax

The process of breaking down the parts of a sentence to understand it is called **parsing.**

- **Partial dictation (for parsing).** These can be used to focus students on morphology and syntax by omitting from the gapped text a key part of the target structure. For instance, imagine teaching the perfect tense of French verbs; you could gap all the auxiliaries to draw attention to these forms. Another example involves word endings in highly inflected languages, which could be gapped to draw attention to the gender and number of nouns/adjectives or to verb tenses and/or conjugations.

- **Parsing grids.** These can be used in combination with partial dictations, except they focus more explicitly on grammatical terminology. Below is a French example where students complete the boxes on listening to sentences 1 to 3 read aloud (see Table 2.4). Field (2009) points out that this task can be used with high-frequency groups of words. In this case, you would stop during one such group and students guess the word that follows.

Table 2.4 A parsing grid

	Subject	Relative pronoun	Verb	Proper noun	Verb	Intensifier	Adjective
1	*Mon frère*		*s'appelle*	*Marc*		*très*	*fainéant*
2		*qui*		*Louise*	*est*		*radine*
3	*Mes parents*			*Julien et Sandrine*		*assez*	

Intonation

Track the pitch. This makes students aware that stress and pitch can mark the ends of meaningful chunks or whole sentences, which helps to segment the message.

1. Read aloud short paragraphs as students follow a transcript. Use rise and fall of pitch to indicate the ends of word groups and sentences.
2. Students mark with upward or downward-facing arrows what they hear your voice doing.
3. Show them your version with arrows on the board, modelling it once more.
4. Students read the same paragraph aloud in pairs, evaluating each other's performance.

Dictation tasks

The following tasks (adapted from Wilson, 2008) will help teach students how to decode carefully and improve their phonics skills.

- **Grading dictation**
1. Dictate some personalised sentences of the type *I get up at 6 o'clock.*
2. Students transcribe the sentence, adding an adverb of frequency to evaluate the statement, e.g. *never, occasionally, sometimes, often* and *always.*
3. Display the sentences and ask students how they graded the statements.
- **False facts dictation**
1. Dictate some sentences, each one containing a false fact. The sentences could relate to general knowledge, or something recently studied in class.
2. Students transcribe and try to underline where they think the error is.
3. Display the sentences and ask students what the factual problem was in each case.

- **Dictogloss.** This widely used activity is a kind of supported dictation which works as follows. The teacher reads a short text several times and students try to produce their own version as close to the original as possible. This can be done individually or in pairs or small groups.

- **Running dictation.** Short paragraphs of L2 text are posted around the walls of the classroom in roughly six locations (to avoid overcrowding). Students work in pairs. One partner rushes to a location, memorises as much text as they can, returns to their partner, the scribe, who writes down what the fetcher has remembered. When the pair think they have finished the whole text they can bring it to the teacher who checks the work for accuracy. The pairs can swap roles at some point of the teacher's choosing.

- **Delayed dictation.** This is a zero-preparation activity which develops important processing micro-skills: holding chunks of language in short-term memory, along with decoding and transcription skills.
  1. Say a sentence students are familiar with, or that contains at least 95% comprehensible input, and tell them to 'hold it inside their heads'.
  2. As they do this, make funny noises or utter random L2 words to distract them for a few seconds.
  3. Finally ask them to write the sentence on mini-whiteboards and show their answers.

Delayed dictation and running dictation are especially good for generating mental rehearsal of language – remember that rehearsing in working memory is more likely to build long-term memory. Other strategies to encourage mental rehearsal are:
- **Wait-time**: leaving a few seconds after a question before eliciting responses.
- **Delayed choral repetition**: leaving a few seconds, then asking the class to repeat on an agreed signal.
- **Delayed copying**: showing a piece of text, giving the class a chance to study and memorise it, then removing the text for a few seconds and asking them to write it down.

Using metacognitive strategies

We have seen that metacognition is about reflecting on and monitoring the listening process. The Listening-as-Modelling (process) approach aims to develop students' self-monitoring skills, namely their ability to:

- identify their general strengths and weaknesses in specific areas of general listening competence, e.g. ability to concentrate at length, skill at recognising words in the sound stream, watching the speaker;

- monitor and evaluate their performance in the above areas and in specific tasks, e.g. skill at transcribing words and phrases, ability to hear inflections;
- develop independent strategies to tackle any identified weaknesses, e.g. practising specific tasks such as transcription;
- make a long-term effort to work on identified weaknesses, e.g. keeping a listening diary, keeping a tally of how specific issues (e.g. anxiety levels; problems with a specific task-type) evolve over time;
- work independently, planning their practice to take advantage of their own learning preferences, e.g. using video or audio, choosing favourite subject matter.

To train students in metacognitive strategies, ideally there needs to be a planned programme consisting of several phases.

1. A **modelling** phase where a strategy is demonstrated. The 'thinking aloud' method works well in this respect. For example, *I'm going to show you how we use our knowledge of L1 to help work out the meaning of a difficult word.*
2. A **scaffolding** phase where the strategy is practised with reminders from the teacher. *Let's listen to this. Try out your strategy and I'll help you along.*
3. An **autonomous** phase where reminders are withdrawn. *Okay, try on your own now.*
4. An **evaluation** phase during which the success of the strategy is assessed. *How did you find that? Do you think that strategy helped you? Could you use it in the future?*

Given the limited time we have available with classes, metacognitive training is best done in small doses as part of other communicative language work to encourage self-monitoring. Here are three simple examples:

- Help students spot intonation patterns by showing a text, reading aloud and using choral repetition to demonstrate how pitch and stress affect meaning.
- Demonstrate how certain key words and phrases give strong clues to meaning, e.g. *but, however, on the other hand.*
- In French, help students spot where words start and end, or liaise, by reading aloud sentences and getting them to do the same. Remind them to be aware of this when doing listening tests.

Sources of listening

As teachers, we are the number one source of input with the unique ability to fine-tune the language students need by instantly adapting to their reactions, slowing down the pace, repeating, separating words and using intonation to support the listening. We can check understanding simply by asking students to do a 'thumbs up' or using a system of coloured cards to show if they are following - green equals yes, red for no. So when conducting teacher-led speaking, e.g. with questions and answers, keep in mind that the main value is in the listening input provided.

Other good sources are the textbook (if you have one) and its digital content, songs, carefully selected audio and video material from the internet and interactive websites. Films are very useful, but they should be chosen primarily for their linguistic accessibility (clarity and speed) rather than their content, unless the goal is primarily cultural. A subtitled film which ticks both boxes is ideal.

A native speaker language assistant can provide excellent additional support, although they may need some training in adjusting their speech to a suitable level, working perhaps in tandem with you in front of the class. The students will have experienced a limited range of language with you as the primary source, so it could be confusing if another speaker departs from that. Additionally, the assistant can record short passages on the topics being taught.

Two practical points: (1) when using an audio or video source, if possible, make sure the treble control is set to maximum and the bass to minimum. This will make speech clearer and (2) do whatever possible to make the classroom as acoustically favourable as it can be; a lot of hard surfaces and high ceilings will reduce clarity. Large examination halls are usually inappropriate for listening tests.

The length and complexity of listening sources will obviously increase with the level of language skill. There is some debate about the importance of listening sources being authentic, e.g. spoken at natural speed, with different accents, from sources designed for native speakers. (Widdowson (2003) uses the term authentic differently, referring to the "specific ways in which language is made communicatively appropriate to context" (p. 93).) Our view is that, in the early stages, authenticity in its first sense need not be a concern. Even with advanced level students, genuinely authentic texts (e.g. radio reports or TV programmes) are too hard to decipher without thorough preparation. Examinations and course books use studio recorded, slowed down versions of authentic material, usually in 'standard' accents and this makes sense. The sensible approach is to start with slow, easy language, giving students confidence. We can then gradually build the length and level of difficulty over the duration of the course.

Narrow listening

Stephen Krashen (1996) coined the phrase **narrow listening**, which means listening to a range of speakers talk about the same topic. This produces, in Krashen's terms, roughly-tuned input. For near-beginners and intermediates the same general idea has been adapted by Gianfranco, but by having students listen to a series of short extracts, each of which recycles very similar language. In this way they hear the same chunks and patterns recycled multiple times, the aim being to make them easier to recall and use fluently later. This kind of repetition is described in the research literature as **input flooding.**

As students listen to each short paragraph read at least twice, they complete a range of exercises such as true/false, matching (who said what?), sentence completion or error spotting. The same sort of exercise can be carried out with reading texts (**narrow reading**). Table 2.5 shows four texts on which various exercises can be designed, e.g. matching, true/false, translation, correcting false statements. Recycled chunks are shown in bold.

Table 2.5 Narrow listening

Miriam My name is Miriam. **I'm** 14 **years old. In my opinion I lead a healthy life.** I'm a **vegetarian**, I don't drink a lot of **alcohol** and I'm active. **I eat a lot of fruit and vegetables**, except bananas. I hate them! **I sleep** at least eight **hours a night. I play** sports at school, and **I am a member of a dance club. I do** modern dance with friends **twice a week. At weekends** I go walking and cycling with my parents **occasionally. I never drink alcohol**.	**Karim. My name is** Karim. **I'm** 15 **years old. I think I lead a healthy life** for someone my age. I am very athletic. For example, **at weekends I play** basketball, football and table tennis. **I am a member of** a basketball club in my neighbourhood. As for food, **I think I eat** pretty well. Not too many burgers and fries, but **I love** pizza. **Other than that, I eat** very little **fruit and vegetables**, except cabbage and cauliflower.
Victor. My name is Victor. **I'm** 14 **years old. I think I don't lead a very healthy life. I eat** too many burgers, fries and sweet things. **I do a little sport** at school, but **other than that I do** exercise **occasionally**. I stay in my room and **I play** video games. **I only sleep** five **hours a night**. My parents say I have to go out to exercise, but I'm too lazy. But I don't smoke and **I never drink alcohol**.	**Susanna. I am Susanna. I'm** 12 **years old. In my opinion, I lead a healthy life** because **I eat a lot of fruit and vegetables,** I exercise and **I sleep** well every night. My favourite activity is dancing. **I am a member of** a dance club. I go **twice a week** with my friends. That's great. **I do** ballet. **Other than that,** I don't eat a lot of meat, but I'm not a **vegetarian. I love** fish, rice and pasta. My parents let me taste wine **occasionally**.

Interpersonal listening

Sometimes called two-way listening, this is where students listen as part of dialogues with the teacher or other students. Much of the listening input they receive is delivered in this way.

Storytelling from a picture sequence

This example of an interpersonal listening task is from Smith (2023). A simple set of pictures (see Figure 2.1) can be sources of a great deal of interpersonal listening and storytelling. A typical teaching sequence could go as follows:

1. Read aloud the narrative, in the first person (past, present or future), pointing to the images.
2. Repeat, along with choral repetition. Focus on one line at a time, until students are confident.
3. Make true/false statements based on the same narrative.
4. Make false statements and ask students to correct what you said.
5. Ask L2 questions to elicit first person responses.

6. Hide some of the images and elicit the story again.
7. In pairs students can recreate the narrative, perhaps alternating one sentence at a time.
8. With some classes, students can then narrate the story to each other without using the images.
9. Produce a written version of the narrative for further exploitation in various ways, including written tasks.

Note how many repetitions there are of common chunks of language. A lesson of this type may look like a speaking lesson, but in fact its main purpose is to provide large amounts of comprehensible listening input.

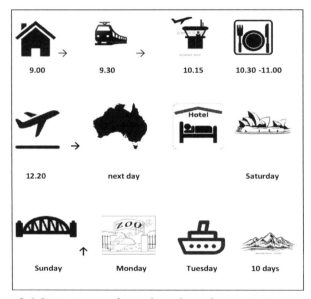

Figure 2.1 Listening and speaking based on a picture sequence

Independent listening

At an advanced level students can use the internet to do independent listening. Try assigning a task a week. Students select their own area of interest and are guided to relevant sites. The task could consist of listening, writing a brief summary of the content in L1 and producing a short bilingual glossary of new words. This could include songs with transcribed lyrics from their preferred genre. This type of task also encourages students to be autonomous learners as they use top-down knowledge of their chosen subject to help with understanding. Listeners can benefit from captions and transcripts on YouTube.

Immersion

The traditional way of providing a quantum leap in listening performance is to offer an immersion experience in the language, e.g. an exchange visit, a study trip or immersion weekend. Evidence suggests this is the single most important thing we can do to raise listening proficiency, not to mention oral proficiency and general motivation. Failing this, native speakers can be invited into school to talk about a topic or their life in general. A bilingual student in the class could perform a similar role. Alternatively, you could ask advanced students to come and talk to beginners in L2. This also lets them see what they could potentially achieve in the future. Or why not set up a film club for advanced students or take them to see L2 films or plays? See Chapter 15 for more about running exchanges.

Task-based listening

Listening can easily be incorporated within a task-based language teaching (TBLT) methodology, but with the main emphasis on listening rather than speaking. TBLT is about trying to reproduce goal-centred, meaning-focused language tasks. Here is an example based on Conti and Smith (2019). This follows the format: **pre-listening**, **while-listening** and **post-listening** (see below).

The Price is Right

Language focus: comprehension of numbers, real estate vocabulary and prepositions.

Preparation: prepare some slides depicting images of houses taken from estate agent websites.

Pre-listening: it is assumed the class knows numbers from 1-100 and a range of simple relevant vocabulary and prepositions. If necessary, review these on the board before the game, e.g. using translation or a matching task with L2 words on the left, L1 on the right. Ensure students are confident with this vocabulary before proceeding. Introduce some new vocabulary as you go along, particularly given that the items will be clearly visible.

While-listening: Invite four students to the front. Describe the house on display, building in repetition. Each student guesses the price of the house. Give them an idea of how much houses cost in general! The one who guesses most accurately gets to stay at the front, while the others return to their seats to be replaced by three new students, and so on. Note that the task allows them to see examples of houses or apartments from the L2 country.

Post-listening: as a 'warm down' activity do some mental math(s) with the class, reading aloud simple additions, subtractions, multiplications or divisions for them to work out and write down as they are read aloud.

Note: tasks can be matched with a wide range of themes such as guessing the age of famous people or the height of recognisable landmarks. Tasks can be matched with a specific communicative objective or language pattern, e.g. describing height, talking about ages, or giving prices.

Steve's zero preparation listening tasks

- With intermediate classes **talk for about two minutes** on what you did the previous weekend. Ask students to make notes in L1, then to feed back in L1 or preferably L2. How much did they understand? You could adjust the task by talking to them, then doing an instant true-false task: *Did I...?*

- **Instant true-false**. With beginners simply make a series of, say, twenty statements in L2 associated with the current topic. Tell students only half of them will be true. Who can identify them all? Use simple, potentially amusing statements: *Paul is a girl. The computer is on the ceiling. My name is Barbie.*

- **'Say the next word or sound.'** For near beginners or low intermediates, simply read aloud a text you have been working on. When you pause, either at the end of a word, or in the middle of one, the students must call out or whisper the next word or sound.

- **'Guess the next word.'** This is an alternative to the above for all levels. Make up an account or description but pause at certain points and students have to guess which word you were going to say next. They could write this on a mini-whiteboard. They hold up their board and you provide instant feedback. They could calculate a score as they go.

- **'Describe a picture.'** With intermediate or advanced students simply think of a picture in your mind's eye, describe it slowly and meticulously and they draw the picture. The best picture could win.

Working with listening texts

This section looks at working with audio or video listening texts, beginning with some general guidance. For beginners, bearing in mind the limitations of working memory and the lack of knowledge they bring to support processing, listening extracts should be very brief, no more than a few seconds at a time, with repetitions. Scaffolding with a written transcript is useful, helping them become not just better listeners, but better readers, as phonics skills improve. If we put ourselves in the shoes of a typical student, imagine how hard listening to audio must be.

With intermediate learners, extracts can be longer, but still usually limited to short paragraphs of speech at a time. Bear in mind that by this level, the range of achievement is very broad in some classes. Even for advanced level students, audio and video extracts would not normally exceed around three minutes, again with ample opportunity for repetitions.

We can use a wide array of activities with a listening text, but here is a general approach:

1. **Pre-listening**. More useful with intermediate level and above. This prepares students for a task, e.g. by activatin their linguistic and non-linguistic knowledge. Below is a selection of possibilities.

- Pre-teaching or brainstorming some key vocabulary to be heard in the text; an odd-one-out exercise could be done.
- Predicting what is likely to be heard, e.g. displaying some statements and asking students to predict which ones are likely to apply.
- Delayed dictation of a small number of chunks from the text.
- Reminders of metacognitive strategies they can use, e.g. warning students that distractors are used in assessment tasks.
- Dictating to students in L2 the questions they will be asked. This prepares them for the content and develops their transcription skills.
- Displaying an image related to the theme of the text as a source of discussion in L1 or L2. Note that even doing this in L1 prepares students for what is to come and gets them ready for what they will hear. This acts as an aid to later recall.

2. **While-listening**. Below is a selection of activities, the choice of which may depend on the nature of the text. For instance, if the text is harder than average, it may be useful to use L1 questions rather than L2, since L2 requires a much higher level of processing (comprehension, as well as formulating accurate written answers). The list is presented in roughly ascending order of challenge.

- True/false (adding 'not mentioned' adds difficulty and is useful for assessment purposes when three options results in a more reliable result).
- Vocabulary to find (*Find the Spanish for...*)
- Ticking off true statements from a list.
- A bilingual glossary of words and phrases to complete.
- Questions in L1.
- Content re-ordering. Students reorder sentences or paragraphs.
- Correcting false statements.
- Sentence completion (either the start or end of a sentence).
- Gap-filling (cloze) using letters, syllables, words or chunks. This can be done either with or without visible options.
- Note-taking in L1 or L2. L1 requires mental translation, while L2 relies partly on transcription, without necessarily total comprehension.
- An information grid to complete in L1 or L2.
- Questions in L2.

3. **Post-listening**. As well as just hearing back answers to activities, the following possibilities are available.

- A discussion about what students found easy and hard and how those difficulties might be addressed (metacognition).
- A follow-up reading or writing task on the same theme, recycling the language heard.
- A focus on a grammatical pattern encountered in the text, e.g. there may have been confusion caused using the passive voice or a verb tense.
- In pairs, students report to each other their answers and any problems they had.
- Reconstructing parts of the text using the 'aural gap-fill' technique, where the teacher starts a sentence and students must complete it.

Assessing listening

How do we know students are making progress with their listening? Since it is not a product we can hear or see for evaluation purposes like speaking and writing, it is less easy to know how much they have understood. Classroom **formative assessment** will help a lot in this context: *Did you get that? Thumbs up? Show me on your mini-whiteboard,* and so on. Teacher-led question-answer work also allows us to gauge reasonably well what students are understanding.

Formal, **summative assessment** is needed at regular intervals, however, and a range of assessment types are used for this. It is important to note that how we assess has implications for how we teach. For example, if assessment is carried out using questions in L1 and we want students to be familiar with the assessment format, we are likely to use questions in L1 in class. But this may constrain the amount of L2 we would like to use. This so-called **washback effect** (see Chapter 13) may lean us towards other assessment types. However, if we were to choose written questions in L2 we would simultaneously be assessing not just listening, but also reading and writing, so the assessment would be less 'clean', less focused on pure listening skill. This is why many assessments feature question styles such as multiple choice from pictures, choosing more than one item from a list of pictures, matching with pictures and choosing letters from a list.

In the classroom it is possible to favour other assessment types such as true/false/not mentioned (as noted, adding the 'not mentioned' makes the assessment more statistically valid), picking correct statements from a list (in L1 or L2), questions in L2 with the requirement to give short note-form answers, matching beginnings and ends of L2 sentences, filling gaps with L1 or L2 words, perhaps from a list of options.

Ideally, assessment should resemble normal classroom practice (to respect the Transfer-Appropriate Processing principle described in Chapter 6) and to allow all students to achieve a reasonable score at least, with the opportunity for the best to get full marks. It is common practice to put easier questions near the start of a test, build up in difficulty, but perhaps provide an easier question at the end to leave students feeling positive!

When assessing listening, keep in mind the principle of test validity (see Chapter 13). In essence, ensure comprehension is tested, not other skills such as writing. If the test includes elements of L2 writing (such as dictation or writing answers to comprehension questions in the L2), then we are testing more than just comprehension of spoken language. A test which combines different skills may have the benefit of reflecting good classroom practice but does not uniquely test listening.

Concluding remarks

We usually get better at what we practise, so to improve listening do lots of it! But listening can be improved by a conscious, structured programme which develops bottom-up and top-down processing skills. The extra attention to decoding (bottom-up processing) is of particular benefit to our less confident students. We have provided examples of the type of listening task which can develop decoding skills. For many more see our book *Breaking the Sound Barrier: Teaching Language Learners How to Listen* (Conti and Smith, 2019). The same book also goes into more detail about how listening is incorporated within Gianfranco's preferred method of instruction, EPI (see also Chapter 12 in this volume).

How often, when a listening worksheet is handed out do we hear *Is this a test*? Listening is best carried out through practice without the accompanying fear of assessment. We have seen that seeing listening activities as comprehension tests makes many students anxious. Guiding them step-by-step through the process of listening not only provides them with the knowledge they need to complete a listening task it also motivates them and puts them in control of their learning.

It must be emphasised, however, that there are no quick fixes for developing long-term listening skills; it takes time and large amounts of recycled comprehensible input, both from the teacher and other sources. It clearly implies teaching largely in L2, valuing it by giving it a serious place in the assessment regime and finding interesting and relevant source material.

3

Speaking

Introduction

This chapter examines the many ways we can develop dialogue with and between students, sometimes artificial, sometimes more 'authentic' (whatever that might mean). Our goal is to help develop multi-skill lessons where students listen, respond, read and write, almost all in L2. We consider the areas below.

Research evidence
- ✓ Input
- ✓ Interaction
- ✓ Output
- ✓ Corrective feedback
- ✓ The oral production process
- ✓ Pronunciation and intonation

Classroom practice
- ✓ Questioning techniques
- ✓ Other types of spoken practice
- ✓ Grammar worksheets used orally
- ✓ Pronunciation teaching strategies
- ✓ Pronunciation teaching activities
- ✓ Accuracy and fluency
- ✓ Information gaps and task-based activities
- ✓ Pair work versus teacher-led work
- ✓ Choosing and changing pairs
- ✓ Working in groups of three
- ✓ Varying our practice

Research evidence

Input

We know that two fundamentals of acquisition are **input** and **interaction**. Input is the language which students hear and read. For input to be useful and 'processable' it needs to be understood. The term **comprehensible input** is frequently used in the research literature and is often associated with the writer Stephen Krashen. Krashen's **Input Hypothesis** (part of the overall **Monitor**

Theory) states that language learners require comprehensible input, represented by i+1, to move from the current level of acquisition (represented by i) to the next level. Comprehensible input is input that contains language at or a little beyond the student's current understanding. Understanding is defined as understanding of meaning rather than of form (Krashen, 1982). For Krashen, the conscious learning and practice of rules only really serves to help students monitor the accuracy of what they are saying or writing if they have the time to do so.

In truth, comprehensible input is a more complex term than it first appears. For input to be understood and processed, the linguistic content of the message is important (phonemes, intonation, morphemes, words, chunks and sentences), but so are other factors, e.g. the student's background knowledge of the world, non-linguistic aspects such as gesture and visual input and, at higher levels, knowledge of social conventions and contexts (Polat, 2016).

Researchers use the term **modified input** to describe language which has been simplified to match the developmental stage a student has reached. Textbooks and teachers therefore use a simplified version of the L2 to ensure comprehensibility. This includes limiting the range of vocabulary encountered to so-called high-frequency words and restricting the range of grammatical patterns. But comprehensibility also involves non-linguistic aspects which may be too hard for some learners (Polat, 2016). Younger learners are more likely to understand language related to their current life experiences than to do with, say, political, historical or social matters.

In the context of speaking tasks, input should not just be comprehensible, but repeatable in students' heads using the phonological loop (see Chapter 2). In this way the input is said to 'prime' students for speaking. **Priming**, a term from cognitive psychology, in linguistic terms, can be when input language sets us up to reuse it in speech. Lexical priming occurs when hearing or seeing one word or phrase makes it (and similar words) easier to process subsequently. Syntactic priming is when, hearing or seeing a grammatical pattern a second time, makes it easier to process (see Chapter 12). In the question-answer sequences later in the chapter, hearing multiple uses of vocabulary and patterns primes students to use them later.

Interaction

Is input enough for acquisition? Nearly all researchers believe not, arguing that learners need to interact with others to make best progress. As Loewen and Sato (2018) tell us, interaction has been a major focus of research into language learning and teaching in recent years. Michael Long's (1981) **Interaction Hypothesis** emphasised the role of dialogue with other speakers. In his view, input alone is not enough for students to make the best progress. Long made two main claims:
1. Comprehensible input is necessary for second language acquisition.
2. Modifications within conversations while negotiating a communication problem help to make input comprehensible to a second language learner.

Is there evidence for this? Numerous studies have lent support. For example, Alison Mackey and Jaemyung Goo (2007) reviewed 28 interaction studies and found positive effects for learners engaged in interaction compared to those who were not.

Output

Interaction clearly requires students to produce **output**. This may come as a surprise but debates have raged in the literature about the degree to which output is necessary for acquisition. Merrill Swain's **Output Hypothesis** argued that constant practice makes learners conscious of their production, helping to move them from processing meaning to complete grammatical processing needed for accurate production (Swain, 1993). Being pushed to produce language makes students better able to notice what they can and cannot say or write. Her evidence came from a famous study of French immersion students in Canada who, despite having good comprehension owing to all the input they received, did not develop accurate oral skills.

Interacting in the classroom is also, quite clearly, a social phenomenon. Students do not learn language in isolation, but within a socio-cultural context. Russian psychologist Lev Vygotsky, who has had a significant influence on educational practice in general, claimed that meaningful interaction among individuals is the greatest motivator in human learning. In language teaching, being able to connect with the teacher and fellow students through oral interaction is one means of creating feelings of enjoyment, progress and self-efficacy. Another researcher, Henry (2021), writes about 'connective instruction', which holds that motivation and engagement increase when students can connect with the teacher as a person. Experience shows this to be true. Successful oral exchanges, where we affirm successful responses and provide sensitive feedback in a supportive environment, largely in L2, are one of the keys to language teaching success.

Corrective oral feedback

A commonly asked question concerns the correction of spoken errors. Should we do it? Which errors should be corrected? How? When? The research in this area is copious and has, alas, produced mixed findings. Two terms are often used to describe how oral errors are corrected: **prompts** and **recasts**. A prompt is an explicit correction of some type, e.g. with the tone of our voice or facial expression, making an error clear. A recast is where we give a correct reformulation of what a student said, without making clear there was an error. This distinction between prompts and recasts may not be clear-cut, since we cannot be sure if a student has grasped that the recast is actually a correction.

Lyster and Ranta (1997) carried out an influential study of how teachers correct in the classroom and which types of correction work best. They found that recasts were the most common type of corrective feedback, but that students only occasionally 'repaired' (i.e. improved) their output as a response. It is pretty obvious why teachers like recasts, since they do not want to discourage students by correcting them. The authors argue that when students do repair their speech, it allows them to automatise the retrieval of L2 knowledge that already exists in some form. But also, when students repair, they draw on their own resources and confront errors which may lead to changes in their hypotheses about the L2.

In a nutshell, there is value in correction, done in the right way, at the right time, with the right students. Be aware that recasts may not be noticed, especially by less proficient students, and be selective with corrections, choosing errors which impede communication and for students who may benefit from the correction. It is a subtle business!

The oral production process

Figure 3.1 shows how the oral production process works (adapted from Levelt, 1989). Alternative, similar models have been proposed.

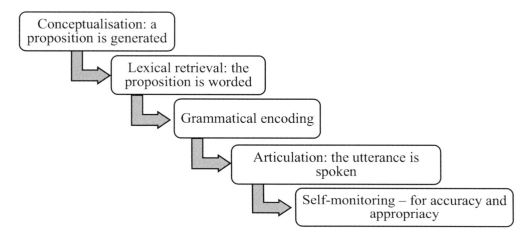

Figure 3.1 A model of the oral production process

For the steps in Figure 3.1 to be carried out students need to have something to say, know the words and phrases needed, have enough grammar for vocabulary to be combined meaningfully, have the articulatory skill (pronunciation) to speak and to be able to monitor and self-edit when needed. Sounds complex when put like that! In addition, students need to perform these tasks fluently. We return to the issue of fluency in Chapter 7.

Pronunciation and intonation

As O'Brien (2021) reminds us, many teachers would like their students to have native-like speech but accept the more realistic goal of aiming for something easily understood. L2 teaching has sometimes been more focused on comprehension and communication than on the fine detail of pronunciation and sound-spelling relationships. Whereas many teachers focus on the L2 sound system during the early stages of instruction, especially when the L2 alphabet is introduced, they rarely continue to emphasise pronunciation for the rest of the course. There has recently been a greater focus on phonics, notably in England following a government-promoted review of language teaching pedagogy (Bauckham, 2016).

Why has pronunciation sometimes been neglected? The main reason is that teachers want to produce competent communicators, and inaccurate pronunciation only occasionally hinders communication. But also, few teachers are trained in phonology and how to teach pronunciation, so are uncertain how best to do it. Keep in mind that pronunciation is not just about speech, but about having an accurate mental representation of language for listening purposes, so there are good reasons for placing an emphasis on pronunciation. As Erler and Macaro (2011) found in their study of learners of French in England, accurate pronunciation and decoding also contribute to students' self-efficacy, a key component of motivation and their desire to continue learning the subject (see Chapter 16).

Just a reminder that a distinction is drawn between teaching pronunciation and teaching phonics. The latter is about teaching students how to convert the written form of the L2 into sound, namely how letters, when combined, should sound in L2 ('sound-spelling correspondences' or SSCs). Teaching pronunciation, on the other hand, is about getting students to accurately master production of the L2 phonological system.

Studies suggest that explicit teaching of pronunciation can lead to improvement. But Thomson and Derwing (2015) caution that research has produced mixed results and its success may depend on a range of factors, including the goals and focus of instruction, its type and duration and student motivation. For example, the principle of **intentionality** (the desire to learn) is a major element in improvement. Research by Schumann (1986) suggested that a positive attitude towards L2 language and culture is an important factor in developing native-like pronunciation.

How well can high school students pronounce? A common view in the literature is that older children and adults cannot acquire native-like pronunciation beyond a 'critical age' (the first few years of life). Research by Bialystok (1997) and others suggests, however, that older learners can also master L2 pronunciation, but it remains true that, in general, older adults find it easier to acquire vocabulary than accurate pronunciation.

Research also indicates that acquiring pronunciation in L2 is not the same as doing so as a young child acquiring L1. The brain interprets new sounds in relation to the L1 system which is already firmly entrenched. Unless they are skilled mimics, students adapt unfamiliar phonemes to the closest match they can find in their L1 phonological system. Typically English native speakers mispronounce uvular and rolled 'r's and vowel phonemes. This is an example of what is called **negative transfer** from L1 to L2.

From the field of cognitive science, a reminder that the storage of sounds in working memory lasts barely two seconds (Baddeley & Hitch, 1974). If students are not given the chance to 'rehearse' sounds in their short-term memory, they are less likely to be able to reproduce them accurately.

Research also suggests that apps may play a useful role in improving pronunciation. In one study by Barcomb and Cardoso (2019), Japanese learners of English improved their pronunciation by playing a series of online gamified activities on Moodle. Interviews suggested the students perceived using the site as enjoyable, anxiety-reducing, and pedagogically useful.

Classroom practice

All the ideas given here have the aim of developing fluent oral production. Remember this does not mean 'speaking like a native speaker' but being able to manage simple conversations using a relatively limited range of vocabulary. Just as we do not expect maths students to be Einstein, we cannot expect most of our students to be fluent L2 users.

Questioning techniques

Let us begin by thinking about how we can use questions in the classroom to generate input and interaction. Questioning in language lessons is not usually the same as in other subjects. As language teachers, we often use questions to further the goal of acquisition, not just to engage in authentic dialogues. In the early stages of language learning especially, questioning is not always used in a genuinely communicative way. *What TV programmes do you like?* is an example of a genuine question which elicits an unpredictable response – there is an information gap between the teacher and student, or between students. In contrast, *Is the dog brown or black?* may be useful for practising the language but is not really an authentically communicative question since both we and the student can see what colour the dog is. Questions of this second type are called **display questions**.

Is this a problem? Not necessarily, pedagogically speaking. Although asking a student, *Is the book on the table or on the chair?* is logically inauthentic, the interaction can nevertheless contribute to the language learning process. This is because it allows them to hear and understand meaningful input, and to respond easily, thereby practising pronunciation and developing control of new vocabulary (*book* and *table*) as well as grammar (in this case using prepositions).

As students build up their proficiency, questions are likely to become less artificial but, even at an advanced level, a question on a text may fulfil this same 'artificial' role of eliciting the use of a structure or item of vocabulary, particularly where difficulties in pronunciation or grammatical details may be involved. This form of questioning is a key part of our repertoire if we wish to remain in the L2 and provide the input learners need.

Table 3.1 shows a hierarchy of question types, from easiest at the bottom to hardest at the top. Using a variety of question types to recycle the same language patterns, based on a source such as a picture or sentence, is sometimes called **circling**. By using a range of questions, we circle round the same language, generating many repetitions.

In the easier questions the language needed to respond is provided, allowing a degree of simple repetition. With the highest-level question students must both decipher the question and provide their own language in answer. This act of retrieval from memory is more demanding.

In a skilled questioning sequence with beginners, start with the easiest questions and work up towards the hardest. When learning to teach it is wise to plan out question sequences in advance;

with experience this becomes second nature. Note also that being skilled with questioning techniques allows us to differentiate between faster and less confident learners. A useful technique is 'return to student' where, if one has been unable to answer or has answered inaccurately, we go to a number of other students, then return to the first to give a successful response.

Table 3.1 Question types

Question type	Example
Open-ended question	What do you think of lions?
Question word question	Where is the lion?
Multi-choice	Is this a lion, tiger or giraffe?
Either/or	Is this a lion or a tiger?
True/false	There is a lion. True or false?
Yes/No	Do you like lions?

So what does this look like in practice? Imagine the class is looking at a picture of some classroom items. Below is part of a teacher-student(s) dialogue:

Teacher	Student(s)
Is the book blue? Yes or no?	*Yes.*
Yes, the book is blue. Repeat: the book is blue.	*The book is blue.*
Is the book red?	*No.*
Is the pencil red?	*Yes.*
Yes, the pencil is red. Repeat: the pencil is red.	*The pencil is red.*
The ruler is green. True or false?	*True.*
True. It's green. Repeat: the ruler is green.	*The ruler is green.*
Is the ruler green or red?	*Green.*
Yes, it's green. Repeat: the ruler is green.	*The ruler is green.*
Is the bag green, black or red?	*(It's) black.*
Yes, it's black. Repeat: the bag is black.	*The bag is black.*
OK, is the bag black, green or red?	*Black.*
Great! It's black. Repeat: the bag is black.	*The bag is black.*
Where is the black bag?	*On the table.*
Yes, the black bag is on the table. Repeat.	*The black bag is on the table.*
What is on the table?	*The black bag.*
Excellent! The black bag is on the table.	
Repeat. The black bag is on the table.	

At the end of a sequence it is possible to check in L1 or L2 that students have understood.

Any problems with that? Did you all follow (thumbs up)? How did we say…?

Of course, when you see the dialogue above written out, it appears very artificial (some teachers would even reject it for that reason), but novice learners are happy to play along with this process, particularly if we explain why we are doing it. In the process of a ten-minute exchange of this sort, students are getting lots of easy, repeated comprehensible input and a chance to practise their pronunciation and embed vocabulary. If they hear the word *bag* twenty times, they are more likely to remember it without having to learn it from an app or a list. In addition, the language being used is all 'connected', i.e. we are not teaching vocabulary as isolated words, but in the context of full utterances. This important point is dealt with in more detail in Chapters 5 and 12. The goals of input and interaction have been achieved and we have been able to provide a little corrective feedback along the way, e.g. on pronunciation or grammatical gender.

Sequences like the above can go very quickly and work either with students putting up their hands or with hands down (known as **cold-calling**). We could interrupt a hands-up sequence by saying we are going to ask the next question via cold-calling. In this case we would select someone either at random or, better, based on whether the question is well-matched to the student. This helps to ensure all students are on board and understanding. We can also bring fun and humour to such sequences by feigning surprise or insisting that something is true when it clearly is not.

Teacher	Student
The book is blue.	*No!*
Yes, the book is blue!	*No!*
OK. The book is red.	*Yes!*
So, the blue book is on the table.	*No! The red book!*

In addition, we can turn the session into a writing one, with students writing down answers they hear, either in a notebook, on a tablet or a mini-whiteboard. This provides more active involvement for the whole class and creates a multi-skill task.

With some classes students may play the role of teacher. Some take to this really well once they see how it works and their classmates respond keenly. This general approach to structured, hierarchical question-answer can work well with classroom items, PowerPoint images, sentence builders and simple texts. We have gone into some detail on this because it is a tremendously useful skill if one of the key aims is to maintain L2 use during lessons while building up lexical and grammatical knowledge.

Other types of spoken practice

Question-answer is only one type of the many oral activities and interactions we can carry out with students. Here are some others from which you could build your own repertoire. Note the element of 'gamification' in some of these. These have been ordered, broadly speaking, from the least demanding and most structured to more spontaneous, demanding tasks.

Consolidation of language items

- **Whole class choral repetition** or **phonics** activities, including whispering, shouting and singing are common practice. This can include building up phrases backwards, e.g. *I would like to go to the cinema* becomes *cinema... to the cinema... to go to the cinema... I would like to go to the cinema.* Choral repetition has the merit of giving students confidence without putting them in the spotlight. 'Part group' repetition (small groups, rows, pairs) may also be used. This adds a small element of variation.

- **'Word association'** is a useful activity focusing on meaning, not grammar. One student utters a word, then the next has to quickly produce the first word which comes into their head. The activity can lead to interesting discussions about how words are connected in the brain and is an example of metacognition – thinking about how we think and learn.

- **Aural gap-filling**. This is where we read aloud a passage, occasionally pause and the students have to say what comes next. They enjoy rising to the challenge of this type of short-term memory task, if the ground has been well-prepared beforehand. The same can be done at sentence level by saying *complete my sentence.*

- **Chanting or singing** verb conjugations, the alphabet, days, months and numbers. These can be made up or found online. Although reciting items in order has its limitations (at a later stage students may resort to going through the whole list in their head or even out loud before they find the item they are looking for), it is an aid to memory, particularly when associated with melody. It is important to remember the limitations of rote-learning verb paradigms. A student may be able to recite a verb, but then be unable to choose the right form when producing a sentence.

- **Cumulative games**, e.g. *I go to the market and I buy....* As the game develops, each student adds a new item to the list, having remembered all the earlier ones. This challenges short-term memory. The task could be done in small groups or pairs. If managed as a whole class activity, it is possible to differentiate between students by leaving those with the best memories until later in the process. Hints such as mimes or gestures can help the process along. The best classes may be able to accumulate 15 items or more.

- **'Aural anagrams'** with a partner. Partner A reads aloud the letters of a word in a jumbled order and partner B must work out the word. Model this activity yourself. Although this does little for general proficiency, it is useful for getting students to use letters spontaneously rather than just in alphabetical order.

Reading aloud connected language (chunks and sentences)

- **Reading aloud** individually or as a group from text on the board. This is useful to help establish sound-spelling links. Reading aloud can be done from a worksheet, homework task or textbook. Students can do this in pairs, taking turns to say a word, phrase or sentence until someone runs out of ideas. An amusing variation is to split the group in two as a choir leader and 'conduct' from the side; each side must be ready to swap reading (or singing) at a moment's notice. **Shadow reading** is when the teacher and class all read aloud together.

  Incidentally, reading aloud is one of the best ways to develop phonics skill over time. Furthermore, reading aloud develops an accurate phonological memory for words and phrases, useful not only for speaking, but also for listening (see Chapter 2). It is harder to recognise words and phrases in the stream of sound if our memory does not hold an accurate representation of what they sound like. Reading aloud games are an integral part of the EPI approach described in Chapter 12.

- **Paired dictation.** Partner A dictates a text to partner B. Each may have a partial version of the same text, with different gaps each to fill in.

- **'Sentence Stealer'.** This is most easily explained in four steps:
  1. Display a list of twelve numbered L2 model sentences which students have been practising.
  2. They each have four blank cards and are asked to secretly write on each card any one of those sentences or simply the number for it.
  3. The game consists of 'stealing' as many cards as possible from others in five minutes. Student X reads to student Y any of the four sentences; if a sentence that X reads is on one of Y's cards, X can 'steal' that card. To make it more fun students play rock, paper, scissors (repeating the three words aloud in the L2) to win the right to guess first.
  4. The student with the most cards at the end of the game wins.

The game can be developed a little further, adding an element of memory to go with the reading aloud aspect. After playing the first game for five minutes, display a list of the same numbered sentences, but with gaps. The number and nature of the gaps would depend on the class. This time students write the number of the sentence from the board. Then the game proceeds in the usual way, except this time they must produce their sentences from memory (referring to the gapped sentences on the board). More gaps can be created in the displayed sentences as the game proceeds, to provide a further challenge.

- **'Sentence chaos'.**

  1. Display 10 sentences on the board.
  2. Put students in groups of three: two players and a reader/referee.

3. The referee decides on a set order of sentences (different from the arrangement on the board) and reads them out twice, at the beginning of the game. The 10 sentences are always visible. The referee keeps a note of the order by writing down the sequence of numbers.

4. The two players try to repeat the sentences in the same order. They have five lives. Every time a player makes a mistake the other has a go until they run out of lives. The one who stays alive, or has managed to reproduce the longest accurate sequence of sentences, wins.

Controlled and semi-controlled activities

- **Question-answer sequences.** These are usually teacher-led, but do not have to be. They can be practised first, led by the teacher, then done in pairs or groups.

- **Making up true/false statements**. Pairs make up true or false utterances based on a picture, text or sentence builder. Partner A makes up a statement, Partner B says if it is true or false. If false, Partner B can correct it. An alternative would be for partner A to just make up false statements for partner B to correct. The teacher can also take the lead on this, of course.

- **Asking the teacher questions**. In many classrooms, because it is traditional for teachers to ask questions and students to answer, they may lack practice in asking L2 questions themselves. This activity can work well with easy texts, combining reading and speaking skills. A sentence can be displayed on the board, then students asked to note down or discuss in pairs which questions could have produced the answer. For example, take this sentence:

    Fred went to the cinema with his friends at 8 o'clock.

    Possible questions, with varying degrees of plausibility, include:

    Where did Fred go? Who went to the cinema? Who did Fred go to the cinema with? At what time did Fred go to the cinema? What did Fred do last night/week/Sunday?

- **Class surveys.** For example, *What subjects do you like and why?* This is an example of a 'milling around' task. We need to be confident that the class will respond well to moving around the class and that the students are using L2 nearly all the time. They collect answers which can be collated with the teacher.

- **Simple transformation drills**. For example, read a sentence and ask students to alter it by transforming it in some way. They might change present to past, present to future or affirmative to negative. These make very good lesson starters if we want to bring the class together and have them focus properly on us. They provide an excellent opportunity for **retrieval practice** (recalling language from memory) and can be tailored to the level of the class.

- **Substitution drills** are where a sentence is given and students change one part of it. Consider combining both substitution and transformation. An example is provided later in this chapter.

Fluency-building activities

- **3/2/1 task**. This is where a student gives a talk about a subject for a given time, e.g. three minutes. They then give the same talk in two, then a third time in one minute. The aim is to build up spoken fluency with the task.

- **'Just a minute.'** The game where one speaker must try to talk about a topic for one minute. If they hesitate very obviously or just stall, then another person in the group intervenes and attempts to finish the minute. And so on.

Unrehearsed, spontaneous activities

- **Making up a story one word or chunk at a time.** This can be done as a whole class activity or in small groups, once the task has been modelled. It makes students pay great attention to syntax and meaning and can produce amusing results. This can be an excellent 'filler' task or plenary (an activity to round off a lesson, recapping earlier work). Although they are not producing full sentences, a good deal of thinking and language processing is needed.

- **Performing** a **sketch, dialogue or short play**. Younger students derive pleasure from writing dialogues. They usually need to be based on existing models. Be aware that this type of activity can take some time and can become uncontrolled if not managed carefully. Plays are an integral part of the AIM (Accelerated Integrated Methodology) approach, used in some schools, mainly in Canada. See their website at *aimlanguagelearning.com*.

- **Role-playing**, for example, parent and child situations, crystal ball, agony aunt, palm reading. Simulations like this work effectively with intermediate and advanced students. A parent-child scenario with older learners might be: 'You have found a small amount of cannabis in your child's bedroom. Imagine the dialogue between you and the child.'

- **'Speed dating'**. Students are given a strict time limit of about two minutes to talk to a fellow student. When the time is up, they change seats and move on to someone else. This task has a couple of advantages. Firstly, they must work under time pressure which adds a sense of urgency to the task; secondly, although they are essentially repeating similar material multiple times, the change of partner makes the task seem less repetitive. In other words, the repetition of language is made more stimulating.

Grammar worksheets used orally

Chapter 6 discusses the teaching of grammar in more detail, but this section looks at how we can use grammar worksheets to generate oral activities.

A worksheet either printed off for students or displayed from the board can be a useful source of input and interaction. Coursebooks and other resources often lack practice examples and allow too few opportunities for repetitive practice and consolidation of vocabulary and structures. Without recycling, language is less likely to become fixed in long-term memory.

One such worksheet might consist of a set of statements which have to be adapted in some way so that they can demonstrate and practise skill with grammar or vocabulary. For example, a simple past tense can be practised like this example of both substitution and transformation:

Change each sentence into the past and then change one element.

Example: Question: *Today **I'm playing** tennis with **my friends**.*
                Answer: *Yesterday I **played** tennis with **my dad**.*

This sort of repetitive exercise is characteristic of the audiolingual approach described in Chapter 1. In audiolingual terms, the idea is that by practising something many times it may become a habit. Nowadays, we are more likely to frame this process as rehearsal in working memory, leading to stronger long-term memory (see Chapter 5). Some argue that pattern drills of this type are not conducive to learning, but we agree with Butzkamm and Caldwell (2009) who say that they can be usefully exploited but got a bad name by association with some more extreme versions of audiolingual and audiovisual courses.

How can we exploit this kind of worksheet to the best effect? Here are some approaches, each with a reflection on its advantages and possible drawbacks. Hopefully this will encourage a careful analysis of how to interact with the class by choosing the most effective approach.

1. **Teacher-led approach:** read out a prompt, get a student to answer hands up or cold-called, then get others to repeat, then the whole class to repeat. Hands up allows quicker students to be selected as good role models before weaker ones take their turn. The teacher-led approach is highly effective for attentive classes, supplies lots of L2 input and allows us to pick out specific students. Differentiation is possible and listening is practised. It may be easy to maintain class control, while they get to hear good models.

   One thing to emphasise here is that such a task demands great attention from classes and only one student speaks at a time, except when there is choral repetition. A brisk pace is needed or attention will quickly wane. Many find answering in class embarrassing. Some claim that putting pressure on students in this way may hinder their learning (we learn less well when anxious), but with sensitive handling this need not be an issue, especially if combined with other approaches.

2. **Pair-work approach**: after some whole class practice as above, quickly move to pair work where partners act in turn as teacher and student. Pair work means they get to speak and listen a good deal in L2. They can help each other and there is little embarrassment factor as the pressure is off. On the other hand, class control needs to be good so that students do not speak too much L1 or waste time. It is possible to insist on a 'no L1' rule. They may also hear wrong answers and poor models of pronunciation, so do not get optimum exposure to the language.

3. **Coaching approach:** rather than having students complete practice exercises in the above ways, this involves using a worksheet split in half with students completing the activities in pairs. For example, translating short sentences into L2 or choosing words from a list in a cloze (gap-fill) exercise, each student explains what they are doing to their partner who watches and listens and, if necessary, questions and critiques. This process reinforces the method in both students' minds and lends itself particularly well to differentiation because stronger students can be paired with less confident ones for coaching purposes. On the positive side, this helps build cooperative spirit and there is a focus on strategies and *metacognition* ('thinking about learning'). On the downside, L1 will be used a good deal and students will not hear the best oral models. Once again, classroom management needs to be effective.

4. **The student acts as teacher**: after a brief demonstration, ask a volunteer, preferably a higher-achieving one, to step up and run the class, as mentioned in the section on question-answer. Although the oral model will be less good (unless, for example, we have a bilingual student in the class), they may listen extra hard and find the process amusing and motivating. The volunteer will learn teaching and leadership skills. On the other hand, as with point (1), each student may not end up saying very much and the focus is more is more on listening. Is that a bad thing? Not if we have decided in advance that the exercise is largely about listening.

5. **Using mini-whiteboards:** adapt approach (1) to involve more students actively by giving each a mini-whiteboard or coloured marker. As an answer is given, they must all hold up their board with true/false or a marker indicating whether they think the response is correct or wrong. This guarantees more involvement from all students, even though the approach is teacher-led.

6. **Combine skills**: use approach (1) but as attention wanes quickly go to oral prompts with written answers. Then the class could simply work individually or in pairs doing written responses to written prompts rather than spoken ones. This means that all students are actively engaged in listening to good models, reading and writing. It may be good for class control and silence will be the norm. On the downside, it is hard to check they are all keeping up and writing accurate answers. It is hard to differentiate between students if the same pace is maintained for the whole class. When working alone there is more chance for them to go at their own pace and ask questions.

7. **Give answers, students choose prompt:** this is a simple variation which helps to vary the lesson and provide a fresh angle. Let us say you have a sheet with 15 answers to some imaginary questions; do not read the answers out but give a question and the students must supply the correct answer from the sheet. This can be done in pairs. On the plus side this may be an easy way into a worksheet. They do not have to create an utterance, just read one already supplied. The focus in this case is on comprehension rather than production. On the other hand, it is often easier therefore less challenging as they do not need to show much syntactic skill.

8. **Supply alternative answers, students choose the best one:** again, this has the merit of making a worksheet more approachable for those who are less confident. A student could read aloud a prompt, then the teacher supplies two answers (a) and (b) and the class votes for (a) or (b). This is good for listening comprehension. There is little pressure to perform, and all students are involved. On the downside, little production is needed and we need to watch out for a peer pressure effect if there is voting.

9. **Introduce a competitive element**: students working in pairs can award points for correct answers. They often like competitions. On the other hand it may lead to arguments and too much use of L1!

10. **Get students to make up their own examples:** once a group seems to have mastered a point, let them make up their own examples or even write their own worksheet. This allows them to be creative, maybe humorous, and to show off their use of the new point. It also provides an excellent homework assignment which allows students to compare work in the next lesson, try out their worksheet on a partner or the teacher and reinforce the language acquired in the previous lesson. There is little to criticise, but we need to be sure they have all mastered the point, or it could be a disastrous homework, reinforcing error or misunderstanding.

Pronunciation teaching strategies

The research referred to earlier, along with our own experience of these issues, suggests several classroom strategies.

■ If we emphasise pronunciation from the very early stages of teaching and sustain that emphasis, students will see it as important and give it due attention. When pronunciation practice is fun and produces greater motivation, it is more likely to be effective.

- Developing positive attitudes towards the L2 and its culture is important. Students who dislike French culture may be less likely to want to sound French. We can encourage them to practise the language orally with L2 speakers outside the classroom, perhaps via social media.

- We can raise awareness of the perceptual mismatch which occurs in working memory to avoid them developing an L1-influenced pronunciation. This means focusing on the differences between L1 and L2 phonemes that students may perceive as identical.

- If we know the sound system of the students' L1, we can anticipate the barriers to accurate L2 pronunciation and plan teaching accordingly.

- Frequency of exposure and practice in L2 pronunciation is vital. Better a few minutes every day, within the context of communicative work, than occasional pronunciation lessons. If students are getting lots of comprehensible input with regular focus on decoding and pronunciation, progress is more likely.

- In teaching pronunciation and decoding skills we can prioritise those sounds that enhance or hinder students' noticing and understanding of key grammar features (e.g. in French 'é' versus 'è' for the understanding of verb/noun/adjectival endings).

- We can favour apps which allow students to hear and say words, chunks and full sentences rather than just read them.

- We can make sure we are rigorous in our expectations when doing choral or individual repetition, if that is part of our teaching repertoire.

Pronunciation teaching activities

Here are 10 tried and tested activities which can help develop pronunciation skills:

1. **Practising letter/sound relationships with pictures**, e.g. PowerPoint slides. Show a picture of an item of vocabulary with a letter highlighted in the word or a phrase containing that word. Read aloud and students repeat. Alternatively, show a series of words sharing the same sound-spelling correspondences.
2. **Demonstrating sounds with lip shapes**: say the sound and students repeat. E.g., for the French vowel 'u' or German 'ü' ask them to make an 'oo' sound with lip rounding, then say 'ee' while keeping the lips rounded. If they do this correctly, they will produce the accurate French or German phoneme.

3. Playing with **tongue-twisters, rhymes, sayings and songs**. This helps us to get students to see the fun value of just playing with sounds in a non-threatening way.

4. For French, displaying and practising combinations of **letters which produce the same sound**, e.g. *o, eau, ot, au, aux, ault, eault* and so on.

5. Using **arm gestures to demonstrate accented** letters. This can be amusing. The French 'ç cedilla' poses a particular challenge, but a cocked leg works well!

6. Repeating **words without their consonants** to focus on good vowel sounds. Consonant-free words could even be chosen for students to work out.

7. **Choral reading aloud from the board**. This is tremendously useful for novices especially, who have to look carefully at spellings while hearing the sounds. Choral repetition must be done well to be effective, so it is important to insist on a unified response from the class. Try delayed choral repetition, whereby students respond on a signal after a few seconds. This gets them to rehearse the language silently over and over again.

8. Displaying **a picture of the human vocal tract** to give a clearer idea of where articulations occur.

9. Teaching **some basic phonetics**, referring to the vocal cords, vocal and nasal cavities, the role of the tongue, lips, alveolar ridge, soft palate, hard palate and uvula. This may help students master particularly awkward sounds such as the uvular 'r'. Explain that babies go through all the vowel sounds when they babble. Demonstrate changes from one vowel to another. Talk about why words for 'mother' in different languages usually start with an 'm', how diphthongs vary by accent in English and which sounds in your own first language non-native speakers find difficult.

10. Practising **pairs of similar sounding phonemes** in L1 and L2, highlighting the differences in articulation.

Accuracy and fluency

One of the best things to happen in language teaching over recent decades is the movement away from accuracy at all costs to a greater emphasis on general proficiency or fluency. We now recognise that getting the message across is more important than doing it with total accuracy. But of course we would like accuracy too and as teachers we should usually aim for this without at the same time hindering or discouraging communication. With this in mind, we can plan oral activities with the focus on EITHER accuracy OR fluency (See Chapter 7). It was Brumfit (1984) who emphasised this distinction. You can even share it with classes: *"Today I don't want you to worry about being absolutely correct, just have a go! This is a fluency activity, make as many mistakes as you want!"*

Fluency activities might include information gap tasks, task-oriented discussions, dialogues, guessing games or general oral discussion. In these cases the teacher would be primarily a listener, rather than a corrector. We may even back off completely, take a well-earned rest and let students get on with just the occasional reminder if they go off task. With fluency tasks we can tell the class the focus is most definitely on meaning. In contrast, accuracy activities might include question-answer to practise a grammar point previously presented, structured drills, written grammar exercises, repetition, pair work tasks with a focus on grammar, such as 'battleship(s)' (see below) or paired dictation. In these cases we correct where necessary because for accuracy tasks the focus is on form.

It is possible that some language teachers still tend to focus on accuracy too much. Why? Firstly because they are good at it themselves and sometimes come from an era or educational background where it was more highly valued. Secondly, because in the school setting, making judgements as to whether something is right or wrong is an expectation, and thirdly assessments, for all sorts of reasons, still place a considerable emphasis on written skills where, despite mark schemes and rubrics which reward successful communication, accuracy still counts.

Gianfranco's five-step approach to developing speaking skills

See Chapter 12 for how the types of activity described below are used within Gianfranco's EPI approach at various points in the MARS-EARS cycle.

1. **Modelling phase**: model the L2 phoneme and/or how to transform the L2 graphemes (letters) into sound.
2. **Description and analysis**: the differences between similar (but not identical) L1 and L2 phonemes are clearly explained (or arrived at inductively by students). For instance, when teaching the difference between a typical Spanish 't' and typical English 't', demonstrate and explain what is happening physically.
3. **Receptive awareness-raising and discrimination**: students practise matching the L2 phonemes with letters/combinations of letters and discriminating between these and the similar L1 sounds (e.g. they listen to the word 'bonjour' first uttered correctly and then by a speaker pronouncing 'j' the English way).
4. **Productive phase involving controlled practice**: the L2 phonemes and/or related graphemes are practised with drills designed to produce the L2 sounds (e.g. easy role-plays and simple tongue twisters).
5. **Productive communicative practice phase**: to develop automatic use of language. Semi-structured communicative tasks such as surveys, interviews, role-plays, information gaps' or oral picture tasks are useful ways to train students in pronunciation and decoding. Before they begin a task, focus on specific aspects of pronunciation, e.g. a word or sound that will cause difficulty.

Information gaps and task-based oral activities

Another of the best ideas to emerge from the communicative movement in language teaching is the notion of the **information gap**. The idea is that, if students have a genuine need to find something out or to exchange information, they are more likely to want to talk and the communication will be more authentic.

It is easy to set up information gap tasks to generate discussion. Often these activities take minimal preparation and students enjoy them.

- The game of **Battleship(s)** is a type of information gap activity which is widely used and can be the basis for work on vocabulary or verb forms. Battleship(s) is an amended version of the traditional game using a grid of about 8 x 6 cells. For example, along one axis verb infinitives are placed; along the other, subject pronouns. Students play the game by combining subject pronoun and infinitive into correct verb forms for each cell.

  Three-chunk translation battleships is a variation where phrases are given along both axes, as well as in a selection of boxes in the grid. Table 3.2 shows an example. Students see the L1 and translate to L2 for their partner, who must identify the right cell.

Table 3.2 Three chunk battleships

	with my parents	with my friends	with my friend Alex	with my friend Jade
I go to the train station	every day	sometimes	often	occasionally
I go to the large park	on Saturday	on Sunday	at the weekend	sometimes
I go to Paris	sometimes	occasionally	often	every weekend
I go to the new pool	occasionally	at the weekend	sometimes	often

- At the simplest level, pairs of students can play a guessing game. E.g. each writes a list of five things they did at the weekend and tries to guess the other's list using only yes/no questions.

- Each student has a list of items they bought at the supermarket which their partner must guess.

- Pairs of students have partially completed diary extracts or school timetables and they have to find out the missing information by asking each other questions. Each partner has different gaps in their information.

- At a more advanced level a class could solve a 'jigsaw' murder mystery with each student given different key information including red herrings. By sharing information orally they try to solve the crime (see an example in Smith (2023).

- In pairs, students plan a set of weekend activities. Each partner has a list of their likes and dislikes along with a list of useful language, see Table 3.3 as an example. Together they must plan their weekend over the phone.

Table 3.3 Weekend plans

STUDENT A	STUDENT B
LIKES: shopping, going to the movies, board games, listening to music, swimming, going to the beach	**LIKES:** meeting up with other friends, listening to music, swimming, going for walks
DISLIKES: computer games, sport, going to cafés, going for walks	**DISLIKES:** shopping, going to watch movies, computer games, sport, going to the beach

> *On Saturday morning, shall we go to the shops?*
> > *No, I don't like shopping. Do you want to come to my house?*
> *Okay. I'll see you at 10.*
> > *What shall we do in the afternoon?*
> *Would you like to watch a film at the cinema?*
> > *Yes, good idea. I like films.*
> *And in the evening?*
> > *Shall we play on the computer?*
> *No, I hate that. Do you want to play a board game?*
> > *No. Would you like to go to David's house?*
> *Okay.*

Another useful trend to emerge in recent decades is the use of **task-based activities**. Here the focus is on completing a useful task rather than on the language itself. Students must solve problems or negotiate meaning to achieve a goal. If they are motivated by completing the goal, they may be more likely to use L2 in a natural and authentic fashion. These often work particularly well at an advanced level. Below are some examples of tasks.

- Plan a dinner seating arrangement based on the characters, gender, political views and family relationships of the guests (Ur, 1981).

- Plan a short holiday in a city destination using tourist material they have been provided with.
- Plan a day of television watching using a TV listings page in L2.
- Establish a set of rules and a house cleaning rota for sharing a home while at university.
- Compare the CVs of several job applicants for a specific post using a set of job criteria.
- Write and record a news broadcast using stories supplied or newly written ones. Alternatively, students can be given a list of breaking stories for the day, they discuss their order of priority, then record a broadcast. This can be played to their peers.

Example speaking task. 'Organising a party'

In this example, several 'sub-tasks' can contribute to a final goal: making a short video with a partner advertising a party you have planned. The classroom sub-tasks and communicative goals involved are summed up in Table 3.4.

Table 3.4 Communicative goals and sub-tasks

Communicative goal	Sub-task leading to final task
Talking about what people will want to eat and drink at the party.	Oral class survey as a 'milling around' task. Drafting a shopping list.
Talking about what music people will want to listen to and dance to.	Preparing a written survey, e.g. on a Google Form. Drafting a list of music tracks.
Talking about what clothes people will wear.	Fashion show. Students bring in clothes and describe what they will wear.
Talking about what we are going to do at the party.	Preparing a digital or paper poster advertising the party.

Pair work versus teacher-led work

Since the rise of the communicative approach in the 1970s there has been a move away from teacher-led oral work towards other forms of dialogue, notably pair and group work. How do we get the balance right of teacher-led and pair or group work? This is worth thinking about carefully.

Reasons for doing teacher-led oral work

- It allows us to carefully control the input students receive.
- It provides a lot of listening input, released in small manageable chunks. So teacher-led question-answer, drilling and discussion should not just be seen as oral activity, but, more importantly, a reflection of the reality of communication, with listening playing an important role.
- It is part of a whole pedagogical approach which assumes grammar and vocabulary can be internalised by controlled practice.
- It can be effective as a class-controlling activity. We control the pace as the only person talking.
- It can be entertaining and motivating for students when done well.
- It can be an effective way of differentiating between faster and slower students. With a hands-up or hands-down approach, we can direct harder, more open-ended questions at those who are more proficient, easier closed questions at those less proficient.
- Cleverly scaffolded question sequences can encourage students to infer language rules on their own.
- Many students enjoy taking part in whole class question-answer work. Younger ones especially often enjoy showing off what they can do.
- A no-hands-up approach should encourage all students to listen intently and be ready to answer when called upon.
- At higher levels the teacher-led approach allows us to adapt instantly to students' answers, challenging them further and taking conversation in interesting directions.
- It is highly adaptable. All kinds of variations on question-answer can be used, e.g. giving false statements to be corrected, seeking questions to answers, getting a student to play teacher at the front, doing true/false or instant multi-choice and so on.
- It is a useful lesson starter or 'warmer'.
- It brings the group together and lets us review previous work, giving the class confidence in what they have already learned.
- Although frequently an artificial form of communication, students are willing to play the game, especially if we explain to them why we are doing it.
- It can be part of a multi-skill activity, e.g. ask a question, and students answer orally then write down the answer.
- Skilled teacher-led oral work allows us to keep the class running in L2.

Reasons against doing teacher-led oral work

- Only one person can speak at a time, so it is highly inefficient. Pair work is far more productive; group work less so since there are fewer opportunities to speak.
- Teacher talk places high demands on concentration so can be counter-productive with some classes. It can also be boring if done without skill and enthusiasm.
- Although we are in control, teacher-led work can place demands on our energy and, at higher levels, oral skill. If teacher proficiency is limited, the quality of input will be low.
- We can never be certain if students are listening, even with a hands-down approach. They would appear to be very inactive most of the time.
- With both a hands-down and hands-up approach students are under pressure to perform in front of their peers. Many students dislike this and some argue that it hinders progress. They may prefer pair or small group work where there is less pressure to be correct.
- If the main role of teacher-led work is to promote listening comprehension, there may be better ways to do this. Question-answer exchanges are, as we have seen, usually very artificial in a classroom setting.

Further reflections

In teacher-led questioning, as with many classroom activities, much depends on how well the task is managed. Some teachers are very skilled with question-answer and thrive being the centre of attention with classes enjoying the process. Others may be more comfortable and successful developing listening in other ways and promoting oral fluency primarily through pair and group work.

Remember, of course, that these approaches are all rooted in our explicit or tacit view of how languages are learned. Some practitioners believe proficiency only emerges through receiving large amounts of comprehensible input. Proponents of the Teaching Proficiency through Reading and Storytelling (TPRS) approach (see Chapter 19) value question-answer (circling) primarily because it provides lots of meaningful input and repetition, not because it provides opportunities to speak or practise grammatical structures. They believe that spoken fluency does not improve through the process of speaking itself, but rather through listening and reading. In this view, conversation is only useful as a source of more comprehensible input. This is all in line with Stephen Krashen's **Input Hypothesis** (Krashen, 1982).

But most teachers and researchers assume that the very act of practising speaking and interacting with others makes students better speakers. Recall that Swain (1993) and Long (1996) proposed that we need to produce language to be able to notice what we can and cannot do and get responses from another speaker.

Choosing and changing pairs

There is some limited research evidence which suggests certain pairings work better than others. Storch (2002) investigated how pairing types affected learning outcomes. She identified four types of paired interaction: 'collaborative', 'dominant-dominant' (where each student was reluctant to listen and engage), 'dominant-passive' and 'expert-novice'. She found that the 'collaborative' and 'expert-novice' pairing retained more language over time.

Tian and Jiang (2021) concluded from their study with quite proficient Chinese learners of English at university level that it might be wise to pair low-level learners with high-level peers to produce more opportunities for **negotiation of meaning** (the process that speakers go through to reach a clear understanding of each other) and avoid generating too much L1 use. This might further learners' L2 production and learning.

Ramage (2012) advocates some flexibility with the pairing up of students. They may have a regular partner who sits next to them, with whom they work happily and productively. We can easily vary things, though, by matching students of similar prior attainment for some tasks and different for others. In the latter case the more confident can help those who are less so.

Sometimes just randomly varying partners can spice up a lesson, as long as we do not end up with unproductive students sitting together. The mere fact of changing pairs during a task can enliven a relatively mundane pair work activity. Ramage suggests labelling students as A's or B's, then, during the activity, telling A's to stay seated while the B's move around. This can be part of the popular 'speed dating' paired activity where students move quickly from one partner to the next, repeating the same set of questions. In any case, allowing unproductive, chatty students to sit together is a mistake.

In many beginner classrooms there are assigned places to sit, which dictates to some extent who works with who. This does not preclude changing places for specific paired tasks.

Working in groups of three

There are good reasons for using groups of three rather than a simple pair. The third member of the group can act as a 'referee' for some types of activity. An example is the fun game devised by teacher Dylan Viñales called No Snakes No Ladders. This is an oral translation board game. The board is a track made up of about 30 squares (see Table 3.5). Each box contains a short L1 sentence to be translated. The chunks become increasingly difficult as the game progresses.

In groups of three students (2 players + 1 referee) players take turns rolling a dice. When a player lands on a box, they have 10-15 seconds to translate the sentence into L2. The referee then tells the player (with the help of the answer sheet) if their translation is correct. If it is, they get another go and advance to the next box. They translate the next sentence, and so on. If their translation is incorrect, the referee reads out the correct version twice for the players to try to memorise it for the next round. The student who is closer to the finishing line after ten minutes is the winner.

Table 3.5   No Snakes No Ladders board

24 I did some work	25 I ate my breakfast	26 I took the train	🏆
23 I visited a museum	22 I saw my uncle	21 I went to the park	20 I watched a YouTube video
16 I listened to a song	17 I watched a TV programme	18 I played a computer game	19 I read a blog
15 I drank a beer	14 I visited a castle	13 I ate some pasta	12 I went for a walk
8 I saw my friends	9 I went to the cinema	10 I watched a movie	11 I rode my bike
7 I played tennis	6 I did my homework	5 I read a book	4 I ate some rice
➡	1 I played football	2 I went to the shops	3 I listened to music

Varying our practice

For most classes, best practice is likely to involve a combination of teacher-led work and pair or small group work. Pair work is generally superior to group work since students get more chance to speak and are more likely to remain on task. Beginners respond well to teacher-led work, but as they grow older, they are less inclined to respond and answers may be limited to the very confident few. Cold-calling is a possible response to this. By intermediate level an oral activity can be briefly modelled before moving quickly to pair work. This also adds variety to lessons which may frequently end up being divided into sections of 10 minutes or so (see Chapter 19 for more about lesson planning).

Once familiar habits have been established, students slip into pair work mode with no fuss and communicate largely in L2. It is important that the bar is set high with expectations for pair or group work. Classes need to know very clearly that too much L1 is unacceptable, unless the task is of a meta-linguistic nature, e.g. explaining a rule of grammar or giving feedback about some written work. With advanced level groups, which are often much smaller and include more confident young adults, teacher-led work may come to the fore once more, as we seek to challenge students with more stimulating questions. We need not worry if pair work becomes noisy, as long as the noise is productive. A quiet word here and there may be enough to keep the volume at acceptable levels.

Concluding remarks

Managing classroom oral work is one of the most important skills we need as a language teacher. It develops with time and depends not just on natural flair, but on a principled set of skills which can be worked at from the start and deliberately practised. It takes a good deal of empathy with students - we need to have a keen sense at every moment when they are starting to flag, what stimulates or amuses them, what irritates them, what they find easy and what they find hard.

When it goes well, we may experience the same pleasure as an actor on stage, but we do not need to be a full-blown thespian for it to succeed. If we work at our techniques, show flexibility and really listen to students, we can produce some very enjoyable experiences for us and them. It is through effective management of oral work that we build up a solid, trusting relationship with classes.

4

Teaching in the target language

Introduction

If you are a training to be a teacher or are newly qualified, the issue of teaching in the target language (L2) may be a major concern. As you observe lessons and talk to your colleagues there may be little apparent consistency: some try to teach largely in L2, while others are happy to jump frequently from L1 to L2. As a result you might justifiably ask yourself a few questions. Will I lose control of the class if they do not understand? Will it stop me building up a rapport with my students? Should I feel guilty if I use L1? Should I write comments in exercise books in L2? Are my skills good enough? Should I be using 100% L2; if not, what percentage? Is it the best approach anyway? Is it possible if there is no culture of L2 teaching within the department?

The issue for most teachers is not the principle that L2 use is a good thing, but just how much you should use and how best to use it. In this chapter we consider the following areas.

Research evidence
- ✓ Input and interaction revisited
- ✓ Categorising L2 use
- ✓ In favour of L1 use
- ✓ Getting the feel right

Classroom practice
- ✓ Building a repertoire of procedures
- ✓ How L1 might be used
- ✓ What if it is not working?
- ✓ Input and output tasks
- ✓ Awkward questions about L2 use
- ✓ Working as a departmental team

Research evidence

Input and interaction revisited

Here is Principle 8 from Rod Ellis's 10 Principles of Instructed Language Learning:

> *The opportunity to interact in the target language is central to developing second language proficiency* (Ellis, 2005).

As noted in the introduction to this book, there is no unambiguous research evidence to suggest any one general teaching approach is better than another. But researchers agree that comprehensible input and interaction (classroom communication) are fundamental to progress, so being able to run a classroom largely in the L2 is both a necessity and a challenge. Based on a review of studies in several countries, Turnbull and Arnett (2002) found that there is near consensus that teachers should aim to make maximum use of L2, while Vold and Brkan (2020) write that exposing students to the L2 is essential for the development of communicative language abilities.

The American Council on the Teaching of Foreign Languages (ACTFL) (*actfl.org*) recommends that L2 should be used 90% of the time. Although such a precise figure is questionable, it does have the merit of sending a clear message about the importance of L2 teaching. This guidance is a reaction to the reality of many classrooms. In ELT classrooms, Kerr (2019), citing Levine (2014) suggests that L1 is used between 20% and 40% of the time. One might imagine that the figure is similar in many world language classrooms.

Molway, Arcos and Macaro (2022), in their study comparing L2 use by teachers in Spain and England found that studies that have investigated the ideal balance of L1/L2 tend to conclude that the L2 should be used for around 80–90% of all communication.

Interestingly, Dewaele, Botes and Greiff (2022), carried out a study of 332 students around the world about anxiety, boredom and enjoyment in language lessons. They found that students reported they enjoyed lessons most when teachers used the L2 a lot. This might need unpacking, since it is possible that teachers with the best language skills may be both more confident L2 users and more confident teachers generally.

Categorising L2 use

Ernesto Macaro (2001) identified three ways to categorise L2 use:

1. **The Virtual Position**. The classroom should be like the L2 country. There is no value in using L1 and it should be excluded.
2. **The Maximal Position**. There is no value in L1 use. But because perfect teaching and learning conditions do not exist (e.g. the teacher's skill is lacking), then you have to resort to L1.
3. **The Optimal Position**. There are pedagogical advantages to L1 use. Learning may be enhanced by principled use of L1.

In recent years, guidance has moved towards (3). Teachers and researchers have become less doctrinaire about L2 use, partly owing to research which shows the positive value of using L1, translation and **code-switching** (going from L1 to L2 and vice versa), particularly with novices and near-novices. Macaro (2000) argues for the benefits of L1 use in the classroom: beginners use it to help them decode text; all learners use L1 to help them write text and L1 tends to be the language of thought, unless the student is very advanced or is in the L2 country. It is naïve, therefore, to think that we can stop them thinking in the L1 – they will always do so.

In their research review from 2022, the English schools inspection body Ofsted takes the following view:

> *Teachers' use of the target language should be carefully planned within the scheme of work. It should support and complement the scheme of work and build systematically on learners' prior knowledge, reinforced by English when needed.* (Ofsted, 2022).

In favour of L1 use

Some writers even more enthusiastically endorse the use of L1. For example, Butzkamm and Caldwell (2009) attack "monolingual dogma" and write of the L1:

> *Rather than a liability, it is the most valuable resource, indeed the critical one, that a talking child brings to the classroom.* (p. 13).

They cite studies which claim that a bilingual approach is more successful than a monolingual one. They also describe their five-point programme for principled use of L1 and L2:

1. Teachers use the sandwich technique for most unknown expressions.
2. Students may insert L1 expressions when needed; teacher springs in with the appropriate equivalent or tries to reformulate the student's contribution in the L2.
3. Teacher and students retain and keep track of expressions introduced.
4. Teachers and students alike exercise self-discipline and consistently use the L2 expressions that have been made available.
5. All L2 teachers agree on functional L2 use in all classes, i.e. the L2 is and remains the primary vehicle of communication.

The sandwich technique is where you utter an L2 word or phrase, then translate it into L1. Butzkamm and Caldwell argue this should not be done on an ad hoc basis but planned for and embraced.

The same writers enthusiastically argue that teachers have been the victim of a monolingual orthodoxy over the years, where L1 use is used begrudgingly, as a last resort (Macaro's Maximal Position). They welcome the L1 as a source of knowledge to be exploited, not feared; a source of skill, not error. This view has been taken on board by many teachers, more so in the UK than the USA where the 'monolingual' view still prevails in research guidance, e.g. from ACTFL.

Whether you believe L1 is a help or hindrance to learning, we can agree that for language to stick in students' minds they need to hear and read as much of it as possible. Researchers usually argue that the implicit, unconscious route is the most powerful – we pick up language simply by using it, communicating with it. This is much more important than describing it. In this sense, as

Bill VanPatten puts it (2017), language is not 'subject matter'. As students hear and see repeated examples of language they understand, it tends to stick. Repetition of comprehensible L2 is needed. Students will only be able to activate words and grammar if they have heard and used them multiple times, unless they are unusually gifted.

Getting the feel right

Hazel Crichton (2009) wanted to explore successful L2 use by five teachers in Scottish schools. She found that they all combined considerable use of L2 with a warm, supportive approach. By using L2 extensively, the teachers also created, in her view, an atmosphere in which it appeared to be less unnatural for students to use L2 themselves. She found that the teachers also showed an interest in the wellbeing of the students, asking them about absences and discussing a variety of subjects with them in exchanges which were designed to be overheard by the whole class:

Teacher: *Où est Rachel? Absente? Oui? Bonjour C. Ahhh! C'est bien. Tu étais absent, oui? Tu étais malade? Oui? Oh, c'était grave? Serious? Oui? Tu étais à l'hôpital? Non? Au lit? Au lit, oh. Mais il est bien de revoir Calum, non? Non? Il est bien de le revoir. Good to see him again, non?* Student: *Oui!* (Crichton, 2009).

She also found that the teachers showed sensitivity to the level of the students' productive capabilities by creating conversations which they could sustain without becoming stressed about having to think about the form of the language when giving an answer. Being exposed to natural, 'real' language, not necessarily part of the syllabus, was valuable in terms of increasing awareness of the language and developing the ability to understand everyday dialogue.

In the conclusion of her paper (Crichton, 2009) she writes:

> *The teachers' constant interaction with the learners together with their responsiveness in adjusting their own language to their listeners' level of understanding ensures that the pupils do not feel overwhelmed by the TL and so are more likely to stay engaged.*

An important takeaway from this sort of study is that use of L2 is founded not just on theoretical issues, but on skilled and subtle human interactions undertaken in a caring environment. One factor to keep in mind is this: if we do not take L2 use seriously and make it our prime means of communication, then students are not likely to either.

Classroom practice

Building a repertoire of procedures

Firstly, it is worth posting on classroom walls key language which the teacher and students will commonly use: instructions, making excuses, asking permission, asking for repetition and expressing confusion (*I don't understand*, etc.). But L2 use is not primarily about comments in students' books, writing lesson objectives on the board in L2, posting signs in L2 so children can ask if they can go to the toilet; it is about classroom interactions through the process of presentation and practice of language material. These interactions can be between teacher and student or between students. We considered a large range of these in Chapter 2.

The ability to run classes in L2 is founded on having a clear, practised repertoire of interactive procedures which enable us to stay in L2 while ensuring students are always understanding. As soon as they fail to understand what is going on they lose confidence and interest. One of the merits of the EPI approach by the way (see Chapter 12) is that all the language presented and practised in sentence builders is comprehensible, since it is all translated into L1. Students are given every opportunity to understand with receptive comprehensible language before they proceed to more challenging productive activities.

Similarly, the Knowledge Organisers used by some teachers, notably in England, contain parallel translations of sentences so that all the language can be understood. They can serve not just as reference documents, but as tools to exploit in various ways in the classroom.

Smith (2023) includes a chapter about building a repertoire of procedures to making planning faster and thus reduce workload. New teachers can find planning very time-consuming, but with experience this becomes much easier as successful, tried-and-tested procedures are developed. We return to this in Chapter 19.

How L1 might be used

In general we suggest limiting the use of L1, for the reasons given above, but to use it in a principled fashion. Some words and phrases are easily explained with gesture, a picture, definition or because they are cognates. Others are harder so you have to use your skill and be what Macaro (2010) has called a 'dictionary designer', i.e. judgment is used to decide what methods are best to help students understand words or expressions. Sometimes an explanation in L2 might be best, sometimes a translation will be more efficient and avoid any confusion. Other ways of getting meaning across without translating include:

- **aural gap-fill**. Give a phrase or sentence with the L2 word missing;
- give a **synonym or antonym**;
- give a **paraphrase** or near synonym;
- **contextualisation** (if the L2 word were *bread* you could say: *you buy it at the baker's*);
- **definitions**;
- **pictures**;
- **gestures**.

These are all good because they provide more language input while simultaneously avoiding code switching from L2 to L1 which may encourage students to get lazy and expect translations. It is wise to avoid the temptation to constantly sandwich since students may think they do not need to listen to the L2. We need to plan but also develop a feel for when that little bit of extra support should be supplied which may serve the purpose of facilitating classroom interaction. It is important to make clear to the students that these are real-life strategies they can employ themselves when interacting in L2. It also helps if all members of a department are following the same policy.

But there are occasions when L1 use can be recommended:

- **To explain complex activities** - it saves time and ends up allowing for more L2 use.
- **To give complex cultural information**. There needs to be some room for the teacher to tell stories, amuse, explain, and build up a relationship.
- To deal with **behaviour management** issues in most cases.
- To sometimes **set out the goals** for the lesson. There should be no doubt in the students' minds over this, so occasionally it may be better done in L1.
- **To 'ease' a class into a lesson**, depending on their mood. A better connection might be made by saying a few words in L1 to start. In reality, all sorts of issues can present themselves at the beginning of a lesson, so adaptability is the watchword.
- **To put work into context**. For example, if the goal is to work on a text on a certain issue, would it better spark the class's interest by briefly dealing with some key points in L1 or showing a short video? If this leads to greater commitment to the text later, it is worth doing.
- **To explain grammar and give notes**. With really fast classes and more advanced students it may be possible to do this in L2. Care is needed, however. Clarity is vital, and perhaps especially so when a grammar point needs to be understood.
- To do certain types of **formative assessment work**, e.g. looking at model exam questions, target setting, checking how much students have understood at the end of a lesson and so on.
- To give **complex feedback** in exercise books and orally. Is it possible that we make a closer psychological bond with most students by using the mother tongue with them? The exercise book or homework sheet is one of the most intimate links we have with a student.
- **To talk** with classes **about language learning**.
- **To set homework assignments** (usually) - there must be total clarity for this. It can be sone in L2 first, then have a student interpret.

What if it is not working?

If we know our technique is sound, but we are losing the class and need to resort to L1, then it is not the end of the world. In this instance, after some L1 input, when we have the class's confidence, we can go back to L2. It is more important for to survive and build relationships than lose credibility with students over an ideological point of language teaching pedagogy! As we have seen, this is not necessarily a defeat, but a conscious strategy.

To help things along, it is well worth explaining to a class why we are using L2. Let them into your 'secret'. Why not tell them about child language acquisition and how you are trying to tap into their natural language acquisition abilities? Why not teach them some simple learning theory? We might say: *"When you were tiny you learned to speak and understand your own language by the age of about 4 and nobody gave you vocab to learn, homework or tests. How did that happen? Can we try and make the same happen in the little time we've got together in class and for homework?"* Or: *"Let's think about how we memorise things. How many times do you think you need to see or hear something to remember it? Do you think you learn best when you are relaxed or anxious?"*

Try working in bursts of L2 for up to ten minutes (no L1 at all), then release tension by allowing some L1, perhaps using that time as an opportunity to check understanding with students. Be very assertive when necessary, e.g. if L2 pair work is going on, and too much L1 is heard, nip it in the bud to ensure good habits and clear expectations.

L2 use is about maximising meaningful input and opportunities for student output. If using the L1 helps this along, that's fine.

Input and output tasks

When planning a lesson it is worth reflecting on whether the activities are primarily about providing input (listening and reading) or allowing opportunities for output (speaking and writing). Many activities (the best ones?) contain elements of both.

Input tasks (focus on exposing students to language)

- **Listening to recordings** and doing comprehension tasks.
- **Listening to the teacher** while doing question-answer or drill style work.
- Watching and listening to a **video**.
- **Reading an article or story** and doing oral or written comprehension on it.
- Doing **extensive reading**.
- Using a **picture for oral discussion** led by the teacher.
- Doing a **question-answer sequence** when introducing new grammar or vocabulary.
- Doing a **cloze** (gap-fill) **task** with the focus on **meaning**.
- Playing **bingo**.
- Doing a **crossword from L2 to L1** or with the focus on sentences in L2.

Output tasks (focus on activities which supply little or no new input)

- Doing a **grammar-translation** task (e.g. translating from L1 to L2).
- Writing a **composition** 'cold', i.e. with little help from a source text.
- **Memorising** a talk or essay for an assessment.
- Doing a **cloze exercise** with the focus on **grammatical accura**cy.
- **Memorising** a vocabulary list for a test.
- **Recording a talk** on a digital device.
- **Solving anagrams**.
- Doing a **crossword from L1 to L2**.
- Practising **learned conversations** with a partner.
- Creating a **grammar presentation**.

Effective L2 teaching should feature input tasks with a focus on meaning, along with ample opportunities for output. It will also strongly feature input at whole sentence or paragraph level, i.e. chunks of connected language rather than isolated words.

Awkward questions about L2 use

Students are very easily confused, especially when L2 is not used with skill or carefully selected for difficulty. Weaker students struggle with the concentration required, especially if the teacher talks too much with few contextual clues. If not supported by explanation in L1 some students may struggle to have a feel for what they have achieved. "What did I learn today?" The nature of language learning is cumulative, so it is not always easy to provide steps they feel they have mastered. Returns may be long term rather than short term; this needs explaining to students.

We recognise that L2 use requires great teacher skill and a degree of fluency which not all teachers have. It also requires a simpler version of normal speech which is more comprehensible yet still right. For example, we may use more cognates such as, in French, *réaliser* rather than *se rendre compte* (see Chapter 5 about why we choose to teach some words over others). We need to use a method which works for us. The idea that students will internalise rules by pure exposure and practice may seem fanciful, given the lack of regular contact time most receive.

Steve's tips for L2 teaching

- Have some sort of sign or signal indicating when only L2 is allowed.
- Apologise to the class for using L1 to set the right tone and show you are one of them.
- Give rewards to students who consistently use L2 or who use L2 spontaneously.
- Make maximum use of gesture, realia and pictures.
- Set challenges, e.g. *I am going to talk to you for 3 minutes about my weekend in (L2). Write down notes in L1 and I'll see how much you picked up* (then check understanding in L2: *Tell me in in (L2) anything I did..*
- If a student asks something in L1, give a quizzical look and say you don't understand.
- Use cognates where possible if the class needs them.
- Slow down your speech, but not too much.
- Use plenty of aural gap-fill: *I'm going to start a sentence, you finish it,* or *I'm going to end a sentence, how would you start it?*
- Do not be overly concerned with accuracy, except when the task demands it. Decide if the aim of the lesson or activity is to focus on accuracy or general proficiency.
- Use mini-whiteboards to keep all students active during L2 work.
- Use students as interpreters after you have spoken in L2. Choose one as 'interpreter for the day'.
- Use L2 talk as students walk in, e.g. counting to 20 (books out by 20), reciting the alphabet, chanting/singing days and months.
- Make the focus of computer/tablet work on input (e.g. listening, interactive grammar and comprehension) rather than devoting too much time to producing 'artefacts' where non-linguistic activity takes too long.
- When a student makes a mistake, sympathetically recast (i.e. reformulate) their response in a correct form to provide further input.
- Use L2 with colleagues in front of the class, perhaps talking about the class itself. Visitors such as the head teacher or principal will often be happy to play along.

Working as a departmental team

We have heard teachers say: *"I use (L2) consistently, but I have colleagues who don't"*. This is an issue for departments to work on through team meetings, continued professional development and personal targets. A consistent departmental approach will benefit students in the long run. Would it not be a good thing if students feel let down when they do not receive plenty of L2 input? It is not unreasonable to claim that they get better at what they practise. If we do lots of speaking and listening in L2, they will get better at it.

Alison Chase (2015) argues that it is essential for a department to develop, implement and monitor an L2 policy to ensure a degree of consistency across all members of the department. If teachers share the rationale behind it and implement similar practices, this should result in better outcomes for students. Once the rationale is explained, Chase suggests a number of frameworks departments might use. Two of these are:

> *1. Teachers of languages should always remain in L2 but may use the occasional single word of L1 to avoid unnecessary confusion. Where students speak L1 their contributions will be acknowledged but they will then be helped to word these contributions in L2.*
> *2. Teachers of languages should use L2 whenever it is beneficial to students' language learning and L1 should only be used in limited situations where it is common sense to do so.* (Chase, 2015 p. 124-5).

She then lists several statements which could further encourage consistency across a department, summarised here.

- The expectation is that L2 will be the main means of communications within the classroom.
- The expectation is that student to student L2 use will be encouraged, monitored and celebrated.
- New vocabulary or language will, initially at least, be introduced in L2.
- At least one exclusively L2 activity should be included in every lesson.
- It should be insisted upon that students always use L2 in situations where they know the required language or can access it from displays around the classroom.

Consistent application of an L2 policy will undoubtedly bring benefits to both students and teachers.

Concluding remarks

In this chapter we have tried to reinforce the idea that L2 use stems naturally from an approach founded on structured practice and meaningful input. We must acknowledge that students are different. Some may thrive on an approach founded strongly on L2 use, others may prefer a greater element of the analytical, cognitive, puzzle-solving approach. It may be sensible, given the still uncertain nature of research in this field, to cater for all needs while making sure that students are exposed to large amounts of comprehensible L2. When teaching in L2 the most skilful teachers manage to balance these requirements, creating a sympathetic, caring environment where students feel at ease contributing to classroom interactions, unafraid of making mistakes.

5

Vocabulary

Introduction

Students, especially the quicker ones, pick up vocabulary unconsciously through exposure in context. Most words in both L1 and L2 are probably learned incidentally, through communication, and extensive reading and listening. In any case, as Nation (2022) points out, there are too many words to teach directly. So it is safe to assume that if we provide repeated input over a long period, students will improve their mastery. Most teachers feel, however, as do we, that what researchers call **explicit instruction** is essential for beginning students whose lack of vocabulary limits their reading and listening ability. In this chapter we consider:

Research evidence
- ✓ The importance of vocabulary
- ✓ The mental lexicon
- ✓ Fluency
- ✓ Receptive and productive knowledge
- ✓ Formulaic language
- ✓ Incidental and intentional learning
- ✓ Building memory
- ✓ Levels of processing
- ✓ Information processing
- ✓ Forgetting
- ✓ Spaced repetition
- ✓ Retrieval practice (the testing effect)
- ✓ Chunking

Classroom practice
- ✓ How do we 'teach words'?
- ✓ Vocabulary teaching strategies
- ✓ Selecting the vocabulary to teach
- ✓ Recycling the vocabulary
- ✓ Encouraging deep processing
- ✓ Developing fluent recall
- ✓ 20 ways to work with vocabulary lists
- ✓ Using apps and other digital tools
- ✓ Learning vocabulary via a sentence builder
- ✓ Learning vocabulary through extensive reading

Research evidence

The importance of vocabulary

Applied linguist, David Wilkins, famously wrote: "While without grammar very little can be conveyed; without vocabulary nothing can be conveyed" (Wilkins, 1972 p. 111-2). Knowing words and multi-word units (chunks) is central to proficiency. Despite our best efforts, however, we often find that students have not retained as much vocabulary as we would like, particularly when it comes to producing it from memory for speaking and writing. What can we do to help them learn and retain vocabulary more effectively?

Beatriz González-Fernández and Norbert Schmitt (2017) also highlight the clear importance of vocabulary knowledge in language acquisition, stating that it is a key predictor of overall language proficiency. The more words we know and can use, the more proficient we are. Students often say that their lack of vocabulary is the main reason for their difficulty in understanding and using the language (e.g. Nation, 2022).

The mental lexicon

It is unclear how vocabulary is stored and processed in the **mental lexicon**, or **mental dictionary**, but vocabulary knowledge is not just about knowing the meaning of individual words; it means having all sorts of knowledge about words and the connections between them. For example, learning one item has an effect on learning others (Meara & Wolter, 2004). Evidence shows that L2 vocabulary learning is partly about establishing connections through exposure to words in varying contexts. In short, the more contacts you have with a word, in varying situations, the better you will remember it.

What does 'knowing a word' mean? Nation (2022) describes a framework (see Table 5.1) summarising what knowing a word means. This includes the word's *form* (e.g. spoken, written, word parts), *meaning*, e.g. what it refers to, its associations, collocations (what it goes next to) and grammatical functions, and its *use*, e.g. what words you can use with it and when you can use it.

Researchers have also described vocabulary knowledge as having three dimensions: *breadth*, *depth* and *fluency*. Breadth refers to the size of a person's lexicon, i.e. the number of the words for which they know the meaning (Nation, 2022). Depth refers to how well a learner knows a word across all the three dimensions identified by Nation (see Table 5.1).

Table 5.1   Nation's (2022) three dimensions of knowing a word

Form	• spelling • pronunciation • morphological knowledge (knowledge about affixation)
Meaning	• knowledge of word-meaning • knowledge of the role of context in defining meaning • knowledge of synonyms and antonyms
Use	• knowledge of correct usage • knowledge of collocations (i.e. knowledge of how L2 words combine in natural L2 usage) • knowledge of when to use and not use a word

Breadth

Breadth has been considered the most basic aspect of vocabulary knowledge, and learners with larger vocabulary sizes are more proficient language users (Meara, 1996). Breadth is about superficial knowledge of words. But definitions of breadth are complicated by the fact that we talk both about words, e.g. *bake,* and word families: *baking, bakery, baker*, but to give an idea of the number of words needed at intermediate level (e.g. in the GCSE exam in England, Wales and Northern Ireland), around 2000 words would be typical (either for receptive or productive knowledge).

Breadth and depth can interact, e.g. the more words you know, the more examples of word parts like prefixes and suffixes you will know - so breadth develops depth (Qian, 2002), provided that there are many encounters in a large variety of linguistic contexts. For example, just using a vocabulary learning app is not sufficient. Breadth usually develops before depth, so beginner and intermediate students have more difficulty putting sentences together.

Depth

Depth of vocabulary refers to a 'robust' knowledge of words, the many different facets of words, including how they sound (phonology), their written form (orthography), other forms of words (morphology), their grammatical use (syntax), meanings, and how they relate to other words (semantics), and how they convey meaning to other people (pragmatics). While breadth implies having a superficial knowledge of meaning, depth of knowledge seems to play the main role in determining success in complex linguistic and cognitive tasks such as listening comprehension

(Vafaee, 2016). So students may have a superficial knowledge of word meanings but fall short in tests where connected language is used.

Breadth usually develops before depth, meaning that beginner and intermediate students have more difficulty putting sentences together (Vafaee, 2016). As Qian (2002) notes, vocabulary knowledge develops cumulatively. Hence, words acquired at earlier stages are likely to have more depth than recently learned ones.

Fluency

Fluency is about how fast and effortlessly students can recognize, process or access the form and meaning of a word for language use (Vafaee, 2016).

Nation (2007) states that fluency benefits from specific training where students, once they have learned a word explicitly, need to do repeated practice in its retrieval in increasingly complex contexts for it to be internalised. For the teacher, this can mean increasing over time the rate at which input is delivered, and providing gradually longer texts.

One dimension of fluency is a student's ability to hold chunks in working memory as they process input. The larger the chunks our working memory can process at any one time, the more fluent processing is likely to be. Some researchers believe that working memory capacity is genetically determined and cannot be altered by teaching (e.g. Field, 2009); others (e.g. Nation and Newton, 2009) believe it can.

An important point to make concerning fluency is that it is **modality-specific** (Nation, 2007). We should not assume that simply because students are fluent in the oral production of vocabulary, they will be equally fluent in recognising it when listening or reading. We sometimes come across students who can utter long, complex sentences quickly and accurately, but who struggle to understand simple questions.

Fluency is also context and task-specific. This means that how fluently vocabulary is recalled depends on how similar the tasks are. Think of how you might transfer skill in one sport to another (Segalowitz, 2010). The most fluent students are those who can transfer their fluent recall across different topics and tasks.

Overall, it is worth spending as much time as possible on depth and fluency during listening tasks, not focusing exclusively on breadth. Unless vocabulary retrieval is fast, it is not useful in real time communication or under exam pressure. Remember, as mentioned above, that fluency also results from repeated exposure to vocabulary across a wide range of contexts. This is why recycling vocabulary over and over is so important.

Receptive and productive knowledge

The distinction is made between receptive and productive knowledge. The former unsurprisingly develops first. One study (Nemati, 2010) found that receptive knowledge may be five times greater than productive. So students typically recognise words but cannot recall and use them.

Although quoted figures vary, research suggests that learners require 2000-3000 words to understand about 95% of spoken English - enough for good comprehension (van Zeeland and Schmitt, 2012) and to hold basic conversations (Treffers-Daller and Milton, 2013).

Vocabulary acquisition is an incremental process. Different aspects of word knowledge are learned at different rates. Some aspects seem to be learned in order. For example, Norbert Schmitt (1998) found, in a study of 11 words, that spelling, derivative information, associations and different meanings for a word (polysemy) were acquired in order. Webb (2007) found that aspects of word knowledge were acquired in parallel but at different rates.

In addition aspects of word knowledge are picked up gradually, along a continuum ranging from zero knowledge to precise knowledge (e.g. Henrikson, 1999). Finally, receptive mastery precedes productive mastery. One researcher (Fitzpatrick, 2012) found that aspects of vocabulary knowledge sometimes regress.

Formulaic language

Formulaic language consists of idioms, lexical chunks and collocations. These terms are sometimes lumped together and called multi-word units. In English it has been calculated that these occupy between a third and a half of all conversation (Conklin & Schmitt, 2012). In general, isolated words and formulaic language should both form part of vocabulary teaching, but there are good reasons for emphasising the latter. It is more efficient for working memory to process whole chunks rather than isolated words. Wood (2010) argues that speech fluency is largely about chaining together familiar chunks of language (for more about this see Chapter 12).

Incidental and intentional learning

Incidental learning means picking up words where vocabulary acquisition is not the main goal. Learning occurs with little conscious effort. Lots of learning occurs this way, although uptake can be slower and more uneven. This is because the number of exposures needed to learn 'unconsciously' is high. How many exposures? This is hard to say and depends on the individual student. In one study of Chinese learners of English (Teng, 2019) 14 exposures to words in a graded reader were needed for them to be recognised, and 18 for them to be actively produced.

Research suggests that incidental learning through listening requires even more exposures (e.g. van Zeeland and Schmitt, 2013). Nevertheless listening tasks are a good source of incidental vocabulary learning. However, aural input is fragile (Nation, 2022) and for incidental learning to happen students need to understand 95-98% of the words (Nation, 2022; van Zeeland and Schmitt, 2013). In both listening and reading, high frequency words are more quickly acquired than low frequency words.

Intentional learning means deliberate attempts to learn new words. This can be through direct instruction such as call and response flashcard work, matching tasks, gap-fill, or through personalised learning from lists. As mentioned above, there is research to suggest that intentional learning is efficient (e.g. Webb, 2007). Laufer and Rozovski-Roitblat (2011) found that intentional exercises (practising words out of context, synonym and antonym work, selecting the right meaning from options, writing the words in sentences) led to better recall, both short and long-term, than incidental approaches. Bilingual word lists and flashcards have been found to be useful. Meaning-focused output (e.g. writing new words in sentences) is also supported by research. Other research suggests that the best approach is to combine intentional with incidental learning, where the latter reinforces the former. Boers (2021) notes that intentional learning is enhanced by telling students, before they read a text, that they will be tested on the target words at the end of the lesson. In sum, intentional learning is more efficient than incidental, but it needs to be reinforced by implicit exposure through repeated encounters.

Building memory

As we shall see, learning and teaching strategies that engage all the senses including visual (seeing and perceiving), auditory (hearing and speaking) and tactile (touch and movement) increase the chances of both storing and retrieving vocabulary. Gesture can play a useful role in memorising words, e.g. Macedonia (2014) found that gestures accompanying L2 vocabulary learning create 'embodied representations' and enhanced word learning.

Stories are also conducive to building memory. Bower and Clark (1969) tested the memorability of words embedded in stories versus a random list of words. Students were asked to memorise and recall 10 sets of unrelated words. The control group remembered the words in any order they wanted. The 'story' group constructed a story that contained all the words, one story per set. When asked to recall the words the students who constructed stories were able to remember six to seven times as many words compared to the random set.

Stories need not just be read or heard. Co-creating stories with classes, common in the TPRS approach (Teaching Proficiency through Reading and Storytelling), allows for frequent repetitions of vocabulary, and also helps create emotional connections with the language (see Chapter 19). When students' imaginations are engaged it is more likely language will be recalled.

Levels of Processing theory suggests that we recall information, including vocabulary, better when we learn it at greater depth. Figure 5.1 shows how this works, based on a seminal study by Craik and Lockhart (1972).

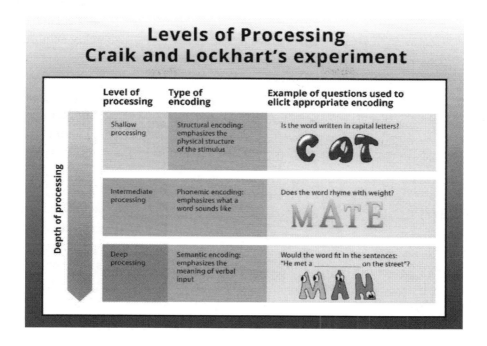

Figure 5.1 Levels of processing (from Smith and Conti, 2021)

The more contexts and meanings through which vocabulary is introduced, the more pathways are created in the brain. This is called **deep processing**. Appealing to all the senses also allows for the information to be stored in different regions across the brain, allowing for greater interconnection. Sounds tend to be stored in the left hemisphere, images in the right.

Research has also demonstrated that successful memory construction takes place when new content is linked to old: when new knowledge **schemas**, as they are called in the literature, are built on old ones.

It is worth noting another aid to memory, namely the **production effect**. Research shows that learners retain lists of words better when they read them aloud (e.g. Forrin and MacLeod, 2018). It is thought that memory is made stronger since speaking involves three elements: auditory, motor/articulatory (the physical act of speaking) and what's called a self-referential component. The latter is the idea that we process our own voice differently to other people's. Writing words down, another motor activity, also aids memory – more so than typing, it is thought (Smoker *et al.*, 2009).

Information-processing

Let us look in some detail at what happens in the brain of a student, as explained by **information-processing theory**.

When vocabulary is learned, it is stored in **long-term memory** (LTM), but is not stored randomly. Research on slips-of-the-tongue and aphasia (a language disorder which impedes comprehension and expression) suggests that the neural connections we make between words are determined by associations. These include the physical aspects of a word as well as its semantic, social and emotional features.   Words are associated at the physical level based on their spelling (graphemic level) and sound (phonological representation). Words that look and sound similar (alliterate, rhyme and chime) are more likely to be strongly associated. For example, when we attempt to retrieve the word *dog* from LTM, the brain activates all the monosyllabic words starting with 'd' and ending in 'g' (e.g. *Doug, dig, door*, etc.). Interestingly, even the anagram of *dog, god* may be triggered. This phenomenon explains slip-of-the-tongue errors, which are like 'computing mistakes', whereby we retrieve a near homophone instead of the word we need.

Words are also strongly linked by meaning to each other. Synonyms and other words that refer to items frequently associated in real life are also activated during retrieval. Going back to the *dog* example, words like *pet, bone, puppy, tail* and *bite*, amongst others, are activated during retrieval, each being more or less activated depending on: (1) how often you have processed (receptively or productively) those words in conjunction with the word *dog* in the past; (2) how frequently, in your experience, the items those words refer to, are associated with the idea of 'dog'.

In a fluent L2 learner with a sizeable vocabulary, there is also an association between an L2 word and its L1 (and L3, L4, etc.) translation(s). So the word *dog* in the brain of a speaker of Italian, French and German relates to the words *chien, cane, Hund,* etc. Consequently, when the brain searches for the word *dog* in one language, all the words in the other languages are activated too. This explains why some learners, when struggling to find an L2 word retrieve an L1 word instead of its L2 equivalent.

In sum, the more connections we have, the more likely we are to retrieve any word we need effectively. Successfully retrieving a word depends firstly on the strength of the memory trace (how often we have processed that word) and secondly on the availability of cues which help us find that information. The more words we know in L1 and L2, and the more world experience we have, the easier it is to recall L2 vocabulary.

What does this all mean for the language teacher? Before we come to this, let us consider why students forget words.

Forgetting

A first point to make is that we tend to forget things very quickly in general. Think for a moment about how quickly we forget someone's name at a party, or how we must rehearse in our head or out loud a phone number we have been given. German psychologist Hermann Ebbinghaus investigated forgetting, and produced his famous **forgetting curve**. He carried out experiments with short nonsense words of three letters, then tried to remember them at various time intervals after the initial learning (Ebbinghaus, 1885). The results of his experiments were clear and have been replicated many times since (see Figure 5.2).

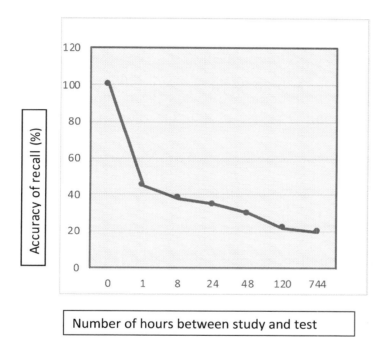

Figure 5.2 The Ebbinghaus forgetting curve

Figure 5.2 The Ebbinghaus forgetting curve

The reason we often fail to retrieve a word is not necessarily that the word has disappeared from memory. It may be that the context in which the word was learned has not been replicated. For example, if a student learns a word highlighted in red on the whiteboard while sitting near a specific classmate, the colour red, the teacher's whiteboard and the classmate are all possible retrieval cues for that word. The absence of these three factors may prevent recall. This implies that the more associations created by the student in learning a word, the more likely they are to remember it. The phenomenon of recall being associated with the context in which an item was learned is called **Transfer-Appropriate Processing.** It means that if we test an item of vocabulary in the same way that the item was first learned, it is easier to recall.

Another possible reason we forget is that when we take in new information, a certain amount of time is necessary for changes to the nervous system to take place so that it is properly recorded. If this **consolidation** process is not completed, we lose the information. Consolidation has even been shown to occur during sleep. Without **rehearsal** of L2 vocabulary, 60% of it is thought to be forgotten within 48 hours of having been 'learned'. This is why we need to recycle the information repeatedly until it is stored permanently in long-term memory.

Forgetting is also modality-specific. This means we might forget one dimension of a word rather than others. For instance, we may not recall the pronunciation of a word, but may recall its spelling. We may recall its meaning, but not its collocations (the other words it tends to keep company with).

Finally, words can be forgotten because of what cognitive psychologists call **interference**. This is when two words have similar meanings or sound similar. So, in French, a student may forget the meaning of the words *fraise* (strawberry) and *framboise* (raspberry), since, in this case they are both red berry fruits and both begin with /fr/. Interference can be proactive or retroactive. Proactive interference is where knowledge we already have interferes with how we learn new information. Retroactive interference is where new information disrupts our existing knowledge.

An example of **proactive interference** would be when students have learned a set of German verbs in the perfect tense, which are all conjugated with the auxiliary verb *haben* ('to have'), as in *Ich habe gelernt* – ('I have learned'), then they are taught that some verbs take the auxiliary *sein* ('to be') as in *Ich bin gegangen* – ('I have gone/been'). But they may forget to use the auxiliary *sein* with verbs that require it.

In contrast, **retroactive interference** would occur when students begin a second modern/world language which adversely affects their knowledge of the first new language they studied.

Spaced repetition

Research is clear that memory develops more effectively when encounters with information (in this case, vocabulary) are spaced out over time (e.g. Carpenter, 2017). This is called the **spacing effect** or **distributed learning effect**. Between each learning episode the brain has a chance to consolidate the learning. You could say that spacing is an antidote to forgetting. To counteract the forgetting that Ebbinghaus measured, opportunities to revisit vocabulary are needed.

Is there an ideal way to space out learning encounters? It has been suggested that the optimum time lag between learning episodes might be just at the moment a learner is about to forget (e.g. Bjork and Bjork, 2011), but of course this would be impossible to predict for any or every student in a class. In general, research is not clear about this, particularly when spacing intervals are tested outside laboratories, in real classrooms (Rogers & Cheung, 2018). Perhaps the best that we can say is that spacing is important (e.g. Bahrick *et al.*, 1993), but so is the memorability of each encounter and the depth of processing involved. It is also sound practice to make repetitions most frequent at the start of learning, then gradually reduce those repetitions over time.

Retrieval practice (the testing effect)

It is widely recognised in education these days that the act of retrieving something from memory reinforces learning. A seminal study by Jeffrey Karpicke and Henry Roediger (2008) on the learning of words in Swahili clearly demonstrated the merits of testing. This has even led some schools to mandate the use of retrieval practice quizzes at the start of every lesson. The evidence for the effectiveness of retrieval practice is enormous. With vocabulary, the effect should be more obvious than with grammar. The former involves retrieving word meanings, whereas the latter is about a building a system of knowledge, which is much harder. In this sense, teaching vocabulary is easier than teaching grammar.

Essentially, when students are actually tested on material, rather than just practising it, the learning gains are far greater. The day-to-day low-stakes recall tests which language teachers are familiar with – vocabulary quizzes, quick translation, "do now" tasks which require retrieving language from previous lessons – all of these have value.

For a much more detailed treatment of memory, with a special focus on language teaching, see Smith and Conti (2021).

Chunking

Research has, therefore, given us some important leads about teaching vocabulary. In general terms we would agree with this advice adapted from the work of researcher Joe Barcroft (2004):

1. Present new words frequently and repeatedly within meaningful input.
2. Do not necessarily force students to say new words when first encountered.
3. Progress from less demanding to more demanding vocabulary related activities.

Let us focus on Point 1. The main way students will acquire vocabulary is by hearing, seeing and using it in connected language. This develops both breadth and depth of vocabulary knowledge. Given the time constraints most teachers work under, priorities need to be set. Is it better for students to spend 20 minutes learning words from a list or app? Or could these 20 minutes be better spent using the vocabulary in, for example, easy aural or written texts, sentence builders or dialogues? Given that word knowledge is much more than just knowing the meaning and form (which a list provides), it is better to encounter and use words alongside other words.

So, the evidence from memory research clearly suggests that we should prioritise chunked language over the teaching of isolated words. That is not to say there is never a case for learning isolated words. There is little wrong with presenting some new simple vocabulary via, for example, flashcards, but even with simple concrete vocabulary, it can be placed within a phrase.

On a PowerPoint slide, for example, instead of just displaying the word *cat*, you could always place it within a phrase or short sentence such as *I like cats* or *We have a cat* or *My cat is black*. Many students will find it easier to recall a whole chunk of that type than making up a sentence from the single word *cat*. In addition, a phrase or sentence carries more communicative clout than a single word. For much more about this, see Chapter 12 on lexicogrammar.

Classroom practice

How do we 'teach' words?

A key point to make from the outset is the importance of students spending time learning vocabulary orally and aurally. Only then will they be able to both pronounce words and recognise them in speech. This is because students need to have an accurate phonological representation of words and multi-word units, not just a more superficial knowledge of what words look like. Learning spellings from apps or lists is not enough. Nation (2022) provides a list of ways teachers typically use to get across the meaning of new words to classes. We can do so by:

- performing actions;
- showing objects;
- showing pictures and diagrams;
- defining the new word or phrase in L1, including giving example sentences;
- defining and giving examples in L2, including using synonyms or antonyms;
- providing contextual clues, e.g. what words nearby help you understand?

To this list we can add:

- providing glosses with texts (lists of word meanings in L1 in the margin, above or below);
- providing partial glosses, e.g. with letters missing;
- using gestures.

Vocabulary teaching strategies

Here are some specific teaching strategies which make good sense.

1. In any given lesson teach words that are related semantically and grammatically. This is often done by textbooks anyway. Some research suggests that closely related words interfere with each other in memory, so be aware if this might be the case with individual words. In French, for example, it may be wise to avoid teaching the words *cour*, *court* and *cours* in close proximity owing to their phonological similarity. These three homonyms have very different and multiple meanings (e.g. playground, court and lesson).

2. When teaching new words try as far as possible to hook them with previously learned vocabulary which alliterates, chimes or rhymes with the new vocabulary. This can be turned into a game in which students are given the task to find, to a time limit, a rhyming or alliterating word for the new L2 vocabulary.

3. Try to ensure that, from the early stages, students are aware of the word class an item belongs to. This provides them with an added retrieval cue in the recall process. For instance, they could be asked to categorise the words into adjectives, nouns, adverbs, etc., or to brainstorm all the words they learned that day in those categories.

4. Find as many opportunities as possible for students to relate words, especially the challenging ones, to their personal and emotional life. For instance, when learning colours they could be asked to match each colour to an emotion or physical state. Or, when learning food, ask them to say which fruit, pastry, drink, etc. they identify with and why.

5. Students could also do activities requiring them to perform more elaborate semantic associations between new and previously learned vocabulary. For instance, create 'lexical chains', i.e. given two words quite far apart in meaning, students produce an associative chain of words that links those two items in some way, logically or otherwise. For example: *old lady, cats, cat food, cans, aluminium, factories, pollution.* This can be fun and does not require knowledge of complex vocabulary.

6. Activities involving semantic analysis of words, such as odd-one-out, definition games, sorting vocabulary into semantic categories, matching lexical items of similar or opposite meanings, also creates further associations (deep processing).

7. Be careful when teaching cognates that are orthographically or phonologically very close in the two languages. These sorts of L2 cognates can cause difficulty as they are so closely associated with their L1 translation that they can result in retrieval of the L1 form. For example, French words ending with the spelling *ation* being pronounced as 'ation' in English - think of a words like nation or natation.

8. Review the vocabulary across as many contexts as possible and as often as possible until it has been fully acquired, especially during the two days following the initial teaching, when most forgetting usually occurs.

9. In languages which have genders, be consistent in using either the definite or indefinite article in the early stages. If students get to hear a word with the same article many times over, it is more likely they will remember its gender without needing to learn it by rote. They become quite competent with gender over time in this way.

10. Extensive reading contributes greatly to vocabulary acquisition. Where possible, and where time allows, it is wise to give students the opportunity to read texts for pleasure. Finding texts at the right level can be a challenge. There may be a mismatch between students' cognitive maturity levels and their L2 proficiency. One solution is to make use of parallel reading texts presented with L2 on the left and L1 on the right.

11. Digital text manipulation tasks, e.g. *textivate.com*, *sentencebuilders.com* and interactive exercises, such as those that can be found at *languagesonline.org.uk,* can combine exposure to vocabulary with the opportunity to use it repeatedly and meaningfully.

12. Place an emphasis on verbs – these are sometimes neglected in favour of nouns. There is good reason to practise lots of verbs together with nouns. In his workbook series Gianfranco refers to 'verb pivots' – verbs presented and practised within lexicogrammatical patterns.

Selecting the vocabulary to teach

In putting the course together, or adapting an existing one, we are often largely influenced by the choice of words in a textbook or by prescribed lists provided by examination awarding bodies. However, we should bear in mind a range of other factors. One obvious approach is to base decisions on vocabulary choice on a **frequency list**. This is based on a **corpus**, i.e. a collection of texts (spoken or written) actually used by L1 users. Corpora are often used for linguistic research. At first view it seems logical to teach the words most often used, but it is not so simple, since a decision has to be made about the source of the corpus – should it be drawn from conversational speech or written sources, for example? Other significant factors in vocabulary selection include the ones listed below.

- **Teachability**. Concrete vocabulary may be taught early on since it can easily be illustrated through pictures or demonstration. This is particularly relevant when a direct method, L2 only approach is used (Richards, 2001).
- **Learnability**. How easy or challenging the vocabulary is in terms of length, pronunciation, spelling, meaning, part of speech, grammar, word order in a sentence, etc.
- **Relevance.** How relevant the vocabulary is to learners' interests, background and cultures.
- **Semantic relatedness**. Words which are more strongly semantically inter-related have a better chance of being retained. We can hold semantically related words (e.g. *cat, dog, bird*) better in working memory than unrelated ones (e.g. *desk, pillow, mouse*) (Kowialiewski *et al.*, 2022).
- **Similarity**. Vocabulary may be chosen because it is similar to words in the L1, e.g. English and French have many cognates such as *table*, *football* and *musique*.

- **Availability**. Some words may not be frequent, but are readily available in that they come to mind when certain topics are taught, e.g. classroom vocabulary such as *pen*, *pencil case* and *chair* are worth teaching early on (Richards, 2001).
- **Coverage/defining power**. Words that cover, include or help define the meaning of other words might be useful, e.g. *seat* might be taught since it covers *chair*, *stool* and *armchair*. Other examples such as vehicle, container and dwelling may not be high-frequency words, but are worth teaching.

Another key factor to bear in mind is relevance to students' age range and interests. For teenagers it makes sense to teach words about school, popular culture, common pastimes and future plans. In addition, the choice of vocabulary might be influenced by issues of the day that are considered important, such as climate, pollution, human rights, diversity and inequality. Finally, students may wish to learn vocabulary relating to their personal interests, e.g. a favourite pastime or current event.

If a teacher does not make their own resources, or they are a novice teacher, it may be useful to draw up a list of words and multi-word units for students to learn to ensure that systematic recycling occurs throughout the lesson and from one lesson to the next. The best textbooks help with the recycling from one unit to later ones. Some, however, are overloaded with vocabulary, so there is no need to think we have to 'cover' everything. Coverage does not equal learning.

In addition, consider which lexical items students need to learn **receptively** (for recognition only) and **productively** (for use in speech and writing), receptive learning obviously being easier. Consider also how 'deep' the teaching of the vocabulary item is going to be. Which levels of knowing a word are we going to teach, bearing in mind what 'knowing a word' means (see Table 5.1).

The number of words selected per lesson depends largely on our learners and how systematically we want the words to be recycled. About three or four chunks of information is the maximum amount working memory can hold. The amount of stimulus constantly received by the brain quickly overloads our working memory. Learning and memory use also quickly cause fatigue. The more intense the learning, the quicker students tire. In our experience, with a high-achieving group (i.e. students with highly efficient working memories) we can aim at up to 20-25 words or lexical chunks receptively (especially if the words include cognates) and around 10 to 15 productively, in an hour-long lesson.

Recycling the vocabulary

Plan for several recycling opportunities throughout the lesson, e.g. through listening, speaking, reading, writing and gestures. Ensure students process each word receptively and productively at least ten times during a given lesson. Since research shows that students notice adjectives and adverbs less, greater attention could be given to them. They can be used frequently across many fields of vocabulary and so represent a great way of helping recycle both nouns and verbs in a different context. Ensure recycling includes activities like the ones below.

- **Higher order thinking skills**, e.g. odd-one-out, matching with synonyms, inferring meaning from context, etc. The deeper and more elaborate the level of semantic analysis of the L2 lexis, the more likely students remember.
- **Communicative activities** involving information gaps and negotiation of meaning; a large body of research indicates that these activities significantly enhance vocabulary acquisition.
- Working on **spelling**.
- Working on **phonological awareness**.
- **Manipulating the grammar** associated with the word (endings, noun-verb-adjective).
- **Semantic and phonetic associations** with previously learned vocabulary.
- '**Inferential strategies**', e.g. understanding texts in which the vocabulary item is needed to grasp the meaning of an unfamiliar word.
- A **competitive element**, e.g. word games.
- **Developing self-reliance**, e.g. by using dictionaries and by creative use of the vocabulary, such as putting words and chunks into sentences.

It is worth stressing correct pronunciation of new words from the very early stages as associating sounds with spellings (phonics) helps vocabulary recall. Try to make work as relevant as possible to students' own interests. It is also advisable to ensure that words are practised in context, not in isolation. If games or wordplay are used, try to favour the use of words within meaningful sentences. This also contributes to developing general listening and reading skills.

When visuals are used, they should be as clear as possible (see Chapter 10). If using visuals to present new words, many teachers like to show the spellings at the same time. This is a justifiable approach, even though often discouraged in the past since it was thought to produce poor pronunciation, influenced by the L1. Better to get sound-spelling correspondences sorted out in the early stages, in our view.

The use of striking pictures, anecdotes, jokes or sound effects makes the input more arresting and therefore more memorable. Some students will enjoy taking advantage of mobile technology using the many apps available, possibly competing with others, to help set words or chunks to memory. Apps often involve associating images with words and use computer algorithms to select words which may not have been mastered.

Encouraging deep processing

We can use various ways to foster the deep processing of vocabulary:

- **Elaboration**. This includes encouraging inferring (working meaning out from context), sorting/categorising words, creating sentences with a new word.
- **Distinctiveness.** Find ways to make words stand out or be memorable. An example is the **keyword technique** where you think of an L1 word (the keyword) which sounds like the L2 word. A mental image must be established to connect the keyword with the new word or information. For example, if the word to be learned is *pasto,* (grass in Spanish), a keyword that sounds similar must be introduced. The word 'pasta' can be used as a keyword since it sounds similar. The student is then asked to combine the meaning of the new word and the keyword through mental imaging. For the word *pasto*, a mental image can be formed of pasta growing like grass. When seeking the Spanish for 'grass', this memory is activated to recall the image.
- **Personal association.** For instance, associating adjectives with members of one's family
- **Stories.** Using vocabulary in a story which makes an emotional connection in some way is likely to make it more memorable.

Developing fluent recall

Most teachers think of fluency in terms of speaking naturally or smoothly, but as we shall see in Chapter 7, it is also used about the other skills of listening, reading and writing. It takes time for fluent recall to develop, but we can devote lesson time to tasks specifically aimed at developing fluent retrieval. Nation (2014) suggests these principles when planning fluency tasks:

1. The focus should be on receiving or conveying meaning.
2. There is no unfamiliar language, and content is largely familiar (thus limiting extraneous cognitive load).
3. There is some pressure or encouragement to perform at a faster than usual speed.
4. There is a large amount of input or output.

Many retrieval tasks can include pressure to encourage rapid recall. One widely used example is **Disappearing text**. After working on a written text displayed on the board, a second is shown with words or chunks missing. Students note what is missing to a time limit - orally, in pairs or on mini-whiteboards. A third text can be displayed with different, or more, gaps to fill. A retrieval task based on images is the famous **Kim's Game**. A set of pictures is shown and practised, with images removed in subsequent slides. Many other examples of lexical retrieval tasks can be found in Conti and Smith (2019). A general pedagogical point is that when teachers work at a brisk pace and expect students to do so, fluent recall is more likely to develop (see Chapter 7).

20 ways to work with vocabulary lists

Many teachers work with textbooks containing lists of vocabulary. Despite its limitations, traditional vocabulary learning has value and receives some support from research. For example, Hunt and Beglar (1998) include providing opportunities for intentional learning as one of their seven principles

That said, learning from lists can be an off-putting task in class and an uninspiring homework to set. We also have to deal with students who do not complete their homework or who simply cannot set words to memory very easily. Explain that it is more effective to study words regularly over several short sessions. Make sure they are aware that, as most forgetting occurs immediately after initial exposure to a word, repetition and review should take place almost immediately after studying a word for the first time. These behaviours can be modelled in class to illustrate the point by teaching ten words at the start of a lesson and testing them at the end without further input and then comparing in the next lesson with another similar ten, which are reinforced systematically.

To make vocabulary learning more stimulating, what else can students do with lists of words apart from just reading and memorising them? Below is a checklist of 20 possible procedures. Remember that many of these work at the isolated word level. We suggest using a mixture of techniques, favouring the use of vocabulary within chunks, sentences or longer utterances.

1. Students **cover the words and test themselves** or ask someone to help.

2. For slower students make the vocabulary test into a **matching task**. Write L1 words on the left and L2 on the right. Students link them with lines. Alternatively, number and letter each word. For faster students the matching task could consist of words and their definitions.

3. Students **write the words out** over and over – L1 next to L2 and vice versa – do more and more from memory each time.

4. Students **record the words** onto a digital device or phone and listen back. Some will happily do this on the way to school before a test.

5. Students **write the words on post-it notes** and stick them up around their bedroom.

6. Give students **partly spelled words** to complete, e.g. with vowels missing.

7. Set **crosswords** with definitions in L2. There are websites which allow you to produce crosswords extremely quickly, e.g. *armoredpenguin.com*.

8. Students **play a partner game**: each person gives a word from a list or on a particular topic; the first one unable to give a word loses.

9. Students play **'running reporter'**: a vocabulary list is put somewhere far away, e.g. at the back of the classroom. One student runs to the list and tries to memorise as many words as accurately as they can and runs back to their partner who writes them down. The first pair to finish the list correctly wins.

10. Ask each student to write ten words in L1 from a list they had to learn (using this list makes them revise). They pass their list of ten items to a partner, and each **translates their partner's list**. Then they check their partner's translation with the original list to be learned.

11. Get students to cover up the L2 words. You then **supply the first syllable or sound** of a word, and they must complete it with the rest of the word. Students produce their responses orally or in writing. Then do the same but supply the **last sound or syllable** of the word.

12. Give **oral definitions** of words and students write the answers. This is harder but provides good general listening practice. If it is a test, make sure they have been warned about the format. You can use synonyms and antonyms as part of this. Recommended only for more able groups.

13. Play **word association**. This can lead into various directions, but works well with large fields of similar vocabulary, e.g. food and drink. It can be done as a whole class or group activity.

14. Do **'aural anagrams'**. Spell words with the letters jumbled up. Students guess the word as fast as they can. This encourages careful listening and reinforces knowledge of the alphabet. You can make it a team game or get students to play the game in groups.

15. Makevoneoenormouscwordafrombtheulistlyouahavergivenythem.
    Place extra letters between the words. The added letters spell out another word or message.

16. Play **'strip bingo'** or **word bingo**. In strip bingo students write a list of about 12 words or chunks (from a list you have displayed) on a strip of paper. Read aloud the items at random, repeatedly. Each time a student recognises a word at the top or bottom of their strip of paper, they tear it off. As words are torn off, new words/chunks appear at the top or bottom of their strip. The winner succeeds in removing all their words. In word bingo, a list of L2 vocabulary is displayed. Students select around eight of these words. You read out the words at random as if playing bingo. The winner is the first to have all their words read out.

17. Play a **dominoes** game. Make up dominoes with words and definitions or translations. You supply pairs of students with a set of dominoes and they play to a time limit.

18. **'Running to the board'** games. Write up words on board in a random pattern. Create two teams, give each student a number so each team has a person with the same number. Give a definition or translation and call out a number. The first student to rush to the board and touch the word gets a point. Alternatively, get two students to stand by the board and do the same activity. Change pairs every few minutes. They enjoy this type of competitive activity, but you need to make sure it is both safe and under control.

19. In pairs, one student turns their back while the other **draws a word with their finger** on the first person's back. The first person tries to guess the word. This is an amusing activity for students and gives them more opportunity to say and hear the words. Alternatively, in pairs one spells out a word in the air and the partner must guess it.

20. Produce **gap-fill texts** into which students insert vocabulary they have learned. This has the merit of supplying extra language input and letting them see the words in context.

Using apps and other digital tools

At the time of writing, popular apps for vocabulary learning include Quizlet, Blooket and Memrise. While there is clearly some value in having students set words to memory, it is worth weighing up whether the time spent doing so might be better spent on activities which involve using new words in context. This has the potential to produce greater depth of knowledge. As we have mentioned, apps which allow them to hear words as well as see their spellings and meanings are preferable.

Digital tools which engage students in hearing, seeing and using vocabulary in context have a great advantage. Again, at the time of writing, tools such as language-gym.com, sentencebuilders.com and languagesonline.org.uk serve a useful purpose. Gamifying the learning and introducing a competitive element further motivates vocabulary learning.

Incidentally, although several studies have indicated that gamifying vocabulary learning is motivational, we have found no study which compares its effectiveness with traditional ways of memorising vocabulary.

Learning vocabulary via a sentence builder

Could vocabulary learning be made more productive and enjoyable? If you wish to move away from traditional vocabulary learning and testing based on word lists, consider this alternative. Within Gianfranco's EPI approach, the sentence builder is usually the starting point for a lesson sequence. Many teachers have embraced their use in recent years.

We have seen that 'knowing a word' is much more than knowing its meaning or knowing how to write it down accurately in a test. Really knowing words also means knowing what they sound like, what other words they keep company with, when and how they are used, how they relate to other forms of the word (e.g. *play - player - playing*), not to mention their relationship with synonyms, antonyms and L1 words.

To recap, every minute spent learning isolated words could be spent using these words in context, in connected, meaningful sentences or chunks. Rehearsing language in this way is more likely to enable students to later retrieve useful chunked language to make meaning. Learning words in meaningful multi-word units or whole sentences builds a deeper understanding of vocabulary and is more productive communicatively. Put differently, memorising chunks and sentences provides better 'surrender value' - more learning for the time spent. In addition, it may be more enjoyable, creating more motivation, more self-efficacy and more learning.

In practice, here is one way to do it. Provide students with a sentence builder they are familiar with, or even similar to one used in class. Tell the class to practise reading aloud at home as many sentences as they can in, say, 15 minutes. Suggest they record this on their phones. Suggest also, that within the time they allocate, that they close their eyes and say the sentences from memory. (Closing eyes is a good way to avoid distraction.) Advise them, furthermore, to divide the time up so that their practice is spaced out, e.g. between other bits of homework.

Then, in class, tasks could include:

- From memory, producing as many sentences as possible to a time limit.
- Working with a partner, each student gives a sentence until one cannot (competitive element).
- Write down as many sentences from the sentence builder as possible.
- As above, but add new, adapted sentences, slotting in alternative words.
- Do a gap-fill activity using sentences from the sentence builder.
- Do a traditional L1 to L2 written test (harder) or L2 to L1 test (easier).
- Give sentence starters. Students must finish the sentence.
- Harder: asking questions, the answers supplied by students from their sentence builder.

This process is likely to be more enjoyable and productive than a traditional single word vocabulary test. All the practice done in the process will leave long-term memory traces - chunks of language that students can call upon when trying to converse or write.

Learning vocabulary through extensive reading

We return to the topic of reading in Chapter 8, but it is worth saying here that a good deal of vocabulary can be acquired incidentally while doing extensive reading, such as using graded readers. It is worth devoting some of the valuable time at our disposal to silent reading in class. There is a range of age-appropriate readers available, some of which provide parallel translations to make sure the language is always comprehensible. An element of free choice can be introduced, but keep in mind the importance of the reading input being both interesting and comprehensible. If readers are unavailable, consider producing parallel texts on topics which will interest your students. An AI tool can do this quickly and can also provide comprehension questions to accompany the texts.

Concluding remarks

Knowing words and multi-word units is at the heart of everything. It is more important than grammar. When students are exposed to large amounts of high frequency vocabulary and given the opportunity to make as many connections as possible, they can achieve a lot. Interacting with aural and written texts, communicating with the teacher or peers, playing games, using sentence builders, co-creating stories, using apps or word lists all contribute to breadth and depth of lexical knowledge and skill. It is always a pleasure to see and hear students using new language they have encountered, practised or just set to memory. If we do not provide frequent, spaced out and reinforced exposure to high-frequency, relevant vocabulary, students are unlikely to develop the knowledge and skills they need to communicate.

6

Grammar

Introduction

Grammar may be defined as the system and structure of a language, usually taken as consisting of syntax (word order) and morphology (including inflections). Researchers sometimes make the distinction between pedagogical grammar (the rules we find in grammar books) and grammar as 'mental representation' (what is in our heads and invisible).

Knowing grammar, implicitly (and maybe explicitly – 'knowing the rules'), is necessary for using a language competently. How we get students to achieve this competence has been hotly debated in the research over the years. Do we teach rules? Do we draw their attention to grammatical structures and practise them? Or do we let nature take its course and allow students to gradually pick up the rules through hearing and reading large amounts of comprehensible input?

This chapter considers the areas below.

Research evidence
- ✓ Two types of grammatical knowledge
- ✓ The interface question
- ✓ Does teaching grammar help?
- ✓ Focus on <u>form</u> or focus on <u>forms</u>?
- ✓ Input and output-based instruction
- ✓ Learned attention
- ✓ Processing Instruction
- ✓ An inductive or deductive approach?
- ✓ Developmental readiness
- ✓ 10 research-based principles for grammar teaching

Classroom practice
- ✓ An inductive approach example
- ✓ Presentation-Practice-Production (PPP)
- ✓ Making the work interesting
- ✓ Making students feel successful
- ✓ Selecting and sequencing of grammar
- ✓ Consolidation
- ✓ Practice activities for major tenses
- ✓ Learning by heart
- ✓ Why agreements are hard to master
- ✓ Assessing grammar

Research evidence

Two types of grammatical knowledge

Hossain Nassaji (2017) reminds us of a long-standing controversy in the field. Does learning develop primarily through explicit teaching and conscious manipulation of structures, or merely through unconscious processes when people are exposed to meaningful input (known as implicit learning)? Psychologist Nick Ellis (2012) points out that implicit and explicit learning are functions of separate memory systems in the brain. Scans show that explicit learning is supported by neural networks located in the prefrontal cortex, whereas implicit learning involves other areas of the brain, the perceptual and motor cortex. So physical evidence suggests a clear distinction between explicit (conscious) and implicit (unconscious) learning.

Explicit learning leads to explicit knowledge, often called declarative knowledge, i.e. 'being able to explain the rules'. This in itself is not much use when it comes to speaking and comprehending in real time. Implicit knowledge is taken to occur based on extensive meaning-focused input, acquired without awareness and stored implicitly (speaking the language without being able to explain the rules).

Some researchers, (such as Ullman, 2006) believe that grammar and vocabulary are stored differently in the brain. They suggest that vocabulary is stored as declarative memory, whereas grammar is stored as implicit or procedural memory. This may explain why using grammar accurately is harder for students than recalling vocabulary. In other words, you might say that the system (grammar) is harder to acquire than its components (vocabulary). Ellis and Shintani (2013) sum up the differences between implicit and explicit knowledge (see Table 6.1).

Table 6.1 Implicit and explicit knowledge (adapted from Ellis and Shintani, 2013).

Characteristics	Implicit knowledge	Explicit knowledge
Awareness	No conscious awareness of rules but knows what 'sounds right'	Consciously aware and can explain rules
Type of knowledge	Procedural, i.e. available for automatic processing	Declarative – facts about the L2 only available through controlled processing
Systematicity	Variable but systematic	Often inconsistent since students may have a partial understanding of the grammatical feature
Use of L2 knowledge	Evident when used for communication	Used to monitor production; used when students lack implicit knowledge
Self-report	Internalised constructions which may not be easily reported	Can be reported using metalanguage (grammar terminology)
Learnability	May be age limits on ability to acquire grammar implicitly	Learnable at any age, but older learners have more world knowledge

It is worth pointing out immediately, that explicit knowledge is much easier to acquire than implicit. It is all too easy to imagine that when students have good explicit knowledge, they can convert this to implicit. In fact it is not easy, as we shall see in the next section.

The interface question

What is the relationship between these two types of knowledge? In particular, can explicit knowledge become implicit? Traditionally there have been three views about this which involve what is called the **interface** between explicit and implicit knowledge.

The **no-interface** position (e.g Krashen, 1982) holds that explicitly, consciously learned language cannot become implicit. Instruction makes no difference - all you need is meaningful exposure to language. The **strong interface** position (e.g. DeKeyser, 1997) holds that implicit knowledge can result from proceduralisation of explicit knowledge, i.e. through explanation and practising the skills you can become proficient. In this view, students can use explicit knowledge to consciously construct utterances in working memory. The **weak interface** position argues that explicit knowledge facilitates the acquisition of implicit knowledge.

Critics of the strong and weak interface position (e.g. Lichtman and VanPatten, 2021) argue that no mechanism has been described to explain how explicit knowledge can become implicit. Brain scanning shows the two types of learning happen in different brain areas. Nick Ellis (2005) has suggested, however, that explicit and implicit knowledge work in cooperation, not separately. Unlike the strong interface and the non-interface positions, the weak interface refers to **noticing** and 'noticing the gap'. Noticing refers to the conscious cognitive effort of detecting and paying attention to language features as a necessity for language acquisition while noticing the gap refers to when learners notice a mismatch between what they say/know and what native speakers say (Schmidt, 1990). This is known as Schmidt's **Noticing Hypothesis**. Scholars do not agree about the extent to which 'noticing' is needed for structures to be acquired (i.e. internalised for spontaneous use). Indeed, by 2010 Schmidt had softened his view on this (Schmidt, 2010).

A final point to note is that DeKeyser's (1997) strong interface position comes with some caveats. He argues that you need a certain set of circumstances for explicit knowledge to be successfully automatised, e.g. learners need to be adult and have a certain level of aptitude. In addition, he argues that there is a difference between automatised explicit knowledge and implicit knowledge. Both involve rapid access to linguistic knowledge, but explicit knowledge involves consciousness about linguistic features, whereas using implicit knowledge requires no awareness (Suzuki and DeKeyser, 2017). In reality, it is not always clear to language learners whether they are speaking based on rules they know or feel (McLaughlin, 1978). For most teachers this distinction may not seem very important, as long as students can use the L2 successfully for their purposes or for an examination.

Does teaching grammar help?

You might be surprised to even be asked that question, but some scholars in the field, e.g. Stephen Krashen and John Truscott, argue that grammar teaching makes little or no difference to developing students' proficiency. Their reasoning goes back to the interface issue referred to above. They argue there is no evidence that declarative knowledge of grammar can become procedural skill. On the other hand, Michael Long (1983) looked at 12 studies comparing learning through exposure with 'instructional' learning and concluded that overall instruction made a positive difference at all levels with both children and adults. Rod Ellis (1990, 1994) and Larsen-Freeman and Long (1991) also found that instruction helped with the rate and ultimate level of acquisition. More recent studies have reached the same conclusion (Norris and Ortega, 2000; Spada and Tomita, 2010; Goo *et al.*, 2015).

Overall, the empirical evidence favours instruction, but what type of instruction? It has been argued that the studies mentioned here only really measured improvement in the accuracy of certain grammatical forms. But the Spada and Tomita (2010) study found that grammatical improvement was measurable even in spontaneous speech. Kang, Sok & Han (2018), having analysed 54 studies from 1980 up to 2015 found that instruction was useful, especially for beginners, but that implicit instruction had a longer-lasting effect. However, let us be clear – explicit grammar teaching probably helps our students less than you think. Using the language is much more important.

Pawlak (2021) examined the evidence about whether grammar is better acquired through explicit instruction or by picking it up implicitly through input and usage. He reminds us that the rules and patterns of **pedagogical grammars** (the type we find in grammar manuals and textbooks) have little to do with the mental reality of learners' **interlanguage** (the unconscious mental model of grammar that learners are developing as they learn). He notes that just because students have explicit knowledge of pedagogical grammar, it does not mean they can apply it in real time. Nevertheless, he suggests, following DeKeyser (2012), that students who have relatively little contact time with the L2 can rely on 'automatised explicit knowledge' to get them by since they do not have time to build a large foundation of implicit knowledge. (In practice, most teachers would not be too worried whether students are using implicit knowledge or automatised explicit knowledge!) His conclusion is:

> ...the predominant goal of GI (grammar instruction) is to help learners develop implicit knowledge, or much more realistically in many contexts, automatise the explicit knowledge they have at their disposal. (Pawlak, 2021).

He also cites Nassaji and Fotos (2011) who stated   "... teachers should be eclectic in their pedagogical approach."

Focus on <u>form</u> or focus on <u>forms</u>?

This (confusing) distinction was put forward by Long (1991). **Focus on forms** means traditional, point by point grammar teaching typically used in a grammar-translation, audio-lingual or oral-situational approach. Each grammar point is isolated and sometimes taught in quite a decontextualised, not very meaningful manner, e.g. getting students to do substitution drills where they have to change the tense of the verb in a fairly random sentence. In contrast, **focus on form** is about dealing with grammar explanations and brief practice when they arise incidentally but the focus is on meaningful interaction. It could also involve giving corrective feedback, such as recasts (correct reformulations of a student's response) or simple correction.

The term **synthetic syllabus** is used to describe a course based on building up the language from its component parts, e.g. grammatical forms. Textbooks, and indeed most language courses, take this sort of 'lego' approach.

There is research to suggest that focus on form (grammar in a meaning-focused context) can more effective, (e.g. Ellis, 2008; Nassaji and Fotos, 2004). But, according to Shintani (2013) overall there is no real evidence yet that one approach is better than the other. Much of the research in this area is problematic because there are no clear definitions of what constitutes focus on form and focus on forms instruction.

Input and output-based instruction

Should the focus of grammar teaching be on input or output? Input-based teaching refers to approaches involving the processing of input. This assumes that students' attention can be drawn to grammatical forms through activities where the aim is to understand input for meaning (not form), e.g VanPatten (2015). This is known as **Processing Instruction** (PI) (see below). Some studies support this approach over traditional grammar teaching (e.g. give the rule and practise, as in PPP, described later). Critics argue that this type of instruction only improves comprehension, not the ability to produce accurate grammar. Input-focused teaching can also involve 'flooding the input' with the language features you want the class to develop (e.g. in narrow reading and listening tasks).

In contrast, output-based instruction draws attention to structures through eliciting and practising output. This would be more in line with traditional PPP grammar teaching. DeKeyser (2010) suggests that output tasks will help develop output whereas input tasks will help develop comprehension. By this view you get better at what you practise.

Learned attention

We acquire grammatical patterns by hearing and seeing them as input, but what we pay attention to is partly dictated by what we know about our L1 and what we think is significant. This means we do not pay equal attention to every grammatical feature – this is what is called **learned attention** (Ellis, 2012).

For instance, English speakers learning Spanish may not notice Spanish masculine or feminine endings of nouns and adjectives in the input, because the notion of grammatical gender does not exist in English. Similarly, English learners of French may not notice that a French verb is in the simple future because in English the simple future is cued by the word 'will' whereas in French it is indicated by an inflectional change to the verb ending. For English learners of German, the issue is even more complex owing to word order and cases. This blindness to grammatical features is called **blocking** (Ellis, 2012). One implication of this is that simply providing input is not enough, we have to make sure we get students to focus on the features they may ignore. Ways to make grammatical features more salient (noticeable) include:

- Enhancing written text through colour, bold fonts or underlining such things as adjectives, articles or verb endings.
- Exaggerating the sound of important morphemes like verb endings, e.g. the sound of the past participle in French.
- Making facial expressions when pronouncing certain morphemes.
- Using explanation and translation to highlight the difference between L1 and L2.
- Using the 'dodgy translation' technique, e.g. translating German *Ich bin gegangen* as 'I am gone', rather than 'I have gone' to remind students that the verb *gehen* takes the auxiliary *sein* in the perfect tense.
- Using form-focused exercises such as: 'Choose the right ending', 'Listen and correct' and 'Spot the silent endings'.

In sum, to enable students to see and hear L2 features blocked by learned attention, grammar teaching is partly, about redirecting their attention when they read and listen to L2 input, by training them day in day out to focus their eyes and ears on parts of the L2 words and sentences they would not normally see or hear because of their L1 processing habits.

Processing Instruction

Connected with learned attention is **Input Processing** (IP) theory, which attempts to explain how students turn input into 'intake' by analysing input while their main attention is on meaning. VanPatten's (2015) model lays out a set of principles interacting in working memory, which has limited processing capacity and focuses on some things more than others. Content words and phrases are searched out first, since these provide most meaning. We also tend to focus on the first content word(s) in a sentence. Further, when content words and a grammatical form are both present and create meaning, students pay attention to the words, not the grammar. A key idea in the IP model is 'communicative value': the more a form has communicative value, the more likely it is to be processed and made available for acquisition. In contrast, forms with no or little communicative value are least likely to get processed and, without help, may never be acquired. In English, words like *cat*, *happy* and *play* are more likely to be processed than *that*, *which* and *by*.

Activities can be designed which force students to notice the link between form and meaning. For example, if you were doing a drill to practise tense manipulation and included time phrases such as *yesterday* or *tomorrow*, then they would not have to pay attention to the verb tense since the time frame is provided elsewhere in the sentence. As mentioned in the previous section, the ending would not be salient. So you might omit the time phrase to force students to notice the tense form.

In his detailed review of studies on IP, Boers (2021) concludes that, although the idea seems promising, the evidence for its effectiveness is so far mixed. Nevertheless, language teachers would be wise to keep IP in mind.

An inductive or deductive approach?

In an **inductive** approach to teaching grammar students hear or see input, maybe use it and are then asked to work out the rules for themselves, perhaps with guidance from the teacher. In a **deductive** approach, a rule is given with examples, then students are asked to do various practice tasks to internalise the rule. Research is not yet clear on which approach works best, though in his review of many studies Boers (2021) expresses a slight preference for concisely presenting rules first. In reality, whether we opt for one approach over the other depends on the class and the point of grammar being dealt with. Some patterns are much easier to identify than others.

Boers argues that because classrooms involve so many variables, it is wise to adopt a varied approach. Here is the sequence he describes as evidenced by research:

1. Draw students' attention to L2 words/phrases/patterns.
2. Explain the meaning or function of the items/pattern with the aid of examples, or, if thought possible without a high risk of confusion, ask students to work them out themselves with the aid of examples, and then confirm.
3. Engage students in content-oriented activities with input texts that illustrate the use and meaning of the items/pattern.
4. Possibly elaborate briefly about a property of the item that may make it easier to remember.

5. Provide opportunities for the students to retrieve the items/pattern from memory. This can be done in diverse ways. For example, a modified version of the input texts from Step 3 could be used to cue recall of missing items (e.g. gap-fill). In the case of certain grammar features, it could be done through the kind of interpretation practice proposed in Processing Instruction (exercises which force students to make form-meaning links with the grammar, for example a verb ending). Recall of meaning can be prioritised if the aim is to encourage receptive knowledge; recall of form if the aim is to foster productive knowledge.

6. Engage students in communicative tasks likely to elicit the target items/pattern. Ensure opportunities for improvement (e.g., feedback) between the tasks or task repetitions. Although there are more language-focused steps in this ensemble (steps 1, 2, 4 and 5), the content-focused activities (steps 3 and 6) would take up more time, thus creating a balance overall between the two broad approaches.

Developmental readiness

Natural orders

Experienced teachers are well aware of the fact that students pick up certain vocabulary and grammatical structures far more easily than others. Some language just seems to stick. Why might this be? One thing the research literature has told us is that the language we remember depends in part on how *learnable* it is. What does this mean?

To start with, research evidence suggests that the sequence in which humans acquire the morphemes in their first language (e.g. verb endings such as the -*ed* on the end of past tense verbs in English) is predictable (Brown, 1973). Research was then carried out showing that the same applies to L2 learning (e.g. Dulay and Burt, 1974). This became known as the **Natural Order Hypothesis,** the idea being that learners acquire grammatical forms at their own rate and in a similar order. It is sometimes said, therefore, that language learners have an **in-built syllabus** which affects what they can and cannot easily acquire. More recently, some researchers prefer to talk of an **Ordered Development Hypothesis**. Lichtman and VanPatten (2021) write:

> *The evolution of the learner's linguistic system occurs in ordered and predictable ways and is largely impervious to outside influence such as instruction and explicit practice* (p. 11).

But this is a much debated and messy area of research. Some doubt the extent to which natural orders apply in second language acquisition (Kwon, 2005). Factors such as frequency, inherent difficulty of the grammar and differences between the L1 and L2 may come into play (see below). Others suggest that the social context may influence sequence of acquisition, for example whether the language is being learned in a formal classroom or in other social settings (Ellis, 2015).

One thing is safe to say: teaching can only have, at best, a partial effect on the order in which learners acquire grammar. Remember that by *acquire* we mean possess the internalised ability to use grammar, not just explain it. In other words, the grammatical system needs to be in procedural long-term memory, and this takes time.

Transfer

If you analyse your own use of another language, how much is it influenced by the grammar and vocabulary of your first language(s)? Quite a lot, we suspect. Research suggests that the differences and similarities between the L1 and L2 can affect the acquisition of a structure both positively (if the structures are the same across the two languages) or negatively (if they are different). This phenomenon is referred to as **cross-linguistic transfer**. Transfer must be kept in mind when weighing up learnability and how you go about teaching a structure.

Processability Theory

The basic idea underlying Manfred Pienemann's (1998) **Processability Theory** is that at any stage of development a student can understand and produce only those L2 linguistic forms which the current state of the 'language processor' in the brain can handle. They may be ready to acquire a new structure, or not ready. This varies from language to language, and from one individual to another. You will have noticed how students seem to be able to pick up some structures more easily than others.

A real difficulty, however, is knowing the developmental stage a student has reached (Meisel *et al*, 1981). How many error-free examples are needed in spontaneous speech or writing to decide if a student has internalised a grammatical form? Knowing if they are ready or not for a structure is therefore hard to gauge and, in the end, comes down to the teacher's knowledge of each class and each individual. In reality, because the range of natural aptitude and achievement in any class is considerable, deciding when to move on is bound to be a compromise.

Textbooks can compound the difficulty. They typically work through grammatical structures in a set order which may correspond poorly with the needs of individual classes and students. The same structures can be reviewed every few weeks or from one year to the next, but this degree of distribution is inadequate for many when it comes to building long-term memory. Curriculum design and teacher pedagogy need to consider any possible mismatch between grammar being taught and students' developmental readiness to understand and use it. Therefore, an important takeaway for language teachers is that, because a traditional grammatical syllabus fails to take account of a student's current state of second language development, you have to select the most important structures, supplement the textbook and build in more practice.

In sum, whether students are immune to the order in which you teach grammar or not, it is important to have a sense of whether they are **developmentally ready** to acquire new grammar.

10 research-based principles for grammar teaching

1. **Do not make learning grammar rules the focus** of language teaching (Ellis and Shintani, 2013). Grammar teaching can reduce enjoyment (Graham, 2022). In particular, make the grammar content lighter with students with lower language-analytic ability, i.e. being able to derive rules by analysing language. Grammar teaching is more suitable for high-aptitude learners (Suzuki and DeKeyser, 2017).

2. **Combine the use of explicit and implicit learning** (Ellis and Shintani, 2013). To maximise implicit learning, use highly patterned input, input-flooding and input enhancement, i.e. emphasizing specific grammar items, through phonetic or visual devices (such as pronouncing a verb ending louder, highlighting a preposition, colour-coding case endings in German). Another way to maximise implicit learning is to exploit input at every level (Ellis, 2015), through intensive reading and listening.

3. **Introduce new structures in familiar linguistic contexts**, e.g. with known vocabulary, to decrease cognitive load (Smith and Conti, 2021). Practise new grammar structures in sentences which are simple, short and where vocabulary and pronunciation create less cognitive load.

4. **Gradually phase out scaffolds**. Move gradually from receptive processing to highly controlled, then semi-controlled and finally unplanned production. The rate at which you do this depends on the class. Research suggests that successful acquisition of a grammatical feature correlates with success in the initial retrieval episodes (Boers, 2021). So, go to production when you are confident students will be successful.

5. **Be aware of factors affecting acquisition**, including issues such as L1 positive/negative transfer, saliency (how noticeable features are), regularity, frequency, complexity, phonological issues and so on. Anticipate these in your planning (Ellis, 2015). Above all, consider whether the class is developmentally ready to acquire grammar features, notably younger learners and lower-attaining students.

6. **Compare with L1 structures**. Especially for students with low L1 literacy, explain how you would form and use the L1 equivalent of the target L2 structure first, then draw or **elicit a comparison from the students**. Tribushinina *et al.* (2022) provide evidence that this contrastive approach is effective for primary age children with developmental language disorder.

7. **Consider Transfer-Appropriate Processing**. Remember that if a structure is learnt and practised in a specific linguistic context or through a given task, it is not easily transferred to another. For instance, if reflexive verbs are only practised in the context of daily routine, students find it difficult to transfer them to other contexts (Smith and Conti, 2021). Similarly, grammar is best tested in the way it was practised.

8. **Assess grammar uptake through a mixture of structured assessment** (e.g. gap-fills) and **free-production tasks,** for example, "talk to me about last weekend" (Ellis and Shintani, 2013). Structured assessment tells us if students can do so when there are clear prompts as to what they are required to retrieve; free-production tasks test spontaneous grammar use, so tell us if the target structures have really been acquired.

9. **Use delayed assessment**. Assess the learning of a grammar structure not just **when the retrieval strength is high** (such as right at the end of series of lessons on it), but several weeks later too. This reveals how much has been truly retained. Delayed tests can be impromptu and low stakes, so students are not demoralised if they do badly.

10. **Correct errors directly and selectively**. Research evidence is mixed on error correction, but generally suggests that it can improve grammatical accuracy, both oral and written, if done clearly, selectively, promptly and in a contextually sensitive way (e.g. Ellis and Shintani, 2013).

Classroom practice

After that lengthy look at just some of the research out there, in this part of the chapter we suggest what it means for your everyday practice. By now, it should be clear that 'teach grammar' is a complex term and that we should not for one moment assume that once we have taught and practised a structure (e.g. a tense, adjective agreement, how to form adverbs, the subjunctive), students will be able to use this language spontaneously for themselves. With regard to teaching grammar, Rod Ellis (2006 p. 84) writes:

> *Grammar teaching involves any instructional technique that draws learners' attention to some specific grammatical form in such a way that it helps them either to understand it metalinguistically and/or process it in comprehension and/or production so that they can internalise it.*

An inductive approach example

With the whole class
Consider this script of a lesson which aims to introduce a **past tense**:

Teacher *Come to the board, Anne. How are you? Good! Me too. Anne, please draw a house for me. Draw a house. Good! That's cool! Nice house. (To the whole class) Anne drew a house! Anne drew a house! I'm going to draw an elephant. Here we go. Here's my elephant. Look! I drew an elephant! I drew an elephant! I drew an elephant! Anne, did you draw an elephant or a house? I drew an elephant.*

Anne *I drew a house.*

Teacher *Wow! A house. You drew a house! I drew an elephant. Suzi, come to the board. Hi, Suzi. How are you? OK? Good. Suzi, draw an elephant please. Nice! Cool elephant! Suzi drew an elephant! She drew a beautiful elephant! She drew an elephant. Class, did she draw a house or an elephant? (Choose a student).*

Student	*She drew an elephant.*
Teacher	*Yes, she drew an elephant. She drew an elephant. Everyone?*
Class	*She drew an elephant.*
Teacher	*Again?*
Class	*She drew an elephant.*
Teacher	*Excellent! Yes, she drew an elephant. Did Anne draw an elephant or a house? (Choose a student).*
Student	*She drew a house.*
Teacher	*Yes, she drew an elephant.*
Class	*No! She drew a house.*
Teacher	*OK, sorry. She drew a house. Did Suzi draw a house? (Choose a student).*
Student	*No, she drew an elephant.*
Teacher	*Yes, she drew an elephant. Everyone?*
Class	*She drew an elephant.*
Teacher	*Anne, what did you draw?*
Anne	*I drew a house.*
Teacher	*Yes, very good. You drew a house. Suzi, did you draw a house?*
Suzi	*No! I drew an elephant (stupid!)*
Teacher	*OK. Yes, you drew an elephant. I drew an elephant too. We drew an elephant!*

That was an example of presenting grammar in an inductive way, i.e. the students get to hear the grammar in action and are encouraged to work out the rules themselves. During that question-answer-repetition sequence the phrase *I drew* is heard nine times and the phrase *she drew* (or similar, e.g. *Suzi drew* or *did she draw*) is heard 21 times. In addition they hear the imperative *draw* and brief examples of *you drew* and *we drew*. We know from research that repeated exposure to meaningful language enables those brain connections to be made and for language to be gradually acquired. We also know that memory is reinforced when words are associated with memorable moments. In this simple exchange lasting about ten minutes, which is probably fun for all, we have introduced students to the basic formation of a past tense verb. In L2 we are likely to have chosen a regular verb, easy to demonstrate and to follow phonetically.

In this exchange, unless students are prompted to listen for particular forms, they will just enjoy the moment and be focused on the meaning. For some teachers that might even be enough, others would then ask in L1: "Did you notice anything about how we said *I drew* and *she drew*?" This is your route into explaining what is going on and helping students in subsequent structured practice on other verbs which follow the same pattern.

With groups

Another approach to inductive learning is for small groups to work together to figure out rules. For example, give out pairs of translated sentences (one in L1, one in L2), each sentence containing examples of the grammatical structure being taught. Then supply L1 questions such as: "What do you notice about the ending of the verb?" or "Can you explain in your own words how the rule works?" The students then go on, when ready, to make up further examples of the rule.

This can be developed by moving from the simplest to more complex rules. For instance, groups work out from examples the rule for forming the perfect tense in German in the first person (e.g. *ich habe Tennis gespielt* – "I played tennis"), you then give further examples from which they can work out the other person forms of the verb (e.g. *wir haben Tischtennis gespielt* – "we played table tennis"). In this instance, a 'jigsaw' activity can be done, giving individual words on pieces of paper or card to arrange in the correct order.

Presentation-Practice-Production (PPP)

A well-established approach to teaching grammar is to employ the PPP approach. This emerged in the mid-1970s within the oral-situational and communicative language teaching approaches (Anderson, 2016). Although it has come in for criticism for being reflective of a 'focus on forms'/synthetic approach, it continues to be a staple of teacher training programmes. One merit is that it corresponds with how we expect to learn other things in life. For example, when we learn to play a sport, we expect it to be demonstrated, drilled, then practised more freely. PPP also reflects the traditional role of the teacher – to explain something before it is practised (see Anderson, 2016).

Presentation

For our students to learn something new, they need to be able to perceive and understand it, meaning we have to present new material in a way that is accessible for initial learning. This 'presentation' stage can refer to two elements: firstly, the limited and controlled modelling of a language item when we introduce a new grammatical structure or word; secondly, an initial encounter with comprehensible input in the form of spoken or written texts, along with explanations, instructions and discussions.

Effective presentation requires students to be attentive; it should clearly audible and/or visible, make links with previously learned material and be memorable. It may involve exploiting various senses: sight, hearing and physical movement. When explaining concepts, it must be clear and accessible. We should imagine what they find difficult. They really value a teacher's ability to explain things clearly, so careful preparation is needed for how we will order any explanation, the language used and any illustration provided. Teachers in training may even write these details out.

During presentation bear in mind the advantages of being concise, using judicious repetition and paraphrasing, checking that students have followed what you said. By the way, some might say they have understood, but actually have not, so it is wise to ask them to do something with the knowledge they are picking up. Anything which helps them remember what was said is useful: effective tone of voice, a humorous illustration or anecdote, or getting a student to present the material once more. For younger students, it may also help to suggest that they are 'language detectives', being trained to solve the mysteries of the language.

One dilemma when presenting grammar is how much to simplify the explanation. If we over-simplify this may be at the risk of complete accuracy. If we explain every detail, students may be left feeling confused. An appropriate balance is needed which suits the particular class.

If we wish to present the grammatical point in context, which also has the benefit of providing meaningful language input, the full range of approaches we describe in Chapter 2 can be used: pictures, objects, sentence builders and PowerPoint flashcards, for instance.

At some point we may want students to write down the rules, with examples (in their own words, if they are able to). This has the merit of giving them time to digest the rules as they are explained again. In addition, it can be a useful quiet time after a period of oral practice. Alternatively they can be given a stick-in handout or more self-motivated students can be referred to the grammar pages of their online or printed textbook, if they have one.

Practice

Once an item has been presented, it is time to move to the practice stage. This involves using the grammatical feature in controlled exercises such as gap-fills, drills and 'closed' speaking activities such as tightly structured question-answer sequences (Anderson, 2016).

Researchers talk about moving from **controlled practice** (sometimes labelled 'pre-communicative practice') to **free practice** (production). The idea is that students gradually master a point until it becomes automatised to the point where they can use it independently. For this to happen the practice needs to be copious and built up in stages, from easier to harder. Controlled practice is often done by drilling style tasks using oral prompts, worksheets or exercises from a textbook or presented from the front. With controlled practice the teacher offers more support than with free practice. Whatever the activity, it must be clearly presented to the class, so they know *exactly* what they are meant to do. If this requires an explanation in L1, then do it. Let us now look at some examples of controlled practice.

Types of controlled ('pre-communicative') practice

The following example of this type of mechanical exercise, with minimal changes from step to step, practises the future tense with low intermediate students:

    Example cue: *Today **I am playing** <u>tennis</u> with my dad.*
    Example answer: *Tomorrow **I'm going to play** <u>football</u> with my friends.*

Here are some ways to exploit exercises of this kind, along with the pros and cons of each approach. Textbooks and other resources are often short of examples, not providing enough opportunities for the kind of copious and repetitive practice needed. Remember that varying the use of these practice types can help to avoid students becoming bored.

1. **Teacher-led approach:** read out a prompt and get an individual student to answer, then get others to repeat, then the whole class. This can be done with hands up or hands down. **Strengths:** this 'old-school' approach is highly effective for attentive classes and supplies lots of L2, allowing the teacher at the same time to pick out specific students. It is good for matching questions to students of different abilities and for providing listening input. It may be easy to maintain class control and they hear good models, i.e. the teacher's. **Weaknesses:** it demands great attention from weaker classes and only one student speaks at a time, except for group repetition. A brisk pace is needed, or attention will quickly wane. Many individuals find answering in class embarrassing; does this kind of pressure aid language learning?

2. **Pair-work approach.** After some whole class practice as above, you can quickly move to pair work where the partners act in turn as teacher and student. **Strengths:** students get to say and listen a lot in L2. They can help each other. There is little embarrassment factor; pressure is off. **Weaknesses:** behaviour management needs to be good so that they do not speak too much L1 or waste time. A 'no L1' rule could apply. They may hear wrong answers and poor models of pronunciation, so do not get optimum comprehensible input.

3. **The student takes the lead and acts as teacher.** After a brief demonstration, ask a volunteer, preferably a more able one, to step up and run the class. **Strengths:** similar to (1), though models may be less good. The class will listen extra hard and find the process amusing. The volunteer will learn teaching and leadership skills. **Weaknesses:** as (1) in as far as each student may end up not saying very much. The focus is more on listening here.

4. **Using mini-whiteboards.** Adapt approach (1) to involve more students actively by giving each a mini-whiteboard or coloured marker. As an answer is given all students must hold up their board with true-false or a marker indicating whether they think the response is correct or wrong. **Strengths**: as (1) plus more involvement from all the class. We get to assess how well they understand; this is a good formative assessment technique. **Weaknesses:** largely as (1).

5. **Combine skills:** use approach (1) but as attention wanes quickly go to oral prompts with written answers. Then the class simply works quietly or in pairs giving written responses to written prompts provided. **Strengths:** all students are actively engaged in listening to good models, reading and writing. This may be good for behaviour management. **Weaknesses:** it is hard to check that all are keeping up and writing accurate answers. Differentiating between students may be more difficult if the teacher controls the pace (when working alone there is more chance for them to go at their own pace and ask questions).

6. **Give answers, students choose prompt.** This is a simple variation which helps vary the lesson and provide a fresh angle. Let us say you have a sheet with 15 prompts (sentences, questions, etc.). Read an answer and the students must supply the correct prompt from the

sheet. This can be done in pairs. **Strengths:** it may be an easy way into a worksheet. Students do not have to create an utterance, just read one already supplied. Focus is on comprehension rather than production. **Weaknesses:** it is often easier therefore less challenging as there is no need to show syntactic skill.

7. **Supply alternative answers, students choose the best one.** Again, makes a worksheet more approachable for less able students. A student could read aloud a prompt, then the teacher supplies two answers (a) and (b). Students then vote (a) or (b). **Strengths:** good for listening comprehension. There is little pressure to perform and all are involved. **Weaknesses:** little production needed; watch out for a peer pressure effect if there is voting.

8. **Get students to make up their own examples.** Once a group seems to have mastered a point allow them to make up their own examples or even write their own worksheet. Here we are venturing a little into free practice territory. **Strengths:** it allows students to be creative, show off their use of the new point and even be amusing. This provides an excellent homework assignment. It allows them to compare work in the next lesson, try out their worksheet on a partner or the teacher and reinforce language acquired in the previous lesson. **Weaknesses:** nothing to speak of, but be sure that all students have mastered the point or it could be a homework disaster!

9. **Sentence-combining.** For example to develop the use of relative pronouns (*which, that*) and other complex sentences students are given pairs of sentences which they must turn into a single sentence. For example:
   1. I bought a new skirt last week.   2. The skirt was blue and white.
      → The skirt which I bought last week was blue and white.
   Or:
   1. I went to the cinema.   2. Then I went to McDonalds.
      → After going to the cinema I went to McDonalds.

10. **Oral translation:** students are given cards with bullet points in L1 and need to translate them into L2. Each bullet point will get them to use a point of grammar, e.g. agreement, verb conjugation or word order).

11. **Using writing mats:** these are usually A4 sheets with examples of grammatical structures in context and vocabulary which can be used by students to make up simple adapted examples for themselves; they are extremely useful for generating both speaking and writing exercises.

Production (free practice)

Within this PPP approach we recommend only moving to free practice once it is felt that enough controlled practice has been done. There is often a temptation to proceed too quickly to less controlled practice, before students are ready for it, i.e. before language has become proceduralised, which can lead to feelings of frustration and lower self-efficacy. We should not be too rigid about this, however. It may be, for example, that free practice reveals a point that has not been mastered well enough, so freer tasks can be used to assess if more controlled practice is needed at the time or later. Much depends on the individual class.

By the way, many teachers are frustrated that students never seem to produce accurate language even after frequent practice. This may be because, as we saw earlier in the chapter, they are simply not 'ready' to successfully internalise the new grammar. Their 'mental representation' of the language will take its own time to mature (see Chapter 20). There is no need be alarmed by an initial lack of mastery by all students in the class - this is normal. Sometimes, we just have to move on, be prepared to recycle the language later, trust that the syllabus will revisit the grammar another time or take comfort in the fact that grammatical accuracy is not the be-all-and-end-all of proficiency. Far from it!

Examples of free practice activities

1. Original or supported **sentence, paragraph or essay writing**. With free writing students usually need some support in terms of bullet points, a template to follow, and some pre-preparation in class. Giving a written task 'cold' may lead to very inaccurate results and over-reliance on direct translation from L1.

2. **Oral presentations with a grammatical focus**. If the goal is to have students practise adjectives of personal appearance and character, they could improvise or read from a script a presentation on three people: a friend, a parent or caregiver, and a teacher. Adjectival agreement may need revision, if this is an issue in the L2. If we were dealing with the order of noun and adjective, we would probably model a slightly different exercise to keep the two issues separate in the first instance.

3. **Storytelling from key words**. Give the class a set of 10 words, including odd or rare ones, to include in an account of an imaginary weekend. This is a variation on the familiar 'what I did last weekend' task. The students can write creatively while making frequent use of the past tense.

4. **'Talk Show':** this can be used by intermediate to advanced students to practise using **question forms**. They can film this task to make it more fun. There are at least three alternatives as to how the talk show can be organised:
    a. Students play themselves.

b. They write out role cards for fictitious people, which are shuffled and handed out.
c. Each student designs their own role card which should all follow the same pattern, e.g. with name, age, country of origin, married/children, job and hobbies.

One group of about four students prepares three topics each and suitable questions as hosts of the talk show. Each host is allotted about the same number of people from the remaining students to interview (ideally no more than five people). Each host draws a certain number of role or name cards (if students play themselves) and tells their group which topics they will be asked about and how they are going to be interviewed.

Then each group, consisting of one host and up to five interviewees, acts out their talk show. This could be done in front of the class, in which case, the rest of the class can ask supplementary questions. Alternatively, each group could film their shows on a mobile device and show their films to the class afterwards or plac6 them on a shared digital area.

5. **'Finding a time to meet':** this can be used by near beginners and low intermediate level students to practise **the present tense** or **immediate future** ('going to') form of the verb. See Table 6.2. In pairs each student has a different schedule for the week. They have to find at least one time when they are both free to meet up by asking each other questions:

What are you going to do on Friday?
Are you going to be free on Friday at 7?

If they cannot meet their partner at the time proposed, they must say why (i.e. say what they are going to do at that time). Supply students with two grids, one blank, the other with their own set of activities. As the information gap activity progresses, each can fill in the empty grid with their partner's activities.

Table 6.2 Grid for 'Finding a time to meet'

	Monday	**Tuesday**	**Wednesday**	**Thursday**	**Friday**
Morning	shopping in town	revising for an exam	going to the dentist	going swimming with mother	
Afternoon	visiting grandmother	playing on the computer with friend	tidying my bedroom		going to the beach if it's nice
Evening	going to the cinema		party at friend's house	having dinner with visiting cousins	going bowling with friends

Making the work interesting

Although some students will be simply motivated by getting good grades, preparing for a test, or earning 'merit points', generally speaking, practice needs to be inherently stimulating. Motivation has to derive from the intrinsic interest of the activity itself: its (non-linguistic) topic and the task to be done. If activities are just too uninspiring, they will lose interest and the learning aims will not be achieved. Students who are bored lose concentration and may misbehave as a result. If the lesson is interesting they will learn more effectively, will enjoy the process and want to continue learning.

Practice activities can easily become boring if they are not 'spiced up'. This can be done in various ways explained by Penny Ur (1988) in her book *Grammar Practice Activities* and summarised here:

1. **Interesting tasks and topics.** Base practice on topics and tasks students may find interesting. This might mean using a game or an interactive website such *language-gym.com*. As regards subject matter, there is no single recipe for choosing topics, but their own interests might be a guide, as well as current affairs and issues which arouse strong reactions or topics they may not know much about already. Typical areas might include: factual information on matters of general interest, film, music, entertainment and famous people. The teacher's own enthusiasm for the topic or task will also play an important role.

2. **Visual focus.** Use interesting visual support to make practice activities more stimulating. Technology has made this considerably easier, with the possibility of using presentations, moving images, video and the interactive whiteboard.

3. **Open-endedness.** An open-ended task allows for lots of different student responses, so may produce more varied and creative ideas. Borrowing Penny Ur's example, to practise adverbs of frequency, one technique is to supply a sentence such as, *He has coffee for breakfast* and then ask students to insert the word *always*. This example in itself has little interest value, being predictable and purely mechanical. But if they are asked to suggest all sorts of things they *always* (or *sometimes* or *occasionally*) do when, for example, feeling depressed, or when they have a free day, the exercise becomes more interesting for everyone. This can also make a task harder, but can be overcome by supplying helpful language on the board.

4. **Information gaps.** When a gap in information is provided as part of the task there is bound to be a greater element of interest involved. Simple guessing games can fulfil this purpose. For example, when practising past tense verbs give pairs of students two lists (one each) of activities from the previous weekend and each partner must guess, using yes/no questions, what their partner did.

5. **Personalisation.** This means using interaction based on students' own personal experiences. For example, to practise the idea of *I have been doing… for…* (a difficult element of verb use for English learners of French, German and Spanish), rather than doing a practice exercise based on a picture, students can be asked how long they have done certain things in their own lives: *How long have you lived…? How long have you been at this school? How long have you studied/played/learned…?* It is also important to be aware of what activities students engage in outside school; ready-made lists in textbooks may reflect the life experience of different socio-economic or cultural groups.

6. **'Pleasurable tension.'** Games and game-like language practice activities provide what Ur calls a feeling of pleasurable tension (Ur, 1988). For example, if the class is shown a picture and asked to make up sentences in the present tense the objective is somewhat ill-defined and there is no particular challenge involved. However, if the objective is rephrased as: "Make up 20 sentences about the picture in two minutes" or "Which group can get to 20 sentences the fastest?" there is an immediate rise in tension (can we get to 20 or can't we?). This simple 'twist' or rephrasing of the task creates greater motivation.

7. **Entertainment.** Sheer entertainment can add to the interest. For example, exercises based on combining or comparing ideas which are not normally juxtaposed can produce good results. *How many ways can you use a pen?* could elicit amusing uses of *You can use it to…* (typically a modal verb with object pronoun and infinitive). Comparing items which are in totally different categories can produce amusing results, e.g. compare a planet with a giraffe or the Eiffel Tower with a spoon.

8. **Play-acting.** Acting out a role as someone else can make a controlled or free grammar practice activity more stimulating. With near beginners, shopping or café dialogues are an effective way of repeatedly using key structures such as question forms or *I would like/Do you have?*

9. **Literary/cinema extracts.** Some curricula require the teaching of L2 literature and cinema. Poetry often supplies repetitive structures which can be practised then adapted (e.g. the poet Prévert for French). Using an extract from a film, students can describe the actions of a protagonist using a particular range of verbs (e.g. reflexives, intransitive verbs etc.).

10. **Making drills more fun**. For example, to practise past tense yes/no questions ask students to close their eyes while you change five things about your appearance, e.g. remove a shoe, take off a watch, put on glasses, put on a hat, take off a necklace. Students ask questions to figure out the changes made, such as, "Did you take off a shoe?". "Did you put on a hat?" This kind of activity can be fun and, more importantly, goes beyond mechanical responses (from Larsen-Freeman, 1997).

Making students feel successful

For students to feel motivated, they have to feel they have mastered tasks successfully (see Chapter 16). Practice is therefore most effective when it is well sequenced and scaffolded to ensure success at every stage. With this in mind, we suggest the following principles for effective practice:

- In general, use L1 to explain grammar rules so as not to create cognitive overload for students. If they are struggling to understand the message, they are less likely to understand the rules. Identify the cognitive steps that applying the rule involves and teach one step at a time. Some rules are more difficult than others as they involve more cognitive operations, such as changes of word order or inflections which they are not used to in their L1. Each step needs to be mastered so it can be done without thinking. You can tolerate 'over-generalisation' of rules (i.e. when a student applies the normal rule to irregular examples, e.g. saying 'I taked' in English). You need not correct every error; indeed, you can encourage error. After all, it is a rule you are teaching and you want to ensure it has been internalised. To correct an over-generalisation slows down rule acquisition as it sends negative feedback to the brain.

- Avoid presenting grammatical structures in linguistically difficult contexts, e.g. with difficult vocabulary or other grammar points. Keep students focused on the main point and the load on working memory to a minimum. For instance, provide an L1 translation for each L2 example.

- Provide plenty of receptive practice before asking students to produce their own examples. If the approach is inductive (see above), give opportunities to notice, analyse and evaluate the structure in the context of listening or reading texts. This reduces cognitive load since recognition is usually easier than production. For example, take the third person of the present tense of a French *–er* verb (e.g. *elles regardent*): by using lots of modelling on the pronunciation of the silent ending *-ent* students are less likely to mispronounce it later.

- Aim for 'cognitive control'. Teaching should allow students to apply the rule quite accurately and spontaneously in unplanned speech. Remember that for a structure to be fully acquired ideally it needs to be practised across all four skills. This should help them internalise the pattern more effectively.

- Consider using the 'flipped learning' principle, i.e. give students an opportunity to learn about the structure before the lesson, then practise it in lesson time.

- Deliberately using more difficult multi-word units can pave the way for future learning. By memorising more complex chunks of language, students will be better prepared for those structures later in their learning when we can 'connect the dots' by making references back to them. This could include use of 'polite' conditional forms of the verb used lexically at an early stage of the course (*I would like*), or reasons for lateness given in a past tense learned by heart (*I went to the toilet/restroom*).

Selecting and sequencing of grammar

Despite the problems associated with developmental readiness to acquire grammar, we need to decide which grammar to teach and in which order. It is unwise to try and teach too much grammar to students at beginner or intermediate level. The more structures taught, the less the chance that each one becomes internalised. So, it is advisable to limit the range of patterns to the most useful and learnable. What is taught will be partly dictated by the existing curriculum plan, but inexperienced teachers should exercise judgment and seek advice from colleagues about what is most useful and teachable. Effective teachers use exercises from textbooks selectively, evaluating them for difficulty level, interest and quality. Newer teachers may have a less well-developed feel for what students will find hard.

Most textbooks sequence grammar from what is thought to be the easiest to the hardest. This sometimes corresponds with what is most frequently used by L2 speakers. For example, textbooks usually start with the present tense, which is the most used. An exception to this would be, for example, the French subjunctive which is often left to advanced level because the rules for its formation and use are complex. Yet it is very commonly used.

This sequencing is bound to place restrictions on what students are exposed to. Some teachers are reluctant to break away from the strict sequence, whereas others are happy to adopt a freer approach and teach more complex chunks of language, even at beginner level, some of which can be set to memory. Typically, this might involve supplying set structures to help students prepare for an oral or written assessment. Experience shows that some subsequently incorporate these learned phrases into their everyday repertoire.

As we have seen, most courses are organised around a grammatical sequence. They also have a 'spiral' organisation, meaning as the spiral staircase is climbed, students encounter the same structure again on the next floor (such as the following year). If there is the luxury of at least a five-year course, students may get several 'goes' at the present tense, as well as all the day-to-day incidental practice on it.

Within each grammatical area the order of teaching needs sequencing, moving from most straightforward to more difficult, e.g. teaching regular verbs before irregulars. The best textbooks organise this. It does, however, create an issue because the most common and useful verbs tend to be irregular. So grammar teaching cannot be sequenced purely based on simplicity or regularity.

It is generally unwise, however, to expose students to a confusing diet of various structures all at once. We need to be aware at every stage what we think they are likely to find straightforward or confusing. This will vary depending on the language being taught. In French, the mechanics of the perfect tense cause difficulty, whereas in German the perfect tense may be perceived as easier. On the other hand, word order and cases are inevitably harder to master in German. In Spanish the use of the subjunctive becomes unavoidable earlier than it does in French.

Consolidation

Given the limited time we get to spend with classes and, often, the inappropriate frequency and spacing of lessons, it may feel frustrating that grammar is insufficiently recycled and consolidated. We are of the view that it is better to do a limited diet thoroughly, than a large diet superficially - the 'less is more' principle. We also need to take advantage of the principle of **spaced practice** (see Chapter 5) or 'little and often' to embed knowledge and skills.

Homework provides an excellent opportunity to reinforce grammar practised in class and should never be an afterthought. A lesson plan will often involve a teaching sequence with the final activity being homework (see Chapter 19). If there are only two or three 'contacts' a week, homework can provide an extra one or two. It usually makes sense to focus class work as much as possible on oral and aural work, saving the bulk of reading and writing for homework. The availability of Google Translate and AI tools does, however, dissuade many teachers from setting written homework. This is a shame. Longer lessons of an hour or more mean we need to include independent, reflective activities in class, as well as for homework, because it is difficult to keep up full-on oral and aural activities for a whole lesson. The school may also impose restrictions on when homework is assigned.

Practice activities for major tenses

These activities provide repeated practice of verb structures.

1. Present tense

Insert the verb (near-beginner): this can be used as a starter and is a good example of retrieval practice. Display sentences with the verb missing. Students, either individually or in pairs, identify the missing verb. Choose language they have been using in previous lessons. A French example would look like this (the answers are given)

1. *Je _____ la télé dans le salon. (regarde)*
2. *Je _____ les devoirs dans ma chambre. (fais)*
3. *Je _____ français en cours. (parle)*
4. *Je _____ à la discothèque. (danse, vais)*

Start the sentence (near-beginner/low intermediate): display short ends to sentences. Students must retrieve a suitable verb to complete it. For example, display the phrase *with my friends,* students could supply a range of verb forms such as *I play football, I go to school, I go to the mall.*

2. Past (preterite) tense

Picture stories (intermediate). Sequences of pictures on the board with times provide a tried and tested way of practising simple past tense (see also Chapter 10). These can be drawn simply by hand using stick figures (students often enjoy our feeble artistic efforts) or PowerPoint can be used. Include at least 10 pictures depicting a range of activities (a journey, holiday or day out work well). Describe the sequence in either the first or third person (or both) through repetitive question-answer work. If you have drawn single stick figures you can add extra figures for plural subject pronouns (*they* and *we*).

Piling up events (intermediate). Give each student a piece of paper with a verb in the simple past tense (e.g. *I went, I bought, I played*). Start a simple chain of events with the sentence: *Yesterday I went to town and I bought a loaf of bread.* The first student continues, repeating your first sentence, then adding one of their own using the verb they were given. The next continues the chain, and so on until it becomes impossible to remember the whole sequence.

3. Imperfect tense

Past and present. Display pairs of pictures on the board, left and right in two columns, or pairs displayed in sequence, showing a character who used to be poor and who has become rich. On the left your character will be shown with small house, no money, a bicycle, a cap, eating a sandwich and so on. On the right the same character will be seen with a big car, big house, a top hat, drinking champagne and so on. Describe in the imperfect tense what his life used to be like and in the present tense what their life is like now. Make clear any verb ending changes. Either present all the imperfect tense pictures in one go, then the present tense ones, or present them side by side to enable students to hear the immediate contrast. Then proceed to question-answer and repetition work, followed by showing and reading the written forms of the verbs. This an example of the inductive approach described earlier. The task is presented graphically in Smith (2023).

4. Future or immediate future tense

What will you do with it? (From Ur, 1988) For intermediate students. Have a bag containing a collection of easily recognisable objects, such as a cup, a stone, a plate or a box of matches. Alternatively, use a set of picture cards or just the names of the items on large pieces of paper. Display an object/picture/word to the whole class except for one student who must guess what it is. The guesser asks: *what will you do/are you going to do with it?* The others then make their suggestions using a future tense verb. To help them do this, provide a list of verbs in their future forms on the board. After a period of oral practice, students could then write down answers for each object to a time limit.

5. Conditional

Finishing conditional sentences (intermediate and advanced students). Give a sentence using an *if* clause and the conditional (e.g. *If I went to Berlin, I would visit the Reichstag*). Then model an answer. With students new to the conditional write up examples of conditional verbs on the board. With advanced students who have learned it before this is unnecessary. Then simply provide more examples of unfinished sentences beginning with *if* clauses: *If I went to France, if I won the lottery, if I saw a burglar in the kitchen, if there were a fire in the kitchen* and so on. Others may then repeat in the third person what the previous student has said.

Learning by heart

Learning by heart is often called **rote learning**. Should we make use of this to help students internalise grammar? There are no right answers here, but most teachers will include some rote learning as part of grammar (and vocabulary) acquisition. For example, the French perfect tense verbs using the auxiliary *être* can be memorised from their first letters (MR DRAPER'S MT VAN) or German prepositions taking the accusative case could be memorised with their first letters (DOGWUF). A lengthy list of such mnemonics (memory devices) is given for French, German and Spanish in Smith and Conti (2021). We must remember, however, that mnemonics and memorised language are no substitute for real acquisition. A student's performance in a test may not reflect their proficiency.

Many teachers have students chant verb paradigms, sometimes to music. Some encourage them to practise verb conjugation using websites and apps. Whether these activities contribute to the development of proficiency is very much a moot point, but it is possible that conscious setting to memory of grammar can become part of a student's internalised, 'tacit' competence. The analogy of learning multiplication tables or scales in music is appealing. The main problem with memorising verbs or lists is that this knowledge does not transfer easily to new contexts.

As a reminder, the principle of Transfer-Appropriate Processing (TAP) from cognitive psychology suggests that when we learn something, we encode the memory along with the context of learning. As an example, if students learn numbers in a sequence 1-20, they may be very good at reciting the numbers this way, but not so good at using them spontaneously in context. This strongly suggests the need to match the learning context to how we would like them to use the language later and is another reason why we advocate teaching language in chunks, rather than through the learning of isolated words.

All that said, students say they appreciate the clarity that rote learning techniques produce. They may appreciate an apparent mastery, even if such learning out of context is far from the most important way they will develop proficiency. Since L2 acquisition is a slow and cumulative process, it is useful to find ways to make students feel they are making stepped progress. The acquisition of declarative grammatical knowledge, along with functional, transactional grammatical tasks can arguably help achieve this. It is good to be able to say "I can do this now".

Finally, rote learning of language can be useful for some types of examination. For example, if an oral test includes conversation, many students like to prepare learned chunks of language to enhance their fluency. When writing essays they benefit from pre-memorising lists of chunks or sentences which may come in useful.

Why agreements are hard to master

Most readers will be teaching a language where agreements are an important aspect of grammatical accuracy, if not communicative usefulness. We include this section to help explain why students find these hard and what can be done to make the process easier for them.

In our experience, students find it relatively easy to grasp the rules of adjective agreement but rarely apply them with total accuracy. Why is this? And what can we do about it?

If we consider brain function for a moment, when working memory experiences **cognitive overload**, the brain tends to focus only on the most semantically **salient** (i.e. noticeable) features of the output and neglects features which do not contribute much to meaning. However, the picture is more complicated than that. The cognitive operations and knowledge involved in the process of applying adjectival agreement rules in L2 French/Italian/Spanish/German speaking or writing under real-life conditions, require a student to:

- retrieve from memory the required adjective;
- remember to make it agree with the noun in terms of gender and number (not always straightforward as they may be relatively far from each other);
- know whether the noun is masculine, feminine (or neuter);
- know whether it is regular or irregular;
- apply the rule;
- pronounce or spell it correctly;
- decide whether to put it before or after the noun in some languages.

This represents a lot of cognitive operations to perform on the spur of the moment! The cognitive load imposed by these operations is further increased by the fact that there are often other things to cope with in the same sentence, e.g. subject-to-verb agreement.

If our students persistently make 'regular' rather than random errors, these can end up being **fossilised** (automatised) and incorporated permanently in their current mental representation of the language. To try and avoid this we could first consider the three main psycholinguistic causes of the issue, which refer to the seven processes listed above.

1. **The gender of nouns** – the notion that words can be masculine and feminine (or neuter in German) is completely alien to an L1 English native speaker. So we need to ensure from the outset, that students are constantly reminded of this, both explicitly (e.g. through work on the make-up of nouns) and implicitly (e.g. through colour coding of different genders).

2. **Focus on word endings** – a native English speaker focuses on the beginning of words, since there are relatively few inflections which affect meaning. Instinctively they do not attend to the end of words, meaning that students may not improve the use of agreements (word endings) just from hearing or reading L2. To alter this requires lots of practice over time. It is particularly important for German where different case endings add a further complication.

3. **The importance of agreement** – this issue compounds the problem. An L1 English speaker is not only unused to the notion of gender, but also finds the idea of agreement unfamiliar and unnecessary. Their brain automatically places agreement low down the list of priorities. The challenge for teachers is to ensure students are constantly aware of agreement so that it becomes second nature – as it is for any French, Spanish, Italian or German native speaker. By making the application of agreement become second nature, we mean that, whenever an adjective is retrieved by working memory, a *production*, as skill theorists call it, is automatically activated in the student's brain. It operates something like this:

If condition: *if* I use an adjective in a phrase/sentence…

Then condition: …*then* I must make it agree with the noun it modifies.

The speed at which the brain activates the above production plays a big role in determining how efficiently the agreement rule is applied.

The implications of all this are that we need to focus on developing 'processing efficiency' while addressing the issues 1-3 mentioned above, making students more aware of them until, after regular spaced practice, they become automatic. All this, by the way, hinges on the extent to which accuracy needs to be a focus of teaching.

Gianfranco's tips for focusing on agreement

- Colour code masculine, feminine (and neuter) endings.
- When providing vocabulary lists include the feminine and masculine (and neuter) endings of the adjectives. This takes time but is worthwhile.
- Do listening activities involving a focus on endings, e.g. 'minimal pairs', where the feminine and masculine (and neuter) forms of the same adjective are contrasted.
- Do 'error hunt' tasks where students need to identify a set number of agreement errors in a text. They enjoy trying to find them all.
- Do drills, e.g. multiple choice gap-fills; exercises on endings; translations, etc.
- Provide checklists to help students proof-read written essays.

Gianfranco's tips for focusing on gender

- Always present masculine and feminine (and neuter) nouns with the (indefinite/definite) article or any other determiner using colour coding.

- When providing vocabulary lists, make sure that the masculine and feminine (and neuter) nouns are grouped separately. Colour coding as background can be used to enhance the contrast.

- Model and practise gender rules which may work as an *aide-mémoire* in the identification of gender (e.g. in French, nouns ending in *-tion* are always feminine). Make up nonsense words to see if students can guess gender. This may take time but will improve confidence and save effort later.

- After doing a reading or listening activity, get students to identify the gender of a set list of chosen nouns. Quizzes can be done, based on gender identification, e.g. odd-ones-out and gap-fills where the article must be inserted.

- Give a short passage containing gender errors and challenge them to find the errors to a time limit and with the help of a dictionary.

- Reminders and rules can be posted on the wall.

Assessing grammar

It should be clear by now that 'knowing the rules' in the sense of being able to explain them (declarative knowledge), is of limited use for communication. So how do we know they have really mastered grammatical structures, in the sense of having internalised them, being able to use grammar correctly under real-life conditions? We cannot really say 'my students have learned structure 'X' effectively' without evidence of spontaneous and independent use.

It is tempting to think that students have acquired a grammar rule if they can explain it or apply it accurately in the context of specific exercises. This belief could lead to a grammar teaching approach which does not aim at genuine automatisation of grammatical structures, namely the transformation of declarative knowledge into procedural knowledge, resulting in free and independent spoken and written fluency.

It is useful to consider the difference between **performance** and **proficiency**. A student may perform well on a well-defined, rehearsed task, but this may disguise a lack of genuine proficiency. To be sure they have properly acquired a structure, therefore, it needs to be assessed when used independently, maybe under time pressure, for example, when producing connected writing within a strict time limit or, best of all, when conversing spontaneously. Consider, therefore, doing 'on the spot' oral assessments or written tasks. This will give a clearer idea of whether language has been truly automatised.

Concluding remarks

The ability to use grammar correctly is vital to communication in L2. We have seen that this area remains much debated, but that there is consensus amongst teachers that some grammar teaching is 'a good thing'. However, we have also seen that it is far more useful to present and practise grammar in an engaging way and in meaningful contexts instead of teaching grammar as lists of examples and sets of verb conjugations. Much of a teacher's creative skill is expended in finding stimulating and effective ways to do this. If you feel this creativity is lacking, others in the school or on social media are there to suggest ideas.

In addition, 'teacher's books' which accompany courses, synthesise some of the better ideas developed over the years. If we are well versed in methodology, we are better placed to assess whether those ideas are useful or not.

It is no doubt true that students can acquire some mastery of grammatical structure just by meaningful input when it is supplied in very large amounts, i.e. in an immersive environment. For students in a school context, however, we have argued that the route of clear, explicit presentation and explanation with large amounts of meaningful controlled and free practice will lead to good results.

Finally, we agree with Mike Swan (2006) who writes:

> *We should reject nothing on doctrinaire grounds: deductive teaching through explanation and examples, inductive discovery activities, rule-learning, peer-teaching, decontextualised practice, communicative practice, incidental 'focus on form' during communicative tasks, teacher correction and recasts, grammar games, corpus analysis, learning rules by example and heart – all of these and many other traditional and non-traditional practices have their place, depending on the point being taught, the learner and the context.*

7

Fluency

Introduction

In Chapter 3 we showed a model of oral production and mentioned how the complex tasks of lexical retrieval, grammatical decoding and articulation all have to be done fluently. How can we help students do this, whatever level they are working at?

This chapter considers the areas below.

Research evidence
- ✓ What is fluency?
- ✓ Cognitive processing
- ✓ Fluency within a communicative approach
- ✓ Fluency in the curriculum plan
- ✓ Negotiation of meaning – pair and group work

Classroom practice
- ✓ From controlled to free practice
- ✓ The importance of pronunciation
- ✓ Encouraging fluent, spontaneous talk
- ✓ Risk-taking and compensatory strategies

Research evidence

What is fluency?

Charles Fillmore described one of four types of fluency as the "ability to talk at length with few pauses" (Fillmore, 2000, p. 51). This is what many of us think when we describe what it means to be fluent. We have the idea of someone who can speak rather like a first language user. To be 'fluent in Spanish' is to be able to speak quite fast, without too much hesitation and with some accuracy.

Research into fluency tends to focus on temporal measures of L2 production - syllables per second, number and length of pauses and mean 'length of run' - the number of syllables between pauses, rather than general proficiency. It is about how well speech flows.

But there is more to fluency than that. As Segalowitz (2010) explains, when looked at from a psycholinguistic perspective, we can define three types of fluency:

1. **Cognitive fluency**: our ability to mobilise and bring together the underlying cognitive processes responsible for producing fluent utterances - short-term memory, planning, lexical retrieval, choice of grammar, phonological knowledge and so on.
2. **Utterance fluency**: this is what is referred to above, namely how well speech flows - the oral manifestation of cognitive fluency.
3. **Perceived fluency**: judgments made about speakers based on samples of their speech.

Tracey Derwing (2017) points out that massive amounts of input and opportunities to speak are necessary to improve general fluency. In addition, being more fluent encourages students to engage in more conversations which produce more input. But even with more limited input, typical in the average classroom, it is possible to become fluent in a narrow repertoire of language.

A distinction is sometimes made between **lower-order fluency** (fluency at the level of words, phrases and single sentences) and **higher-order fluency** (fluency at the discourse level, i.e. beyond single sentences (Taguchi, 2009).

Cognitive processing

Drawing on research into L1 acquisition, Pawley and Syder (1983) refer to the 'one-clause-at-time' constraint. This means that learners, limited by working memory capacity, can only focus on a single clause at once. They state: "It is the knowledge of conventional expressions, more than anything, that gives speakers the means to escape from the one-clause-at-a-time constraint and that is the key to native-like fluency" (p. 164). By conventional expressions they mean ready-made chunks (collocations, stock phrases etc - see Chapter 12). Their idea is that language learners can compensate for their lack of fluency by falling back on multi-word units. A six-month long study by Wood (2006) showed the extent to which the use of formulaic sequences contributes to fluency.

But other aspects of cognitive processing are also important. Here is a simple model of speech production proposed by de Bot (1992), based on Levelt's (1989) model we saw in Chapter 3.

1. Start with an idea (a semantic notion) that you want to express (the 'conceptualiser', which includes the choice of which language to use).
2. Put the idea into linguistic form (the 'formulator'), where words, grammar and phonology are implemented.
3. Speech is produced by the 'articulator'.

De Bot suggests that L2 learners need a 'feedback loop', as they realise they lack the words needed and must reformulate the language to match what they can actually do. As articulation proceeds, speakers monitor what they are saying for accuracy. Being able to find words quickly is crucial.

Segalowitz (2010) adapted the de Bot model, identifying points where fluency can break down, e.g. in the encoding of grammar, lexical retrieval, phonological encoding, articulation and the speaker's perceptions of their own production. The speaker's degree of automaticity dictates fluency. Fluent speakers perform the process of speaking with little effort, whereas learners must resort to paraphrase and avoidance strategies owing to their limited range of language. This means they may avoid talking about something because they instantly recognise they do not have the words they need. The more words and chunks students have in long-term memory, the easier it is both to retrieve and to paraphrase. In addition, articulation is easier if they have mastered a good level of pronunciation (see below).

If fluency is developed at each level (e.g. phonological, lexical, grammatical) then overall fluency will improve. This might suggest that designing classroom activities to develop each level of fluency should have a beneficial effect at a larger scale. This is the model used in Conti and Smith (2019), where listening skills are broken down into micro-skills which can be practised individually (see Chapter 2). If fluency breaks down at any level, then overall fluency is impaired.

Interestingly, Towell, Hawkins and Bazergui (1996) found that if someone speaks fast in their first language, they are more likely to speak fast in the second. In another study by Derwing *et al.* (2009), it was found that L2 fluency was influenced by the first language of the learners. In this case, L1 Mandarin speakers became less fluent in English than L1 Slavic language speakers. So it is possible that where there is a greater dissimilarity between L1 and L2, fluency is slower to develop. This makes sense if the L1 and L2 share cognates and similar grammatical structures since learners can draw on their existing knowledge to help.

The choice of classroom task affects fluency. Derwing *et al.* (2004) compared three tasks: a picture narrative, a monologue and a conversation. The picture narrative was judged by listeners to be less fluent than the other two conditions. This was thought to be because the picture tasks dictated to some extent which vocabulary could be used. In the monologue and conversation speakers could choose their own language. Foster and Skehan (1996) found the same, and attributed the problem with the picture task to greater cognitive load, but essentially they are referring to the same problem – students are more likely to be fluent if they can choose what to say. This has implications for test design. If students are allowed to do a presentation or hold conversations, they are likely to be more fluent than during a role play or picture task, where the language is somewhat defined by the source.

Fluency within a communicative approach

Gatbonton and Segalowitz (1989; 2005) proposed a specific methodology to develop automatised spoken fluency within the framework of a communicative approach. They called their model ACCESS (Automatisation in Communicative Contexts of Essential Speech Segments). The model for sequencing lessons looks like Figure 7.1

PHASE 1   'Creative Automatisation'

Pre-task: Introduce theme or topic, test learner readiness, demonstrate task, and elicit essential speech segments

Main Task: Learners engage in a task or tasks in which functionally useful utterances are used and elicited naturally and repeatedly

Sample tasks: Problem solving, role-plays, games, simulations

---

PHASE 2   Language Consolidation Phase

Aim: Strengthen learner control of problematic utterances elicited and practised in Phase 1

Sample tasks: Fluency, accuracy and grammatical discovery tasks

---

PHASE 3   Free Communication Phase

Aim: Test the use of practised utterances in context

Procedure: Learners engage in free communication activities that deal with topics compatible with those of the Creative Automatisation Phase

Sample tasks: Problem solving, role-play, games

Figure 7.1 The Gatbonton and Segalowitz ACCESS model

In this model, the authors wished to show that fluency can be developed by combining communicative tasks with a degree of controlled grammar and vocabulary practice. In a high school setting this model might work best at an intermediate level or above. The model is an example of how we can integrate a 'focus on form' approach within communicative lessons.

In Chapter 12 we explain how fluency is integrated within Gianfranco's EPI lexicogrammar approach. His MARS-EARS model (Conti and Smith, 2019) comprises stages where fluency is developed at each level through specific activities.

Fluency in the curriculum plan

Fluency can be a specific goal in any curriculum plan for languages, with planned activities to support its development (see also Chapter 20). In Nation's **four strands** curriculum model, fluency is defined as "being able to receive and produce language at a reasonable rate" (Nation and Yamamoto, 2012, p.168).

The four strands are shown below.

1. **Meaning-focused input**, e.g. reading interesting texts (including easy readers), listening for meaning, watching video, listening to the teacher talking about their own experiences, exchanging messages with a partner online.
2. **Meaning-focused output**, e.g. free writing, sharing messages online, conversation, giving presentations, taking part in less controlled information gap and communicative tasks, taking part in less controlled dialogues, role-plays and sketches.
3. **Language-focused learning**, e.g. using textbook tasks, grammar exercises, controlled oral drills and question-answer, controlled information gap tasks, doing gap-fills, memorising vocabulary, using a sentence builder, using a workbook, using contrived reading texts, doing translation.
4. **Fluency development**, e.g. doing tasks under time pressure, building aural fluency by doing phonological and phonics awareness tasks, doing lexical retrieval listening tasks, doing a communicative task to a time limit.

Nation suggests we should ask four questions about tasks if we want the focus to be on fluency:

1. Is it message and meaning-focused?
2. Is it easy? (familiar material – nothing new)
3. Is there pressure to go faster? (Speed)
4. Is there quantity of practice? (Volume)

Nation's most famous fluency task is the 4/3/2 task (actually from Maurice (1983)). Nation (1989) describes it as follows:

A student spends a few minutes preparing a talk on a given topic, without making notes. The student then pairs up with another and talks for four minutes, as their partner just listens. Then they change partners and do the same again for three minutes. Then they change partners once again and do their talk for two minutes.

The 4/3/2 task has been shown to increase spoken fluency and possibly accuracy (Nation, 1989). (We would note that Nation was working with adult learners who may have had a fair degree of fluency already. The timings are too long for the typical intermediate school student – a better timing might be 90 seconds, 60 seconds, 45 seconds). In any case, the time limit adds an extra level of motivation and the urge to speak more fluently. (See Chapter 3).

Clearly, fluency can be developed by our choice of classroom activities. Prioritising listening and speaking, maximising input and practice, teaching frequently occurring chunks and common discourse markers (e.g. words and phrases like *then, next, after all, finally*) – all of these can be built into the curriculum plan. We can even teach students how to hesitate convincingly by saying English equivalents of 'em', 'well' and 'like'! Rossiter *et al.* (2010) describe an activity where students transcribe a native speaker conversation and identify how the speakers hesitated.

Factors which may work against fluency practice include large class sizes, competing demands of other language skills, time limitations and lack of teacher fluency. Practising outside the classroom is also important. This can be built into a curriculum plan using homework. Study trips, school trips and exchanges are bound to help hugely in this regard.

Nation and Newton (2009) argue that we need a focus on all the language skills for fluency to develop. It is true that each skill supports the other and leads to deeper processing of language, but equally doing lots of listening will lead to listening fluency, doing lots of speaking will build spoken fluency, and so on. It is worth repeating how target language listening and speaking need to take priority.

Negotiation of meaning - pair and group work

For fluent, spontaneous talk to be developed effectively in large classes of the size typically found in high schools, a good idea is to have students do pair or group interaction through tasks requiring what researchers call **negotiation of meaning**, e.g. information gap tasks. Fluency development occurs when students try to put a message across to another speaker, regardless of the mistakes they make. Only after much practice of this type can they develop spontaneous speech.

Incorporating a mixture of teacher-student interaction and student-student interaction adds variety to lessons, making them more enjoyable, raising motivation and thus increasing the rate of acquisition (see Chapter 3). Having said this, some teachers are reluctant to do pair and group work for the following reasons.

1. Students do not always stay on task and lapse into their L1.
2. There is concern about the negative effect of pairing students of different proficiency levels; the higher-achieving students might not be stretched enough if they work with weaker ones.
3. By working with their peers, students might pick up poor examples of language which may become fossilised.
4. Not all students enjoy it.

The first point is a genuine concern and if you are not in full control of the class, it is understandable that you would be reluctant to give students too much freedom to talk. However, several studies have found that they do generally stay on task and tend to use L2 most of the time. What is more interesting, even when they lapse into L1, they tend to use L2 for behaviours which enhance their learning, i.e. (1) to facilitate the negotiation of meaning; (2) to talk about the task (how to conduct it and what the expectations are). Indeed, in some contexts we may even want to encourage students to use a mixture of L1 and L2 and engage in **translanguaging**.

Translanguaging is defined as: "..the act performed by bilinguals of accessing different linguistic features or various modes of what are described as autonomous languages, in order to maximise communicative potential" (Garcia, 2009 p. 140). It is a natural way for multilingual people to communicate and may make particular sense where communities share two or more languages, for example Wales in the UK, where translanguaging was conceived, or in parts of the USA where Spanish or other languages may be commonly spoken in the community. In multilingual classrooms translanguaging can be seen not only as a way for students to "use their full linguistic repertoire" (Garcia, ibid), but also as a way of valuing cultural and linguistic diversity in a context where one language or culture is traditionally seen as dominant.

Studies produce another interesting finding: student-to-student interaction tasks promote a host of 'self-regulation' strategies which assist acquisition and which many teachers observe every day (such as students whispering a word to themselves that they have just heard from a peer or teacher to commit it to memory).

As for the second and third points above, one study by Noriko Iwashita (2001) investigated whether pairing students of different proficiency levels might have adverse effects on the frequency and quality of interaction. She got her students to work in three proficiency pairs: high-high, low-low and high-low. She found that the lower proficiency students gained a lot from working with higher proficiency peers and produced lots of improved language, while the higher proficiency learners were not seemingly disadvantaged.

Finally, as far as the fourth point is concerned, Macaro (1997) found that oral pair work made most students feel comfortable and they reported learning and remembering a great deal. Very few reported negative attitudes towards pair and group work; our experience supports this.

Classroom practice

From controlled to free practice

As we wrote in Chapter 6, to develop spoken fluency and spontaneity we would argue for the importance of starting from an imitative, highly scaffolded (i.e. supported) and controlled (pre-communicative) practice stage in which students receive lots of prompts and support. This involves intensive and lengthy practice, taking at least a lesson if achieving spontaneity is a focus. Oral activities can become increasingly challenging and generate gradually more varied and complex responses. They may include adapting sentences by using different tenses or persons of the verb, changing answers into questions, adapting sentences by changing one word or more, role-plays, dialogues with visual or L1/L2 cues, 'find someone who' tasks, oral translations, classroom surveys and simulations.

This highly scaffolded stage can be followed by a consolidation and expansion phase of less scaffolded practice in which the language is reinforced through activities aimed at strengthening retention. Subsequently, more communicative practice can be done without scaffolding, so-called **free practice** (production in the PPP model described in Chapter 6). This phase can allow for extensive practice when students are encouraged to take risks and expand vocabulary on their own.

The final stage could be called the **autonomous** (spontaneous) stage in which students communicate without scaffolding and in which accuracy is not a concern unless it impedes communication. Errors need not be corrected. When scaffolding materials are removed, the teacher can monitor, help on request and give feedback. Students could record or video themselves talking in pairs without a script. (They are usually, for obvious reasons, keen to work from a written script, but we need to insist on 'letting them loose' to have a go and make mistakes.)

Throughout each phase students can be exposed to an increasingly wide range of questions, since fluent, spontaneous speakers need to be able to react to a range of prompts, some unexpected. Research in L1 and L2 acquisition suggests that the variety, length and complexity of the questions asked play an important role in acquisition. Recall that opportunities for free practice outside the classroom can be created. Students can do timed speech activities such as recording a talk from limited notes, rather than writing something out.

Much of the above may seem unrealistic to some readers. Being able to develop a sequence from 'controlled' to 'free' depends on having adequate time, so for some classes it can be hard to get to the stage where free practice is possible. In this case it may be necessary to cut down the number of topics or communicative goals so that students can be become competent, but in fewer areas. This is likely to raise their self-efficacy.

In Chapter 12 we look at how classes can move from receptive to productive work in a planned way as part of the lexicogrammatical approach called Extensive Processing Instruction (EPI).

The importance of pronunciation

One dimension of fluency is the actual speed of sound production (see also Chapter 3 for more about pronunciation). When our articulators (lips, tongue, palate, etc.) have not mastered the pronunciation of L2 sounds, speech slows down and vocabulary retrieval is hampered, as memory of words is also related to our association of words with sounds. It follows, therefore, that for us to help develop fluency, we should emphasise good pronunciation habits. This means we need to focus on detailed listening and decoding skills, as seen in Chapter 2.

There are ways to ensure that students' speech is intelligible. When doing L2 oral pair work they can jot down the meaning of what their partners have just told them in response to a question. This does slow down the conversation, but (a) it is a real-life task (L2 speakers interpret for their peers all the time) and (b) it makes the listener pay more attention to their partner's language. Suppose you have organised an oral communicative activity such as an intermediate level style interview: you may want to get each student to perform four rounds of interviews; they do the L1 translating or interpreting for two of the four rounds, whereas for the other two rounds, the listener can focus on providing feedback on their partner's pronunciation, range of vocabulary, correct use of tenses or any other language feature(s) focused on in the lesson.

Gianfranco's fluency tips

- Encourage participation and communication via games such as Sentence Stealer and 'Find someone who…'. These 'chunking aloud' games are fun and inclusive. Willingness to join in is one key to fluency development.

- Ensure L2 items are processed many times over through listening and reading, using highly comprehensible language. Then proceed to tasks which become increasingly less structured. This helps build automaticity (see Chapter 12).

- Next, use engaging, gamified tasks aimed at increasing speed of retrieval. Again, language should be feasible, involve highly familiar language, repeated processing, task repetition and working under increasing time pressure.

- Allow planning time and 'priming tasks' which prepare students for fluency activities. Give weaker students the most time for planning.

- When doing tasks which require spontaneous responses, do them twice, inserting a review stage between them. This provides corrective feedback and helps students improve their performance.

- If the aim is fluency, pay little attention to accuracy.

Encouraging fluent, spontaneous talk

Spontaneous talk is when a student takes part in a conversation while 'thinking on their feet', without any pre-planning and without relying on any sort of support (such as vocabulary lists, talking mats, dictionaries, etc.). In other words, spontaneity means unplanned speech production.

Students vary enormously in their ability to speak spontaneously, depending on a range of factors, notably their natural aptitude, their knowledge and their desire or need to communicate. After three years of teaching, some are already capable of using a narrow repertoire of language creatively with little or no help. We hear them playing with the language with their friends and they come out with unexpected utterances in class and in their books. Other students, the majority, with the same teacher and input, encounter great difficulty speaking spontaneously, even after five years of study.

There is no doubt that, while we must have high aspirations for all, in reality despite our best efforts some will struggle to achieve the spontaneity we would love to see. That said, if we optimised our approach to build greater motivation and to maximise input and practice, it is likely that more students than today would achieve some degree of proficiency and that the most able would be even more fluent. It also helps if we have in mind precisely what we expect nearly all our students to be able to achieve after, say, five years and do everything we can to help them reach this goal.

We have seen that spoken fluency is about the automatisation of speech production; the speed at which words are retrieved from long-term memory. This can only be achieved through practice in retrieving language under time pressure. So encouraging oral interaction as much as possible is vital, both between students and between student and teacher. This needs to develop from simple, structured exchanges of the type we have described in earlier chapters (question-answer, drills, information gaps and so on) towards greater autonomy. But spontaneity can be encouraged from the earliest stages, even with our weakest students through everyday classroom interactions – greeting them at the door, chatting with them in the corridor or the playground.

Obviously, the process of acquiring spontaneity in L2 speech production needs to be supported by teaching large amounts of L2 vocabulary (not just nouns but a wide range of verbs, too), of discourse markers (words like *but, and, I mean, well, because*) and by plenty of exposure to comprehensible listening input. Writing using social networks can also play a useful role, as it allows students to converse through the written medium at a speed high enough to practice fast L2 processing, but slow enough to allow for self-monitoring.

Below are some suggestions for activities which help develop spontaneity and fluency.

- **Pair work guessing games**. For example, ask partners to jot down five things they did last weekend. Each person has to use yes-no questioning to guess what their partner did. The first to work out all five is the winner. Put a time limit on the task.

- **Scaffolded situational dialogues** - gapped dialogues with options to choose from, but with the instruction that students should add more of their own. Alternatively, provide ungapped dialogues, but with some words and chunks underlined, that they should change.

- **Interactional writing tasks within time limits**. Students could engage in social network-style communication with their devices or mimic it in their exercise books at home. The sequences of speech bubble trails now available on smartphones facilitate this: templates reproducing these would be a useful model to follow. This encourages students to develop quick reactions and lessen their fear of making mistakes.

- **'Sales pitch.'** In this game students are divided into *buyers* and *sellers*. Sellers are briefed about what they will sell, and each is given time to prepare their sales pitch. Meanwhile, buyers are given receptive practice in the sort of vocabulary they are likely to hear from the sellers.

  - Example: Selling holiday accommodation, such as a hotel, campsite or holiday park.

  - Sellers prepare their information about the accommodation, facilities, activities available, excursions and nightlife. They are given a 'stall' (desk). Buyers go from stall to stall, listening to the sales pitch, taking notes. They then compare notes in pairs and feed back to the teacher on their choice.

- **'Messengers.'** Students are placed in teams of 5 or 6. Each team has a *describer*, two or three *messengers* and two *makers*.
  - The describers have a diagram, map or picture to describe.
  - The messengers listen to the describers and relay what they hear to the makers.
  - The makers reproduce the diagram, map or picture based on the description they hear.
  - Because of the complexity of this task, the messengers will need to return to the describers more than once to recall all the information they need. Good sources would be simple town maps, a diagram of a school, a picture of a family, beach scene or house.

- **Timed writing**. Students are given a picture to write about. They have five minutes to write as many sentences as they can about the picture. After this first attempt, they write down the number of words they wrote. They can compare responses with a partner and feed back to the teacher. They repeat the same task later, for example during the next lesson, and note down how many words they managed to write the second time (adapted from Nation, 2014).

- **'Sentence puzzle race.'**
  - Two students are each given identical or similar jumbled-up sentences.
  - The student who reads out the sentence in the correct order is the winner.
  - A third student acts as timer/referee.
  - As a post-task students could do some L1-L2 translation of the same sentences or write a paragraph aimed at reusing the same or similar sentences (best for higher-achievers). If the aim is fluency building, ignore errors.

Risk-taking and compensatory strategies

We have seen that fluency can be fostered by encouraging students not to be afraid of taking risks and making mistakes. Risk-taking, however, requires some scaffolding too. We can equip students with effective compensatory strategies to cope with communication breakdown, for example, how to make up for a lack of vocabulary. Here are some strategies we can teach:

- **Coinage** – showing students how you can create an L2 word from an L1 word (this strategy does not apply to all languages). For instance: how to get the French for words like *university*, *city* or *proximity* by changing the *y* to *é* or how to obtain the Spanish equivalent of verbs ending in *-ate* in English by replacing *-ate* with *-ar* e.g. *exagerar, alternar, enumerar,* etc.

- **Paraphrase** – teaching how to make up for a lack of vocabulary by using a basic definition or description of a word, e.g. for *glass – you use it to drink water*. Guessing games such as '20 Questions' develop this skill.

- **Approximation** – using a word that is close enough in meaning to the one you need, e.g., *boat* for *yacht*, or *chair* for *stool*, with or without the use of mime.

Teaching these strategies can be a lot of fun. You may be tempted to frown upon the idea of students learning how to produce incorrect language to get the message across, but these strategies are not simply compensatory strategies; they are ultimately learning strategies in that their use usually results in a correction by another speaker which provides the accurate L2 form. Spontaneity requires the kind of risk-taking and creativity that the application of these strategies entails. Compensatory strategies allow a speaker to keep up fluent talk even when they lack vocabulary and grammar; in this sense, they are important communicative tools.

Steve's tips for developing spontaneous talk

- Model to students creative ways to put a message across to another speaker when they do not know vocabulary, i.e. train them in the use of communicative strategies.
- Take any opportunity for students to go to the L2 country or talk to native speakers.
- Incorporate in the curriculum plan assessments and activities which allow some opportunity for spontaneous speech and writing, not just pre-learned answers to questions or memorised presentations, valuable though these may be.
- Have key phrases on the wall to use when they want, e.g. *I would like… How do you say…?*
- Take all opportunities to encourage students to speak in L2 – *I need a pen.*
- Give as much support as possible during pair work, such as literacy mats (key language and vocabulary sheets).
- Reward bravery and risk-taking. Make sure students know that making mistakes during spontaneous talk is not important. Getting the message across is much more important.
- Build spontaneity into routines, e.g. when students enter the classroom, hold up a mini-whiteboard with a key phrase at the door, e.g. *opinion in French* and they have to give an example as they come in. That way each has said something in L2 before they've even settled down. Engage in small talk in L2 with students while they are waiting outside the door.
- Make L2 seem like the natural means of communication and give rewards to students who use language spontaneously.

Steve's speedy starters to build fast recall

Time limits can be set for many simple retrieval starters, fillers or plenaries. This encourages a sense of urgency and quick recall. Below are five simple low-preparation examples for near beginners or pre-intermediate level. These can be done orally, in pairs or in writing using paper or a mini-whiteboard.

- **Insert a chunk**. Display slides with gapped sentences where a phrase can be inserted. These can be designed so that there is just one option or many.
- **Complete my sentence**. Display slides, each with a sentence where the final word is missing. Students add a suitable missing word.
- **Vocab championship**. Think of a football championship where teams compete in each round to reach a final. In this case, the teams are words from a chosen topic, e.g. sports, food, cooking types, countries. For the chosen topic, brainstorm vocab then give students pairs of words to vote on. This produces a winner for each match in that round. The winner proceeds to the next round, until one word wins the final. For foods, assume it will be pizza!
- **Ever-changing sentence**. Display a sentence with a few elements, e.g. time marker, subject, verb, complement (object, place, manner). In pairs students take turns to remove one element and replace it with a new one. This new, altered sentence is the basis for the next change, and so on.
- **Word cloud challenge**. Create a word cloud (or just write on the board) using words from the current topic, or a previous one. To a time limit, individuals or pairs must come up with as many sentences as they can, using at least three words from the cloud.

Concluding remarks

Fluency is one of the toughest nuts to crack. In speech it can only really be achieved through huge amounts of practice and exposure. But fluency can also refer to fluent cognitive recall, fluent pronunciation, fluent decoding when listening and reading. For students to be fluent they need the following:

- Plenty of vocabulary, especially high-frequency vocabulary. The more they know the more they will be able to communicate.
- Practice in manipulating multi-word units to adapt them effectively to various linguistic contexts.

- A classroom climate which encourages one-to-one oral interaction and risk-taking and which prioritises fluency and communication over grammatical accuracy.

- Extensive controlled and highly scaffolded one-to-one oral practice which leads to free practice. This should aim at developing transferable communicative routines, whose automatisation will ultimately lead to spontaneity.

- Independent vocabulary learning, and seeking oral interaction opportunities outside the classroom. An exchange trip where students stay with a family would be ideal.

- Practice in compensatory strategies, i.e. ways of keeping going by working around difficulties.

- Lots of listening which models useful language and communicative routines.

We can plan for all this carefully and work towards it by applying the principles above while creating a supporting, non-judgmental learning environment conducive to risk-taking. Ultimately, the extent to which students become fluent L2 users will largely hinge on the amount of vocabulary they know, the listening and reading input they have received, the speaking practice they have done and their willingness to take risks. But we cannot expect students to perform miracles. We sometimes have to say something along these lines: "Does the physics teacher expect you to be like Einstein after five years? Then we cannot expect to become fluent speakers of another language in that short time. Well then, you can learn to cope in a range of everyday situations if you listen and practise hard enough."

8

Reading

Introduction

The main role of L2 reading is as a source of meaningful input which furthers language acquisition. It also serves to widen students' intercultural knowledge and improve their general literacy. Reading naturally integrates with the skills of listening, speaking and writing to create multi-mode lessons and lesson sequences. In this chapter we shall consider the areas below.

Research evidence
- ✓ What is reading?
- ✓ Top-down and bottom-up skills
- ✓ Reading strategies
- ✓ Extensive reading
- ✓ Intensive and narrow reading
- ✓ The role of phonology
- ✓ Reading aloud

Classroom practice
- ✓ Using strategies
- ✓ Developing top-down and bottom-up skills
- ✓ Exploiting narrow reading
- ✓ Exploiting extensive reading
- ✓ Reading aloud activities
- ✓ Assessing reading
- ✓ Teaching with written texts

Research evidence

What is reading?

Reading, unlike listening and speaking, is not a natural skill that humans are biologically predisposed to acquire. But like listening and speaking, it is a complex, dynamic process involving a range of skills, micro-skills and knowledge. William Grabe (2013) points out the following aspects which allow us to comprehend written texts:

- Recognising words rapidly and efficiently.
- Using both grammar and vocabulary to process sentences.

- Employing a range of strategies and thinking skills, e.g. setting and changing goals and monitoring comprehension.
- Using background knowledge.
- Evaluating texts depending on a reader's purposes.
- Processing texts fluently over an extended period of time.

Both L1 and L2 reading ability correlates well with vocabulary knowledge. Reading therefore requires both a large knowledge of vocabulary and rapid word recognition. Research on English L1 eye movement tracking reveals that good readers recognise words in a few hundred milliseconds, and they move their eyes ahead about eight letter spaces per focus. The average silent L1 reading rate for adults in English is 238 words per minute for non-fiction and 260 for fiction (Brysbaert, 2019). When we read, we focus on about 80% of the content words and about 50% of the small function words (Grabe, 2009). Much research suggests that, as with L1 reading, it is important to establish clear letter-sound correspondences (phonics) from the beginning (e.g. Woore, 2022). In addition to vocabulary knowledge, knowing grammar, both syntax and morphology, has been shown to improve reading performance. Ultimately, reading skill only develops with extensive exposure to meaningful written text. To quote Suk (2017), "Reading ability is only likely to develop gradually when L2 learners are continually exposed to abundant meaningful input, or extensive reading" (p. 73). For a detailed treatment of issues surrounding reading, see Grabe and Stoller (2019).

Top-down and bottom-up processing skills

Research shows that both top-down and bottom-up processing skills contribute to reading proficiency. As with listening, **top-down** involves using previous knowledge about the topic and context of the text to infer meaning. **Bottom-up** processing refers to the way a student reconstructs the meaning of a text through knowledge of vocabulary, grammar, sound to letter relationships and sociolinguistic features such as the connotations of words.

Reading strategies

Anderson (2003) classifies language learning strategies into seven major categories: cognitive strategies, metacognitive strategies, mnemonic or memory related strategies, compensatory strategies, affective strategies, social strategies, and self-motivating strategies. **Metacognitive strategies** are those conscious learning strategies that oversee, direct and regulate the learning process. These involve thinking about learning processes: planning, monitoring, evaluating and adjusting them (Vandergrift, 2002).

Several early studies identified relationships between certain types of reading strategies and successful and unsuccessful L2 reading. For example, Carol Hosenfeld (1977) studied high school students in the U.S. reading French, German or Spanish. 'Successful' French readers did several things: (1) they kept the meaning of the passage in mind during reading, (2) they read in what she termed 'broad phrases', (3) they skipped words unimportant to total phrase meaning, and (4) they had a positive self-concept as a reader. By contrast, Hosenfeld's 'unsuccessful' French readers (1) lost the meaning of sentences as soon as they were decoded, (2) read in short phrases, (3) seldom skipped words as unimportant and viewed words as equal in their contribution to total phrase meaning, and (4) had a negative self-concept as a reader.

How successful are reading strategy programmes? A major classroom study by Robert Woore and colleagues (Woore *et al.*, 2018) followed 900 Year 7 students in England (Year 7 is the first year of high school, so these were largely novices). Over the course of a year they worked with eight 'pedagogical texts'. The students were divided into three groups: (1) focused on extra phonics teaching, (2) focused on extra metacognitive strategies and (3) with no particular extra focus ('texts only'). The results of the study were mixed, with the 'strategies' group showing slightly higher levels of self-efficacy by the end. The study concluded: "An integrated approach to French reading instruction – combining explicit instruction in both Strategies and Phonics with the use of appropriately challenging, engaging texts – is more likely to be beneficial than any of these approaches in isolation" (Woore *et al.*, 2018 p. 7).

As with listening strategies, it is likely that to be most effective, a major structured programme would be needed. In general, our guidance would be to train students in strategy use within the general sequence of lessons. Higher-achieving students use strategies unconsciously, partly carrying over their skills from L1 reading, so benefit less than weaker ones from strategy training. This does not mean teaching strategies on an *ad hoc* basis, since you can plan for and introduce those likely to be most useful.

Extensive reading

Extensive reading means reading very easy, enjoyable, or different types of books or materials for pleasure or to build reading skills. It is generally agreed by researchers that extensive reading in L2 is important. Within Paul Nation's 'four strands' model of the curriculum, discussed in Chapter 7 (Nation and Yamamoto, 2012), extensive reading is strongly advocated. Some scholars, e.g. Krashen, argue that this 'sustained silent reading' or 'free voluntary reading' is really all students need to become better readers. There is little controlled research evidence to support this, though common sense suggests that lengthy reading of highly comprehensible language must be useful.

Nakanishi (2015) carried out a meta-analysis of many studies and concluded that "extensive reading improves students' reading proficiency and should be a part of language learning curricula" (from the abstract). At the very least, extensive reading provides a constant recycling of well-known and partially known material in contrasting situations which will help fully implant the language into long-term memory. The problem is finding time for this in a busy school programme. The figure of 95-98% is often quoted as the number of words in a text that a student should already know in order for it to be easily understood (Nation, 2006). Glossing a text helps where the unknown vocabulary percentage is higher.

Intensive and narrow reading

In contrast to extensive reading, **intensive reading** in class this involves working with a text in a variety of ways, e.g. hearing it read aloud, reading silently, reading it aloud, talking about it and manipulating language contained within the text. This sort of intensive work generates repetitions, memory for vocabulary, morphological and syntactic awareness, and vocabulary knowledge. Extensive reading is assumed to be relatively fast and meaning-focused, whereas intensive reading is slower and more focused on detail and language form, in addition to meaning. Intensive reading with associated listening, speaking and written tasks creates more repetitions, thus more chance of vocabulary being internalised.

Along with the concept of narrow listening, proposed by Krashen (2004) (See Chapter 2) he also proposed **narrow reading**. This essentially involves reading several interesting texts on the same topic, with each text recycling some vocabulary and structures. A few studies have demonstrated the effectiveness of this technique, including one by Kang (2015) with 61 high intermediate level learners, which demonstrated that narrow reading considerably facilitated students' understanding of word meanings and the ability to use them appropriately.

Within the EPI approach (see Chapter 12), narrow reading, like narrow listening, involves a much tighter focus on chosen language patterns, repeated many times over. The resulting **input flooding** (also known as **input seeding**) should benefit memory and acquisition, a finding borne out by a few studies summarised in Boers (2021), e.g. Sánchez-Gutiérrez *et al*. (2019).

The role of phonology

Research into cognitive skills shows clearly that poor readers have difficulty with phonological processing, i.e. the processing of sounds (Walter, 2008). There are a few reasons why efficient phonological processing predicts a high level of reading proficiency. Firstly, the establishment of a clear phonological mental representation of a word appears to be the most important requisite for success in early L2 vocabulary acquisition for young L2 students. Secondly, phonology plays a role when retrieving words from memory. This is because when we learn a word, we encode it through its phonological representation, (i.e. the way we hear it). Thus, when we see a word, we 'hear' it in our heads before retrieving its meaning from long-term memory. In other words, the sound of a word helps us remember it. Doing this rapidly means that, as we read, the brain can free up cognitive space in working memory. This means there is more space available for higher levels of cognitive processing, such as the analysis of grammar and meaning.

In summary, research suggests the need to develop top-down and bottom-up skills, increase vocabulary, develop reading strategies, provide opportunities for intensive and extensive reading, and make sure students have the chance to establish strong links between sounds and words.

Reading aloud

Although reading aloud by students has not always been favourably viewed in L2 classrooms in the last few decades, its usefulness in developing lower-level processing efficiency has been widely confirmed (Gibson, 2008). Research has shown that reading aloud helps in many ways.

- It develops students' accurate phonological representation of vocabulary (Gibson, 2008).
- With its focus on connected texts, it raises awareness of rhythm, stress and intonation, by using connected texts rather than decontextualized vocabulary items, e.g. Kato (2012).
- It significantly improves the speed of silent reading (Suzuki, 1998).
- It improves listening ability (Kato and Tanaka, 2015).
- It can boost motivation (Shinozuka *et al.*, 2017).
- It helps with memory recall, especially when you repeat aloud to another person (Lafleur and Boucher, 2015; Forrin and MacLeod, 2018).
- It helps develop oral fluency by (1) training the articulators, i.e. all the organs involved in the production of sounds and (2) exposure to self-generated listening input, (Seo, 2014).
- It develops decoding ability which in turns facilitate processing and learning vocabulary. Erler and Macaro (2011) revealed how poorly many students can turn written language into speech, and how this tended to discourage them from continuing with French.
- It helps students to break down sentences into chunks.

Classroom practice

Using strategies

To improve students' reading, we recommend, the strategies below, following, Harris (1997).
- Recognising the **type of text**; poem, newspaper article, brochure, etc.
- Examining pictures, the title, etc. for **clues to meaning**.
- Going for **gist**, skipping inessential words.
- Using **punctuation** for clues: question marks, capital letters, etc.
- Using **knowledge of the world** to make sensible guesses.
- **Substituting** L1 words, e.g. 'she *something* on her head'.
- **Analysing unknown words**, breaking a word or phrase down and associating parts of it with familiar words, e.g. German *hochgewachsen* (the meaning in English 'lanky' is derived from *hoch* (high) and *gewachsen* (grown))

- **Saying the text out loud** and identifying chunk boundaries; how a sentence breaks down and which parts of it to work on at one time.
- Identifying the **grammatical categories** of words.

As with listening, if we wish to train students in these strategies, there needs to be a planned programme. As a reminder, this involves:

1. **A modelling phase** where a strategy is demonstrated, e.g. the thinking aloud method. For example, *I'm going to show you how you can identify where the verb is in the sentence,* or *This is how you relate word endings to those in L1.*
2. **A scaffolding phase** where the strategy is practised with reminders from the teacher. *Let's look at this paragraph and see if you can spot all the verbs or find endings which help you work out the L1 meaning.*
3. **An independent phase** where reminders are withdrawn. *Okay, try on your own now.*
4. **An evaluation phase** during which the success of the strategy is assessed. *Do you think that strategy helped you? Could you use it in the future?*

If you prefer to work more 'opportunistically', after working on a written text, students can be asked to consider aspects which impeded their understanding and what they could do to overcome them without using the dictionary. Specific strategies can be suggested, e.g. using cognates, punctuation, parts of speech and linking words. It may be useful to show that every word does not have to be fully understood, bearing in mind that in L1 we often do not understand everything, and this does not impede understanding of the overall message.

Developing top-down and bottom-up skills

To practise both sets of skills, simply giving students reading comprehension tests, marking them and giving scores is not enough. Just as with listening, we can do a good deal to teach students how to read. The 10 activities below are recommended.

1. **Pre-reading tasks**: these (a) elicit background knowledge of the topic and context of the L2 text while modelling useful reading strategies and (b) present and practise the key vocabulary in the L2 text.

2. **Recycling the text**: through several activities to exploit its full linguistic potential across the lexical, grammatical and cultural dimensions. Such activities will involve word-recognition or finding L2 equivalent of L1 words in the text.

3. **Scanning the text**: to search for synonyms from a list of L2 words. This builds vocabulary and makes students focus on individual words.

4. **Grammatical analysis**: e.g. underlining parts of speech, highlighting linking words and analysing sentences using an online text manipulation programme such as *textivate.com* or a site such as *languagesonline.org.uk* or *language-gym.com*.

5. **Comprehension questions**: in L1 or L2, true or false, split sentences, gap-fill or multiple-choice comprehension questions.

6. **Post-reading tasks**: these consolidate vocabulary and grammar, e.g. odd ones out, categories, answering questions in L2, rewriting a text from a different perspective, translating or writing a summary.

7. **Real-life reading activities**: to enhance student motivation and effectively scaffold independent internet-based reading outside the classroom, reading activities can include activities the students perform in real life, whether for pleasure (e.g. reading media gossip about a pop-star, movie synopses, reviews of video games, short stories, poems or magazine articles) or to accomplish a task (checking the train schedule, researching information for a piece of homework, finding out where to buy a given product at the cheapest price, buying groceries or clothes from a shopping website or booking a holiday online).

8. **Student-driven text selection**: give students a degree of choice as to what is read in class. This can be done fairly easily where they have tablets, personal computers or mobile devices. When this is not possible, carry out a survey to find out what they are interested in and select texts accordingly. There is no need to be afraid about departing occasionally from topics in the syllabus.

9. **Reading longer texts**: this can become a habit amongst students, starting with simplified readers, using parallel texts and even reading short stories, perhaps adapted. Reading clubs can be set up with the support of school librarians, parents or older students. Song clubs can focus not only on listening, but on reading lyrics. They could keep a diary of their reading. Teachers need not feel guilty when their students just get on with silent reading!

10. **Web-related learning strategies**: advise students about the most effective approaches to developing reading skills on the web. This could include where to find resources suitable for their level, modelling ways to exploit such resources effectively, how to use online dictionaries or forums, how to store and organise new vocabulary they come across and even how to use it for self-teaching, e.g. by using apps such as Quizlet, Blooket or Memrise.

Exploiting narrow reading

Here are some ways this can be incorporated into your lesson planning:

- Ask advanced level students to **source online L2 news stories** based on the same event, then get them to share and read, perhaps providing general exercises to support the reading. These could be simply to summarise in L1 or L2 the main points of the story.

- **Authentic forum posts** can be copied or adapted to provide the basis for narrow reading tasks, such as matching opinions to writers, finding vocabulary or summarising in L1 or L2.

- **Reviews** of hotels, restaurants or holiday destinations from sites like *Tripadvisor* or *Booking.com* can provide multiple texts on a similar topic. You can adapt them as necessary to make sure L2 vocabulary is being recycled.

- Simple **teacher-made 'adapted authentic' texts** which relate to students' own interests can be made into an effective lesson plan, for example, hobbies, attitudes to school, TV or film reviews. This type of contrived text allows you to recycle identical patterns multiple times and is a staple of the EPI approach.

- Table 8.1 is an example in Italian (from Conti and Smith, 2019) where the texts were used for narrow listening. In this case it is only the text in bold which changes, the rest (the input flood) is nearly all identical.

Table 8.1 Beginner-level Italian narrow reading texts on the topic of leisure

TEXT 1 - Mi chiamo **Franco**. Nel mio tempo libero di solito gioco a **scacchi**. Adoro giocare a **scacch**i perché è **emozionante** e **divertente**. Mi piace anche molto **giocare ai videogiochi** ma è **malsano**. Non **faccio sport** perché è **faticoso** e noioso. Ogni tanto vado **in discoteca con i miei amici** nel week-end.
TEXT 2 -Mi chiamo **Maria**. Nel mio tempo libero di solito gioco a **pallone**. Adoro giocare a **pallone** perché è molto **competitivo** e divertente. Mi piace anche molto **arrampicare perché** è **sano e divertente**, ma è un po' faticoso. Non **gioco al computer** perché è noioso e **malsano**. Ogni tanto vado **al centro commerciale con i miei genitori** nel week-end.
TEXT 3 - Mi chiamo **Sonia**. Nel mio tempo libero di solito gioco a **pallavolo**. Adoro giocare a pallavolo perché è molto **emozionante** e **avvincente**. Mi piace anche molto **fare equitazione** perché è **rilassante** e **appassionante**. Non **gioco alla playstation** perché è **una perdita di tempo**. Ogni tanto vado **in chiesa** e **al cinema con la mia ragazza** nel week-end.

Examinations and textbooks often contain examples of several short texts on similar topics, so by using these techniques in class you are helping prepare your students effectively for assessment. A typical way to approach narrow reading is to supply roughly six short texts, then work through several tasks which engage them in careful reading and recycling of vocabulary. Exercise types include:

- identifying words in the texts from **definitions** in L2;
- identifying words or phrases from L1 **translations** (i.e. 'find the Spanish');
- **rearranging the order** of some statements in L1, using one of the short texts as a source;
- finding **synonyms and antonyms** from the texts;
- doing **true/false/not mentioned** tasks;
- answering **questions in L1**;
- **reading aloud**;
- **matching** L1 or L2 statements with each text.

Exploiting extensive reading

We have seen that while **intensive reading** provides a basis for comprehension, language analysis, vocabulary building and discussion work, **extensive reading** involves reading at length for enjoyment. Material for extensive reading should usually be selected at a lower level of difficulty than for intensive reading. The purpose of an extensive reading programme is to train students to read fluently in L2 without the help of the teacher.

The challenge, however, is to find reading materials which are both interesting and set at the right level. If a ready-made set of graded readers is unavailable, a reading programme can be produced by the teacher, perhaps using adapted resources form the internet. Various publishers have a selection of stories or short novels, e.g. in French, German and Spanish, which are cleverly selected for near novice and intermediate students and which many teachers enjoy using. AI tools have become a fast and effective way to generate texts at a chosen level.

A significant issue for teachers is the lack of classroom time available for extensive reading, when so much else has to be done. Even so, it may be possible to devote a regular amount of time, perhaps 20 minutes per week, or five minutes at the start of lessons, for personal reading. At advanced levels, where there may be more time for extensive reading, it usually forms a key part of courses. As well as any prescribed reading, students can be encouraged to do weekly reading from the internet. Cartoon books can be a useful way to do extensive reading at high intermediate and advanced levels. Parallel texts are another means of helping them understand interesting reading material. The school library can include a range of interesting reading for enjoyment, including translated popular novels and non-fiction picture books.

When helping students to read at length, advise them not to go too slowly, looking up every word, but just enough so that comprehension is maintained. They may like to keep a record of new words they encounter, perhaps in the margin of a printed text, in a notebook or electronic device. Mention that if they discover they are not interested in the text, they should not persevere too long.

Reading aloud activities

Given the importance of phonology and phonics in reading, it is good practice to regularly read aloud from texts and play read aloud games. Keep in mind also the added advantages of letting students read aloud from written text.

- Allowing the most confident students to perform. Some enjoy showing off what they can do, and this may reinforce motivation.
- As a source of comprehensible (self-generated) listening input to the reader and the rest of the group.
- It may be a good activity for class behaviour management. Classes usually listen respectfully to their peers reading aloud.
- Helping develop a student's confidence in speaking in front of others - a good life skill.
- As a formative assessment opportunity. After someone has read, others can comment on what was good about it.

The following points are worth noting, however.

- When not carefully prepared and scaffolded after much receptive input, it is a scary activity for some students, so reading aloud in pairs is often preferable. It is important to lay a lot of emphasis on the teaching of decoding skills and pronunciation from day one of the course.
- If the ground is poorly prepared, public reading aloud may open a student to ridicule from their peers.
- A trick of the trade is to have students cover their ears as they read aloud individually. This lets them hear their own voice without distraction from others.

Getting students to read aloud 'around the class' in a predictable order is usually poor practice. Reading aloud in front of the group may be a stepping stone to paired reading aloud, which has other advantages: everyone is active, students can assess each others' reading and there is no need to feel inhibited, so performance may be better. Paired reading aloud is effective if the quality is good. If students are allowed to perform badly errors may become perpetuated. Here are two reading aloud games which many classes enjoy.

Find your match

This zero preparation game, devised by Gianfranco, works as follows.

1. Students secretly write on mini-whiteboards or on paper one sentence (or more) from a list of about 12 displayed on the board. For example, they might all be answers to the question "What did you do last night?" ("I did my homework"; "I played a board game", and so on).
2. Students go around the classroom asking 'What did you do last night?'. Their task is to find another student with the same sentence. It is important that they always read aloud what they have on their mini-whiteboard or paper.
3. Several rounds of the game can be played in around 10 minutes as they usually find their match quite quickly.

The 'something' game

This game, created by teacher Dylan Viñales, works as follows.

1. Sit students in pairs, back-to-back.
2. Give Student 1 sheet A and Student 2 sheet B. Each sheet has a different version of the same list of sentences; the sentences which are gapped on student A's sheet are complete on student B's sheet and vice versa.
3. They take turns in reading one gapped sentence each, and say 'something' (e.g. *algo* in Spanish) to signal the presence of a gap. (The gaps can target specific chunks we wish to recycle.) When student B hears student A say 'something' they must read out the whole sentence twice, including the missing chunk, while the other writes it down and vice versa.
4. At the end of the game they compare the two sheets to see who was more accurate.

Assessing reading

How do we know students are improving their reading skills? When doing interactive oral work with classes, the feedback we get provides useful ongoing information about understanding, but formal assessment is also needed. The form of assessment may have a strong effect on our teaching, known technically as the **washback effect** (see also Chapter 13). Washback can be positive or negative. Ideally, we want teaching to lead the assessment, not the other way round. This creates positive washback. Teachers often 'teach to the test' and this is fine when washback is positive, the test is appropriate and reflects good pedagogical practice.

If the goal is to assess reading separately from the other skills, we need a form of **discrete skill** testing which does not involve students using other skills at the same time. Otherwise it is hard to know whether we are assessing reading or something else, such as written accuracy. Discrete skill testing leads to question types such as matching with pictures, multiple choice with pictures and multiple choice or questions in L1 or L2. Multi-choice in L2 has the merit of providing even more input, but some would argue it is more confusing to students who must cope not only with the original text, but also with L2 questions.

Discrete skill testing is all well and good, but in normal classroom teaching we want to be integrating skills to ensure maximum use of L2 (combining listening with speaking, plus reading and writing – all reinforcing the same language). Question types which reflect this include questions in L2, multiple choice in L2, split L2 sentences, gap-fill in L2 and choosing options from a list in L2. All these question types have the advantage of providing more L2 input, so make for better teaching, but clearly muddy the waters in terms of assessing reading alone.

Our preference is generally to take the latter approach, i.e. to use 'integrated skill testing' since, because of the washback effect from the test, it is likely to lead to better classroom pedagogy.

When assessing a student's reading ability, we need to be clear what it is we are trying to assess: a knowledge of the general comprehension (gist) of a text, detailed understanding of pieces of information, whether the reader has understood the opinions or feelings of the writer, the ability to read quickly, or even the command of grammar, such as tense usage. Different question types will reflect the nature of what we are trying to assess.

Question types

It is good practice, therefore, that test questions resemble those used in classroom activities. Here is a selection.

- **True/false** in L1 or L2.
- **True/false/not mentioned** – this is statistically better than simple true/false but be very careful when devising 'not mentioned' cues as these can easily cause confusion for students.
- **Matching the beginnings and ends** of L2 sentences – avoid using structures and vocabulary lifted straight from the text.
- Traditional **comprehension questions** in L1 or L2.
- **Translation into L1** – be aware that this is a test of comprehension, not a test in using L1.
- **Gap-fill** exercises in L1 or L2 (with or without options).
- **Matching** L1 or L2 statements to individual short texts.
- **Ticking options** from a series of statements.
- **Multiple-choice** questions in L1 or L2 – note that when using L2 questions an extra element of comprehension is added, not just comprehension of the original text. As mentioned above, when using L2 we need to avoid providing identical vocabulary to that used in the text, so skill is needed in finding synonyms or paraphrases. Three options are enough to provide a statistically valid score.
- **Summary**. This is a higher-level activity which can be done in L1 (easier) or L2 (where written language adaptation and manipulation are required).

We have shown what research tells us about reading and what this might mean for the classroom. On a purely practical note, a teacher's day is busy and tiring. We do not need to be performing all the time. Quiet reading or combined reading and writing activities are a good opportunity for you to have some 'down time' when students actually work harder than you! This can also be an opportunity to see them individually to go over their last few pieces of work and discuss progress.

Steve's zero preparation reading activities

- For advanced students, write on the board some statistics taken at random from a suitable text. Ask them to work in pairs to find the figures in the text and then explain to each other what they refer to, using their own words where possible. When finished, tell them to turn over the text so they cannot look at it. Point at the figures on the board and ask students what they refer to.

- For intermediate and advanced students, write a list on the board, in random order, of some key words or ideas from the text, choosing one item per paragraph. Ask students to sequence them according to the article.

- Ask intermediate or advanced students to design a worksheet based on a text. This would be a good chance to talk about assessment and question types. The task also puts students in the shoes of the teacher, thereby helping them develop their own reading strategies.

- For all levels, after working on a text for some time, ask students to hide it from view. Then read aloud the text, pausing to leave a gap. They must put up their hand to supply the next word or words. Alternatively they could write their idea on mini-whiteboards. Then give the correct answer and move on. Warn students earlier in the teaching sequence that they will do a memory test later, to focus their minds on the task.

- Do a live, improvised true-false reading comprehension. Look through the text yourself and find an interesting fact. Paraphrase it in your own words, either accurately, or else changing some small detail so it is not the same as the text. Ask students to scan the text to see if the statement is true or false.

Teaching with written texts

Teaching with a written text is a nuts-and-bolts skill that all language teachers need, whatever the level of the students. Here is some guidance on how to work with written texts.

Laying the ground (pre-reading)

To prepare students for the text they are going to read, especially at intermediate level and beyond, we suggest asking a few questions or giving a brief introduction to the topic. They guess which points might be covered in the text to arouse interest or provide knowledge about what they are about to read. Some words/phrases from the text can be displayed as prompts.

There are other ways of stimulating an interest in what is to be read: showing a short video, recounting an anecdote from your own experience or eliciting personal experiences from students. It may be useful to do some work on the language they will be reading in the text. Vocabulary manipulation tasks on paper or online are one possibility.

Reading the text aloud or playing a recording of the text

This allows students to hear correct pronunciation and encourages them to read slowly and carefully since they must go at the pace of the reader. It is a good 'settling' activity, but we must make sure that students are actually following the text and listening. Encourage this by saying that after your reading you are going to ask someone at random to say what the gist of the text is or to give a particular fact in the text. Younger students can follow the text with their finger or ruler. Your intonation may also help in deciphering meaning. Reading aloud to the class has the advantage over audio because you can control the pace of delivery.

Finding the L2

This simple task, best done in the early stages of looking at a text, simply involves getting students to pick out vocabulary using L1 cues. It can be done orally, with you asking questions from the front, or perhaps better in writing as then all are involved in the task.

Bilingual glossary completion

Provide two incomplete columns of words, L1 and L2, with gaps to be filled. Alternatively just provide the L1 or L2 words for students to translate. This can be a reassuring task. One of the most common questions they ask is *What does this word mean?* As teachers we often over-estimate how much our students understand. Even words which seem like obvious cognates may not be understood, e.g. when students do not know the L1 word in the first place.

Asking questions

Questions can be in L1 or L2. They may be asked to the whole class with a hands-up or no-hands approach. Students can give oral or written answers. Written answers have benefits: it keeps all students focused, allows time for them to think, practises close listening and reading as well as writing skills. A question-answer sequence can be done orally, then in writing, using the same questions, thus recycling and consolidating language. Alternatively they can write written answers to written questions or ask each other questions in pairs, either writing them down or not.

Questions in L1 have their place but are generally better suited to assessment than language practice. Keep working in L2 as far as possible. One pitfall is to work too superficially - to ask questions or get students to write a few answers without consolidating and using the text to develop further skills. Doing intensive L2 questioning, gives a greater sense of mastery. Over a long period this helps develop control of the morphology, syntax and vocabulary of the language.

Defining words or phrases is an extension of question-answer work. Students, either orally or in writing, have to define in L2 the meaning of an L2 word or phrase.

Jigsaw reading

Students must put some sentences or short paragraphs into the right order. This is an easy task to prepare by cutting and pasting (physically or digitally) and allows them to develop their skill of seeing overall structure and coherence in a text. Not all texts are suitable for this activity, so look for those with a clear development from one point to the next with links from one paragraph to another. Online tools such as Textivate (*textivate.com*) allow students to do jigsaw reading electronically.

Parallel texts

Giving students two versions of the text, in L1 and L2, helps deal with the familiar problem that they want to read about interesting things appropriate to their maturity level but do not have the linguistic means to do so easily. This allows texts with a richer range of vocabulary and grammar to be used. Parallel texts mean that students can see the meaning straight away and you can then do other tasks using L2. An easy variation on this is simply to read aloud an L1 translation of the text as they are reading in L2. This may seem to go against the principle of working in L2, but if it provides a way into the text which will subsequently generate greater motivation and practice it is worth doing.

Asking for synonyms in the text

This can be done as an oral or written task and gets students to build up their vocabulary knowledge. It is a rather more sophisticated version of the vocabulary list completion task referred to above. Asking for antonyms also works but is more challenging.

Students devising L2 questions

To do this well students have to decipher meaning carefully. They can then use the questions with a partner for oral practice. If you give an answer, students can make up the question. They enjoy this and the task can allow for creativity and humour. It also allows them to practise the neglected skill of question formation.

Completing sentences

Once the text has been studied in some depth you can get students to complete orally or in writing sentences for which you give the beginning. This can allow for some creativity and amusement if you give them just a short phrase or even just a word.

True/false/not mentioned

Care is needed in designing tasks of this kind. The distinction between 'not mentioned' and 'false' is often a fine one! Students themselves can make up true/false questions which they then practise orally with a partner or ask the teacher. The latter is a fun and challenging task for high-attaining students. Giving false statements is a slight variation, but one which they enjoy - simply ask them to correct these orally or on paper. Wildly false ones can be amusing.

Multiple-choice questions (MCQ)

This is a good activity for allowing students to show a fine grasp of meaning. Multiple choice tasks should give at least three options and can take the form of a question with three answers or the start of a sentence with three different completions. Good multiple-choice questions are not easy to design; they may appear ambiguous or offer one answer which is far too obvious. Ideally, all the options should be plausible.

Gap-filling (cloze)

Words, phrases or whole sentences can be blanked out from the original text, or from a summary of the text, to revise meaning, structures or vocabulary items. This can be improvised at the end of a lesson or as the starter to a follow-up lesson. Students cover the text, while the teacher reads it to them leaving gaps at key moments which they have to fill. This has the merit of allowing you to choose the number of gaps according to the attainment level of the group. Students enjoy this sort of memory work and close listening is practised at the same time. Gap-filling can also be done as a pair work task.

Summarising from memory

After the text has been studied, get students to summarise the main points to the whole group or, perhaps better, to a partner. Remember that they enjoy such short-term memory tasks which recycle known language.

Metalinguistic tasks

Relevant examples of this activity would be underlining specific parts of speech or cognates, highlighting inflections or link words. These help reinforce grammatical skill and grasp of meaning. This sort of task may best be carried out prior to a genuinely communicative task. It is a good example of thinking or talking about the language rather than using it.

Writing tasks

Many texts are appropriate as a source for free writing tasks, such as imagining an interview with the writer, rewriting an account in a different time frame or writing a summary of a text. These make excellent homework opportunities for intermediate and advanced groups and, naturally, consolidate previously practised material.

Essay writing

This may be a task for advanced level classes who have been working on a topic, film or literary text. An essay is usually the end point, following a series of other scaffolded tasks. It would generally be considered poor practice to set an essay 'cold', i.e. without doing plenty of preparatory oral and written practice beforehand.

Translation

It is easy and useful to set sections of text for translation into L1. We might choose a section of text which is most important, or which contains language material we wish to focus on. Alternatively, we can do **retranslation** which involves making up an L1 text based on, and similar to, the original L2 model. Students use the original text to help them work out the meaning. With this type of exercise the focus may be on the manipulation of grammar, with students obtaining vocabulary from the L2 text.

Working with dialogues

If the text is in the form of a dialogue, it can be read aloud, memorised and adapted, e.g. using a colour-coding system whereby students alter items in colour, replacing them with alternatives which they make up or are drawn from a list. Dialogues lend themselves well to pair and group practice but can sometimes be awkward to exploit in other ways.

One simple way to exploit a dialogue is to underline phrases or words which could be replaced, then supply some alternatives on a separate sheet. Students can adapt the original dialogue using these alternatives or their own.

Concluding remarks

The 'reading lesson' is much more than reading a text and answering questions about it. As we said with regard to listening, we can view reading not just as a source of comprehension, but also as a source of modelled language. Just as we talked of Listening-as-Modelling, we can talk of 'Reading-as-Modelling'. This involves the intensive use of a range of activities which recycle the language.

It is impossible to divorce reading from the other skills of listening, speaking, and writing. To decode a written text you need not only to know vocabulary and grammar, but to be able to decode written language phonologically (phonics). These elements can be practised by the full range of activities we have described in the chapter.

9

Writing

Introduction

You may think that writing is both the least useful and hardest skill. Nevertheless, there are good reasons to focus on writing in the classroom, not least because forms a major component of many school examinations. Writing also acts as a support to the other skills of listening, speaking and reading. Although writing may have the least practical application in later life for the many students who only study a language for a short time, the increasing use of social media provides ample opportunity to demonstrate the important role of writing, so authentic activities can be developed with relative ease.

Writing is not necessarily the most difficult skill to practise since, unlike with speaking, students usually have time to reflect, carefully monitor and review their work. Some prefer writing to speaking for this reason. Others genuinely struggle, however, notably if they have poor L1 writing skills. In addition, in the minds of students (and some school administrators!), writing is equated with 'work' while speaking is sometimes considered more trivial. School inspectors and lesson observers may also expect to see evidence of learning through writing. In this chapter we shall consider:

Research evidence
- ✓ The role of writing
- ✓ The writing process
- ✓ Does instruction help?
- ✓ Error correction
- ✓ Planning and task repetition

Classroom practice
- ✓ Types of L2 writing
- ✓ Interactional writing
- ✓ Writing complex sentences
- ✓ Planning a writing programme
- ✓ Assessing writing
- ✓ Translation

Research evidence

The role of writing

Unlike listening and speaking, which are sometimes described as **biologically primary** skills (i.e. in most circumstances all humans naturally learn to listen and speak), reading and writing are

biologically secondary (Geary, 2008). They are not natural and require specific instruction.

Some scholars take the view that writing, along with speaking, is far less important than listening and reading in the language classroom. They believe that acquisition occurs almost entirely in a natural fashion by students receiving comprehensible input (e.g. Krashen, 1982). In their opinion, the aim of the teacher should be to provide listening and reading input at the right level; nature will then take its course and students will speak (and write) when they are ready. Writing is therefore relegated to a secondary status.

Merrill Swain (1993), on the other hand, noticing, as many teachers do, the disappointing quantity and quality of many students' writing, argues that writing really helps them acquire the language because they notice the gaps and problems in their knowledge. She claims that students need to do written tasks to produce what she calls **pushed output**. This means experimenting with new grammatical structures and vocabulary they may not yet have mastered. In doing so they may notice what they cannot yet do and ask for help or look up information to help themselves.

The writing process

How do students actually compose sentences and texts? There is some debate as to whether they apply exactly the same processes in L2 as they do in L1, but the processes are very similar. As students learn to write in L2 they gradually improve their ability to plan, revise and edit text, search for appropriate words and phrases (heavily influenced by their L1) and attend to the grammatical accuracy of what they write. These mental processes are hard to describe, so researchers explore them by getting students to 'think aloud' as they are writing, or describe what they did afterwards, for example. The responses demonstrate that students must retrieve from long term memory words and rules they know, supplement these with newly acquired language they have looked up and monitor their performance using working memory.

An influential model of the mental processes involved in writing comes from Kellogg (1996). He describes three main processes as follows: formulation, execution and monitoring.

1. **Formulation**: this entails the lower-order processes of lexical retrieval and syntactic encoding which translate the plan into language form, and higher-order processes such as planning content, retrieving ideas from the input and/or from long-term memory, and organising ideas into a coherent plan.
2. **Execution**: the writer uses motor movements to hand-write or type text.
3. **Monitoring**: the writer ensures that the written text matches their intended plan and, if needed, changes are made.

For novices, the challenge is mainly about developing the lower-order skills – knowing words and phrases and, when needed, the grammar to put them together. For some students, execution is a challenge if hand-writing skills are poorly developed. Monitoring may involve both lower-order and higher-order processes.

Does instruction help?

Most scholars seem to agree that specific teaching in writing technique has an effect and that the knowledge required to write is learnable and the skills trainable. In the L2 learning context, while students' ability to write clearly and accurately depends to an extent on their general level of proficiency, certain aspects are either specific to students' writing or may be specifically seen to develop through writing. Research (and experience) shows that targeted instruction can affect:

1. students' written accuracy;
2. their range of structures and vocabulary;
3. overall quality of writing (by explicit teaching of grammar);
4. ability to reflect on and monitor their own written work;
5. essay writing technique, producing more effective and appropriate work;
6. understanding of the cultural and contextual appropriateness of particular structures and vocabulary.

Error correction

Although written corrective feedback is a widely used in classrooms, its status among researchers is controversial, with views ranging from strong support to total rejection. Ferris (1999) claims that there was mounting research evidence that effective error correction (selective, prioritised, and clear) can help at least some students. By contrast, Truscott (1996) argues that research evidence shows grammar correction to be ineffective. However, a recent meta-study (Brown, Liu and Nourouzian, 2023) found that all forms of written corrective feedback had a long-term effect on students' accuracy. They found "robust evidence of the durability of moderate effectiveness of WCF over time" (from the abstract).

So how much correction should there be and what form should it take? Here are various ways to carry out written corrections.

1. Direct error correction
This is where the teacher writes in a corrected version of an incorrect form. This has the merit of clearly signalling to students what the correct version should be. On the other hand, it does not require them to think through the source of the error themselves. In theory, thinking harder (deep processing) should lead to better long-term memory.

2. Indirect error correction
In this case errors are underlined, circled or given codes such as V for verb, T for tense and left for the students to self-correct. The rationale for this is clear: students are cognitively involved in the correction process, think about it more deeply and are more likely to look out for the error in

future. They are not just the passive recipients of correction, but actually doing something about it. By working on mistakes they will become more aware of problems and, in the long term, hopefully stop making them. Yet indirect error correction (IEC) may be less useful than we imagine. Why?

- Errors may be due to lack of declarative knowledge, i.e. not knowing the rule governing the language item. So, for instance, if the student wrote *Ayer voy al cine* (intended meaning: *yesterday I went to the cinema*) because they did not know the preterite in Spanish, they used the present *voy* because they had not mastered (declaratively) the preterite tense.

- Errors may be due to the failure of the student's working memory to cope with the demands of the task: the preterite tense is known, but because their working memory was busy trying to sort out vocabulary choice, word order, agreement as well planning the content, they chose the wrong tense. If asked in isolation to put *I went* into Spanish, there may not have been a problem.

If the teacher highlights the mistake in the first scenario (i.e. the student does not know the rule), the student will not be able to correct it, unless prompted to find out about the preterite by the teacher. In the second scenario, the student might be able to self-correct. So unless the teacher goes through the essay thoroughly with them, they will never find out the real reason for the mistake, possibly leading to underlining one they will never be able to correct. The more advanced and unpredictable the language being employed, the more likely this is to occur.

Another point concerns what we might call the 'surrender value' of IEC. If students have the knowledge to correct the errors pointed out, they are not really learning anything new. While they may learn not to make the error again or that to pay more attention in future, the chances are they will not. Self-correcting when you are cued to see a mistake is totally different from self-correcting while you are proof-reading without being told where to look for the mistake. This is especially true for beginners whose working memory, when proof-reading, is loaded with so much linguistic baggage to attend to that they will not be able to spot every single mistake made.

To make things worse, studies have found that IEC can have a negative impact on motivation in that it causes anxiety and frustration. Imagine being a weak student and being given your essay back with lots of errors to self-correct but with no idea how to correct them.

Another issue relates to the presence of an error the students can self-correct NOT because they know or understand the rule or the context that caused the mistake, but because the change is obvious. For example: *la chien* (in French 'dog' is a masculine word); if the *la* for gender is underlined there is no alternative but to change *la* (feminine) to *le* (masculine), no internalised mastery is brought to bear. Nor can we assume that by self-correcting the student will not make this mistake again. In the absence of follow-up (recycling of that information) and depth of processing, this information is likely to be lost after a few hours. Experienced teachers notice that students frequently make the same mistakes over and over despite correction. (This may be because they are not developmentally ready to acquire certain structures – see Chapter 6.)

3. *Focused error correction*

This is the term used in research to describe the correction of only a certain set of errors in students' work. You might, for example, decide to just correct errors to do with a verb tense or agreements. Some recent studies have suggested that selectively correcting, especially when errors are directly corrected, leads to improved writing (see Potter, Marsden and Hawkes, 2023).

If all this suggests that marking corrections, directly or indirectly, is of questionable value, it may be possible to suggest a further step. For weaker students some selective marking could be done while we make a written or mental note of the type of errors being commonly made. This is then used as the basis for further practice in the classroom so that they are exposed to more examples of the correct language forms. In addition, you may be able to use feedback to help students set their own targets for improvement. If you do this, providing specific, achievable targets is preferable to general ones. For example, better to write or say: "next time I would like you to look up every verb in the verb tables if you are unsure" rather than "pay attention to detail".

Another idea to consider involves giving students some autonomy in triggering the correction process. For example, when writing they may insert questions in the margin in coming across areas they are uncertain about. This may work particularly well for higher-achieving students, providing them with some agency and developing a dialogue with the teacher. Gianfranco has coined an acronym for this process: LIFT (Learner-Initiated Feedback Technique).

Despite the provisos given, it is worth stressing that most students will have an expectation that you have read their work carefully and that error correction signals you have done so and that you care. So here are two takeaways: first, we need to recall that error correction is not just about cognitive processes, but also involves a social and personal relationship between a teacher and a student; second, remember it is very easy to overestimate the value of written correction!

Ellis and Shintani (2013), in their thorough review of the evidence for both oral and written corrective feedback, make the following recommendations (adapted):

- Research shows that corrective feedback can help students focus on accurate form and the cognitive advantages may outweigh any affective drawbacks. (Note: this is clearly a delicate area, where the needs of each student need to be kept in mind. It is likely that younger learners will be more disheartened by error correction).

- The effectiveness of correction depends on students' readiness to acquire the language feature, so sometimes correction will be a waste of time.

- Correction needs to be noticed by students. There is no point in hiding its intent.

- The weight of evidence suggests that direct correction (showing the correct version) is more useful than indirect correction (just highlighting where there is an error).

Planning and task repetition

One useful finding from research is that if we give students a chance to plan their writing, they will produce more accurate and complex work. It may seem obvious, but when students are under time pressure, the quality of writing deteriorates. Planning includes thinking of what to write, structuring the content, setting writing goals, or preparing linguistic aspects (Potter, Marsden and Hawkes, 2023). Ellis and Yuan (2004) found that the quality of planning makes a difference to written production. Uludag, McDonough, and Payant (2021) suggested that the quality of the planning is affected by a student's proficiency. This suggests that writing templates and instructions should match their proficiency and current level. Lower-attaining students need more precise guidance at the planning stage, e.g. through more detailed instructions or bullet point prompts. Potter, Marsden and Hawkes (2023) state that it is reasonable to expect many students, especially the less proficient, to want to start their planning in L1. This then requires strategies to allow them to work from L1 into L2, considering what they can realistically express in L2, based on the "use what you know" principle.

Research in recent years has tried to discover if repeating tasks (written and oral) improves the accuracy, fluency and complexity of the task (Bygate, 2018). The evidence so far suggests that receiving corrective feedback, then repeating written tasks, may be more effective for learners with more efficient working memory and higher language aptitude (e.g. Lu and Li, 2023).

Classroom practice

Types of L2 writing

L2 writing can take many forms. Students can carry out a range of tasks.

- **Copying** single words, phrases or sentences.
- Creating **vocabulary lists**.
- **Translating**.
- **Paraphrasing** and **summarising**.
- Writing **sentences, paragraphs and essays**.
- Answering **comprehension questions**.
- Doing written grammatical **drills**.
- Completing **unfinished sentences**.
- Doing **cloze tasks** (gap-fills).
- **Taking notes** from a spoken or written text.
- Doing **online interactive writing** activities.

- **Writing out presentations** to be delivered orally.
- Writing **blog posts** or **social media posts**.
- **Communicating via social media in real time** or via forums.

In the school context, unlike in other areas of life, most writing is done by hand. Increasingly, however, particularly at higher levels, students draft their writing digitally. This raises questions regarding the use of spelling and grammar checkers, online translators and AI tools, the relative accuracy of handwriting and typing and the fact that examinations are nearly always done with pen and paper. In our experience students tend to make more errors when typing, as opposed to writing by hand, although research on this is hard to find. (There are studies which show that handwriting is better for memory recall, perhaps because of the added motor skills required which somehow deepen the processing.) It is important that, as students approach examinations, they predominantly write by hand to avoid dependence on technology, to maintain clear presentation and learn to plan carefully in advance (since you cannot reorder paragraphs easily by hand as you can with word processing).

From the very early stage of L2 learning students can be encouraged to use the written language in a creative fashion, usually with the aid of scaffolded support. Free writing is best done later in a teaching sequence as a task to reinforce listening, speaking and reading, once controlled writing tasks have been practised. If students are given writing tasks 'cold' they are likely to find them hard, making many mistakes and maybe ending up resorting to online translation.

If there is limited classroom contact time it is possible to assign most written work for home to assess how much language students can master. If there are long lessons to fill, however, consider including time for quiet reading and writing. This allows students to reflect at their own pace, under less time pressure than for oral and listening work. It is a myth, by the way, that lower-attaining students always dislike writing. They will often feel more secure putting pen to paper than having to respond quickly to aural stimuli.

Interactional writing

There is one 'real-life' writing task that most of our students use - communicating via social media or other forms of instant messaging. If we are to prepare them for communication in the real world, we ought to take this into account.

This is one context where we commonly use writing, whether it be (in 2023) via blogs, forums, YouTube, WhatsApp, Instagram, Facebook or Twitter. On these platforms we need to quickly understand written input and respond in writing, promptly and fluently, not necessarily with grammatical accuracy and complexity.

For this we need a sizeable repertoire of high-frequency words, a wide range of discourse functions, the basic tenses and communication strategies (e.g. ways to compensate for lack of vocabulary). Finally, in chatting with an L2 native speaker an effective interactional writer must be able to grasp cultural features in their input, including the jargon and abbreviations used in L2 instant-messaging communication.

Teaching interactional writing skills has the added benefit of preparing students for oral communication as it requires them to process language in real time, almost as quickly as when speaking. It follows that most of the traditional activities we use to foster communicative competence, through both the oral and written medium, apply to the teaching of interactional writing (e.g. information gap tasks and role-plays). In fact the oral practice that takes place in the classroom helps students write interactively.

Writing complex sentences

One aspect of writing proficiency which needs attention with students who have reached a certain level is linguistic variety (both in terms of vocabulary and grammatical structures), clarity, conciseness and, most importantly, the ability to produce complex sentences). Below are some activities which help develop these skills.

1. **Signalled sentence combining**. Give two sentences and instructions on constructing the more complex sentence. E.g. (for low intermediate French):
   J'ai une soeur. [I have a sister]
   Elle s'appelle Marie. [Her name is Marie]   Use 'qui' [who]
   The result would be:
   J'ai une sœur qui s'appelle Marie [I have a sister who is called Marie]
   Signalled combining is useful for drilling a particular grammatical structure or connectives in a controlled linguistic environment.

2. **Open sentence combining.** In this approach, students are not cued. For example, the chunks below:
   J'ai une sœur [I have a sister]
   Ma sœur s'appelle Marie [My sister is called Marie]
   Elle est sympa, aimable et serviable [She is friendly, pleasant and helpful]
   Je me dispute avec elle de temps en temps [I argue with her from time to time]
   Elle est trop bavarde [she is too talkative]
   could be combined as:
   Ma sœur, qui s'appelle Marie, est très sympa, aimable et serviable, mais de temps en temps je me dispute avec elle car elle est trop bavarde [my sister, who is called Marie, is very friendly, pleasant and helpful but from time to time I argue with her because she is too talkative].

3. **The cumulative sentence.** A cumulative sentence contains a main clause and several modifying clauses. Here is an example:

Elle est venue chez nous [she came to our house]

Elle est venue hier soir [she came yesterday]

Elle était habillée en noir [she was dressed in black]

Elle était accompagnée par son frère [she was accompanied by her brother]

Son frère avait l'air triste [her brother looked sad]

These could be combined as:

Elle est venue chez nous hier soir, habillée en noir, accompagnée par son frère qui avait l'air triste [she came to our home yesterday, dressed in black, accompanied by her brother who looked sad]

Cumulative sentences encourage students to vary their output, add metaphoric descriptions, rephrase confusing sentences and eliminate redundant elements.

4. **Whole discourse exercises.** These are more challenging, but also more useful if we are trying to forge effective essay writers, since they do not confine syntactic transformation and manipulation to stand-alone sentences. Whole discourse exercises build on the previous techniques by presenting students with various sets of sentence chunks (about five or six). The task is to create a sentence out of each set and then group the resulting sentences cohesively into a meaningful and logically arranged paragraph.

5. **Decombining**. This means taking a complex sentence and breaking it down into small chunks (the opposite of the previous activities). It is a great learning activity, as by deconstructing texts students become more aware of the writing process, especially when they are required to analyse the choices made by the author.

6. **Paraphrasing.** This is an important skill which develops vocabulary (by forcing them to use synonyms), their grammar (by often having to alter the sentence structure, e.g. from active to passive voice) and use of metaphors, imagery, analogy and other rhetorical devices in more adventurous or advanced students. One very fruitful activity we can do with advanced students is to ask them to paraphrase sentences which sound ambiguous or even obscure, in an attempt to enhance their clarity (the sentence can be given in the L2 with the intended meaning next to it that the author failed to express effectively).

7. **Summarising and shrinking**. High intermediate students often have difficulty writing concisely. Summarising is a very effective way to get them to be concise, especially if they are given a word limit and are not allowed to repeat more than a very limited number of the words included in the original text. Shrinking pushes the summarising challenge a notch further by requiring students to concentrate the meaning of a paragraph into a single sentence.

A word or even character limit can be imposed, here, too. Students can be shown examples from Twitter on how to do this.

Gianfranco's 'writership' activities

- **Answering questions**: as a starter or plenary write a question in L2 on the board. Students have two minutes to write an answer including three details. To differentiate, two questions may be asked, the second being an extension for more fluent students. Intelligibility is the focus not accuracy.

- **Picture tasks**: like the previous task, except the **stimulus** students respond to is **visual**. The rationale is that (a) in social media students must often respond to a visual stimulus such as commenting on a funny photo; (b) it taps into their creativity and (c) it may elicit language beyond the boundaries of the topic being worked on.

- **'What is the question?'**: give students a very short L2 dialogue with questions omitted. They provide the missing questions. This recognises the likelihood of the L2 learner's frequent need to ask questions in transactional situations and practises formulating these.

- Very short **translations with a time limit**: students need to translate what is written on the board using mini-whiteboards or paper. Again, the focus is on intelligibility and fluency rather than on total accuracy.

- **Social media 'slow chat'**: students need mobile devices for this. Using a 'virtual learning environment' (VLE), we can ask them to chat with each other about a given topic. Give out red cards to the chat initiators and blue cards to the responders. The initiators are in charge of asking questions to any of the responders. Every ten minutes the students switch cards. They are given a time limit to answer, which varies from class to class. A similar exercise can be done by passing back and forth a piece of paper, which is immediate, amusing and requires no technology.

- **Agree or disagree**: a simple statement appears on the screen (e.g. *tennis is enjoyable; I like it when it rains; the food in the canteen is great*) and the students must write a response to a time limit.

- **Fluency assessment**: at key stages in the unfolding of a unit of work we can use the first activity above on questions, but ask students a much broader question and give them more time to answer it on paper or on a device. At the end of the allocated time, ask them to stop and write down how many words they wrote. The time-to-word ratio will give an indication of the class's writing fluency.

Planning a writing programme

To gradually develop in students the ability to write at some length quite accurately, with a reasonable range of vocabulary and structures, a sequence of tasks needs to be planned for within each unit. But also a long-term vision is needed of how to get from starting point to destination.

Long-term planning

1. In the initial stages, students can copy-write single words, phrases and short sentences. This can be accompanied by phonics practice as we begin to establish the sound-writing relationships which help them remember words, pronounce and write accurately.

2. The next step might be to move on to scaffolded copying, i.e. completing sentences, filling in missing letters, words or phrases. This, once again, helps develop not just writing, but the other skills of pronouncing well and learning new words. In these early stages you are unlikely to mention grammar very much, if at all. Students may begin to pick up patterns on their own but are more likely to be focused on meaning. Teachers usually limit any verb forms to present tense used with first and third person subjects.

3. Subsequently, students can move on to writing their own sentences or short paragraphs, probably using models or templates to guide them. While doing whole class oral work, you can make partial notes on the board for students to use as a scaffold for their own sentences. Better classes should soon be able to move on to answering questions in L2, making up false statements, writing simple dialogues or changing words in sentences or paragraphs to their own versions.

4. By the end of the first year of learning most students will ideally be capable of writing short paragraphs or dialogues independently (more or less accurately) either with dictionary help or having done some learning by heart to help the process. Work will largely or wholly be in the present tense, using simple sentences without subordinate clauses. Writing mats or sentence builders are a useful aid at any stage.

5. As students increase their skill level, paragraph writing can take a greater role for class or homework. Over a long period, this helps develop their independent use of the language not only on paper, but orally too. By the end of the second year of learning, many students will be able to write short compositions based on a mixture of pre-learned material or with the help of appropriate scaffolds. By now, they may be working in two, or even three, time frames and using complex sentences with linking words and subordinate clauses.

6. And so the process goes on such that after a few years, if all goes well, most of the class will be able to write chunks of at least 120 words with at least some accuracy and with reasonable complexity, within a limited repertoire of topics. We have to be realistic; because of the time constraints imposed by most schools and curricula, only a minority of students will achieve significant competence at writing without formal teacher-led support.

7. For those students who move on to a more advanced level there will still be value in doing controlled practice based on specific grammatical structures, but the bulk of writing is likely to be in the form of answering comprehension questions, writing summaries or paraphrases, translating and, at the most demanding end, writing longer form discursive essays on contemporary topics, film and literature. After seven years of study the best linguists are able to produce sophisticated connected writing.

By the way, to give students a feeling of success throughout the early stages of learning, tasks must be scaffolded tightly enough so that errors are kept to a minimum. In this way, from the motivational point of view, writing becomes a rewarding, not a threatening experience. Self-efficacy is developed (see Chapter 16). That said, some will always find the mechanics of writing in the early stages hard. With the importance of literacy in schools, at the very least the languages department can help to support the strategies in place for learning L1, particularly when there may be many students who have English as an additional language (EAL).

How much dictionary use is advisable? With beginners, online dictionaries such as *wordreference.com* are too advanced, so a small paper dictionary, sometimes called a 'learners' dictionary', is still advisable. This will also back up the efforts of the L1 language department and reinforce L1 spelling. Specific dictionary tasks can be set to help students use the dictionary sensibly. Using a dictionary presents a good opportunity to remind them about parts of speech and grammatical terminology.

Short-term planning

1. The most common practice is to approach a unit via listening, reading and speaking before you move to any form of free writing. This means that writing can be based on recently acquired prior knowledge. Initial tasks are likely to be more controlled, such as oral drills, gap-fill, correcting false statements and answering questions.

2. With novices and intermediate students, as progress is made through a unit, more challenging and creative tasks such as sentence invention and short paragraph writing may be done by some classes. The degree of support given will depend on the class. There is some merit in giving them some freedom of expression, but if the result is highly inaccurate it may end up being frustrating and demotivating for all. With too much freedom, weaker students translate

literally from L1 which results in very inaccurate work. No teacher wants to spend hours writing corrections on writing tasks which were ill-conceived to start with.

3. Translation into L2 of full sentences and paragraphs is a high-order task best done late in a teaching sequence. At lower levels, when doing free writing, students inevitably think of what they want to say, retrieve an L1 word from memory, translate into an L2 word from memory and write it down. If they do not have the L2 word in memory, they look it up or make a guess. Giving sentences to translate provides them with ready-made content and should give practice in retrieving or looking up L2 words. The downside is that students are reading L1 sentences, not L2, so they are receiving less input. This kind of pedagogical choice has to be weighed up. In general at an earlier stage of learning it is better only to require relatively small transformations to be made from forms of the language students have already encountered.

Assessing writing

At the end of a unit of work we need to know how well our students have mastered writing about the topic covered. Question types include filling gaps with individual words, answering questions, writing short paragraphs or longer compositions, often with prompts to help them put an essay together.

Students' answers can sometimes be marked objectively where points are awarded for right answers. For free writing (composition) a simple level-based mark scheme (rubric) can be devised which rewards content (relevance), range of language and accuracy. Normally only a proportion of marks would be allocated for accuracy. Communicating a message unambiguously is the priority. Minor errors are usually classified as any which do not alter the intended message. These include errors of gender, adjective agreement and spelling. Major errors are those which distort or destroy meaning, including the wrong choice of words, omissions and verb tense errors.

Mark schemes need to be looked at carefully. The best ones make it easy to match student work to specific marks and grades. Some 'level based' ones can be vague and difficult to use. Research shows that teachers use these inconsistently. This should be kept in mind when designing our own or looking at those supplied by examining bodies.

The ACTFL (American Council on the Teaching of Foreign Languages) produced some detailed descriptors of writing performance at different levels. Their 'Intermediate Mid' descriptor reads as follows (from their website in 2023):

> *Writers at the Intermediate Mid sublevel are able to meet a number of practical writing needs. They can write short, simple communications, compositions, and requests for information in loosely connected texts about personal preferences, daily routines, common events, and other personal topics. Their writing is framed in present time but may contain references to other time frames. The writing style closely resembles oral discourse. Writers at the Intermediate Mid sublevel show evidence of control of basic sentence structure and verb forms. This*

writing is best defined as a collection of discrete sentences and/or questions loosely strung together. There is little evidence of deliberate organization. Intermediate Mid writers can be understood readily by natives used to the writing of non-natives. When Intermediate Mid writers attempt Advanced-level writing tasks, the quality and/or quantity of their writing declines and the message may be unclear.

This type of statement is quite useful at a general, summative level, and may help in establishing general expectations. Similar statements can be found in the CEFRL (CoE, 2001). However, this type of statement does not allow you to mark or grade a piece of writing in detail. As an example of a mark scheme designed for producing a specific grade for intermediate (GCSE) students of French, German and Spanish, have a look at this, from England's AQA awarding body (in 2023). It is how the category 'Range of language' in a written composition is assessed at the Higher Tier.

10–12 Very good variety of appropriate vocabulary and structures. More complex sentences are handled with confidence, producing a fluent piece of coherent writing. The style and register are appropriate.

7–9 Good variety of appropriate vocabulary and structures. More complex sentences are regularly attempted and are mostly successful, producing a mainly fluent piece of coherent writing with occasional lapses. The style and register are appropriate.

4–6 Some variety of appropriate vocabulary and structures. Longer sentences are attempted, using appropriate linking words, often successfully. The style and register may not always be appropriate.

1–3 Little variety of appropriate vocabulary. Structures likely to be short and simple. Little or no awareness of style and register.

0 The range of language produced does not meet the standard required for Level 1 at this tier.

Mark schemes (known in the USA as **rubrics**) like the above which are 'level based' are not without problems. To mention just one example, the difference between a 'very good' and 'good' answer may be hard to pin down. Experience shows that assessors apply such mark schemes inconsistently, sometimes to the consternation of teachers. Research clearly demonstrates that where a mark scheme is not totally objective (e.g. true-false or multiple choice) examiners produce varying scores. So could non-objective, level-based mark schemes be made more specific, with less room for manoeuvre? Yes, but this in turn may lead to students producing responses even more closely tied to and constrained by the mark scheme. Producing mark schemes is not an easy business!

In an assessment situation, with no dictionary support, many students struggle a good deal with writing. If the assessment style reflects tasks done in class beforehand, they will perform better. Using an unfamiliar question type adds to the cognitive load of a task and will cause students to underperform. An ideal written assessment resembles exercises they have done during the unit of work or whole course (recall the washback and TAP effects!). It is always worth checking the quality of any published assessments, preferably piloting them yourself. Once again, you are seeking to create a situation where students can succeed and feel good about their progress.

Part of the assessment should be hard enough to let your best students excel and achieve full marks. An ideal mark range for a written assessment might be between 50% and 100%. If a student gets a very low mark, you may want to give them a second chance to do better after more revision. If assessment can become a positive experience, a mere extension of their normal work, they will value its importance without fearing it excessively.

Steve's zero preparation writing activities

- With intermediate groups lead a **question-answer sequence** on a topic, e.g. 'Describe where you live' or 'My school'. As students give answers, write up partial answers on the board. Students copy these, filling any gaps as appropriate. If they do not have time to fill all the gaps they complete the sentences at home. They end up with a reasonably or wholly accurate piece of writing which they can use later for oral practice or exam revision. This makes for a multi-skill lesson with all students actively engaged.

- With all levels, when a text has been worked on orally, we can **improvise questions** to which students have to give **written answers**. Offer a little support by starting answers for them when needed.

- With intermediate students and above, make up **L1 sentences** which the class **translates**. These could be delivered orally or written on the board, with partial answers if needed.

- For intermediate students give them a title to write about, without a dictionary. Give a time limit and reward those who **write the most in the time limit** (say, 20 minutes). Titles might include *Last weekend*, *My summer holiday* or *My favourite foods*. If a recent topic is chosen, students should have material to write about.

- Do classic **dictation** based on the current topic. Make sure it is not too difficult and that it comes towards the end of a sequence of lessons. Assess the dictation by counting mistakes or by taking the number of errors from a total, for example 50. Dictation is much easier in German or Spanish than French. In France dictation is frequently practised by young native speakers.

Translation

Whether translation is a useful learning tool is still controversial. Why? Mainly because not much research has been carried out on the extent of its impact on L2 learning. Its use became widespread in language teaching not for any theoretical reason, but because that is the way Latin and Greek had been taught. Moreover, at least until recently, translation has been out of favour with a large part of the teacher community for the following reasons.

- It is associated with the much-criticised grammar-translation approach.
- It is assumed that L1 use in the classroom hampers L2 acquisition.
- Translation is seen by many as a mechanical transfer of meaning from one language to another and not a communicative activity.
- Translation tasks are perceived as boring.
- Translation is seen as independent of the other four skills.
- It takes up lots of valuable time that could be devoted to more beneficial communicative activities.
- Translation is believed to be appropriate only for training translators.

However, attitudes towards translation have been gradually shifting in recent years. As Duff (1994) points out, translation is a real-life task that happens everywhere around the world in a wide range of contexts. In the L2 classroom, students translate for their classmates on a daily basis items they do not understand. When visiting another country, L2 speakers translate for non-L2 speakers signs, notices, announcements, etc. When socialising with people who have different L1s, interpreting is a common occurrence too. In addition when using the internet, our students often draw upon translation in their interaction with social media or other knowledge sources, whether using dictionaries or digital tools. Kern (1994) found most teachers agree that mental translation into one's L1 is inevitable when reading.

Increasingly, studies suggest a helpful role for translation or L1 transfer in students' language learning. In Horwitz's (1988) study the majority of German (70%) and Spanish (75%) students believed that learning a second language is largely a matter of learning to translate from English into their L1. Prince (1996) noted that students often believe learning through translation, with the new word being linked to its native-language equivalent, is more effective than learning vocabulary in context.

Hsieh (2000) reported that translation benefited Taiwanese students' L2 reading strategies and vocabulary acquisition, while enhancing cultural knowledge: 85% of his students reported that translating helped them pay attention to the coherence and contextualisation of an English reading text. Karimah (2020), in a study of undergraduates learning English, found translation was felt to be beneficial for learning. This supported an earlier study by Dagliene (2012).

Gianfranco's lesson sequence using translation

Step 1 – Planning

1. Translation into L2 is often best done as the final part of a teaching sequence. Firstly, prepare the translation to be done at the end of the sequence.
2. Then prepare four or five texts very similar in length and linguistic content to the translation task (narrow reading), with a series of activities based on these. Ensure the tasks include finding the L2 equivalent of L1 words.
3. If time allows, prepare three or four more shorter texts with the same features for narrow listening comprehension. Slightly modify the texts you produced for the reading comprehension by changing a few details.
4. Identify the words and structures you expect the students will have problems with and prepare a set of L1 and L2 sentences which feature them. It is important to make sure the sentences are as similar as possible in syntax to the kind of sentences found in the translation task. Cut in half or gap the sentences in L2 by removing the key items you want them to focus on.

Step 2 – Word level teaching

This can be 'flipped', i.e. prepared at home. Prepare a series of activities which drill most of the key unfamiliar lexical items and the grammatical structures included in the translation task. If possible, use apps such as Quizlet or Memrise for this. At the very least students can be given a list of words to memorise.

Step 3 – Modelling of L2 items through narrow reading

The modelling of L2 items occurs through narrow reading first as it is easier. Dictionaries are allowed. Narrow reading allows for recycling of key lexical and grammatical items.

Step 4 – Noticing key items through listening with gap-fill

Use the gapped/cut-in-half sentences in the L2 that were prepared in Step 1. Say the sentences at moderate speed (the purpose is modelling, so speak clearly) to draw the students' attention to the unfamiliar words or phrases you removed when you gapped them.

Step 5 – Reinforcing modelling through narrow listening

This is the same as Step 3 except that it is done by listening, not reading.

Step 6 (Optional) – Paying selective attention to the key L2 grammatical items through grammar judgement quizzes

This means holding a 'sentence sale' where students are presented with several sentences, some correct some not, containing the key items included in the target translation task. Give each sentence a price. Working in groups with an 'allocation' of $1000, the students must decide whether to buy the sentence the teacher wants to 'sell'. If they choose to buy a correct sentence, they 'win' its value and they also win the appropriate amount if they refuse to buy an incorrect sentence. Conversely, if they buy a wrong sentence or refuse to buy a correct one, they 'lose' that amount. For example, the sentence *je suis treize ans'* (I am 13 years old) is incorrect. Say the sentence is worth $100, those groups who refuse to buy receive $100; those who decide to buy lose $100. The teacher then asks who wants to correct it. Groups who volunteer and amend the sentence correctly get an extra $100. At the end of the game, the group with the highest amount of money wins. The aim is to focus students on the kind of grammatical mistakes they frequently make.

Step 7 – Sentence level translation

This can be done as a whole-class activity or in groups, turning it into a competition. Students translate the L1 sentences prepared in Step 1 to a time limit. The student(s) making the fewest mistakes in each round win(s).

Step 8 – Translation task

Break up the text into sentences and utter one sentence at a time. Using paper or mini-whiteboards, students translate them into L2. Dictionaries are allowed and this can be done to a time limit.

Steve's tips for translating into L2

- Do it very traditionally as a **teacher-led activity** to model chosen translation strategies (i.e. 'thinking aloud'). Students will hear higher quality input than might be the case in a group. Make sure they are all kept busy by writing down agreed answers. Use cold-calling and vigilance where necessary to keep them all engaged.

- **'Running translation'** - like 'running dictation' (see Chapter 2) but the fetcher brings back some L2 for the scribe to translate (with the fetcher's help). Make it a race.

- **'Pick the best translation.'** Provide pieces of L2 with, say, three alternative translations, only one of which is just right. You can make this as subtle as you wish, depending on the class. Students can work individually or in pairs.

- **Gapped aural translation**. Give students a gapped piece of L1 writing. Gaps must be designed to make guessing hard. Then read them the equivalent text in L2. Students fill the gaps using L1. You could make these quite funny and implausible.

- **Matching tasks**: L2 on one side, L1 on the other. Students link up the right pairs. The sentences could be similar but with subtle variations of tense, mood or formality to enhance understanding of these issues.

- **Parallel texts** to provide models. These can be done alongside other comprehension tasks.

- Use **questions in L1** to deliberately elicit translations from the text.

- Use ***textivate.com*** to do scaffolded translation exercises.

Steve's tips for translating into L1

- Explain the rationale for doing translation. Explain it is mainly about building comprehension and reading for detail. Warn students, of course, that a word-for-word approach only works sometimes and it is a chance for them to show off how well they can use L1.

- Allow them to use Google Translate, Deepl or an AI tool to see how well it does and to make corrections where they see fit. They will learn something from the process and, let us face it, if they get the chance, many will do so anyway. Alternatively, avoid setting translation for homework.

- Students work in groups with each group doing a different section of a text. Add a competitive element with a time limit or race. As an alternative, they can work in groups or pairs on the same language, then compare versions.

- Get students to use *wordreference.com*. Give them specific words or phrases to research.

- Give advanced level students phrases or whole sentences to research using *linguee.com*.

- Provide gap-fill partial translations, especially for weaker groups.

- 'Find the translation' - give students a list of quite hard sentences or short paragraphs. Post translations around the classroom (or hide them) for them to find individually or in teams. Make it a race.

- 'Translation dictation.' Students play the role of a written interpreter. The teacher speaks in L2 and they write down their L1 translation to a time limit. The teacher may have to repeat utterances more than once. This has the benefit of also providing L2 listening input.

- Use questions in L1 to deliberately elicit translations from the text.

- Give 'real-life' tasks e.g. a menu to translate, cooking recipes or an advertising leaflet.

Concluding remarks

Most students feel that learning a language is primarily about taking part in conversations which require effective listening and speaking skills. Reading may be perceived as the next most important, informing as it does listening and speaking in contact situations (names of products displayed on signs, etc.). Yet writing is used frequently in social contact situations and supports the other skills in lessons. It also provides us with tangible evidence of progress.

Using the techniques suggested in this chapter, students will make considerable progress, to the point that, by the end of five years (or however long the course is), they will feel able to express themselves, with varying accuracy, using a combination of the skills they have developed helped by online tools.

10

Teaching with pictures

Introduction

Some of us remember, as students of languages, experiencing a diet of projected slides, flashcards of cats sitting on tables and sequences of robotic characters enacting a boring daily routine; if you are younger, you may have experienced a similar diet but via PowerPoint. Is there value in using visual images? Is translation just as good?

This chapter considers the areas below.

Research evidence
- ✓ Working memory and dual coding
- ✓ Do images aid retention?
- ✓ Possible limitations of pictures

Classroom practice
- ✓ Choosing the right pictures
- ✓ Exploiting pictures of scenes
- ✓ 'Picture talk'
- ✓ Pictures for storytelling
- ✓ Teaching new words
- ✓ A sample sequence for using pictures of scenes
- ✓ Using student and teacher photos
- ✓ Picture sequences
- ✓ Sources of digital images and video

Research evidence

Working memory and dual coding

We need to return to cognitive science for a moment. One of the most influential models of memory (Figure 10.1) comes from Baddeley and Hitch.

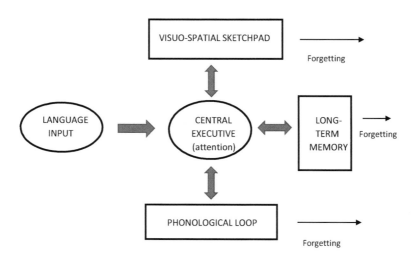

Figure 10.1 A model of memory based on Baddeley and Hitch (1974)

Research is clear that sounds (spoken language) and images are processed separately in the brain. In the diagram, these two routes of learning are described as the **phonological loop** and **visuo-spatial sketchpad**. The **central executive** focuses our attention on the sensory input, whether it be linguistic or visual. Once information is processed in the two areas of working memory, it may find its way into long-term memory. Rehearsal and spaced repetition help this along. In a later model Baddeley proposed that processing in the phonological and visual areas can reinforce each other to strengthen memory traces. This combination of the auditory and visual was already hypothesised by Allan Paivio (1971) and is known as **dual coding**. In essence, we remember more when sound is combined with image – even written language is a form of image.

Do images aid retention?

Research on the benefits of using pictures for vocabulary learning is scarce. Psychologist Richard Mayer (2001) conducted studies which led him to conclude that learners retain words better when they are presented alongside and simultaneously with pictures. Carpenter and Olson (2012) also found an advantage for pictures when learning vocabulary. The value of using pictures in vocabulary lessons was also apparent in a study by Jazuli *et al*. (2019) which showed how, through pictures, low-proficiency Malaysian students improved vocabulary acquisition and gained motivation to learn English. In addition, findings of a study by Na and Nguyen (2022) revealed that, compared with translations. pictures led to better retention. Andrä *et al*. (2020) found that pictures and gestures enhanced vocabulary retention of 8-year-old children both in the short and long term.

One interesting research finding is that when learners are taught using pictures, they are more likely to recall the words when pictures are also used in testing. Similarly, if students are taught using translations, then translations produce better test results (Lotto and de Groot, 1998). This is another example of Transfer-Appropriate Processing described in Chapter 6. The way we learn something affects the way we retrieve it.

Finally, the **Levels of Processing** (LOP) theory from cognitive psychology (Craik and Lockhart, 1972) suggests that if we process words through a range of means (spelling, sound, image, gesture, collocations) better memory performance should result (see Chapter 5). In other words, LOP predicts that recall depends on the degree of depth achieved during information encoding. If a word is encoded in a shallow way, at the phonological level, for example, by only hearing it, the recall of that word will be less efficient than if processed deeply by adding sensory information. Therefore, enriching a word with a picture or through other sensory experiences, makes encoding deeper than simply reading the word.

Pictures can also provide useful cultural input, especially now it is easier to access a wide range of freely available, copyright-free photographs (e.g. from pixabay.com). Like video, they can bring glimpses of L2 cultures into the classroom.

Possible limitations of pictures

Here are some possible objections to using pictures and some counter-arguments.

1. Some pictures are ambiguous; translations are clearer.
   - Some pictures certainly are more useful for some concepts than others.
2. Why not just use an L1 word instead of a picture? The L1 is in students' minds anyway, so we should not shy away from using it.
   - Pictures have the power to draw attention in the classroom. Most information we receive and store is via what we see. We seem to be hard-wired to attend to visual images, especially if they interest us in a particular way, for example, by amusing or surprising us. What will attract a student's attention more, a word or an image?
3. Pictures may place too much demand on memory. Why not use written words to support listening as much as possible?
   - It is true that the written word scaffolds listening, so this needs to be weighed up against the attractiveness of a picture.
4. Showing words in L1 develops literacy in both L1 and L2, both for students with weak literacy and EAL students, who get to see morphological patterns across the two languages.
   - Again, this advantage needs to be compared with attention-drawing, memorable nature of images.
5. Images are more useful for concrete words than abstract.

■ It may be wise not just to use pictures at all costs, with the goal of avoiding L1 use. Enough research evidence supports L1 use for us not to be doctrinaire about this area. The issue of concrete versus abstract words is significant. A study by Repetto, Pedroli and Macedonia (2017) found that the use of gestures was more effective than pictures.

Classroom practice

Choosing the right pictures

Pictures for teaching vocabulary and verbs need to be clear, simple, bold and unambiguous. If possible, they should represent the L2 cultural context. Amusing ones may be fine if they do not unduly distract classes. Displaying pictures on an interactive board allows you to play with the images in various ways. You can make them move, flash up briefly, gradually reveal or blur them and partially obscure them. Pictures to be avoided include any which are unclear, too small, too complicated, or depicting violent scenes and stereotypes (unless the aim is to expose stereotypes!).

Effective visuals may be memorable for all sorts of reasons: they can be beautiful, funny, moving, odd and even unattractive; however, if they elicit some kind of emotional response, they are doing their job in providing an effective stimulus for language work. We know that emotional responses can enhance memory.

Technology makes it easy to find and display a huge array of images, some of which may be used to support work on L2 cultures. However, our instincts suggest that exposure to a mix of both digital and analogue sources of imagery works best: if students are exposed to too much screen presentation it may become counterproductive. For instance, traditional hand-held flashcards can still play a very useful role. It is worth keeping a stock of these, laminated for future use and shared across a department. But the teacher can also, quickly and easily, make simple line drawings or stick men pictures to support a point being made. Pictures can be attached to the wall or the board. Students may enjoy the novelty of 'real', especially when they are not very good. Magazine pictures and brochures may also be a useful source. As can be seen below, pictures depicting scenes are useful, as are 'spot the difference' pictures.

Exploiting pictures of scenes

One approach to exploiting complex pictures is to brainstorm, say, 25 words related to the picture, then categorise them by word type, adding more words of the same type, to the limits of students' knowledge. Another approach is in pairs, where one student has a picture and must describe it to the second, who attempts to draw the image. Simple scenes work well for this. For beginners you could have a plan of a bedroom viewed from above. You would pre-teach a range of useful phrases such as *at the top, at the bottom, on the left, in the top left corner, next to, to the left of* and so on.

Another simple paired activity for beginners is a guessing game to practise simple yes/no questions. Each student has a notebook, mini-whiteboard or a tablet. Student A draws a simple item and student B must guess what they are drawing. As a starter activity a picture could be placed on the board and students use a dictionary to find as many words as possible related to it.

'Picture talk'

This is the name given to an activity used by many teachers using the TPRS approach (Teaching Proficiency through Reading and Storytelling – see Chapter 19). Find a picture online which contains people in a particular setting (see the example in Figure 10.2). The choice of picture can relate to a topic we are working on from the textbook or other sources. If the image requires new vocabulary, display it along with translation.

Display the picture, make statements while pointing, repeating and pausing. Ask questions about the picture and about what you have said about it. Students answer with hands up or via cold-calling. Use questioning techniques to ensure that language patterns and vocabulary are repeated multiple times.

Being able to describe a picture is also a useful skill to practise for some examinations, for example the GCSE in England, Wales and Northern Ireland.

Figure 10.2 Picture talk (Image: freepik.com)

Pictures for storytelling

Along similar lines to picture talk, a simple picture or cartoon might evoke a topic and be used as a pre-listening or pre-reading activity. One enigmatic image, capable of many interpretations, could elicit a whole lesson's discussion with advanced groups. Some pictures may suggest a background story so are useful for generating imaginative discussion with advanced students. Here are two examples with questions to elicit creative responses.

Couple talking

At intermediate level a simple picture, for example of a couple talking (see Figure 10.3), can be the basis for co-created storytelling. *Who are they? Where do they live? What are they called? What do they do for a living? Why are they here? What have they just done? What will they do next?* Students can dictate the story with teacher help (see Smith, 2023). Incidentally, a picture like this could also form the basis of a spoken or written dialogue with some classes.

Figure 10.3 A couple talking (Image: pixabay.com)

A man escaping

Who is he? Where is he? What are his emotions at the moment? Is he running or walking? What is he running from? Why? What will happen next? See Figure 10.4.

Figure 10.4 A man escaping (Image: pixabay.com)

Teaching new words

The most obvious way to use pictures is to teach new vocabulary. This used to be done with pictures drawn on the board or with hand-held flashcards (these remain options). More commonly teachers use PowerPoint slides, displaying clear images of concrete vocabulary, often accompanied by the written word. For a long time, use of the written word with images was discouraged, for fear that students would be influenced by the spelling and pronounce poorly. We suggest showing the words immediately, as it reduces cognitive load and allows sound-spelling correspondences (phonics) to be made immediately. To avoid the written form distorting pronunciation, just ensure that if you use choral repetition, it is done rigorously.

Avoid trying to teach too many new words at once. It is hard to give precise guidelines, since classes vary a good deal, but no more than a dozen at a time is enough. Some classes will be able to recall fewer.

As we saw in Chapter 5, there are good reasons for using words in context, rather than on their own, so it is easy to move beyond isolated words when using slides. Instead of just displaying, for example, *shirt* (when teaching clothing), you could show the phrase *I wear a shirt*. When teaching new, isolated words, decide which article to put next to the word, e.g. in Spanish would you display for shirt 'una camisa' or 'la camisa'? There is no hard-and-fast rule, but keep in mind which article is likely to be encountered most frequently with a particular word. It is important that students regularly hear and see a noun with its article. Gender is acquired naturally this way, as in L1. Steve has produced a screencast about teaching vocabulary with PowerPoint for his YouTube channel.

Other ways of modelling new vocabulary include sentence builders or knowledge organisers with translations, definitions, simple translation, gesture or using objects (see Chapters 5 and 12).

A sample sequence for using pictures of scenes

This teaching sequence has the advantage of producing lots of language from little preparation. It also moves from very controlled activities to much more spontaneous speech and is a good example of controlled, modelled language to free practice, almost all in L2. The activity can work with students of varying abilities, but simpler pictures may be used with weaker groups.

Select the pictures. Select two similar sets of pictures that allow students to answer a range of questions (e.g. *When? How? What? Who?*). For example, Set 1 could include a picture of a Ferrari in a city street, Set 2 a picture showing another means of transport in a similar setting with some variation (e.g. different weather, time of day, different looking people).

Decide on the language focus. In planning the activities decide the sort of verbs and nouns the pictures are likely to elicit. If the focus is on one or more specific tenses, provide practice in time markers (e.g. for the present: usually, every day, always, never).

1. **Brainstorming** – give students the Set 1 pictures and ask them to come up with as many verbs per picture as they can, in groups of two or three. Ideally, some vocabulary building activities should be carried out for about 10 minutes beforehand, drilling in as many verbs as possible, (or the words could have been practised in a homework prior to the lesson using a 'flipped classroom' model).

2. **Modelling via written and aural input** – show on the board L2 sentences (one at a time, based on the Set 1 pictures) and ask students to write on paper or mini-whiteboards, with a time limit, which picture(s) they think the sentences refer to. This can be a listening activity instead, in order to model pronunciation.

3. **Scaffolded written production** – ask students to create one or more sentences for each picture working alone or in pairs. At this stage give a list of vocabulary as support. An app such as Padlet can be used for students to share their output with others. They can take their time over this, but accuracy is not the focus.

4. **Scaffolded oral production** – ask students to work in pairs. Partner A chooses a picture and asks three questions in whatever tenses they have been working on. Put a range of questions on the board. Have students do as many rounds of this with as many different partners as possible. Again, 100% accuracy is not an issue. Go around, help, monitor and provide feedback. This activity, too, is carried out with no particular time limit or pressure on students to communicate.

5. **Eliciting fast written response (teacher led)** – so far, the students have been working with only one set of pictures (e.g. Set 1). Now show three or more pictures on the board from Set 2 which, being similar to the Set 1 pictures, are likely to elicit language already practised earlier. Students must now write as much as they can about each picture *to a time limit*. The aim of this is to recycle the language learned so far but to also focus on developing fluency, i.e. fast retrieval from long term memory under time pressure (see Chapter 7). Encourage the use of specific connectives and one or more tenses. For example, divide the screen into three sections, 'past', 'present' and 'future' and place a picture in each section; students write something like: *yesterday I went to the beach, now I am shopping, later this evening I am going to the cinema with my friends.*

6. **Eliciting fast written response (student led)** – students re-enact part (5) above but in groups of 4 or 5, with one acting as teacher.

7. **Unstructured picture-based conversation without support** – now students do oral pair work again, perhaps with a phone to record, this time with no support and to a time limit. Partner A selects five or more pictures (a mix of set 1 and set 2) for partner B and spontaneously asks questions about them. If a phone has been used, a recording can be sent to the teacher without any editing. If time allows, several rounds can be carried out.

Using student and teacher photos

A great way to personalise lessons and to get to know students is to have them bring in their own photos (or share from their phone). For novices who are learning to talk about their families and friends, photos allow for practice in describing people, their personalities, their interests and what they do together. Keep in mind any potential sensitivities with family photos. You can share your own photos, such as of your family, memorable events from your life, or holidays.

Picture sequences

These make for good oral exploitation, providing lots of repetitive input and opportunities to speak and (later) write. Use a full repertoire of questions (see Chapter 2) to get students to describe each picture individually, then gradually build up the story, eliciting longer sequences from faster students and finally getting them to recount the story to a partner or the whole class. Subsequently, in pairs, they should be able to tell the story to each other. The sequence involves modelling, then recycling the same material in slightly different ways. You could either let them see the whole series at once or release one picture at a time as a slideshow. The latter approach places more stress on memory. The former makes it easier to recount longer sections of the story.

Visit to Paris

Look at the sequence of 12 images depicting a visit to Paris. (Figure 10.5). Arrows indicate arriving and leaving. They could all be displayed at once or presented one by one in a PowerPoint presentation. Typical questions would be:

At what time did you leave the house?
Did you go to the bus station? Where did you go?
At what time did the train leave? Did the train leave at 9.00?
Did you go to Notre Dame or the Eiffel Tower? Did you go up?
What did you do after that? Did you have an Italian meal?
Did you go to Notre Dame next? Where did you go?
When did you get to Notre Dame?   And so on.
Now, who can recount the first three pictures for me? The next three? The whole story?

Figure 10.5 Visit to Paris (Images from pixabay.com)

With this sequence as a stimulus, you can get students to narrate a set of several pictures at once, allowing them the chance to produce longer utterances. This creates a sense of achievement and allows you to differentiate by aptitude.

Once you have worked in the first person (often the best place to start) you could then retell the story in the third person, perhaps in a subsequent lesson, thus recycling previous work and improving mastery. We would want to stress how important it is to return to previous work in a sequence of lessons, adding something new on each occasion.

A sequence of this type offers many opportunities to develop oral and listening skills. The main aims would be to practise the use of time expressions, places and past tense. At the end of a sequence of oral work, students could write up an account in the first or third person to reinforce their oral and listening work.

It is easy enough to design picture sequences yourself. They can even be drawn quickly on the board by hand. Remember that the key aim is clarity and ease of exploitation, not to produce amusing pictures which may be attractive to the eye but of limited use. The same is true of PowerPoint presentations. These may be freely available online. They should be carefully assessed for their efficacy rather than their attractiveness. You can also present picture sequences with text or gapped text to scaffold language.

Sources of digital images and video

There is a wide range of sources for online photos. If you choose to embed photos in Word documents or PowerPoint, be aware of copyright issues and image size although there are many good images which are copyright free and available through the Microsoft clipart library or from sites such as pixabay.com and freepik.com. Even when using images for educational purposes with no commercial gain, always check the copyright status of any image, including clipart and animated GIFs.

When downloading or copying and pasting images note that many images have high resolutions which you may wish to reduce.

Many teachers like to use their own images to bring their personal experience of L2 cultures into the classroom. Pictures of shop fronts, street scenes and signs can be particularly useful.

Sequences of images from a film using the screen capture function of your PC can provide a motivating source for connected imagery. You can obtain more information about how to do this with a range of commercial products or with a simple online search. AI tools can also be used to create images.

YouTube is no doubt the go-to source for video. Remember that you can slow down the speed of the sound and often display a transcript of the text, although, at the time of writing, this is in the form of numbered lines and is not always 100% accurate.

Concluding remarks

It is a cliché that, according to a Chinese proverb, 'a picture is worth a thousand words'. We live in a culture rich with images. Children grow up with photographs, TV, films, video, YouTube, TikTok, Facebook and Instagram. We cannot escape the power of the visual image and, as language teachers, we do well to exploit pictures as a source of cultural interest, amusement, excitement and, most importantly, as an aid to effective second language acquisition. We have seen in this chapter how a well-chosen image or series of images can be used to avoid having to resort to L1, to present, practise and recycle new language, serve as a basis for structured and spontaneous communication, as a support for reading, as well as controlled and free writing.

11

Meeting the needs of all students

Introduction

Our classrooms contain students with all sorts of backgrounds, previous experience and specific needs. Motivation, aptitude and prior knowledge vary. Some have serious literacy issues to address, others are reluctant, anxious learners, while others still seem to thrive as language learners. Cognitive learning processes are common to all, but any practising teacher knows that students vary hugely in all kinds of ways. Language teachers need to be aware of the range of needs and how we can respond to them.

This chapter considers the areas below.

Research evidence
- ✓ Language learning aptitude
- ✓ Personality traits and language aptitude
- ✓ Grouping by aptitude or prior attainment
- ✓ Special needs (Alternative Learning Needs)
- ✓ Dyslexia
- ✓ Teaching students with English as an Additional Language (EAL)
- ✓ Teaching autistic students
- ✓ Inclusive language

Classroom practice
- ✓ Teaching the 'gifted and talented'
- ✓ Teaching lower-attaining students
- ✓ Teaching SEND (ALN) students
- ✓ Personalising learning
- ✓ Working with bilingual students
- ✓ Supporting new students in class
- ✓ Differentiation
- ✓ Transition from primary to high school
- ✓ Cognitive empathy

Research evidence

Language learning aptitude

It is sometimes said that the two key factors for language learning success are motivation and aptitude. Language aptitude has been found to be one of the most important individual variables in second language acquisition (Li, 2015). But, as Catherine Doughty and Alison Mackey (2021) point out it "… is one of the most important, intriguing, messy and often controversial topics in second language research" (p. 1).

Any language teacher knows that aptitude varies enormously in classrooms (as does motivation!). Many are reluctant to use the terms 'high ability' or 'low ability' for fear of labelling students, limiting aspirations or simply in the belief that aptitude is not fixed. However, there is a long tradition of research which shows that aptitude varies and is a fairly fixed trait, i.e. it is not easily altered.

The most famous names in this field are John Carroll and Stanley Sapon who devised a **Modern Language Aptitude Test** (MLAT) (1959). They considered the key factors in aptitude to be:

1. **phonetic coding** (the ability to 'code' auditory phonetic material so it can be recognised, identified and remembered over time - longer than a few seconds);
2. **ability to handle grammar** (being sensitive to the function of words in a variety of contexts);
3. **rote memorisation ability;**
4. **ability to infer linguistic forms, rules and patterns** (with minimal guidance).

Another famous aptitude test was devised by Paul Pimsleur in 1966. He called it the **Language Aptitude Battery** (known as PLAB). His test comprised six sub-tests, each allocated a number of points, which in total add up to 117.

1. **Grade-Point Average** (American terminology) in academic areas other than modern language learning (18 points).
2. **Interest in learning a new language** (8 points).
3. **Vocabulary**: a test of knowledge of L1 vocabulary (24 points).
4. **Language Analysis**: a test of ability to discern the function of language elements in several forms in an unknown language for which English equivalents are given - a discovery test of sorts (15 points).
5. **Sound Discrimination**: the candidate learns aurally three Ewe words (Ewe is an African language) which are similar but not identical in sound. They then must spot the correct word in sentences given aurally (30 points).
6. **Sound-Symbol**: recognition of the written form of English nonsense words (22 points).

It is worth noting that the above tests are primarily about diagnosing the potential of students, including whether they have any disability for language learning. This view sees aptitude as a **fixed trait** which cannot be altered (Singleton, 2017).

Others take a different view, arguing that although aptitude is more stable than motivation, there is evidence that certain components of aptitude might improve during learning (e.g. Kormos, 2013).

Some view aptitude tests as mainly focused on conditions of explicit, conscious learning and since language learning, is largely an implicit process, it needs a test which tries to measure implicit learning ability.

In contrast to Carroll and Pimsleur, Robinson (2005) considered language aptitude as cognitive abilities which we draw on during L2 learning and performance in various contexts and at different stages. This definition suggests a more dynamic view of language aptitude and is derived from the belief that aptitude is sensitive to environmental factors and is either activated or inhibited depending on different learning conditions.

Since the work of Carroll and Pimsleur, research into aptitude rather fell out of fashion, but it has seen a renewed impetus with growing interest in cognitive science. **Working memory** is a recent addition to language aptitude models and an increasing body of research seems to indicate that it plays an essential role. Remember that working memory is one route by which we process and store language input in long-term memory. In particular, it may be that phonological working memory (that capacity of being able to hold language in working memory) plays a role in aptitude. Zhisheng Wen (2016) has been a leading proponent of the idea that working memory is a good predictor of language learning aptitude. Several studies have shown a correlation between working memory capacity and vocabulary learning ability, for example. Working memory seems to be relatively fixed, but as Singleton (2017) points out, some studies have shown that working memory capacity can be developed for specific tasks, if not as an overall ability. So research remains in flux.

One point we would make is that, even if aptitude is a relatively fixed trait, this does not somehow put a ceiling on the progress that can be made. Motivation and hard work remain central to improving proficiency and this is the message to get across to students.

Personality traits and language aptitude

It should be noted that the evidence on how different personality types affect language learning is tentative, since personality type classifications used in research vary and because not enough studies have been carried out. Several findings are worth being aware of, however, some of which are counter-intuitive. The personality types referred to below are taken from Costa and McCrae's (1992) 'Big Five' model. They generate the acronym OCEAN.

1. **Openness to experience**. People with high levels of this trait are intellectually curious, independent in their judgment, appreciate beauty and the arts, are in touch with their feelings, love adventure and unusual ideas. Those with low levels are traditional and conservative.
2. **Conscientiousness.** This denotes thoroughness, punctuality, thoughtfulness and reliability at work. People with this trait prefer planned and structured behaviour to spontaneity and creativity.
3. **Extraversion**. Highly extraverted people enjoy engaging with the external world, are friendly and warm-hearted, full of energy, enjoy playing and seek stimulation.
4. **Agreeableness**. This personality trait refers to modesty, compassion, altruism, tender-mindedness and honesty. Agreeable individuals are friendly, helpful and usually tend to see the best in people. They appreciate good relationships with others.
5. **Neuroticism.** Neurotic people are unstable and impulsive who are prone to negative emotions such as anxiety, anger, hostility, resentment and depression. When under stress, they react with fear and irrational behaviour. They are often in a bad mood.

Whether we agree with these categories or not, after reading the above an experienced teacher may be able to predict which factors correlate more strongly with success in language learning. One obvious answer is openness to experience. Why is this important personality trait associated with language learning? Firstly, it is the factor most strongly linked to intellectual curiosity and flexibility (Biedron, 2011). It goes along with creativity and divergent thinking, which are typical of gifted learners in general. Also, students who are highly 'open to experience' are less likely to be critical of a different culture, and, appreciative as they are of art and beauty, more prone to embrace the language of a country with a strong artistic heritage or concerned with aesthetic beauty.

Another factor that may correlate positively with success in second language learning is conscientiousness, especially in the areas of memory and grammar, and in developing cognitive academic learning ability. This is possibly because conscientious people tend to be more dutiful, hard-working and intrinsically driven to do well in whatever they do. Conscientiousness is said to be the best predictor of the quality of professional activity as well as academic achievement (Strelau, 2000).

Agreeableness seems to be a predictor of success in terms of phonological coding and pronunciation, possibly because highly 'agreeable' individuals tend to listen more attentively and may subconsciously try to use their voice to harmonise with fellow humans more effectively. This is called **phonetic convergence** (Lewandowski and Jilka, 2019).

As for extraversion, its correlation with language learning ability appears controversial. On the one hand, extraverts display lower levels of anxiety and engage in more frequent communication and greater risk-taking. They may therefore develop more effective interpersonal skills and better oral fluency (Dewaele and Furnham, 2000). Dewaele (2009) notes that studies have consistently shown that extraverts have a working memory advantage.

On the other hand, research seems to indicate that extraversion correlates negatively with language aptitude. This may seem surprising, but we must bear in mind, as mentioned above, that other factors can offset the advantage or disadvantage a given personality trait naturally gives you. The extravert may be too impatient to wait for L2 skills to be embedded.

The factor that seems to correlate most negatively with language aptitude is neuroticism, owing to the high levels of anxiety a neurotic person experiences. The evidence suggests these have a strong detrimental impact on cognitive processing, focus on tasks, memory and motivation.

All this can have important implications for learning, especially for students who may not be identified as potentially gifted in general intelligence but may score highly in terms of 'openness to experience'. Moreover, if you have spotted a child with neurotic behaviour, it may be useful to adopt specific strategies to minimise the risk of causing them stressful experiences and vice versa. In sum, if you know your students' personalities to any degree, you may be able to adjust how you interact with them and the type of tasks you set.

Grouping by aptitude or prior attainment

Grouping students by predicted or prior achievement is the main way many schools take account of varying aptitude. In the research literature this is called **tracking**. In schools in England it is not at all uncommon for languages and mathematics classes to be in 'sets' (commonly classes grouped by prior attainment). In the research literature this is described as **between-class ability grouping** (Papachristou *et al.*, 2022). Many object to this principle, either for social, behavioural and philosophical reasons, or because it is thought to be ineffective. To be clear, opponents of ability grouping argue that placing some students in a 'bottom' group creates a 'sink set' mentality, where any lack of self-efficacy is simply reinforced. A social justice argument can also be forcefully made, namely that grouping may end up reinforcing existing socio-economic differences.

It is generally felt by teachers that ability grouping benefits slightly the most able and has a negative effect on lower-attaining students. Research tends to bear this out, e.g. Parsons and Hallam (2014) in a study of 7-year-olds. Hattie (2011) suggests that, on average, ability grouping is not a good way to raise standards. It should be noted in passing that much of the research into this area focuses on maths and reading.

On the other hand, Fleischmann *et al.* (2023) found in their large study of maths learners that placing students of lower attainment in mixed-ability groups reduced their feeling of 'academic self-concept', i.e. they were unhappier to be placed with high-achieving students.

The Education Endowment Foundation (2023) points out that grouping by ability can be ineffective partly because less skilled teachers are sometimes assigned to lower-achieving groups. They also suggest that ability grouping creates negative self-fulling prophecies for disadvantaged pupils, whereby their chances of improving attainment and experiencing success is hampered by "the combination of lower teacher expectations and between-class stratification". There is also some evidence that pupils from disadvantaged backgrounds are more likely to be misallocated to lower sets.

Thus far, there is scant research on the effects of ability/prior attainment grouping on achievement gains specifically in languages in the secondary context. Taking away the non-academic arguments from the debate, it is possible to hypothesise that attainment grouping allows the teacher to more easily match the input and lesson plans to the level of the class.

Grouping can take many forms which vary according to the school context. In very small schools it may be impossible to group by aptitude at all. In other contexts, a reasonable solution may be to have one accelerated class, with a number of parallel groups below. Another variation would be to have two parallel higher achieving groups, with other groups below. Attempts to 'baseline' students at an early stage (i.e. do a baseline test against which future attainment can be assessed) are fraught with difficulty and we would suggest that, if you go down this route, it is best to wait at least a year before considering grouping by aptitude or achievement.

Special Needs (Alternative Learning Needs)

What are SEND and ALN?

Every young person has the right to learn a world language and it is the responsibility of schools and teachers to provide equal access. In the UK the term Additional Learning Needs (ALN) has a legal definition and refers to children and young people with learning, physical or sensory needs that make it harder to learn than most children of the same age.

Young people require special educational provision if they have a disability which prevents or hinders them from making use of educational facilities generally provided. These difficulties can be age-related and may fluctuate over time. Many students with vision impairment, hearing impairment or a multi-sensory impairment (MSI) require specialist support and/or equipment to access their learning, or habilitation support (help with motor skills, movement, speech, etc.). Children and young people with an MSI have a combination of vision and hearing difficulties. Some children and young people with a physical disability require additional ongoing support and equipment to access all the opportunities available to their peers (DfE, 2015).

The SEND (Special Educational Needs and Disabilities) Code of Practice identifies four broad areas of need: Communication and Interaction; Cognition and Learning; Social, emotional and Mental Health difficulties; Sensory and/or physical needs (DfE, 2015). Specific needs relevant to language learning and literacy include hearing impairment and dyslexia.

Dyslexia

In a teaching career we often work with dyslexic students. Dyslexia, also known as **developmental dyslexia**, is a specific learning difficulty (SpLD) that primarily affects the skills involved in accurate and fluent word reading and spelling. It is partly genetic in origin. Figures vary, but according to the British Dyslexia Association, the number of people with dyslexia in the UK is around 10%, with 4% of the population at the severe end of the dyslexia continuum. In the United States, National Institutes of Health research suggests that dyslexia affects 5-10% of the population, with estimates as high as 17%.

Dyslexia operates across a spectrum from mild to severe and levels of dyslexia vary depending on the language. For example, it may be more of an issue in orthographically opaque languages like English, French and Russian (where spelling is not always a clear guide to pronunciation), than in orthographically transparent languages such as German, Italian and Spanish. (But see Hoeft, *et al.* (2015) who believe more research is needed to confirm this.

Deficiency in phonological processing is what underpins the reading difficulties of people with dyslexia and a variety of explanations have been proposed. These include deficits in phonological awareness and verbal memory. Some studies suggest that developmental deficits in reading may also be related to visual processing problems, which are particularly relevant for visually complex stimuli such as alphabetic writing (e.g. Koller, 2012). It is likely that students with poorer phonological working memory struggle most when classroom work focuses only on speaking and listening, both of which demand lots of attention. This suggests that, rather than avoiding writing with struggling students, it should be used as beneficial support.

As far as non-alphabetical languages are concerned, Dehaene (2009) points out that all types of reading involve co-opting areas of the brain which evolved to handle visual and spatial information, not to read – after all, as mentioned previously, reading is not a natural skill (Geary, 2008). The key processes of learning to read are the same for all languages.

Language teachers, in conjunction with special needs coordinators, should be aware of any children with dyslexia and make a particular effort to ensure help is given with decoding issues. Kormos (2017) lists signs to look out for when identifying dyslexic students:

- **Word level reading**: slow pace, inaccurate word recognition, difficulties pronouncing words, difficulties inferring meaning of unknown words.
- **Text level reading**: difficulties understanding key and detailed information, difficulty inferring implied meaning, paying attention to meaning when reading aloud (because of the extra attention needed for decoding).
- **Word level writing**: slow pace, inaccurate spelling.
- **Text level writing**: difficulty organising ideas, coherence, accuracy, proofreading and revision.

- **Listening**: distinguishing similar sounding words, paying attention, remembering information, understanding implied meaning.
- **Speaking**: pronouncing words, accuracy, coherence of ideas.

To support dyslexic students Kormos (2017) recommends strategies, which also make sense for all learners:

- **Multi-modality**: supporting listening with written text, reading aloud, using text to speech.
- **Explicit teaching and awareness raising**: dyslexic students find it harder to learn implicitly, so a greater focus on explanation will be useful. This includes explicit phonological and sound-spelling practice.

All students benefit from training in phonics, but especially those with dyslexia. It cannot be assumed that students will just pick up the relationship between letters and sounds without specific activities devoted to helping the process along. We pay a lot of attention to phonological awareness and decoding activities in *Breaking the Sound Barrier: Teaching Language Learners How to Listen* (Conti and Smith, 2019). In everyday teaching, tolerance is needed with pronunciation and spelling errors, and students should get plenty of opportunity to read aloud syllable by syllable.

Teaching students with English as an Additional Language (EAL)

Although most of our lessons are carried out in L2, we may teach classes with a significant number of students whose first language is not English. At the very least this is worth bearing in mind when choosing to make comparisons with L1. Those who have some competence in more than one language already may be at an advantage, comfortable as they are with the concept of being bilingual.

In England, The National Association for Language Development in the Curriculum (naldic.org.uk) is the professional association for teachers specialising in EAL. They state on their website (accessed in 2023):

> *"Students learning EAL share many common characteristics with students whose first language is English, and many of their learning needs are similar to those of other children and young people in our schools. However, these students also have distinct and different needs from other students by virtue of the fact that they are learning in and through another language, and that they come from cultural backgrounds and communities with different understandings and expectations of education, language and learning."*

In the USA the term **heritage language** is used to identify languages other than the dominant language (or languages) in a given social context. English is the *de facto* dominant language of the USA (not an 'official' language, in fact, but the primary language used in government, education, and public communication); thus, any language other than English can be considered a heritage language for speakers of that language. Whatever the terminology used (you also come across **minority languages**, **community languages** and **home languages**), speakers of additional or heritage languages are a very useful resource in the classroom, bringing, as they often do, cultural and linguistic insights which the class may otherwise be unaware of. Taking advantage of EAL students' L1 will, in addition, benefit their self-esteem.

Worth noting is that EAL students may not be literate in their L1, in which case they will benefit from supplementary classes to raise the level of their L1 literacy; this will also aid their literacy in English (their L2) and in their L3 (e.g. French or Spanish). There may have to be a trade-off on the school timetable between their L2 and L3, if time for both cannot be found. It is possible that a student may also have learning difficulties, so questions arise about how to identify this when their English is relatively weak. The rate at which they learn to cope with 'social' English is a good indicator of their ability. Most young people will pick up what they need for daily living very quickly if they are well integrated with classmates. If they do not, it may be worth finding out how they coped with learning their L1.

Where linguistic support in the EAL student's L1 is available, vocabulary lists can be prepared with three columns: L3, English and L1. If several L1 languages are spoken in the class, the third column can be left blank to be completed in whatever way possible, perhaps even by the students as they work out what a flashcard or other cue indicates. This is a good way to monitor how well they are following, too. Parallel texts (in paired combinations of L1, L2 or L3) can also be useful.

Teaching autistic students

Autism spectrum disorder (ASD) is a developmental disorder that affects behaviour and communication. It affects 1-2% of people so it is safe to say that all language teachers should be aware of ASD and ways to accommodate student needs. Autistic students typically struggle with human interaction, expressing themselves, and adhering to social norms. One of the common symptoms of ASD is the presence of unusual repetitive compulsive behaviours that may interfere with daily activities. ASD students may find it hard to decipher non-verbal signals such as gestures and facial expressions, as well as voice intonation. Many children on the spectrum suffer from hypersensitivity and overexcitability. All these factors present a challenge in the school setting and particularly in a subject like languages where communication is a central goal.

Moghadam, Karami, and Dehbozorgi (2015) outline three ways in which making progress in languages may be helpful for students with ASD:

1. Attempts to overcome social barriers may be useful in the long run. L1 acquisition is an unconscious process, but learning a new language in the classroom requires a degree of more formal, deliberate practice. Knowing an L2 can help a student be more aware of their social skills.
2. L2 learning may help a student on the spectrum to overcome social isolation. A student with ASD gets to understand other people better and make their communication patterns more nuanced.
3. Building L2 knowledge may make a student's life more structured. Many people with ASD feel stressed and frustrated when put into an unfamiliar situation. Learning grammar rules and revising vocabulary may become stress-relieving habits.

Useful practical pointers for teachers include using predictable classroom routines, pairing ASD students with mature and sensitive peers, using timers to help make goals clear and being explicit with instructions, assuming no implied meanings.

Inclusive language

Recent years have seen a growing interest in the use of inclusive language in educational settings and teachers may wonder how to approach this issue in the classroom. While there is a growing awareness among L1 users of gender-neutral grammatical usages, e.g. in French the possible use of *iel* ('they' in English) to avoid choosing the pronouns *il* and *elle* ('he' and 'she'), these are rarely used by L1 users so it must be asked whether much time should be spent on them. We agree with Peters (2020) who writes, "It is not pedagogically advisable to expect novice learners of a language to use relatively rare idiosyncratic grammatical forms that are not part of the standard language while they are still trying to master the basic features of the language" (p. 190). Students should still be informed about language gender issues from an early stage. Indeed, they can be the basis for awareness raising about the whole notion of gender in languages such as German, French and Spanish, not to mention non-sexist modes of expression and gender identity questions in general. Teachers need to be aware of the individual preferences of LGBTQIA students and may wish to have individual conversations regarding preferred language use.

Classroom practice

Teaching the 'gifted and talented'

The term 'gifted and talented' is sometimes used in education to define the highest achieving students. Most definitions focus on an individual's abilities and intelligence, as they consider the gifted and talented student to have a natural skill, above and beyond those of the same age (Winstanley, 2005).

The most proficient linguists have certain characteristics. Some of these align with the research on aptitude.

- Good powers of concentration.
- A desire to learn and work hard.
- An openness to language learning.
- Good mimicry skills, meaning they can discriminate sounds and reproduce them accurately.
- An ability to see patterns in language.
- A desire to be accurate.
- Good short and long-term memory.
- High expectations of themselves and the teacher.

Once such students have been identified, and with these characteristics in mind, we have found the following strategies work well, enabling the highest attainers to progress rapidly.

Teaching lower-attaining students

Clearly, teaching less confident students can be a challenge, but one which many language teachers enjoy most of all. Of course, the general principles and ideas laid out in this book apply to nearly all students, but it is true that memory connections will be slower to form for some.

Since research suggests that lower-attainers may benefit less from explicit grammar teaching (Roehr-Brackin, 2022), the range of grammatical structures and vocabulary presented will be narrower with many classes. Better that this narrower range be mastered than to present an overwhelming amount of material for which they are not ready.

Where students' general literacy skills in L1 are weak, learning a second language may seem less of a priority to some schools and teachers, but it is worth recalling that L2 learning contributes to general literacy and communication skills and language teachers play an important role in teaching students about spelling, punctuation, word morphology, grammatical categories, sentence formation and so on. It is a misconception that less confident students should be doing more oral and listening work, with less reading and writing. Lower-achieving classes may have a tendency (but not always) to be less settled, so teachers need to ensure there are quiet times in lessons when they can read and write at their own pace.

Steve's tips for teaching high-attaining students

- Make sure the most brilliant are challenged with special attention, allowing them to give good examples and giving them oral and written tasks which allow them to extend, e.g. with longer oral answers and lots of creative composition work.

- Always have extra work available for the fastest students.

- Be very critical of average work when you know it could have been better. Students will almost invariably show off what they can do next time.

- Let them know you are smart; able students in particular like their teachers to be well-versed in their subject. In turn, they may want to show how good they can be.

- Do not be afraid to do lots of practice examples, e.g. grammar drills, but vary the challenge and give the hardest examples to the most able students.

- Consider doing a more-than-average amount of traditional grammar-translation work. Research lends some support for this. Higher attainers are good at it and enjoy solving puzzles; not too much, though, as it may limit L2 input.

- Do not be a slave to the course or textbook. Pick and choose, selecting only activities which will stimulate and challenge.

- Use the assessment regime to motivate. High-attaining students are especially motivated by exam success and the idea of getting the highest grades.

Teaching SEND (ALN) students

Hazell (2020) makes several recommendations about working with young people with alternative learning needs. An important aspect is getting to know the individual students on a personal level and working with any teaching assistants allocated to that student or the class. She proposes the following questions are worth asking ourselves:

- What do I need to do to best support this learner?
- What do they require to fully access learning? Examples include using enlarged fonts, earphones or a special hearing device.

- What does the teaching assistant (TA) need to know about the task being carried out? How will I use the TA?
- What factors should I keep in mind about the learning environment? Examples include background noise levels, space, groupings, microphones.
- If a scaffolding mat is needed to help with a task, is it in an appropriate form, e.g. a sentence builder?
- Should I keep in mind anything that happened in the last lesson?
- Do I need a specific discussion with the student or TA?

Hazell reports how some students who struggle in certain subjects can enjoy the different nature of language lessons. She writes about how you can devise games and projects, create conversation strips and sentence builder jigsaws; how you can set up a grocery store in the classroom, raid toyshops and charity shops to find classroom objects ('realia').

Further advice Hazell offers includes:

- Being very consistent with classroom routines, ensuring there are clear 'non-negotiables'.
- Being extra clear and concise with instructions, using dual coding to help.
- Modelling what you are expecting.
- Remembering to wear your microphone when it is needed.
- Allowing students with speech difficulties to record themselves.
- Linking new learning to prior learning.
- Avoiding lengthy reading and writing tasks.
- Ensuring printed materials are fully accessible.
- Allowing students to choose optimal learning partners.
- Having spare resources and a back-up plan.

Personalising learning

Some have argued that using the term SEND may lead us to neglect the fact that all students are different in their own ways. This is undoubtedly true. One way to engage every student to the maximum in their learning and to value them as individuals is to provide them with opportunities to draw on their own experiences. Every student's life is unique. At every level it is useful to tap into their interests, preferences, past experiences, future plans and so on. This is easy to do in a few ways.

1. Make a point of finding out **what interests each student**. Try to get to know at least one thing about every one of them. (This is also useful for developing your relationship with the class.)

2. Provide frequent opportunities for students to **talk and write about themselves**, e.g. their family, home, routines, hobbies, school life, holidays, favourite foods, clothes, websites, TV, music, and so on.

3. When working with texts, as well as asking questions about the content of the text, look for opportunities for students to **relate the content to their own experience**; allow them to express opinions and points of view. The ability to do this is often specifically assessed in examinations.

4. For certain students you may even have to **tailor a specific programme of work**. This may be the case if a student has been absent or has a special need (e.g. a bilingual student).

Working with bilingual students

We may have to deal with having a bilingual (native speaker of L2) student in class, i.e. one who is already very proficient in the language being taught. They are probably fluent orally, have excellent listening and reading skills, but varying degrees of written skill. What can be done to make the most of their existing aptitude?

If they are there in the first year of high school, then it may be wise to keep them in the same classroom as their peers. They are settling in socially, making friends and may feel cut off if you send them somewhere else to study. If they are already established at the school, it can make sense to have them do the work you set elsewhere, as they may prefer silence, access to books or a computer. You could have a weekly meeting time, perhaps during the regular class to monitor their work.

Most students are enthused by the prospect of taking exams sooner than their peers. Consult with them and their parents/caregivers to see if this will be motivational. Will the school allow it? A bilingual child will usually do very well in examinations designed for non-native speakers but will need specific guidance on examination techniques. You would also need to be certain that the maturity level of the assessment is appropriate.

Once you have talked things through and established what work they might benefit from, there is a range of possibilities:

- Provide **advanced level texts** with exercises.
- Provide a menu of **challenging** online interactive **grammar, listening and reading tasks**.
- Suggest **novels or non-fiction to read** according to their interest and maturity. The student could write a book review, or existing resources used at advanced level may be adapted.
- Provide **challenging sources of listening** which will broaden their range and interests. It is better to provide some structure to the task than just leaving the student to browse.
- **Involve them** with the rest of the class. They could help with pair work, give easy presentations and help you present dialogues.

- They might enjoy **coaching individuals** with their work, even older ones. This would be good for their self-esteem, provide a useful service and be good experience for the bilingual student.
- Suggest that the student **writes a blog** for the rest of the class and their family to follow.
- **Set grammar exercises or translations** to do. L1-L2 translation will benefit their command of structure and spelling. L2-L1 translation will help develop their use of L1. If bilingual students have a weakness, it is usually with their L1 written accuracy.
- Attempt to **find them an e-pal or traditional pen pal**, if they do not already have Facebook friends who speak the L2.

Supporting new students in the class

Two common situations arise when we have to support new students arriving in an existing class.

Scenario 1 Audrey, a 13-year-old fluent French speaker from La Rochelle arrives in a British school.

In a case like this, Audrey may have excellent spoken fluency and comprehensions skills, but her written accuracy and grammar may be shaky. Once her skills have been diagnosed, several steps can be taken to include and support her:
- Make sure she stays in the class, at least most of the time, so that she can settle in socially.
- Value her skills and use them to support other students, e.g. in pair work and milling around activities.
- Do 'special person interviews' with her so students can learn about her and her background. This offers useful intercultural competence opportunities (see Chapter 15).
- Offer her the opportunity to take an exam designed for older students in the school. This is often a great motivator.
- Provide a specific programme of work. For instance, if useful, provide a grammar and writing workbook to help her firm up her written accuracy; have her read fiction and non-fiction and write reviews; practise exam past papers; be sure to allocate homework time to her tasks and monitor her work periodically.

Scenario 2 David arrives in an American high school from another school where he studied French. He has to begin his Spanish course two years behind the other students in the class. He has done no Spanish.

This is a less than ideal situation but happens quite often. The school management team may decide that David has to join the class, catch up and do any required exams. Catching up in 'linear' subjects like languages and maths (where new work depends to a large degree on knowing older work), is harder than with, say, history, geography or art. Below are some steps which could be taken.

- Devote some one-to-one time to work through beginner resources.

- Get the help of an older, proficient student to do some private tuition at least once a week. This may particularly appeal to keen linguists and potential teachers of the future.

- Assign tasks using a preferred digital technology and apps.

- Involve the new arrival with the class in chosen classroom activities which may be accessible, e.g. starting a new topic.

- Have the new arrival sit next to a volunteer 'buddy' or 'mentor' who will help with classroom tasks and homework.

- Provide resources such as earlier textbooks, worksheets, parallel texts, knowledge organisers and sentence builders. The latter are particularly valuable when every language item is translated.

Differentiation

There are usually said to be three types of differentiation: **by task, by outcome** and **by support.** In language lessons the first would involve setting different tasks for different students. This could mean across attainment groups (different groups following a different scheme of work) or within individual classrooms where, for example, different students would be given separate tasks. The second type of differentiation, used more commonly, involves setting open-ended tasks which elicit student responses at different levels (essay writing is a common example). Differentiation by support involves assisting students in different ways.

There is considerable debate around the question of differentiation. In practice, at high school level, differentiation by task can be hard to plan for and execute. Attainment grouping (sets) clearly plays a useful role in this regard. In second language classes, where students usually follow quite a tightly organised course based on grammar and/or topic progression, and where the teacher frequently takes the lead in modelling new language, most teachers set the same tasks for all students and exploit differentiation by outcome and support. It is also argued that giving easier tasks to some students in the same group reflects a lowering of aspiration for those students and that all students should be encouraged to assume they can achieve the highest standard. This is where our knowledge of the nature of the group comes in, part of the craft of teaching.

Differentiation by task can, in fact, be achieved in quite subtle ways in the classroom. When doing teacher-led oral work, questions and other interactions can be pitched to enable all students to reach their potential (see Chapters 2 and 3). (This is one argument against **random questioning**, a practice which does not allow you to exercise your judgment in selecting questions for students.)

When setting up pair or group work it is possible to vary the groupings according to ability and personality type to allow everyone to do their best. This can be a very subtle business which depends on the group, their abilities, characters and behaviour. It is usually wise to avoid placing more challenging students together. It may be tempting to place boys next to girls – some school language departments do this as a matter of policy, mainly in the belief that girls may have a calming influence on the boys.

Gianfranco's tips for differentiating tasks

- When setting an exercise with a certain number of examples, ask some students to do more.
- Set plenty of open-ended compositional work. Give a minimum word limit and invite students to do more if they are able; set them the challenge.
- During pair work make sure that students who finish a task quickly are given more to do.
- Where possible, use graded readers to allow students to stretch themselves.
- Consider the merits of differentiated worksheets with extension tasks.
- When asking students to do an oral presentation, vary the target length.
- Maintain a list on the notice board of external activities aspirational students might like to do, e.g. details of twinning activities, films on at an art house cinema, festivals, and suitable films, TV series and podcasts.

Transition from primary to high school

Students arrive in secondary schools with varying experience of language learning. In a typical novice class at age 11, some have done our subject before, to varying degrees, some have done a different language, and some have done barely any language learning at all. Not to mention those who come with other languages they have acquired before the age of 11. This presents a dilemma. It would clearly be wrong to take no account at all of prior learning, but nor can it be assumed that previous learning was effective and durable. Realistically, as Conlon (2016) points out regarding transfer from primary (elementary) school to secondary, there can be neither a seamless web nor fresh start. She advocates a dialogue between the two phases to establish what students have done. This means, at the very least, secondary teachers having some knowledge of their prior experience. Another way to find out this information is by asking students themselves with the aid of a questionnaire. This also has the benefit of letting them share their personal experience with the teacher. Questions to ask might include the following.

- Do you speak another language fluently?
- What languages have you studied?
- How long did you study the language?
- What type of activities did you do?
- How many words, phrases or sentences can you write down?
- What did you enjoy about your work?
- What challenges did you face?

Further information can be obtained from any general tests done at primary level and any baseline tests carried out at the start of secondary. Since these do not involve a specific test of language aptitude, numerical data must be handled with caution.

The question that obviously arises is what to do with the information. The only pragmatic solution is to work on the basis that (1) in a sense every student is a novice on our specific course and (2) prior knowledge can be recognised and developed. This means adjusting classroom questioning and feedback in very subtle ways to take account of each student's experience. Students (and parents/caregivers) can be quickly frustrated if previous work is not acknowledged, and many are keen to show what they can do. Previous knowledge is to be celebrated and built upon. Where a student arrives with a great deal of prior knowledge then specific work needs to be assigned to enable them to be stretched appropriately. This could be in the form of workbooks, graded reading or specific written or oral tasks.

If there has been a dialogue with local feeder schools, you will also have an idea what meta-language the students may be aware of, memorisation techniques they may use and other language awareness lessons they may have done. But let us be clear. Transfer is an intractable issue for which there is no easy solution. Secondary teachers should recognise that work done in primary schools usually enthuses children and, at the very least, gives them language awareness which helps them as they start their secondary education.

Cognitive empathy

How do we match our teaching to the cognitive and emotional needs of our students? **Cognitive empathy** refers to the extent to which we perceive or have evidence that we have successfully guessed someone else's thoughts and feelings (Hodges and Myers, 2007). For teachers, it is about the ability to match every aspect of teaching (e.g. lesson planning, classroom delivery, feedback, target-setting, homework) to their students' cognition ('the mental action or process of acquiring knowledge and understanding'). In simple terms, it is about empathising with what goes on in the students' minds.

To some extent, formative assessment strategies address this issue – setting objectives, getting feedback, acting on it and moving students forward. Data obtained through baseline testing is also of some use. However, it only provides a snapshot of students' cognition at a specific moment in time. We believe that cognitive empathy requires four main skills areas.

- **An awareness of the cognitive challenges** posed by L2 learning in general and by the specific language items being taught, especially in the planning of a lesson. Why do my students seem to find listening hard? What will they find hard about learning the subjunctive in Spanish?

- **An understanding of how students respond to such challenges**. This involves an awareness of how individual variables affect cognition e.g. age group, gender, personality types, culture, etc. How well will my beginners understand grammatical explanations compared with older students?

- **Metacognition.** Effective teachers instinctively see the importance of marrying their teaching to the cognitive needs of their students, but they also:
  - constantly reflect on their practice as cognitively empathetic teachers, both before, during and after their lessons;
  - use their own past experiences as language learners to enhance their levels of cognitive empathy;
  - start and maintain an ongoing 'metacognitive dialogue' with their students, e.g. through feedback;
  - actively seek ways to further their understanding of the students' cognitive needs.

- **Methodological knowledge and skills**. We also believe it is important that teachers be able to distinguish between more or less valid theories and research. In past years, for example, the hypotheses of **multiple intelligences** and **learning styles** (e.g. VAK – Visual, Auditory and Kinaesthetic) gained a good deal of traction and were applied too unquestioningly. If someone tells us, for instance, that we do not need to teach grammar in the classroom for students to progress, we need to be able to evaluate that claim. If we are told that students need to translate to learn a language, we should be able to critically assess that statement. In other words, if teachers are well versed in theory and methodology, they are more likely to empathise on a cognitive level with their students.

We would also add another skill set, particularly relevant today as teachers debate the merits of technology. We might call it 'meta-digital awareness'. We need to know how a given technological device, programme or app effectively enhances learning. Alas, there is little research to guide us on the most effective ways to use technology, so we can only use our best methodological knowledge about how students learn languages.

Concluding remarks

In this chapter we have made it clear that every classroom contains a diverse range of students. In a sense, every student has a special need, whether they have lower or higher aptitude, a certain type of personality, a specific language learning history, future plans, language learning disability or specific behavioural characteristics. It is always worth reminding ourselves of this simple fact. In the hurly-burly of a teacher's life, with many facing several classes of 30 students per week, each one different, each one at a different stage of learning, it is admittedly not easy to keep up with the personal needs of every single learner. But that is our challenge.

When thinking of the wide diversity of needs in our classrooms, here is an appealing analogy for your consideration.

> *Teaching is a bit like gardening. You have a group of individual specimens with their own precise needs and qualities and your job is to get them to flourish to the greatest possible extent. But, as with gardening, you often need to focus on one specimen at a particular moment. You can't do it all at once... That's real differentiation: pushing, prodding, nudging, stretching... slow, subtle, nuanced, a step at a time, working around the class from lesson to lesson, to the greatest extent you can manage* (Sherrington, 2014).

12

A lexicogrammar perspective: EPI

Introduction

In this chapter we delve into the concept of lexicogrammar and examine how one approach, EPI (Extensive Processing Instruction) applies lexicogrammatical principles to a practical teaching methodology. We consider:

Research evidence
- ✓ What is lexicogrammar?
- ✓ Words and grammar intertwined
- ✓ Multi-word units
- ✓ Working memory
- ✓ Cognitive load theory
- ✓ Priming
- ✓ A skill acquisition perspective

Classroom practice
- ✓ Extensive Processing Instruction (EPI)
- ✓ The MARS-EARS pedagogical cycle
- ✓ Communication and curriculum

Research evidence

What is lexicogrammar?

For a long-time language learning was held to be about knowing how to retrieve words from memory, then combining them using a knowledge of grammatical rules. You could call this a 'dictionary and rules' view of things, where grammatical rules define a sentence skeleton which is fleshed out by words.

More recently, researchers have tended to move towards a perspective that vocabulary cannot be separated out from grammar in this way. The word **lexicogrammar** is used to describe this way of looking at vocabulary and grammar. In this view we learn a language through hearing, seeing and using multi-word units (chunks). As Michael Lewis put it, language is "grammaticalised lexis, not lexicalised grammar" (Lewis, 1993, p. 24). Words and chunks are the starting point.

According to so-called **usage-based** theories of acquisition, we pick out and string together chunks and patterns based on a sub-conscious statistical analysis (the ones we encounter most often, the ones which are not acceptable), and gradually learn to chain them together in utterances. As Andringa and Rebuschat (2015) put it: "Statistical learning holds that language learning results from our sensitivity to the distributional properties of the input" (p. 188).

This **chunk and chain** process. receives support from an analysis of child language use which shows that, rather than combining words with grammar to make novel sentences, very often children use ready-made chunks. A 15-month study by Kenji Hakuta of a Japanese child learning English found evidence of initial use of prefabricated chunks which were later sub-consciously analysed and used to make further language development easier (Hakuta, 1974). To summarise, we begin by using prefabricated chunks, then become more creative as grammatical patterns are picked up. Worth noting is that adult language users also use ready-made chunks much of the time (estimates ranging from 40% to 80% of the time, depending on context).

By the way, the usage-based view of acquisition stands in contrast to the **generativist** idea that we acquire language by slotting words into underlying grammatical rules which we acquire thanks to innate language-specific learning mechanisms.

One possible conclusion for language teachers to draw is that we could attempt to emulate this type of learning by constantly modelling multi-word chunks, centred around the most useful words. This is likely to be more productive than a words and rules approach. Indeed, some writers have suggested that for many students, given the limited time we have with them, being able to manipulate and combine a repertoire of useful chunks, together with vocabulary knowledge and a narrow range of grammatical rules is the best we can hope to achieve (e.g. Lewis, 1993). If we only have students for, say, three years, then a chunking approach makes particular sense as long-term grammatical mastery will not be achieved anyway. In summary, working with chunks reflects to a good degree how we pick up our L1 and can also be recommended for L2 learning.

Words and grammar intertwined

To exemplify how vocabulary and grammar are intertwined, in Conti and Smith (2019) we wrote about the French adjective *beau* (*beautiful*). To be able to claim you know it, besides its pronunciation, spelling and meanings, you also need to know its masculine and feminine forms, how it is pluralised, its position in relation to the noun it accompanies and how it changes when preceding a noun beginning with a vowel. This shows that you cannot really know a word without knowing how it behaves grammatically. Lexical knowledge depends on some grammatical knowledge. We could equally put it the other way round – knowing the grammar of adjectival agreement depends on knowing the form of the words. The interdependence of lexis and grammar is even more obvious if we consider words not on their own, but as interacting with other words in the chunks of language and patterns in which they often occur. Look at use of the word *good* in English; we can identify specific recurring syntactic patterns such as:

- *to be + good + at +* (verb) *–ing* (e.g. to be good at skiing, keeping appointments, making friends);
- *to be + good + at +* noun (e.g. to be good at languages/science);
- *to be in a + good +* noun (e.g. to be in a good state / mood / condition).

Multi-word units

Many terms are given to frequently occurring combinations of words – multi-word units, lexical chunks, stock phrases are just three. In fact, every word in a language is involved in a complex network of patterns and relationships. A distinction is made between lexical patterns (**collocations**) and grammatical patterns (**colligations**). Proficient speakers use a huge number of such language patterns which students need to become aware of over time.

Collocations are common multi-word units such as *to have dinner, to break a record, a worthy cause, to waste time* or *spick and span*. Words are attracted to some more than others, e.g. we talk about *express trains*, but not *express cars*. You can have a *quick look*, but not a *fast look*. Words are closely linked in the mind so that one word triggers its associated collocates (Willis 2003).

Colligations, by contrast, work at the syntactic level and refer to how words form specific grammatical patterns with other words. Words colligate (are tied together) with certain grammatical patterns. Examples of colligation patterns are:

- verb + *-ing* (*I went swimming*);
- verb + pronoun + infinitive (*I want you to go*)
- verb + infinitive (*I began to understand*);
- verb of perception + adjective (*it sounds fab, it looks great*);
- *with/without* + possessive + noun (*with my approval; with my family*);
- *a* + noun + *of* + noun (*a pack of wolves, a box of chocolates, a kilo of potatoes*).

In the early stages of learning a language in the classroom students rely a lot on rehearsed multi-word units. It has been suggested that learners need to build up a large stock of these before they begin to establish an internalised rule system which allows them to become more creative language users (e.g. Pawley and Syder, 1983; Skehan, 1998). This is called an **exemplar-based approach** to L2 development (Taguchi, 2009). Skehan (1998) also suggested that we have two developing language systems, one memory-based, one rule-based. A teacher takeaway here is: give students the chance to hear, see and use lots of ready-made chunks and they will have a solid grounding for future language development. This is one of the principles behind lexicogrammar approaches and, as we shall see, EPI in particular.

Working memory

There are other reasons to support the use of chunking. Effective language processing and learning partly depends on how well working memory performs. Apart from automatic (implicit) processes which bypass our conscious attention, all processing of information (visual, auditory, etc.) is performed by working memory. When students read or listen to L2 input, translating a passage into L2, planning an essay or performing an oral task, it is working memory that does most or all of the work, as they consciously think of the next word to write or what a particular phrase means, for example.

But working memory is finite and fragile. Whether we are processing input from the outside world or retrieving material from long-term memory, working memory can hold information for only about 10 to 15 seconds. After that, we forget, unless a conscious effort is made to keep information there by focusing our attention on it. Think of how we say aloud a phone number to keep it in our head and how this stops us thinking of anything else.

Now, when we try to memorise a phone number, we chunk it into groups of, say, two, three or four numbers. Chunking means compressing larger units of information into smaller more meaningful ones, so that they take up less cognitive space. So, for instance, as we learn to read, instead of processing texts one letter at a time, we learn to chunk the letters into words and words into phrases or sentences. This allows us to read quickly and easily.

Furthermore, when it comes to bits of language, because we have grammatical knowledge which binds words together into meaningful units, a whole sentence of, say, eight words, can be held in memory much more easily than a random list of the same words. Look at these two sets of eight words, then try to remember them afterwards:

PONG BROTHER WITH THE PING HIS PLAYED BOY
THE BOY PLAYED PING PONG WITH HIS BROTHER

The second set was much easier to remember, of course, and might count as one chunk of language in working memory because the words are bound together by our knowledge of grammar, its relationship with meaning and our usage. The more a string of words is used, the stronger the associations become in long-term memory and the easier they are to retrieve. So, thinking back to those two sets of words, whereas we have never come across the first one, we are familiar with the sentence pattern underlying the second (Subject + Verb + Object + Complement). This familiarity makes the sentence easy to chunk, even if it is the first time we have seen it.

To summarise, by grouping commonly co-occurring words and treating them as one larger whole allows the brain to process greater amounts of information. Chunking allows the class to cover plenty of information quickly. Instead of students processing every individual word in a sentence, what each word means and how it relates grammatically to the one next to it, they deal with ready-made chunks. Instead of building fluency one word at a time, they are doing so one phrase at a time.

Cognitive Load Theory

Tied in with working memory and chunking is the issue of cognitive load. A student in a languages classroom is confronted with some serious challenges: an adult talking in a new language, a stream of PowerPoint slides to look at, text to read, instructions to process and an enthusiastic teacher waving their arms about and urging quick responses. Some cope with all this input more easily than others, who struggle to handle the burden on working memory.

This is where the idea of **cognitive load** comes in. This is the amount of information, in our case language, that we must process in working memory at any one time. Put very crudely, it is about how hard we have to think. But as we know, working memory is fragile, has short duration and a very limited capacity. It is also hard to focus on more than one task at the same time. For example, it is known that language learners cannot focus simultaneously on both the form and meaning of a spoken message. They must be prompted if we want them to concentrate on the form.

Consider these three key points (Smith and Conti, 2021):

1. Some things are inherently harder to learn than others, e.g. forming the future tense in French is easier than forming the *passé composé* (perfect tense).

2. The way we present and practise new language affects how successfully it will be taken up, e.g. simultaneously teaching a new grammatical structure with new vocabulary will make it harder for students to focus on one or the other.

3. Finding the right level of challenge is vital – we do not want tasks to be too easy or too hard. For example, with a proficient intermediate class we rarely teach new vocabulary via flashcard slides.

Corresponding with these three issues, a well-known model of cognitive load claims it comes in three forms: ***intrinsic, extraneous*** or ***germane*** (Sweller, 1988). Psychologists argue about the precise definitions of these, and even whether it is possible to divide cognitive load into such neat categories. However, this way of looking at it is useful to teachers who want to understand how working memory can be made to function efficiently and maximise long-term memory. Keeping the input comprehensible and chunking are two ways to control cognitive load.

Priming

This brings us to another important concept for language learning. Speaking our L1 at normal speed seems pretty effortless. We can do this because every time we utter a word or phrase, we sub-consciously associate it with previous and possible future words or phrases. Our vast experience with the language gives us a huge range of possibilities because we have heard or read so many possible combinations. This subconscious process of words affecting the following ones is called **priming**. One word or phrase primes the next.

In second language learning the term priming takes the form of **semantic (lexical) priming, phonological priming** and **syntactic priming**.

1. **Semantic or lexical priming** is when a listener, hearing the word *bread* will recognise words like *baker, butter, knife* more quickly than unrelated words like *chair, cement* or *lightbulb*. For example, if you present the word *transport* a second time, a student processes it faster.

Michael Hoey's (2005) **Lexical Priming Theory** maintains that each time we encounter a word we make a subconscious note of collocations and colligations (see above). Through multiple encounters with that word (**repetition priming**) we become primed to associate it with the most commonly recurring elements. (Think of how, when you enter a word in Google other words immediately appear after it, based on frequency of search or your own previous searches.) As we mention elsewhere, this suggests we should consider teaching vocabulary in chunks and sentences to encourage the lexical priming effect. In this way, retrieving chunks from memory becomes more fluent and effortless.

2. **Phonological priming** is when a word primes another which sounds similar, such as rhyming words. *Light* primes *night* and *bite*. Any teaching which encourages students to notice phonological similarities will help them remember words and phrases. Rhymes are a good example.

3. **Syntactic priming** (also known as structural priming) is when speakers tend to use the same grammatical structures as those they have recently heard or read (Bock, 1986).

This is why it is good to repeatedly use high frequency grammatical patterns in the expectation that students will pick them up both in the short and long term. This can be done, for example, by means of sentence builders, question-answer sequences or other meaningful oral drills, as well as flooding input language with the patterns you want students to pick up. Sets of short paragraphs, each one containing examples of the same grammatical structure, worked on intensively with a range of exercises, can supply the input and interaction needed to encourage syntactic priming. This is the narrow listening and reading described in Chapters 2 and 8 respectively.

A skill acquisition perspective

So far, we have described lexicogrammar and argued why it might form the basis of a teaching methodology. Now let us add another element. Skill acquisition is one of several competing theories of how we learn new languages. It is based on the idea that skilled behaviour in any area can become automatic through repeated pairing of stimuli and responses.

Skill acquisition draws on John Anderson's Adaptive Control of Thought theory (ACT), which he called a cognitivist stimulus-response theory (Anderson, 1982). ACT distinguishes **declarative knowledge** (knowledge of facts and concepts, such as the fact that adjectives agree) from **procedural knowledge** (knowing how to do things in certain situations, such as understand and speak a language), as discussed in Chapter 6.

Researcher Robert DeKeyser (2003) has argued that through practice we can **proceduralise** declarative knowledge of language over time (recall the Interface described in Chapter 6). But he is clear that this only works in some conditions, with some structures and with some learners - typically adult learners with good analytical skills. The theory also claims that the kind of knowledge which can be automatised is very specific and does not transfer to other areas. For example, if we practise speaking we get better at speaking; if we practise listening we get better at listening. To support this claim, experiments have been carried out (e.g. with invented languages) to see if automatisation can take place. They suggest that acquisition of production or comprehension skills is less apparent if only the opposite skill is practised. There are, therefore, different knowledge stores related to different skills. DeKeyser defined 'practice' as "specific activities in the second language, engaged in systematically, deliberately, with the goal of developing knowledge of and skills in the second language" (DeKeyser, 2007, p.1).

Practice can include drills, but DeKeyser argues that **meaningful drills** with the expression of real feelings and thoughts are better than **mechanical drills** aimed merely at practising forms. He says that the transfer of declarative to procedural knowledge is likely to occur when the practice resembles natural communicative activity. This is tied in with the theory that memories are best retrieved when the conditions under which they were created can be replicated (Transfer-Appropriate Processing, see Chapter 6).

So in some conditions knowledge 'that' (declarative) can become knowledge 'how' (procedural). For example, we can learn the rules of how to form a verb tense, then with practice these rules can become internalised so that we can produce correct utterances without thinking about the form of the language. Specifically, a student may have learned to use the perfect tense of French regular verbs in the context of a structured communicative drill. At the beginning they could do the task slowly, having to retrieve and apply the relevant grammar rule consciously (declarative knowledge) and after several repetitions of the task they have mastered it. This is called **routinisation**. If the grammar pattern can then be applied in a wide range of contexts, this is referred to as **automatisation**.

When students have routinised the task (i.e. can perform it easily and speedily) and there are few errors, this is where the typical grammar test, for instance, indicates the student has 'got it' and can apply the grammar rule accurately when doing a similar task (although not necessarily in other tasks). If they can apply the rule to new contexts, e.g. in spontaneous speech, the grammar is automatised.

Objections to skill acquisition theory

The theory has been criticised, for example by Ellis (2009) for a couple of reasons. It does not take account of learners' **in-built syllabus** - the fact that we tend to acquire grammatical structures in a certain, rather fixed order. And secondly, the fact that we seem to acquire lots of knowledge and skill incidentally, without passing through a declarative knowledge stage. So skill theory may be relevant to language learning, notably in school classrooms, but it is far from the whole picture.

Skill theory takeaways

There is evidence that, as we feel intuitively and from experience, that 'practice makes perfect'. We can teach a rule and practise it to the point where comprehension and production become automatic in limited contexts. With some higher-achieving students we see this regularly. It does seem, to some extent, that practising speaking makes for better speakers and practising listening makes for better listeners. But it really is not that simple. The power of implicit, unconscious learning and the fact that some students are clearly more ready than others to acquire new structures means that skill acquisition is only one part of the equation.

Indeed, some would argue that skill acquisition plays a minor role and that it is largely through interacting with input we understand that we become more proficient speakers in the end. In other words, receptive input ultimately benefits output far more than just practising speaking. It is easy to argue, however, that where you only have a limited time (say three years with mixed-achievement groups), the amount of input is not enough to produce proficient speakers so goals need to be limited and may depend relatively more on the acquisition of a narrow range of automatised skills.

The truth about this is unknown, but it would be surprising if both perspectives did not have value. In school settings, where time is limited, teachers may well be right in their assumption that skill acquisition has a role to play, even if results are often disappointing. Would results be any better if no attempt were made to make declarative knowledge procedural? Some say the result of that would be a lot of confusion in students' minds.

Classroom practice

Extensive Processing Instruction (EPI)

All this brings us finally to EPI! This is a methodology devised by Gianfranco, and used widely in schools in the UK and elsewhere. It is founded on the notion of lexicogrammar and combines both implicit (picking up the language through repeated exposure and use) and explicit (explaining and practising in a controlled way) learning modes. Teachers often associate the method with the use of **sentence builders**, a particular type of substitution table containing chunks of language translated into L1. See Table 12.1 for an example which has a focus on the use of superlative forms in French.

The sentence builder is the starting point for a detailed sequence of lessons which stresses the importance of recycling, many times over, chunks or patterns of language. The sequence begins with primarily receptive use of language and gradually moves from controlled to more spontaneous production.

Table 12.1 *An example sentence builder (French)*

Noun	Relative pronoun	Verb phrase	Verb + pronoun	Noun
	que *(whom)*	**j'aime le plus** *(I like the most)* **je n'aime pas** *(I don't like)* **je respecte le plus / le moins** *(I respect the most/ the least)*	**s'appelle** *(is called)*	**Madame** ……….. **Monsieur** ………
La prof **Le prof**	**qui** *(who)*	**a le meilleur sens de l'humour** *(has the best sense of humour)* **m'aide le plus** *(helps me the most)* **me donne le plus de devoirs** *(gives me the most homework)* **me donne les meilleures notes** *(gives me the best grades)*	**enseigne** *(teaches)*	**l'anglais** *(English)* **l'EPS** *(PE)* **le français** *(French)* **la géo** *(geography)* **l'histoire** *(history)* **les maths** *(math(s))* **les sciences** *(science)*
	avec qui *(with whom)*	**je m'entends le mieux** *(I get along best)* **je ne m'entends pas** *(I don't get along)*		

The MARS-EARS pedagogical cycle

The precise teaching sequence, which is highly prescribed when the method is fully embraced, is described by the acronym MARS-EARS (see Table 12.2).

The emphasis is on mastery of a chosen range of language rather than superficial coverage and favours the use of chunked language over the learning of isolated words and verb paradigms. Grammar is taught explicitly during the sequence of lessons in the form of a 'pop-up', not at the start as in a classic PPP approach. A major feature is the aim to engender **self-efficacy** in students (see Chapter 16) - a feeling of confidence that language can be understood and used successfully. Many teachers who have adopted the method report success in this regard. Resources such as workbooks, sentence builders, narrow reading and listening tasks associated with the method are often closely aligned with the requirements of the GCSE syllabus in England, Wales and Northern Ireland, but are applicable to other contexts.

Table 12.2 The MARS-EARS pedagogical cycle

1. Modelling	Constructions, chunks and words are presented and modelled aurally using sentence builders displayed. Sentences are read out which students translate into L1 on mini-whiteboards.
2. Awareness-raising	Awareness is raised of any phonological or grammatical issues you want students to notice (pop-up grammar).
3. Receptive processing	Students do LAM and RAM (Listening/Reading-as-Modelling) tasks containing 95-98% comprehensible input and input-flooding. The aim is for them to hear multiple occurrences of the patterns to strengthen their receptive learning. This phase lasts long enough to be sure that students have developed a solid receptive knowledge.
4. Structured production	The receptive knowledge acquired through listening and reading is now converted into productive knowledge through **pushed output**. This means using highly structured tasks which force students to produce orally and in writing every word/chunk multiple times. With beginners to pre-intermediate learners, this phase unfolds as follows: 1. Chunking aloud tasks (e.g. Sentence Stealer) 2. Oral paired retrieval tasks (e.g. No Snakes No ladders) 3. Communicative drills 4. Communicative tasks
5. Expansion	Two things happen in this phase: (1) the chunks are 'unpacked' to help students understand them. This resembles a grammar lesson, except that they have already memorised the chunks and have become aware of the underlying grammar through exposure and use; (2) the chunks are practised with old and new vocabulary and structures over time through systematic recycling.
6. Autonomy	The teacher decides if the students have reached a degree of autonomy from the sentence builders. This may involve receptive or productive tasks, e.g. communicative tasks carried out without scaffolding.
7. Routinisation	Automatic retrieval (both in the receptive and productive skills) is developed. This requires task repetition and performing these more and more quickly. This phase would typically take two to four lessons.
8. Spontaneity	A communicative task is carried out to assess spontaneity.

Advantages of the approach include the fact that all language is comprehensible, it is recycled many times to enable it to be more easily remembered and the use of chunking makes best use of students' limited working memory capacity. The focus on listening and speaking is notable, as is the gamified nature of many of the tasks associated with the method. Furthermore, a strong emphasis is laid on Listening-as-Modelling (see Chapter 2) rather than listening for testing or just comprehension. Activities are chosen to model the process of listening at different levels: the phonological, lexical and grammatical.

A curriculum based on EPI is tightly structured over a year and more in order to ensure patterns are revisited multiple times within communicative contexts. The phrase 'less is more' is sometimes used to suggest that teachers should focus on mastery rather than 'coverage' (see also Chapter 6 about consolidation).

Communication and curriculum

The starting point of the MARS-EARS cycle is choosing the communicative goals we want students to achieve. Traditional Communicative Language Teaching (CLT) uses the notion of **communicative functions**, i.e. the purpose for our verbal and non-verbal communication. Examples of communicative functions are: *asking questions, describing people, apologising, making excuses, reporting an event in the past, talking about the way one used to be* (Finocchiaro and Brumfit, 1983). The choice of language structures and lexis is based on the principles of high-frequency, learnability and usefulness in real-life communication.

The communicative functions chosen can be broken down into sub-functions. The example in Table 12.3 shows twelve functions and their sub-functions. These could form the basis of a curriculum of about two lessons a week over three years from beginner level. So for instance, the function *Describing and identifying people, including oneself*, is divided into the sub-functions *giving personal information, describing personality, describing physical appearance, expressing likes and dislikes*, etc.

Table 12.3 12 communicative functions and their sub-functions

Describing and identifying people, including oneself (providing personal data, describing appearance, describing personality, etc.)
Describing places, objects and natural phenomena (describing location, size, appearance, weather, etc.)
Creating questions (requesting information - including directions, making invitations, asking for an opinion, etc.)
Expressing one's feelings (expressing positive and negative emotions, reacting to events, providing reasons for one's emotions/reactions)
Making arrangements (making suggestions, inviting, accepting, refusing, etc.)

Comparing and contrasting (expressing likes and dislikes, supporting an opinion, explaining preferences, talking about the best and the worst of someone or something, etc.)

Describing routine behaviour in the present (talking about what one usually does, indicating time, expressing a purpose, etc.)

Describing routine behaviour in the past (talking about what one used to do, indicating time, expressing a purpose, etc.)

Describing past events (setting the scene, sequencing events, evaluating the consequences of actions and events, etc.)

Making plans for the future (indicating time, making predictions, hypothesising, discussing probabilities, etc.)

Indicating agreement and disagreement (expressing opinions on events and phenomena, explaining why, supporting an argument, providing examples)

Solving problems (describing the problem, providing solutions, discussing possible consequences, arguing for and against)

For a current, more detailed exposition of EPI, we suggest reading Conti and Smith (2019) and Gianfranco's blog at gianfrancoconti.com.

Concluding remarks

The notion of lexicogrammar has been explained, along with concepts such as working memory, cognitive load, chunking, priming and skill acquisition theory. A methodology which takes account of this research, combining elements of implicit and explicit learning has been described. Our belief is that this methodology can be an effective solution for teachers and students in high schools working with certain types of syllabus.

Through its combination of implicit and explicit learning, strong focus on comprehensible input, phonology, phonics, recycling of useful chunked language through all four skills and a degree of gamification it has been shown to enjoyable and effective with many classes. Perhaps more fundamental than a specific methodology, however, is the principle that it is through intensive repetition of high-frequency, chunked, useful, comprehensible language in both input and output, that students are most likely to make progress. In contrast, an approach which relies significantly on the learning of isolated words and grammar rules is less likely to work for most, possibly all students.

13

Assessment

Introduction

Assessment plays an important role since it is vital to inform students of their progress, determine their strengths and weaknesses and provide feedback. What teachers assess, how and why sends a clear message about what is worth learning, how it should be learned, and how well they are expected to learn it. As we shall see, assessment has a direct influence our teaching.

In this chapter we have brought together research and classroom practice by considering:

✓ Formative assessment, with practical examples
✓ Summative assessment (validity, reliability, washback, practicality, authenticity, the piloting of tests, assessing fluency, types of question, etc)
✓ Putting grades on work
✓ Marking and feedback
✓ Putting grades on work
✓ Assessing speaking

Formative assessment with practical examples

There are commonly said to be two types of assessment, one called formative, the other summative assessment. Precise definitions vary, but in a nutshell, formative assessment is about activities, including questioning, quizzes and tests, that provide feedback. This allows the teacher to respond and help students become more responsible for their own learning. Other terms which have been used in this context include **responsive teaching** (Fletcher-Wood, 2018), **adaptive teaching** and **assessment for learning** (Black *et al.*, 2002). Formative assessment is based on the idea that all students can improve and are actively involved in their own learning. Formative assessment helps teachers identify concepts that students are struggling to understand and skills they are having difficulty acquiring.

Formative assessment takes place on a day-to-day basis during lessons, allowing teachers and students to assess progress and adapt teaching and learning. It begins with the principle that good teaching starts from where our students are, rather than where we would like them to be, and because what they learn from their classroom experience is often unpredictable, we need to know where they are in their learning before we decide what to do next (Wiliam, 2021). If a teacher and student understand what has been achieved to date, it is easier to plan the next steps. As learning continues, further formative assessment indicates whether teaching plans need to be adjusted to reinforce or extend learning. Formative assessment may not be formally recorded at all but will influence future lesson and curriculum plans.

Examples of formative assessment can be found in Jones and Wiliam (2007).

- Sharing learning objectives and success criteria with students, the aim being to enable them to develop the capacity to own and monitor their own progress as independent language users. This needs to be supported by developing students' meta-language, i.e. how to talk about their subject and their learning.

- Using effective questioning to enable all students to take part in lessons, whatever their personalities and degrees of confidence; this could include use of cold-calling.

- Using the 'question basketball' technique. This means asking a question to a random student, then choosing another for an evaluation of the answer, then another to provide an explanation of why the answer is correct or incorrect.

- Using 'wait time': a strategy to encourage students to reflect on the quality of their answers. Examples of prompts include: "What can we add to X 's answer?" or "Do you agree with X's answer?"

- Using response systems which involve all students at once to assess their progress in the lesson, e.g. asking if a word is correct and asking them to respond with thumbs up or down. This can create what Jones and Wiliam call a 'teachable moment', when the teacher asks a student "You thought this was correct/incorrect - can you tell me why?" This technique can also be used with multiple choice answers and cards, mini-whiteboards or digital voting systems such as Mentimeter (mentimeter.com).

- Getting students to act on feedback. It may seem hard to encourage them to do this. One simple technique is to tell them that there are errors and provide time in class to put them right. The errors could be classified by spelling, verb endings, gender, missing words, etc.

As language teachers we are engaged in formative assessment much of the time, as we mentally record and respond to students' answers, observe what they write on their mini-whiteboards, monitor pair work, grade written assignments and tests, and so on. End-of-unit tests are particularly useful formal sources of information as we plan the next steps.

Wiliam (2023) reminds us that it is all too common to work through a curriculum plan without adapting sufficiently to students' needs, so some are often left behind in our desire to cover everything in the curriculum. For language teachers, this is a reminder that the curriculum or textbook may be overloaded, especially with grammar, and that we need to respond sensitively to what students can do at every stage. In general, it is better to master less material well, than more material badly, as mentioned previously.

Summative assessment

A summative assessment may be a written test, an observation, a conversation or a task. It may be recorded through writing, photographs or other visual media, or through a recording. Whichever medium is used, the assessment shows what has been achieved.

The goal of summative assessment is to evaluate learning at the end of a unit of work, year or course, comparing it against some standard or benchmark. Summative assessment is often termed 'high stakes' if it contributes to a school's accountability system or is a recognised public exam. Information from summative assessments can be used formatively when students or teachers use the results to guide their future work, e.g. to set targets. Here are some issues relating to summative assessment. Pachler et al. (2014) summarise the reasons why we do summative assessment:

- To generate information for students about their learning.
- To ensure that learning objectives have been reached.
- To motivate students.
- To gather data for reporting.
- To select students for groupings or for opportunities in later life.
- To identify strengths and weaknesses in students.
- To provide certification.
- To fulfil statutory requirements.
- To measure standards which may be used to hold teachers accountable.

We need to consider a range of issues concerning summative assessment.

Validity and reliability

A test is considered **valid** when it reflects the test-takers' ability in a particular area and the test does not measure anything else. Validity is a complex concept in testing, but Brown and Abeywickrama (2010) summarise the main points. In order to achieve validity a test should :

- measure only what it claims to measure;
- rely as much as possible on empirical evidence;
- involve performance that samples the test criterion;
- offer meaningful and useful information about a test-taker's ability;
- be supported by a theoretical rationale.

A test is considered **reliable** if it is administered on different occasions and similar results are obtained. Brown and Abeywickrama (2010) suggest the following ways to ensure that a test is reliable:

- It is consistent in its conditions across two or more tests.
- It gives clear directions for scoring or evaluation.
- It has uniform mark schemes (rubrics) for scoring or evaluation.
- It lends itself to consistent application of those mark schemes by teachers.
- It contains items or tasks that are unambiguous to the test-takers.

Some types of test question are more reliable than others. Multiple-choice and true/false questions are more reliable than essay-style questions. An essay or conversation is assessed using a level-based mark scheme, which is inherently unreliable, since evidence shows that different teachers will give different grades. A multiple-choice question is objective and reliable but lacks validity if the aim is to assess the use of grammar and vocabulary in spontaneous production.

Research on assessment and Transfer-Appropriate Processing theory indicate students do best on tasks when they are familiar with them. When they are not familiar with a test type, anxiety and higher cognitive load are the result. By doing a task repeatedly prior to an assessment, students develop strategies which ease cognitive load. To take a simple example, it would be unwise to test knowledge of grammar through translation into L2 unless they had had a good deal of practice at that skill.

Bearing in mind test validity, a mark scheme (rubric) has to place appropriate emphasis on the skills you wish to test: if you have been working on a range of areas, e.g. accuracy, fluency, vocabulary range, and grammatical complexity, you would not wish to assess students primarily on accuracy.

When it comes to assessing grammar, we need to be clear whether we are assessing declarative knowledge (knowing the rules) or how grammar is used spontaneously (procedural knowledge). If grammar is tested through gap-fill (cloze) tests, the focus is on declarative knowledge of structures, but not necessarily the extent of the students' actual control over them (i.e. the ability to use grammar in real conditions, in relatively spontaneous speech or written output). An oral picture task, spontaneous conversational exchange or written composition would be more accurate ways to assess the extent of a student's procedural knowledge, i.e. their real control over grammar and vocabulary.

A word about listening at this point. Listening is usually assessed solely through comprehension tasks. This does not test an important set of listening skills, what we might call 'listenership', i.e. the ability to respond to another person in real conversation. If we only test students through comprehension tasks, the grade we give only reflects one set of listening skills (comprehending a text), but not the one they need the most in real-life interaction, listening to another speaker as part of a conversation.

Washback

At this point it is worth returning to the important concept of washback which was referred to in Chapters 8 and 9. As a reminder, washback is "the effect of testing and assessment on the language teaching curriculum that is related to it" (Brown and Hudson, 1998 p. 667). It is also used to refer to the influence that a test has on teaching and learning (Hughes, 2003). Positive washback is when a test is aligned with and has a favourable effect on teaching materials and procedures. For example, if we think that summarising is a valuable classroom activity, if summary is used in an exam we can say the exam has a positive washback effect. In contrast, negative washback would be the result if a test question did not align with what we consider good teaching practice. For example, if we believed that too much translation was an undesirable in class, the inclusion of translation in an exam may have a negative washback effect since we would feel obliged to do a good deal of translation practice in preparation for the exam.

An example of a possible mismatch between teaching and assessment is when an exam requires students to infer the meaning of unfamiliar words. This would assess not language learned during the course, but **compensation strategies** (in this instance guessing meaning from context). Although compensation strategies can be taught and are important, a valid test needs to assess them only on what has been taught and not on strategies. A test like this might be perceived by students and teachers as unfair.

Practicality

Practicality refers to the logistical, practical, and administrative issues involved in the process of designing, administering, and marking (grading) a test. Bachman and Palmer (1996) define practicality as "the relationship between the resources that will be required in the design, development, and use of the test and the resources that will be available for these activities" (p. 36). Practical issues typically involve the types of room needed for listening tests and the time it takes to do individual speaking tests. Other issues concern the practicality and reliability of doing online testing and the difficulties involved with using video resources for listening. Video is appealing, and arguably more authentic, but administering video listening tests for large cohorts of examinees is problematic.

Speaking assessments present a particular challenge. You will want to find ways to avoid these impinging upon your class time. You may consider holding them outside class time: assessing pairs of students during the lesson, doing **continuous assessment** over a year (keeping a record of a student's performance), assessing individuals while the others get on with another speaking task or prepare for the assessment. A classroom assistant may be able to play a useful role in this context. Digital recording devices or a phone can be used to record summative tasks being carried out in groups or pairs as you go round the classroom: you need to get students to accept this as the norm so that they do not clam up when they see you approaching!

There are other practical issues to be aware of. In formal tests it should be impossible for students to copy others' work. Tables can be arranged to discourage this or, if space is limited, they may place a bag or other barrier on the table. Conditions need to be adequate for listening tests: background noise should be at a minimum, tone controls of any audio device should be set with the treble to maximum and bass to minimum and you should be clear how many times you intend to repeat an item. If an item is judged to be too fast or unclear, be flexible and play the item more times (unless doing a formal exam). For routine school tests, exams and open-ended assignments, have measures in place for those who finish well before the majority to avoid the possibility of distracting behaviour.

Handing back tests or examinations, and going through them with the class, can be a challenge. Students tend to get quite excited and have so many questions that good order may be compromised. One solution is to provide a set of model answers to work on quietly, allowing them to check that their work was correctly assessed.

Authenticity

Authenticity in language assessment has its roots in communicative language teaching (CLT). It is about producing tests which resemble real-life language use. Authenticity is regarded as one of the main ways to judge how useful a test is for language assessment (Bachman and Palmer, 1996). In the 1970s some writers rejected the ideas of reliability and validity, arguing that they are not reconcilable – you cannot have both. Within the CLT approach, communicative tests were supposed to be judged subjectively and qualitatively by a sympathetic assessor (Fulcher, 2000). Authenticity and real-life assessment tasks became the key concepts underpinning CLT.

In world language classrooms, we still see a nod to authenticity with test types such as role-play, unscripted conversation, comprehension of street signs, food labels and leaflets, listening to authentic or adapted audio extracts and the use of social-media posts and authentic or adapted authentic texts. Lip service is paid to authenticity in questions such as "Write a social media post in which you talk about yourself and your interests".

An issue here concerns the washback effect. If the form of the assessment involves a task with at least some elements of real-life language use, this may help generate more motivating lessons which seem relevant to students. This is a selling-point for task-based approaches, where they may be engaged with problem-solving activities, using language spontaneously. The problem remains, however, that the assessment of real-life tasks may lack reliability, which, for high-stakes exams, is a key factor. We should not expect to see the early demise of multi-choice, gap-fill and comprehension questions.

Piloting tests

Administering a test without piloting it can be problematic even if the test comes from a widely used textbook assessment pack. Ambiguous pictures and solutions, speed of delivery, inconsistency and test validity issues are not uncommon flaws of some course books' assessment materials. The first use of an assessment reveals any problems, so it is better to pilot the test first, perhaps with a colleague. If the test has issues, it may need adapting. This could mean reading aloud a transcript to slow it down or insert pauses, altering the questions to make them simpler or harder, or omitting certain sections of the test. The aim is to achieve a standard that is achievable by all. If one aim is to produce a rank order of students, then the test needs to be challenging enough to produce a range of scores, ideally no less than 50%.

When it comes to setting larger scale tests, such as end-of-year exams, experience should help with planning the following year's paper. Issues to address for revision might be: some questions turned out to be too easy, or confusing; the exam was too short or too long; grades were too high, low or failed to discriminate adequately between students.

Assessing fluency

Fluency is an aspect of language performance that is often neglected in summative assessment even though it is the most important indicator of the level of control someone has achieved in comprehension and production. While fluency is often a criterion in speaking test assessment, in reading and writing this is not the case.

Let us look more closely at assessing written fluency. In speaking, fluency (responding quickly and maintaining a flow at reasonable speed) is a relevant aspect of speech to measure, but in writing, which traditionally allows for reflection and checking, we rarely assess quick response speed and flow. Only in test situations do students really have to write under time pressure and, even then, the time allocated generally gives them time to think carefully about what they are producing.

Given that, one of the few authentic ways students may use their L2 writing is in interpersonal, social networking situations such as instant messaging, as we saw in Chapter 9. We could easily include an element of speed work both in teaching and testing by including a task to be done within a strict time limit. This could be, for example, a set of instant messaging-style prompts or questions to which the student must provide quick responses in whole sentences or mini paragraphs. The emphasis would be on successful communication rather than accuracy. Perhaps not all would complete the task, but if it is explained that the aim of the assessment is to see how well they can respond quickly (and they have been trained in doing this), this could be viewed as an acceptable way to assess written fluency.

In essay writing, you could assess fluency by setting a time and word limit for the task and note down the time of completion for each student. We usually do not differentiate between those who score equally across accuracy, complexity and vocabulary, but who do differ substantially in terms of writing fluency, i.e. the time-to-word ratio. There is no doubt that speed is a useful measure of both oral and written fluency.

Discrete skill and integrated-skill assessment

If you wish to test one skill, listening for example, you may be tempted to do so by excluding any requirement to read, speak or write in L2. By including these other skills it may be impossible to know for sure whether you are just testing listening (test validity). This presents a dilemma, since generally in the classroom you would not wish to isolate skills in this fashion. For example, to stay in L2 and maximise exposure, you may want to combine a listening task with spoken or written responses in L2.

In this context you will need to keep in mind the risk of the washback effect referred to earlier. Just because the assessment concerns a 'discrete skill' does not mean you have to use discrete skill classroom activities all the time, but you will need to 'teach to the test' to some extent so that students are familiar with the test format. It is also worth bearing in mind that if the instruction for a task is in L2 it is quite possible that students will misinterpret what they must do. Where instructions are typically given in L2, they need training in recognising the instructions and format.

Types of test question

Table 13.1 shows some common test question types, along with advantages and disadvantages.

Table 13.1 Common test question types

Question type	Advantages	Disadvantages
True/false/not mentioned	3 options give reliable scores for rank ordering (more reliable than just true/false)	Can be confusing and hard to create, e.g. the difference between false and not mentioned may be confusing for students
Written L2 questions	Integrates skills of listening, reading and writing; positive washback	Hard to be certain what is being assessed, comprehension or written skill; text may be understood, but questions not
Written L1 questions	Tests comprehension reliably	Negative washback (may promote too much L1 use in the classroom); discourages integrated skill practice
Multiple choice	Objective and reliable	Only tests certain things, e.g. comprehension, vocabulary and grammar; possible negative washback effect; lacks test authenticity; time-consuming to design
Gap-fill	Objective and reliable; can test grammar and/or comprehension	Lacks test authenticity; possible negative washback
Free writing	Tests procedural knowledge and language skill; gives some choice to students; has some test authenticity; positive washback	Hard to grade reliably; does not force students to produce targeted language
Photo card	Tests procedural knowledge; open-ended; gives students some freedom; positive washback.	May be hard to assess reliably
Matching (e.g. starts and ends of sentences)	Objective and reliable; can test grammar and comprehension	No authenticity; answers may be obtained without much comprehension if students look at the form of the language
Conversation	Students have control over the content; positive washback; emphasises procedural knowledge	May encourage too much rote learning; not easy to assess reliably; time consuming
Role play	A degree of authenticity; particular language can be targeted	If prompts are in L2 there may be confusion; students have little control over content

Multiple choice questions (MCQs)

MCQs can be used for both summative and formative assessments. Well-constructed MCQs are an effective way to assess listening and reading and to find out what students know. Writing good multi-choice tasks is an interesting challenge for teachers and examiners. The assessment statisticians say that three options are as effective as four, although four or more choices are often given on exam papers. For an even more subtle use of multiple choice to limit the chance of guessing a correct answer, you can design questions with, say, two correct answers out of five, or multiple selection.

It is important with multi-choice for assessment purposes that all options be 'in play'. That is, the distractors must be plausible to the student. When the aim is to reveal the range of skill in a class (e.g. for a higher stakes summative assessment), a good multi-choice question should allow most to get the answer right. A good balance of outcomes would be around 70% get the right option, with the other two options getting about 15% each. A question which attracts equal responses for each option is a poor one. Some examination awarding bodies pilot questions and reject those which produce unwanted outcomes, i.e. which do not produce a valid comparison between students. See Xu *et al.* (2016) for more on MCQs.

Types of mark scheme (rubrics)

In formal assessments or public exams there are two types of mark scheme. The first is a more objective points-based scheme with one mark for each answer and little or no doubt about the correct answer, such as true-false and multiple-choice questions. The second is a level-based scheme, commonly used to assess speaking and compositional writing. This is inevitably more subjective since, as research and experience clearly show, humans apply such schemes inconsistently. Inconsistent marking by examination boards is a common complaint among teachers. If a languages department is using level-based mark schemes, it is advisable for teachers to spend some time trying to agree common standards when applying the scheme or else for one teacher to mark across the board.

Regarding essay grading, you might think that providing a detailed mark scheme would improve the accuracy of marking (it does), but it also leads to students jumping through hoops, e.g. shoe-horning set phrases, expressions of opinion and verb tenses to satisfy the marking criteria. This can stifle creativity.

Marking and feedback

Marking is often considered the bane of teachers' lives, so it is worth asking why we mark students' work and if there are ways of limiting the load. Here is our own list of reasons for marking which we deliberately put in order of importance.

1. To check students have done the work.
2. To show students you care about their work.
3. To check they have understood the work.
4. To show where they have gone wrong and what was done well.
5. To build your personal relationship with each student.
6. To give them more detailed feedback.

Let us elaborate. **Points 1 and 2** are key and are sometimes overlooked in this era when so much research is being done into the role of feedback. The most important thing about a piece of work or homework is that it is completed and that it is done with care and attention. We know that improvement in language skills comes with input and interaction. The more practice students do, the more proficient they become. If they know we are going to read their work and assess it on a regular basis they are more likely to take it seriously and put the time in. If we only collect work in to mark twice a term, we may quickly discover scruffy exercise books and careless work.

Point 3 is vital. We hopefully set work that is accessible to our students, not too easy, not too hard. We hope they do not make too many errors. If they do, it is likely the task was poorly set. If every student gets everything right, then it is at least possible that the work was too easy. Regular marking gives you some of the vital feedback you need on the effect of your teaching.

Point 4 may be over-valued. Corrections are useful, but in a sense, if there are errors, the damage is already done. The question is, has the student done the work and thought things through? How much do you think you should correct? With the fastest students you may wish to be fussy and correct everything, be hyper-critical with accuracy and range. This will, you hope, encourage them to do even better in future. With weaker students, if the work is riddled with mistakes, then you may choose to correct selectively, probably focusing on one important area such as verb errors. To smother work in red (or green?) ink is discouraging and unless there is a recognised system in place to respond positively to corrections, they are unlikely to give them more than a cursory glance.

Point 5 is significant. In lessons with 30 students it is not easy to find much one-to-one time. A well-chosen comment on a piece of work - a humorous remark, an acknowledgement of extra effort for example - unseen and unheard by others, can help you establish a personal relationship between you and the student. This can go a long way in the classroom.

Point 6 is much discussed and there is ample research evidence that feedback aids learning. Hattie (2011) places feedback in his top ten of interventions which can aid achievement. Should the feedback be in L2? Quite possibly, but a word or two in L1 may carry more psychological weight. Writing "wow!" or "amazing!" or "nice touch!" or "ouch!" in the margin will have a stronger reinforcing effect than its equivalent in L2.

Remember that this is your chance to build a confidential rapport with the student and to provide private feedback. You may do that more effectively working in the mother tongue. Detailed feedback needs to be clear too; L2 feedback may be confusing. Your comments in an exercise book are a tiny fraction of the comprehensible input your students get. You do not need be overly concerned with staying in L2 all the time.

The influential psychologist Carol Dweck (2012), as part of her 'growth' theory of intelligence, suggests the following principles when giving feedback.

- Avoid giving person-directed praise, e.g. "you're good at this"; rather give process-directed praise such as "that was a good way to work out what the reading passage meant" or "you tried very hard to construct more complex sentences".
- Give task-oriented praise that focuses on the criteria for success, e.g. "there are far fewer spelling mistakes this time" or "you got your auxiliary verbs right".
- In as far as possible, make summative assessments more of a private than public event, encouraging a student that they are not being compared with others but with their last performance to see how they are improving.

Putting grades on work

There is no clear answer to this question. Many teachers believe grades are a source of extrinsic motivation (see Chapter 16), others that they encourage students to value the grade, not the learning. Both views have merit. The research on grading is mixed and complex. Guskey (2019) summarises studies going back over half a century. He finds that grades have their limitations, but are not inherently good or bad. They are labels attached to levels of student performance, describing in an abbreviated fashion how well they have performed. The labels can be letters, numbers, words, phrases, or symbols. They can serve formative purposes by helping students know where they are on the path to achieving specific learning goals. On the other hand, it is undoubtedly true that many look more at the grade and less at any corrections or formative comments we write on their work. (This issue can be handled by requiring students to respond to comments or write corrections.)

Your department or school may well have a policy on allocating grading and on marking in general. Some school policies are quite prescriptive in this regard. In some school cultures students may even be disappointed not to receive a grade. Because grading is such a complex and subtle process, you might consider grading 'tactically'. A very high-achieving student may be disappointed if you drop them to a lower grade if their work is marginally less careful than usual. It is probable they will try extra hard next time. The converse may apply to lower-achieving students. They may be delighted with a higher grade and try harder next time.

So marking will sometimes spoil a weekend, but language teachers can take some comfort in two things: it is a pleasure to mark really good work and we are not history teachers; their marking probably takes a good deal longer!

Assessing speaking

As we have seen, speaking is the skill which presents the biggest assessment challenge. If you teach several classes of 30 students, it takes a great deal of time to assess each one individually. Should you formally assess at all, once a year or more regularly? What are the other students doing if you are assessing an individual? If you choose to assess outside the lesson, how does this impact on your own time?

When you assess, how do you balance pre-learned, memorised material against more spontaneous talk? How do you allocate marks for pronunciation, complexity, fluency (speed? maintaining flow?), grammatical accuracy and relevance. Do you wish to assess presentational language or inter-personal speaking? If both, what should the balance be? How do you cope with students who have a special need, such as stuttering or poor hearing? How do you handle those who get into a panic when they have to perform one-to-one? Here are four general organisational models which teachers could adopt, notwithstanding any existing policies your school or department may have.

1. **Informal approach**. Keep a general record of student response during lessons, allocating a grade every few weeks. Grades can be monitored particularly carefully during any pair or small group work tasks. If students are told in advance that pair or group work will be graded, this will add some more pressure to the task, but should also obtain a superior performance. This approach is less time-consuming than others, but you may feel that only a one-to-one assessment is fair to all.

2. **An annual or biannual speaking assessment.** With this approach, emphasise the importance of the assessment, raise its status and allow a good amount of time to prepare. With novice students, the bulk of the assessment would focus on pre-learned material but, where possible, some element of unpredictability should be introduced. It is important to bear in mind, however, that many students have difficulty producing spontaneous speech, so they need the opportunity to show off what they have learned. There is nothing wrong with this. In other school subjects, rote learned material plays an important role and there is no reason why this aspect should not be part of assessment for language students.

    Time constraints might mean you are limited to no more than 3-5 minutes per student. They can come to the front or, if your classroom allows for it, you might be able to have a more private area. While you are assessing one student, the others can be preparing in pairs for their own assessment. In this way, they will not be able to listen to those being assessed. If you are fortunate enough to have a classroom assistant, they can monitor the work of the others.

3. **Unit speaking assessments.** In this model, a brief oral assessment is conducted at the end of every unit of work. That might mean every four to five weeks. This has the merit of not 'putting all the eggs in one basket', so students can afford to have the occasional bad day. On

the other hand, it is very time-consuming and may take time away from other work you want to do with classes. Technology can make the process less burdensome.

4. **A technological approach.** Although you would probably wish to include an element of interpersonal speaking with the teacher, digital technology does provide other ways to assess. Students can record individual and pair work, or individual presentations. They could do this on a regular basis, sending you their work which you can assess at your leisure. Digital platforms make this easy to monitor. The parameters for the work would have to be clearly laid out, so that students do not engage in unfair practice or just read aloud.

   If you have access to a language laboratory, you may be able to assess individuals in real time, while other students are getting on with another task. The others may not even know an individual is being assessed. If they can work in pairs using the lab, you can listen in to assess. At some point, however, many students will need to have the experience of being tested by the teacher in preparation for high-stakes examinations such as the GCSE, International Baccalaureate or A-levels.

5. **Surprise tests**. This may seem a bit unfair on students, but giving an impromptu test has the advantage of lowering pre-test stress and reduces the chance of them rote-learning responses. So you get an instant assessment of what they can do based on their current level of knowledge and skill.

In terms of what to assess, mark schemes (rubrics) should reward a range of skills, but in particular the successful delivery of unambiguous messages. Getting the message across is by far the most important thing to reward. This implies that other marks are likely to favour clarity (e.g. accurate pronunciation and intonation), flow of language, range of language appropriate to the task and, least important, accuracy. Minor errors (those which do not have an impact on meaning) can be virtually ignored. Even more significant errors, such as verb tense errors, may not deflect the listener too much from the intended meaning. At all stages in the language learning process, students need to know that actually communicating takes priority over being accurate. The same principles apply to writing. Assessment mark schemes and task rubrics should reflect this.

Concluding remarks

Many teachers may find the fine detail of assessment less of a priority and even less interesting than the creative aspects of classroom pedagogy and management. Nevertheless, it is an integral part of the teaching process and it is useful to be aware of the main issues involved. Most teachers find themselves working within a statutory environment where it is important to be fully aware of any assessment principles and mark schemes. They would be well advised to read carefully, at the earliest opportunity, any official documentation relating to exams their students are taking.

14

Teaching advanced level students

Introduction

One of the great pleasures for language teachers is the opportunity to work with students who have gone beyond the novice and intermediate stage and can begin to communicate at a more advanced level. They may be doing a compulsory course or, as is often the case, they will have opted to study the language to a higher level and so bring greater levels of motivation to the classroom. In addition, by this stage there may be a closer match between their level of maturity and their ability to understand and use the language, so it becomes possible to work with more substantial and potentially more stimulating subject matter.

We refer elsewhere to two somewhat conflicting views of how students acquire second languages. Firstly, the 'natural' approach where learning a second language is seen to be much like learning a first language as a child. Secondly, the skill acquisition theories where language learning is thought to resemble, to a degree, any form of learning and where greater stress is laid on conscious attention to the form of the second language.

At an advanced level it should become possible to take advantage of the more natural approach. There are two reasons for this. First, you often get to spend more time with students working at advanced level so there is more opportunity to expose them to large amounts of meaningful input. Second, by this stage many will have a sound knowledge of the essential rules of syntax such as verb tense formation and morphological rules. This means you should be able to spend less time presenting and practising new structures and more time just using the language for authentic communication, for example discussing topical issues, cultural matters such as film and literature and whatever themes form part of the course you are teaching.

Many of the same techniques you use with novice and intermediate students still apply at advanced level. Skilled questioning and other interactions, creative use of pair and group work, judicious use of translation and appropriate choice of authentic and near-authentic listening and reading resources all continue to play a role. But at this higher level you can focus more closely on written skills, broadening vocabulary and higher-level grammatical structures. Even at this stage some will need teaching from scratch, so there is still plenty of room for presentation and controlled practice.

233

This chapter considers:

- ✓ Task-based activities
- ✓ Teaching film and literature
- ✓ Essay planning and writing

Task-based activities

One by-product of the communicative movement in language teaching was what are known as task-based activities. At all stages, but especially at advanced level, it is possible to design language learning activities where small groups work together to perform a task and achieve a specific objective. The idea is that they will be more motivated to communicate when they have a non-linguistic goal to achieve. Students use L2 to work together, negotiate, take decisions and arrive at an outcome.

Here are three examples which have worked effectively with our classes.

1. **Newsroom.** In this task, small groups of students play the role of news reporters who are given a list of stories for the day. They must discuss the relative importance of each story and decide on a running order. They then write a script for their news bulletin which they subsequently record on video and play back to the teacher and their peers. They can give each other specific roles: news anchor, roving reporter, interviewee and so on.

2. **Dinner party.** In this example, taken from the book *Discussions that Work* by Penny Ur (1981), students in a team must organise the seating at a formal dinner. They are provided with a list of characters, each with a pen portrait, and a set of criteria for the seating plan. Men must sit next to women, and members of the same family should not sit together. The guests are deliberately chosen to have disparate qualities, e.g. different ages, religious or political beliefs, personality traits. The students negotiate their solution, then present it orally to the teacher and their peers.

3. **Weekend break.** Here students are provided with tourist information for a particular city. Each is also given their own personality portrait, including their likes and dislikes. Between them, students must plan their activities for a weekend city break. They subsequently present their solution to the rest of the class, justifying their choices.

All the above tasks generate a good deal of enthusiasm, language input and opportunities for listening and speaking. The challenge for you as the teacher is to ensure that the enthusiasm of the students does not lead to them using too much L1. These tasks also imply the use of certain functions of language, such as agreeing, disagreeing and suggesting. Provide phrases such as *we could…, why don't we…, what if…, I agree, I disagree, we ought to…* If you wish to add more structure to such tasks, adding a greater focus to specific language, you can ask them to use certain phrases a given number of times. Students are very adept at doing this and enjoy incorporating phrases in their conversation repertoire.

Making text work more communicative – 'Ask the experts'
(from Conti and Smith, 2019)

This activity gets students asking and answering questions about a written text.

- First, print off **four short paragraphs** on a chosen topic. When combined, these should form a coherent whole, e.g. the description of a city, information about a famous person or key points in a discussion about the climate crisis. Second, write and print off **about 10 questions** on the topic.

- Explain the activity in L1. Four students are chosen (or volunteer) to be 'experts' on the topic. Each expert has one of the four printed paragraphs. The remainder of the class works in pairs, with each pair having a set of questions. One partner is a scribe, the other a seeker of information from the experts. The seekers have to obtain answers to their questions from the four experts, then report back to the scribe who notes them down.

- Monitor as students move around seeking answers to their questions and reporting back to the scribes.

- The pairs then discuss the written notes and prepare to feed back. The four experts can join in with pairs to help.

- An alternative version does away with the pairs. Each seeker of information simply notes the answers to summarise to the teacher or to write down as a summary.

Teaching film and literature

The themes we teach may be largely dictated by the course being followed and will often be closely linked to L2 cultures. Topics can be chosen by how well they lend themselves to producing communicative lessons. This may mean considering students' own interests and concerns, but bear in mind also that our role is to broaden their horizons to new knowledge and issues. At this point in their development students are often keen to debate topics and develop their understanding.

Even if the course is founded on L2 culture do not avoid issues pertinent to the students' own cultures: current affairs and dramatic world events lend themselves well to classroom discussion as it is quite possible to go *off piste* from time to time.

At advanced level film and literature are an integral part of many courses, while students can also choose to explore other areas of cultural interest such as history, art, music and politics. We now look in detail at the teaching of film and literature.

Film

Choosing the right film

Films are, of course, an excellent source of authentic listening and provide an outstanding way of learning more about L2 cultures. They often feature in advanced level courses. Students, familiar as they are with the medium, enjoy movie watching and, with the aid of sub-titles, are exposed to large amounts of meaningful language input. Sometimes we have a free choice of which film to teach. But we may also be constrained by a list of films from the syllabus. In either case, we should choose one which corresponds with our own tastes as well those of our students. If we are enthusiastic about the film, it is much more likely our students will be too. We also need to take into account speed and clarity of the dialogue and whether the film is appropriate.

When teaching with an examination in view, bear in mind the availability of support materials for studying the film. The school library should be stocked with supporting resources (books on films or directors from the L2 country and at least one extra copy of the DVD, if that technology is still used) and online resource links should be shared with students. These are invaluable when working together on the film. There are specialist websites which provide ready-made support materials such as lesson plans and handouts, but these should be assessed for quality and may need adapting. One to recommend is *dolanguages.com* by Steve Glover. Or else design in-house resources. Consider collaborating with other colleagues in person or online when creating support materials. Facebook has professional groups dedicated to individual films.

Try to source DVDs or other digital copies with useful bonus features which will enhance teaching. Some films are viewable online, of course, but you may wish to supply individual copies if students need to study it in detail or review it several times. Consider creating a blog or shared area of the school's digital platform on which links, reviews and ideas can be shared.

How to approach films

Pre-viewing

If studying a film in detail or working on it in preparation for an exam, it is a good idea to do some tasks preparing students for the content of the film. This could mean looking at the life of the director, briefly studying the setting of the film, if this is important, or the historical context. Some themed vocabulary work can be done if the film features a particular range of lexis. Also introduce a range of generic language which students will find useful when reading and discussing the film: character, themes, plot, structure and film-making terminology.

They may benefit from a general introduction to film-making, looking at the history of film, directorial techniques, types of shot, types of film, and roles in the film-making business. At some point they will need to understand and use language such as close-up, long shot, panning, dolly shot, zoom, freeze frame, cutting, editing, framing, soundtrack, camera angle, establishing shot and so on. Introduce this language early or bring it in at appropriate times when viewing the film.

Studying the film

There is a wide range of oral, reading and writing tasks to do when studying a film. Remember that a film is just one example of authentic spoken language, therefore the full spectrum of tasks used with any listening resource can be employed. Research evidence suggests it is best to show films with sub-titles. A study by Guichon and McLornan (2008) of French undergraduates learning English found that after viewing a 3-minute BBC news report, students who had access to captions (in English) were better able to produce a detailed summary of the information after viewing the report.

After the first viewing it is common to watch sections of the film in sequence with handouts to be completed in class, at home or during personal study time at school. These might be in the form of comprehension questions or, at a simpler level, matching tasks, gap-fill, true-false statements or ticking correct statements. Traditional comprehension questions are effective because they generate a good deal of listening and reading comprehension, as well as oral interaction. Some teachers like to provide a plot or scene-by-scene summary with timings marked in the margin to help students locate key moments. Alternatively they can do this themselves. Vocabulary lists which follow the sequence of the film can be supplied. Other useful tasks you could add to your repertoire now follow.

- Using still images as a basis for oral description and prediction of the storyline.
- Showing the first scene - what came before?
- Showing an extract without sound or listening with no image.
- Playing the soundtrack and having a tick list of words for the moods created.
- Doing matching tasks (beginnings and ends of statements).
- Correcting false statements about the film.
- Cutting off the final few frames for prediction.
- Re-ordering the plot for jigsaw reading.
- Who said what? Matching characters and quotations. Or, who could have said what?
- Open dialogues – imagining the other character (e.g. dialogue on the telephone) or imagining what the people in the scene are thinking.
- Rewriting a scene from the film – how else could it have started or ended?
- Writing and possibly filming a brand-new scene (an imagined deleted scene).
- Performing or writing an imaginary interview with the director.
- Doing research on the director or a main actor for a presentation or essay.
- Watching interviews with the director and actors online.
- Doing listening gap-fill, statement identification or matching tasks on sections of dialogue.
- Doing written gap-fills on characters and themes.
- Writing a film review.

- Finding film reviews in L2 and producing worksheets as if students were the teacher.
- Where relevant, learning about the characteristics of the film school being studied, e.g. the French New Wave or Italian neo-realism.
- Re-enact and film a scene as role-play. This may appeal strongly to students with an interest in drama.
- Defining film-making terms from a list.
- Finding and translating online L2 reviews.
- Designing a classroom display e.g. with film posters, reviews, pictures of actors.
- Writing an analytical essay.

Here is one approach to organising the teaching.

1. Do some pre-viewing work based on the theme of the film and the language of film.
2. Watch the film through for pleasure.
3. Watch the film in sections supported by handouts to be used for language reinforcement, comprehension and discussion. These might include lists of vocabulary.
4. Work with textual material on the film, e.g. reviews, analysis, biography of the director, character analyses. Provide a scene-by-scene summary.
5. Show video material where available, such as interviews with actors and the director. Use these for listening, speaking and writing practice as well as to develop further knowledge of the film.
6. Do a selection of the numerous tasks listed in the bullet points above.
7. When preparing for an exam, analyse mark schemes (rubrics) and show examples of model essays.
8. Have students write essays late in the teaching sequence, once skill at paragraph writing has been scaffolded and developed. Provide them with detailed feedback. Copy the best examples to share (with permission).

Literature

For a detailed treatment, we recommend the book *Teaching Literature in the A Level Modern Languages Classroom* by Katherine Raithby and Alison Taylor (2020). Just like cinema, literature offers insights into L2 culture, but it also offers a chance for students to read challenging language at length, widening their command of structure and vocabulary. If a text must be chosen from a prescribed list in preparation for an examination bear in mind, as with film, not just personal interests, but those of the students, the accessibility of the language and availability of support materials such as criticisms, study guides and websites.

They will need individual copies of texts or digital versions which they can annotate. Digital extracts can easily be displayed and manipulated on a whiteboard. Consider using a visualiser to display printed text from paper. The school library should be stocked with a small range of printed resources: at least one extra copy of the book in case a student mislays their own copy or leaves it at home, any published study guides in L2 or L1, and any accessible works of criticism in L1 or L2. A list of web links to reviews, summaries and criticism should be provided.

How to approach texts

Pre-reading. It is a good idea to prepare students for the content of the text. This could mean looking at the life of the author, briefly studying the setting of the book, if this is important, or the historical context. Do some themed vocabulary work if the text features a particular range of lexis. Introduce some generic language which they will find useful when reading and discussing the text: character, narrative point of view, themes, plot, structure, style, imagery and rhetorical devices.

Give students the opportunity to read the text for themselves if they can cope with it, but this could present a risk if they are likely to find it demoralising to read a major text on their own. An L1 translation of the text is a useful aid.

Studying the text. There is a huge variety of oral, reading and writing tasks to be done when studying a literary text. Bear in mind that the texts are just a lengthy example of written language. Therefore you can employ the whole range of tasks you might use with any text.

One possible approach

1. Do any pre-reading work, e.g. background on setting, theme or author.
2. Read chapter by chapter, or section by section. Set reading for a week ahead with a worksheet for guidance. Expect about two to three hours to be spent on this.
3. A week later use the worksheet as a basis for class discussion, explanation and clarification (wholly or largely in L2). Establish a regular pattern and high expectations for punctual and thorough work.
4. When the book is finished, begin reviewing themes using a range of exercise types. Make use of other sources: critiques and study guides. Some of these might be in L1.
5. When working towards an examination, prepare by studying mark schemes (rubrics) and practising essay writing.

Essay planning and writing

Experienced teachers need to be closely acquainted with any syllabus documents and devote a good deal of time ensuring that students practise examination style tasks and study mark schemes and rubrics. One area which always requires particular attention at this level is essay writing. Students need clear advice on writing with relevance, clarity of structure, and coherence while employing a wide range of accurate language. It is a good idea to help them by providing example essays, lists of useful phraseology and to model with them the process of putting together an essay.

In the early stages of developing essay technique, students may be limited in their writing as much by a shortage of ideas as any insecurity over their language skills. Therefore it makes sense to work through a topic, develop their understanding and range of ideas, brainstorm essay points and deal with essay structure before they are let loose on the task. Teachers are often frustrated by students' lack of written accuracy. Although mark schemes tend to put more emphasis on relevant content, we do need to help them improve accuracy and quality of language.

Advanced level students need to have effective essay planning modelled for them. As well as essay plans, they should be able to see and analyse examples of effective essay writing. It is a good idea to supply lists of useful phrases and grammatical structures they could use in a range of contexts. One approach to the traditional discursive essay on a topic of interest is as follows:

Introduction. Put the question in context, e.g. Why are people talking about this issue? Why is it important? Has a recent event made it topical? How about starting with an interesting fact or statistic? Then say what you are going to do in your essay.

Body of Essay. Write one main idea per paragraph and for each paragraph write:
1. What is your point?
2. Where is your evidence?
3. What does this evidence mean?
4. How is the evidence relevant to the essay title?

The acronym PEAL (or PEEL) is sometimes used to remind students.
- P = Point: start a paragraph with a clear topic sentence that establishes what the paragraph is going to be about. The point should support the essay argument or question.
- E = Evidence/Example: a piece of evidence or an example is used to support the initial point and develop the argument.
- E/A = Explain/Analyse: an analysis of how the evidence/example supports the point, giving further information to ensure that the reader understands its relevance. This is where critical thinking skills are applied, giving real depth to an answer.
- L = Link: to complete the paragraph, link back to the essay question, showing how the paragraph is relevant.

One way of getting the idea of coherence and structure across to students is to say they need to imagine they are taking their reader on a walk and should not leave them behind at any time.

Conclusion. Sum up the main points you have made throughout the essay. Do not introduce new ideas. Give your opinion or a general reflection on the issue if possible.

Essay checking

When we ask students to check their essays we should suggest they run through the text several times, each time checking a particular type of item, e.g. first time, adjectival agreement; second time, verb agreement; third time, gender; fourth time, articles and so on. What they check may depend on the language being studied. Students being students, they will often fail to do this once they think the task has been completed. To encourage them to build this approach into routine habits, get them do it in class before they hand work in, or swap their work with a partner to do the same.

Students like to read other students' work – it provides them with more input and helps them see how effective or ineffective their own work is. After correcting work, it is valuable to spend some one-to-one time with students helping them assess their own performance and providing further advice and suggestions for improvement when they write their next piece. As we know from our own experience we get much better at essay writing with attention to technique and practice.

Essay marking

Essay marking is time-consuming and there is some debate about how best to do it. It is worth recalling the technical distinction between **errors** and **mistakes.** In the language of applied linguistics, errors occur when the student simply does not know something, i.e. there is a gap in their declarative knowledge. Mistakes are more like lapses, inaccuracies which occur owing to the working memory's failure to handle the task. We find both types in student essays although identifying which type it is can be tricky. The word error is used here to refer to both.

As explained in Chapter 9, research suggests it is not worth underlining errors for students to correct any more than directly correcting or not even correcting at all. However, most teachers at advanced level correct them all and either write in improved versions or just underline or circle errors allowing students the opportunity to correct themselves. If they know their work will be read carefully and corrected, they are more likely to do it to a high standard. In some cases, e.g. simple adjective agreement, verb tense and gender, students are instantly able to correct, partly because there are very few alternatives. In other cases, where there is an issue of imperfect style or choice of vocabulary it is best to write in an improved version. Evidence suggests (e.g. Conti, 2001, 2004) that when we point out where an error has occurred, in well over half the cases students can make a correction.

Some teachers have codes which they write in the margin, e.g. T for tense, A for adjective. Others may adopt a system of double underlining for major errors where meaning is seriously hampered) and one underlining for minor errors such as gender and agreement. Whichever approach is adopted, students appreciate consistency and it makes life easier for the teacher.

In one study about error correction John Lalande (1982) compared the effects of two different types of correction on the writing of students learning German. On getting back the marked essays they were asked to correct their mistakes and re-write the entire essay. For the experimental group, this involved interpreting codes. The control group's essays were marked in the traditional way, i.e. with all corrections noted by the teacher in the expectation that students would include them in a rewritten version. As the course progressed, the experimental group monitored the frequency and recurrence of error types by referring to charts in which they logged their mistakes. It was found that "the combination of error awareness and problem-solving techniques had a significant beneficial effect on the development of writing skills" and "effectively prevented students from making more grammatical and orthographic errors." (Lalande, 1982 p. 148).

In the case of some students who make numerous errors of a basic nature, consider marking selectively. There are two good reasons for this. Firstly, there are only so many hours in a week! Is it really worth the time spent for little gain? Secondly, students are unduly discouraged by seeing their work covered in corrections, whether they be simple underlining or direct corrections.

If the ground has been carefully covered before they come to write, and the essay is the culmination of a teaching sequence, they will make fewer errors. Do not be worried about giving them chunks of language to recycle (set phrases, idioms and structures) – these may well become part of their internalised language in due course. But bear in mind too that students will also take pride in finding their own turns of phrase from the dictionary. 'Double tick' these to show you value the fact they have made an effort to impress. Students need to feel they have made a good job of their essay, so it is important they are given every chance to do so. Occasionally it is clear that nowhere near enough time has been devoted to an essay. In this case, a firm line is called for and work should be rewritten to an acceptable standard. The issue is far less likely to recur.

Online translators and AI

It has become a bugbear for teachers in recent years that some students resort to using online translators, usually Google Translate. From late 2022, AI tools from Microsoft and Google have been exacerbating the issue. How much should we worry about these developments and how can we deal with the situation?

It is worth saying, firstly, that students can learn a good deal from online translators and AI tools which improve all the time and are very effective. We can design tasks which encourage their use. For example, at advanced level it would be valid to set a passage of L1 to translate into L2 using online translation, asking them to comment on or correct the version produced.

If a piece of writing has been translated by computer or generated by AI, the student will not have gone through the process of retrieving, checking and typing/handwriting. Their brain will not have made the repeated connections with vocabulary and rules for these to have become internalised. They will also miss out on the enjoyment of finding their own solutions, solving puzzles, showing off their knowledge and skills.

If you have asked for some L2 to be written or presented orally and discover it has been computer-translated or written by AI you will need to have some firm sanctions up your sleeve to discourage this from being repeated. It is usually easy to spot if a student has had extra help. In an assessment situation they will not have access either to a dictionary or a portable device, so they require repeated practice at retrieving language from their own memories. This is, of course, a simple case of honesty, so you will wish to make your expectations clear.

Nevertheless, many schools have stopped assigning written homework in recent years, preferring to give vocabulary learning tasks or even material to read or watch before the lesson, in the flipped learning style.

On the other hand, from the teacher's point of view AI offers several opportunities.

- Generating texts with exercises about films, authors, directors, literary styles and cinema schools.
- Assessing written work with the aid of a mark scheme – at the time of writing early evidence suggests AI can assess quite accurately. This could be an additional tool to support your own judgment.
- Producing corrected versions of written essays.
- Designing worksheets with a range of question formats.

Concluding remarks

Teachers develop very close relationships with their advanced level students, possibly closer than at any other stage of education. It is common to see enormous progress as they begin to develop real proficiency. If we can provide them with an immersion experience in an L2 country, we can accelerate the acquisition process and seriously improve levels of motivation.

At this level we can also expect students to be developing their independent study skills to a considerable extent. This will help if they are preparing for study at university in languages or another subject. Encourage them to read and listen more widely at this stage. One practical way to do so is to set a weekly reading or listening task whereby students choose their own online article or video report and write a brief summary of its content in L1 along with a short bilingual glossary of new words or phrases. This can be checked on a weekly basis without marking or grading. They can build up their own reading and listening diary as they go along.

Additionally we can work with students individually to help them find lengthy reading material, fiction or non-fiction. Popular L2 novels (not too long), translated novels from L1, cartoon books, websites on particular topics work well. Assign some personal reading time within the curriculum plan. Those applying to university to study a language are usually expected to have taken on some significant reading of their own before they leave school. It might be useful for them to make brief notes on what has been covered in a personal learning plan which is discussed periodically with individual students.

15

Intercultural understanding

Introduction

One unique aspect of language learning is its capacity to open students' minds to different cultures, to enable them to value and evaluate both new cultures and their own and thus to become better educated, tolerant and discerning citizens. What is commonly called **intercultural understanding** or **intercultural competence** is rightly considered to be a hugely important aspect of citizenship and social cohesion in our multi-cultural societies.

The internet has meant that teachers are able to access authentic resources such as texts, pictures and video, which make it far easier to bring L2 cultures into the classroom. This is vital, as images and information in textbooks can date quickly. The availability of such resources makes it easier to see the L2 being used in its social context and to confront any ill-informed views or negative stereotypes students (and teachers) may have. In this chapter we consider the areas below.

- ✓ The big picture
- ✓ The five *savoirs* in practice
- ✓ Intercultural competence within the curriculum plan
- ✓ Authentic resources
- ✓ Teaching culture though L2
- ✓ Content-Based Instruction
- ✓ Immersion visits
- ✓ Online projects with an L2 school
- ✓ Culturally Responsive Teaching

The big picture

The role of intercultural understanding has been debated over the years with, at one extreme, culture seen as an aid to language learning and, at the other, language learning viewed as a means to access culture (Kelly, 2014). A Council of Europe document talks of developing "…open, reflective and critical attitudes in order to learn to take a positive view of, and derive benefit from, all forms of contact with otherness. It seeks to mitigate the ego-/ ethnocentric attitudes which arise from encounters with the unknown" (CoE, 2016).

At the national level, bodies which set the agenda for language learning these days always place culture among their aims for language learning. In England the National Curriculum for Key Stage 3 (age 11-14) states: "Learning a foreign language is a liberation from insularity and provides an opening to other cultures. A high-quality languages education should foster pupils' curiosity and deepen their understanding of the world" (DfE, 2023). The ACTFL in the USA, talks of 'World-Readiness Standards' with Culture being one of the five Cs, along with Communication, Connections, Comparisons and Communities. There we find, for example: "Learners use the language to investigate, explain, and reflect on the relationship between the practices and perspectives of the cultures studied" (ACTFL). In Australia, the New South Wales K-10 syllabus talks of: "intercultural capability (as) the capacity to exchange, understand and create meaning between people and across languages and cultures and is developed in all focus areas" (NSW Curriculum K10 Syllabus).

Yet the intercultural dimension is rarely assessed, even if texts are usually set in some sort of cultural context. An exception is the A-level examination in England, Wales and Northern Ireland, where knowledge and analysis of literary texts and films are assessed independently of linguistic skill. This is in contrast to the GCSE examination, in which only language is assessed. (This may appear to be inconsistent.) This suggests that traditionally culture has been something of an add-on in language courses, with textbooks largely driven by grammar and topic. Most teachers probably ascribe secondary importance to it as they concentrate on improving students' linguistic skills and preparing them for examinations.

In the research literature there is disagreement about whether culture should really be part of a languages course. Garrett-Rucks (2016) suggests that assessing intercultural competence would cause it to be taken more seriously. Agar (1994) argues that cultural competence emerges naturally from the language learning experience, whereas writers such as Libben and Lindner (1996) take the position that acquiring cultural competence and linguistic competence are very different things. Some writers try to integrate the notions of intercultural and communicative competence (ICC).

The Council of Europe has formulated a series of competences required for democratic culture and intercultural dialogue, which is targeted at schools. It includes aspects of intercultural understanding, as well as language competence, and aims to empower learners to act as competent and effective democratic citizens (see Figure 15.1)

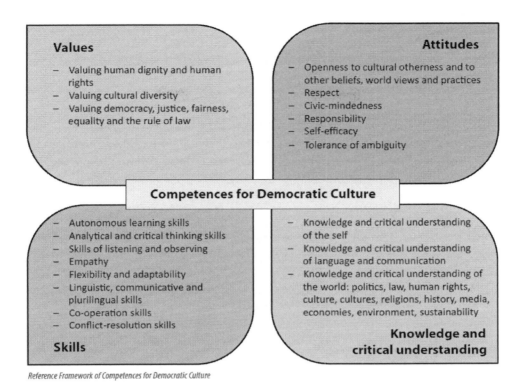

Reference Framework of Competences for Democratic Culture

Figure 15.1 Reference Framework of Competences for Democratic Culture (CoE 2018 p. 38)

Mike Byram (1997) created the five **Savoirs** model of **Intercultural Communicative Competence** which has been influential in the literature. He views language learning as a communicative, interactive and meaningful endeavour. Language learning is seen from a cultural and personal perspective and is part of a journey towards understanding beliefs, values and behaviours which are different to one's own (Byram, 2021). The five *savoirs* are listed in a much-simplified form below.

1. **Savoir. Knowledge** (of self and other, of relationship to society).
2. **Savoir être. Attitudes/Values** (curiosity, openness, approaching the new with imagination).
3. **Savoir comprendre. Interpreting/Relating** (developing new perspectives through comparison).
4. **Savoir apprendre. Discovery/Interaction** (developing research skills, exploiting cultures).
5. **Savoir s'engager. Critical Cultural Awareness** (valuing the attitudes of others, 'decentring' the self).

Byram's model is a useful one for language teachers in framing how we might view intercultural understanding and competence. Developing the above qualities, skills and attitudes is a sound objective – some would argue ultimately more important than the development of linguistic skill.

In the next section we explore how the five *savoirs* might be reflected in classroom practice.

The five *savoirs* in practice

1. **Savoir**
   This is what many of us would consider as central. Lessons include information about L2 countries/cultures, including the use of authentic materials, images, film, literature, visiting speakers, factual information about customs, geography, transport, science, heritage, food, history, language and so on. The choice of classroom activities can include some of these elements at all levels.

2. **Savoir être**
   Lessons involve encouraging curiosity through brainstorming activities; using texts in which people talk about their lives, enabling comparison with one's own life; conversations about L2 cultures – both in L1 (at novice levels) and L2 (at higher levels). E-twinning projects and especially exchanges can play a huge role.

3. **Savoir comprendre**
   Lessons and tasks that allow careful reading, analysis, interpretation of texts in order to achieve a change of perspective; at higher levels, creative tasks working with literary texts (e.g. writing new scenes, new endings); projects where students experience a situation from a different cultural point of view (how does the Mexican school system work and what is a typical day); role plays and games which help develop new perspectives.

4. **Savoir apprendre**
   Zoom/Teams conversations with L2 speakers; online research projects; asking questions in L1 or L2 to a visiting L2 speaker, such as a Foreign Language Assistant.

5. **Savoir s'engager**
   At advanced level, comparing how two countries deal with aspects of diversity; discussing a text about trans issues; at lower levels, in L1 discussing views about stereotypes; talking in L1 or L2 about problem issues in one's own country, e.g. treatment of prisoners, drugs policy, school systems.

Intercultural competence within the curriculum plan

Commonly used schemes of learning in schools feature lists of grammatical structures, vocabulary items, transactional situations, language functions, learning strategies, types of activity and topics. The curriculum can be broad in scope or so detailed and directive that they even specify the content of individual lessons. If we value intercultural competence, we will want the scheme of work to contain aspects of L2 cultures and, bearing in mind models of cultural competence, activities to encourage exploration, research and discussion of cultural issues.

The Nation and Macalister (2010) model of curriculum planning (see Chapter 20) is based on three key aspects: the **needs** of students, **principles** of language learning in the particular context and **environment** (e.g. school, timetabling, teachers). Planning for intercultural competence needs to take account of these three strands. Questions to be asked include:

- What are we planning to teach?
- How shall we sequence the content?
- How shall we assess it, if at all?
- How will the content be embedded in lessons?

Byram (2021) suggests one model for incorporating intercultural competence into a communicative language teaching framework. The curriculum would comprise three elements: 1) linguistic competence 2) communicative competence, and 3) intercultural competence.

With respect to linguistic competence a typical goal would be 'know that adjectives agree for gender and plurality'; a communicative goal would be 'know that a colloquial expression can be used with friends, but not teachers'; an intercultural competence goal would be 'stereotypes are a hindrance to good communication and interaction'. As it stands, few curriculum documents go into this level of detail with respect to intercultural competence.

In text books, common examples of cultural topics which contribute to the Byram (2021) *Savoir* (Knowledge) strand include food customs, education systems, holidays and festivals, transport networks, geography, famous people, film, television and radio, music, simple poetry and literature. At an advanced level culture receives a sharper focus with topics including politics, immigration and integration, history, environmental issues, rights and responsibilities, longer works of literature, film, art, scientific research and charitable work. At this level, students' greater proficiency allows for quite sophisticated L2 discussions.

Textbooks often include textual material and information in teachers' guides to supplement the students' existing knowledge of L2 culture. If this is lacking, the internet makes it easy to source reading material which can either be used in its original, authentic form or, more commonly, adapted to the level of your class. For example, if you are studying education in the L2 country, rather than just using textbook material, you could use an authentic school website as one of your sources. When studying food, you could source school canteen or restaurant menus online. With listening material it may be possible to adapt the source, e.g. by slowing down spoken text, but an activity type can be adapted to make it more accessible to your students, e.g. by making use of more L1 or by focusing on receptive activities more than productive ones.

Authentic resources

Do not worry if your textual material is 'adapted-authentic' rather than authentic (i.e. produced for a native speaker audience). In terms of student motivation, it is important for the text to be linguistically accessible, plausible, and to have the potential to produce stimulating, communicative lessons.

So a sound pedagogical sense is needed when choosing textual sources of cultural interest. Is the material interesting to students? Does it contribute to intercultural competence? Is it at the right level? Crucially, can it be the basis of an effective lesson featuring L2 communication? Some texts may be interesting enough in themselves, but can we actually do anything with them once we have done the reading or listening? We always need to weigh up the value of sources with these points in mind.

Textual subject matter from L2 countries can open up stimulating cultural discussion. We could find material on, for example, policies on integration and multiculturalism in L2 countries, differing education, healthcare and political systems, as well as specific issues such as bullfighting in Spain, the 35-hour working week in France, transport networks, regional identity and separatism, the protection of the French language, migration to Germany, welfare provision differences.

At intermediate and advanced levels films and music make for excellent sources of authentic cultural input through L2. Watching a movie with L1 subtitles is an effective way to engage students with cultures while providing extensive listening. Most teachers feel that this is an excellent way of killing two birds with one stone, namely covering culture and extensive listening. Three French films where the language is clear and culturally significant are *Au revoir les enfants, Les Choristes* and *Être et avoir,* all set in schools, two within a historical context. For Spanish we would recommend *Volver, El laberinto del fauno* and *Ocho apellidos vascos*, while for German you could try *Good Bye, Lenin!, Das Leben der Anderen* and *Die fetten Jahre sind vorbei.*

Songs too, when well-chosen for theme and clarity, fulfil a similar role. See Chapter 18 on using song and drama for much more detail on this. Pictures are a further excellent source of cultural information. Textbooks sometimes provide them, but they can easily be sourced online or from your own collection: houses, shop fronts, market stalls, street scenes – all can play a useful role and be a starting point for L2 practice. See Chapter 10 for ways to exploit pictures. Literary sources are much harder to find below advanced level, although there are a few tried and tested ones which often feature in textbooks. It may be possible to find or adapt short extracts from stories, plays or novels.

For general reading, using parallel texts is a useful way to access cultural material beyond the current level of students. Topics which may suit the parallel texts approach at beginner and intermediate levels include sport, wildlife, celebrities, television, film, music, festivals, scientific discoveries, food and drink.

Teaching culture through L2

There is plenty of room in language lessons for talking about culture in L1. Most teachers have personal knowledge and experience they want to share and, particularly with novices and pre-intermediate classes, this is better done in L1. There are interesting discussions to be had comparing L1 and L2 cultures which allow teachers to explain, dispel myths, open minds, share anecdotes and seek students' own views and perspectives. Think of Byram's five *savoirs*.

Talking about food is an easy and obvious way to engage students in discussion. With beginners do food tastings or liaise with a colleague to arrange some food preparation. This can be combined with lessons on healthy eating and comparisons of diets between countries. In terms of listening for intermediate students and above, recipe videos are useful and easy to find online. Teach about traditional dishes while doing a structured intensive listening task. (Then why not ask them to make the dish at home?)

If a native speaker language assistant is available, they can play an effective role in talking about culture from deep personal experience. Lessons based on interviews with visitors to the classroom also work.

In addition, students often enjoy those special lessons when we do something like a food tasting or dress up in costume (beware stereotypes though!). Sometimes lessons are not just for linguistic gain, but to have a memorable, fun experience. This may coincide with a relevant festival.

With intermediate and advanced classes a good deal of explanation can be in L2 which also offers an excellent opportunity for extensive listening practice. Unlike an audio recording, we can adapt our delivery to the class, adjusting pace, choice of structure and vocabulary to suit the needs of students. We can repeat, clarify, paraphrase, check understanding and use occasional L1 to make messages interesting and comprehensible.

As we have seen, well-chosen listening and reading texts set in a cultural context provide an ideal platform on which to build L2-based lessons. We can deploy our usual repertoire of oral techniques to discuss texts while simultaneously broadening students' knowledge of L2 cultures: questioning, true-false, correcting false statements, gap-filling, matching, instant quizzes and so on - all of these mean a text can be exploited to meet intercultural aims through L2.

Content-Based Instruction (CBI)

This comes in a few variations which all have in common the fact that the content or task set in a cultural context takes priority over the language as the main focus. It can be seen as a methodological approach in itself. **Project-Based Learning (PBL)** is akin to both task-based learning and what is known in Europe as **CLIL (Content and Language Integrated Learning)**. The following definition of CLIL (and by extension CBI) from Coyle *et al.* (2010 p. 1) is clear:

> *A dual-focused educational approach in which an additional language is used for the learning and teaching of both content and language.*

When you think about it, this approach is the one often used when we teach at advanced level where the language becomes little more than the medium through which a cultural topic, film or literary text is taught. At this level much basic grammar and high frequency vocabulary is already quite familiar to students and the focus becomes the content more than the language itself. This is definitely meaning-focused work. With that in mind, many language teachers are already familiar with something loosely resembling PBL or CLIL. If there is a difference between the two, it is that PBL provides students with a tangible goal for learning, often in the form of a project leading to a presentation. CLIL, on the other hand, is a more general term which does not necessarily involve carrying out projects. Whatever the terminology employed, the main point is that content takes precedence over language. The approach may appeal to those who feel that traditional language classes, focused primarily on vocabulary and grammar, lack interest for many students who may be more motivated to engage with texts and tasks about stimulating intercultural content.

With younger classes in high schools the CBI/PBL/CLIL approach is used rarely, but it does have its supporters. How does it work and what are the implications of the approach in terms of incorporating culture into lessons?

PBL involves students working for an extended period to investigate and respond to an engaging question, problem or challenge mainly through the medium of L2. It is attractive because of a problem which language teachers often recognise: the discrepancy between students' cognitive levels and the level of their L2. Put simply, it is hard to find material which is easy enough for classes yet important and engaging. It could therefore be seen as an antidote to lessons about pencil cases, daily routines, holidays and hobbies. In the context of culture, PBL offers several possible advantages:

- It can provide contexts relevant to students' needs and interests.
- It promotes both linguistic skill and general cultural knowledge.
- It may allow for a more creative use of language than with traditional form-focused approaches.
- It may provide particularly good contexts for widening students' understanding of both their own culture and others.
- It may be more motivational than traditional language-focused learning.

A common way this is put into practice in schools is through interdisciplinary modules where language teachers work alongside colleagues in other subject areas in teaching a topic, partly through the medium of L2. The project may be led by the language teacher, whereby students see the work as both linguistic and cultural, or by another department, when the language work may be perceived as an add-on to the main content. Here are other ideas for a more content-orientated approach.

1. **Using the Google Arts and Culture** website as a basis for a topic about art. Particular pictures could be described, stimulating L2 discussion followed by personal research on a particular

style, artist or period. It may be possible to collaborate with the art department of the school. The aim of the project could be to produce a guide for younger students.

2. **Using websites of L2 charitable organisations**, students could summarise the work of charities and voluntary organisations. The focus would be on reading, note-taking and summary with a particular project in mind, for example, sponsoring a child in the developing world. They could produce a PowerPoint or Prezi, for example.

3. **Using the websites of well-known sports clubs or sports people**, students could use L2 material to produce pen portraits. At a simple level the activity can be scaffolded by producing gap-fill templates or information grids to complete. At a higher-level they could write imaginary interviews with sports personalities. One outcome might be an imaginary journalistic interview in L2.

4. As part of a topic on healthy lifestyles, students could use **health and nutrition websites** to find health statistics for a country and summarise healthy living advice. For French a good place to start is the site *mangerbouger.fr*. They could produce a guide or oral presentation on healthy living. Again, lower-level students can be supported with scaffolded resources.

5. American French teacher and blogger Don Doehla has used this project based on **restaurant menus**:
    Students play the role of a restaurant owner who needs to develop and create a menu for their restaurant established in one of the L2 countries. Their menus must have at least five categories, and twenty-five items, all authentic dishes of L2 cultures. They must decide on an appropriate name, create an address, phone number, website and Twitter account name, all consistent with examples they find online from authentic restaurants. Their menu items must be priced in the local currency. The students then do a speech either in small groups or for the whole class in which they talk as the restaurant owner, suggesting good dishes, specialities, etc. They must say at least 15 sentences, and can either present live or on video. As much linguistic support as the class needs can be supplied.
    Don Doehla's work can be found here (accessed 2023):
    http://www.edutopia.org/blog/world-language-project-based-learning-education-curriculum-don-doehla.

6. The class could **produce an L2 newspaper, blog or website** rooted in L2 culture. L2 input could be provided in the form of example features (weather, horoscopes, crosswords, news items). Then students could work in groups to produce their own material to be shared with other classes, younger students in the same school or a partner class abroad.

7. Students could take part in a **letter, email or social network exchange** with a partner class in another country. The aim would be to exchange information on aspects of daily life to produce a comparative presentation in L1 or L2. The teacher would provide support and guidelines for the exchange. For example, would they communicate in L1 or L2? Would the emphasis be on reading comprehension or written output?

8. Intermediate and advanced students could **research an L2 singer or group**. They would listen to songs online, research the artist's website and produce a PowerPoint presentation about the artist with examples of lyrics and song videos in L1 or L2.

It is worth reiterating that projects of this type are time-consuming, and we need to be clear what the aims are when setting them up. Is the language emphasis on input or output? The former may end up placing more stress on the content and be more motivational for students. If they must produce L2 material, although the task becomes more challenging, many will find it hard, time-consuming and they may lose interest in the project content itself. As teachers, we do not necessarily have to judge the success of a cultural project by the spoken or written outcome. If a good deal of interested listening or reading has been done, this is still valuable; indeed some would say all the more valuable. So, in short, consider the 'opportunity cost' (i.e. what do we lose by adopting this approach?) of CBI tasks, as with any language learning activity.

There is evidence to suggest, e.g. in Pachler *et al.* (2014) that a good deal of classroom practice seems to be a 'weak' version of CBI where project-based lessons still adopt a traditional Presentation-Practice-Production model with a fair amount of focus on forms and structures, even if focus tends to be more on vocabulary and learning strategies than grammar. If pressed for time in covering the language of the syllabus this may feel like a sensible compromise for those who hesitate to take on the full CBI approach. The kind of resources used are more likely to be authentic or adapted authentic, with perhaps a broader range of grammatical and lexical input than might be expected for the students' language level.

Does it matter if the level of language is less comprehensible? If we believe that broadly comprehensible, motivating input is a key driver of acquisition we are likely to be more sympathetic to CBI. If we believe that focus on grammatical form, pre-selection of vocabulary and careful sequencing for difficulty of language are vital, we may be more sceptical. Teacher commitment to this approach is a crucial ingredient. It would be easy to imagine that most language teachers, brought up on form-focused, PPP approaches are a little uncomfortable with PBL, feeling that it is somehow 'wishy-washy' and distracting from the main task of serious language learning.

It is possible to see CBI as a useful model for those students who are unlikely to continue with languages for very long and for whom the traditional drip-feed, form-focused approach seems futile. Why not let the focus be on more interesting content, vocabulary building and a more bilingual, parallel texts approach? In this view, intercultural competence takes priority over linguistic progress (see Chapter 20 for consideration of curriculum goals).

Steve's tips for incorporating L2 cultures

- Decorate the classroom with posters showing iconic images from L2 cultures (places, artwork, cultural icons).
- Get students to make a list of items they have at home produced in other countries.
- A contentious point, but consider giving your novice students L2 culture names. They may find this amusing too.
- Display food packaging or menus from L2 countries.
- Play L2 background music while students are working.
- Have a large map displayed at the front of the room. It can be used in a few ways, e.g. pointing out regions, cities, geographical features such as mountains and rivers, teaching compass points, teaching the weather, talking about your travels, asking students to talk about theirs.
- Watch short videos in L1 or L2 about cities or regions from an L2 country. Why not show these as they enter the classroom?
- Display two or three clocks from different time zones.
- Have students bring in items, clothing or food which represent their own or family cultures.
- Do specific end-of-term research projects where students are given or can select their own cultural topic.

Immersion visits

As many of us have experienced, there is little doubt that a prolonged stay in an L2 country, whether it be a family exchange, study course or work experience placement, is the very best way for students to become more motivated as they become intimately acquainted with the culture. Teachers who organise stays abroad regularly report how greatly the interest and linguistic skills of most of their students have increased. Perhaps your own experience of an exchange visit ultimately led you to become a language teacher.

There are many practical reasons why it may be difficult for our students to spend time in an L2 country. But we would urge teachers to look at any possibility of making it happen. In most cases a family-based exchange is the most valuable and cost-effective way of being immersed in the language and culture. Social-networking means this is a less daunting experience than it might have been in the past, even if some purists regret the fact that this also means the immersion is no longer total, given the ease of communication with friends and family at home.

A family-based exchange is most suitable for intermediate students and above, despite the administrative hurdles to be overcome. Depending on the demands of the school, school board or governing body, questions such as health and safety, the vetting of families and child-protection need to be addressed head-on, particularly if there has been no history of such types of visit. There are also decisions to be made regarding the timing of an exchange. Is it less disruptive to teachers and students to use vacation time? What is the school's policy on visits during term time? Is there a suitably matched partner school with committed colleagues willing to put in the time and preparation required to make it a success? How long should the visit last? Is a week enough?

When organising an exchange for the first time, advice should be sought from other teachers, perhaps online, since there are several practical steps which can help an exchange run smoothly. These include how best to match students, what types of organised visits to arrange (cultural? fun?) and how to involve guests in school life. It is important for our own reputation and peace of mind to plan very carefully in view of possible disruption to colleagues' lessons.

If there is a group of 30 visitors:

- How will they fit in classrooms?
- Could you split them up and share them around other student hosts in different classes?
- Will all colleagues in other subject areas be happy to host visiting students in their classroom?
- What happens during sports lessons? Will the guests be expected to take part? Could the PE teacher prepare an activity to involve the guests?
- Could you arrange any special school events to involve your guests, e.g. a reception involving the school's leadership team and local press, a sports event or party?
- Should special lessons or activities be organised for the visitors, presented by a colleague, e.g. music, cookery or local history?
- Can a computer room be booked for students to put together a presentation about their visit?
- During excursions, how do we ensure students do not split off into two national groups, e.g. by having them sit with their partner on a bus?

As far as matching partners is concerned, students should complete a detailed questionnaire beforehand, as it is vital for teachers to bear in mind shared interests, social background, family size and any health issues such as allergies to pets. Because it is rare to get a perfect match in the number of boys and girls, it is wise to ask in advance if any students/families are happy to receive a partner of the opposite sex. The issue of gender-identification may also require consideration.

Preparation before the exchange begins is important. Ideally students should have the opportunity to begin communicating before they meet. Parents/caregivers may also enjoy getting to know the partner's family.

During an exchange they can be asked to carry out projects which get them to communicate in L2. At the very least they could write a diary or blog, incorporating pictures they have taken, or record interviews with their partners or other friends. They could collect realia for the classroom back home. Advanced students could gather information for a project related to their course. Despite the inevitable challenges of the experience, plenty of schools have organised successful exchanges over many years and students and staff have derived huge benefit from them.

Study trips, where groups attend lessons in another country and follow a cultural programme, are also of great value. However, they are likely to be considerably more expensive and less 'immersive' as students will spend more time with their L1 peers. It is easy to find recommendations from fellow teachers about the best organisations to use, or it may be possible to organise a study trip with teachers in other departments, e.g. history or geography.

Cultural holidays, i.e. without formal study, are also tremendously exciting for students and these may suit novices too. Although the linguistic challenge may be limited, the direct contact with an L2 country and culture can lay down useful motivational foundations for the future. An element of linguistic challenge can be built in by having simple L2 guided tours, street surveys to perform, a simple diary to keep or information pack to complete in L1 or L2. The area visited can serve as a thematic focus for future lessons on return.

Students frequently report that stays abroad were one of the most memorable things they ever did at school. It is a tremendous opportunity we can offer, particularly for those who would not as a matter of course visit an L2 country. However, don't underestimate the amount of time and energy required to make these visits happen; shadow a colleague for a year, if possible, before attempting to organise one yourself.

Online projects with an L2 school

Many schools have some kind of international link which enables students to engage with L2 speakers. The traditional letter exchange still has its place, although the internet has obviously opened exciting possibilities where the only barriers tend to be practical and technical, e.g. can the school's internet provision cope with multiple students streaming online if conferencing is used? Are there timezone issues to bear in mind?

Pachler *et al.* (2014) suggest this possible sequence for an online project:

Preparation: Coordination between the teachers of both schools.

Phase 1: Students introduce themselves, their schools and their environment in writing and pictures.

Phase 2: Question and answers, exchange of information.

Phase 3: Exchange of detailed answers based on research; follow-up questions.

Phase 4: Analysis and comparison of results.

Phase 5: (Joint) presentation of results (e.g. creating a display, brochure, newspaper, video/audio recording or web pages), summary of learning outcomes, project outcomes, goodbye letters.

Examples of projects include the following.

1. **Social network exchanges** via social media are one way to go, if they are authorised within the school's social networking policy; check with the IT coordinator or leadership team if there are concerns. A private group could be set up for the students to communicate with L2 students, perhaps with a specific project in mind. It may just be establishing contact before an

exchange, maintaining contact after an exchange, or sharing information on a curriculum topic.

2. **Communicating via Zoom/Teams**. Here, the issues are practical: how to time the communication in school time, especially if different timezones are involved; how to liaise with the L2-teaching counterpart. Should students do their chatting at home? If so, do they all have access to the tech? What guidelines should be established for L1 and L2 use? There may be some merit in seeing this more as a listening opportunity, than a speaking one. In reality, students will come up with their own solutions and that may be fine as long as both languages are in play ('translanguaging'). Conversations held online can be recorded for use later.

3. **A shared blog**. At advanced level students could share ideas on a controversial topic as the basis for a presentation or piece of writing such as a journalistic article. Possible topics include 'My country's policy on euthanasia', 'Drugs policy', 'School exams' or 'Pressures on adolescents'. At a more prosaic level, they could share opinions on music, film and TV programmes.

4. **Writing individual blogs** is another way to share cultural experience. In some ways, this is the easiest option in terms of organisation. Students in both countries set up their own individual blogs using a free platform such as Blogger. URLs are shared and they read each other's material on a given topic. One idea might be to share music lyrics and videos, with comments in L1 or L2. Once again, guidelines for L1 and L2 use could be established.

Culturally Responsive Teaching

The term culturally responsive teaching (CRT), first coined in the USA, refers to teaching which is sensitive to different cultures both within and outside the classroom. "It is an approach that empowers students intellectually, socially, emotionally, and politically by using cultural referents to impart knowledge, skills, and attitudes" (Ladson-Billings, 1994). Since writing the first edition of this book, issues to do with diversity, racism and gender, have come even more to the fore and attracted growing interest in the educational sphere, as in wider society. Language teachers need to be aware of some of the issues at stake. Although there is insufficient space to do full justice to this area, a few points are important.

Culture in general is defined in various ways, one of which is the norms, beliefs, and behaviours passed down from one generation to the next. These partly explain why a student might express themselves in the way they do, or why another might not feel comfortable looking you in the eye when you speak to them. These aspects of culture can affect student-teacher as well as student-student relationships. CRT attempts to bridge the gap between teacher and student by developing an understanding of the cultural nuances that may cause a relationship to break down and may ultimately result in achievement being compromised as well.

A cornerstone of CRT is having cultural knowledge of the students. With 'getting to know you' questionnaires, students can be asked what name they would like used, how they identify, their interests, the activities they enjoy and what they would like to learn. In ethnically and culturally diverse classrooms, this may be especially useful.

Activities can be planned which value diversity, e.g. students can present about their linguistic or cultural background; traditions and festivals can be celebrated through texts, projects, culinary lessons, learning some words or phrases in a student's heritage language, or any other new language. Artwork from different cultures can be used as the basis of a speaking and listening lesson. A 'cultural bulletin board' could be set up in the classroom to highlight a different country or region of the world each month.

With intermediate and advanced classes, texts could be chosen to highlight aspects of history or culture which make students reflect on cultural dominance and power relations. The term decolonising the curriculum refers to identifying, acknowledging and challenging the ways in which colonialism has impacted upon knowledge and learning as well as society more broadly. This means including in the curriculum a range of voices which go beyond the dominant Western perspective. In practice, in advanced lessons, this might mean choosing texts which allude to subjects such as slavery, racism, the displacement of peoples (refugees and asylum-seekers), economic and linguistic dominance, child labour and language use in developing countries.

Some language teachers may feel these issues are peripheral to their main goals. This is understandable when the immediate priorities are preparing students for the next exam, but it only requires some awareness and intentionality to be a culturally responsive teacher, and actually where better to cover these issues than in the language classroom?

Concluding remarks

One of the unique contributions of language teaching to the school curriculum is the raising of young people's awareness to a wider, global dimension. We talk these days of internationalising the curriculum and 'global citizenship'. Students do not need to travel to have a global outlook and, indeed for many of them, much of the exposure they will receive in adolescence comes from school. The successful language learner should have an open mind, be curious about things beyond their immediate experience, and be a responsible citizen. As teachers we have a duty to nurture these qualities. If we can develop intercultural understanding alongside linguistic skill, all the while working in the L2, so much the better.

Many students find the cultural aspects of language learning the most exciting and memorable of all. We have shown that integrating L2 cultures into a language course is both important and feasible. In a sense, learning a language is as much about discovering new cultures and ways of thinking as acquiring the language. If we can combine teaching culture with working in the target language, then so much the better.

16

Motivation

Introduction

This book is mostly about practical ideas for language teaching based on experience and research, but all teachers know only too well that learning mainly happens when students want to learn. One of the biggest challenges facing new teachers is how to generate the motivation to learn.

This was recognised by two pioneers of motivation research, Robert Gardner and Wallace Lambert (1972). They showed that, although language aptitude accounts for a good deal of individual variation in achievement, motivational factors can override aptitude. In some language learning environments, many people seem to master a second language, regardless of their differences in aptitude. In the classroom setting, many teachers will say that, although aptitude and general intelligence count for a great deal, motivation goes a considerable way to predicting success. Because of the central importance attached to motivation by teachers and researchers alike, it has been the subject of a great deal of research in recent decades. This has enabled several models to emerge.

In this chapter we integrate research findings with recommendations for pedagogical practice. We consider the areas below.

- ✓ Instrumental and integrative motivation.
- ✓ Intrinsic and extrinsic motivation.
- ✓ A framework for motivation.
- ✓ Motivation and classroom practices.
- ✓ Ten commandments for motivating language learners.
- ✓ Ten theories of motivation and their implications.
- ✓ Strategies for increasing self-efficacy.
- ✓ Language learning anxiety.

Instrumental and integrative motivation

Gardner and Lambert coined the terms **instrumental** motivation (language learning for more immediate or practical goals, such as mastering basic conversation for a professional role) and **integrative** motivation (language learning for personal growth, cultural enrichment and a desire to integrate into the L2 community). This distinction has its uses, but in schools it is difficult to distinguish clearly between them. For many students, the instrumental goal may be simply to pass an examination as a means to a further goal, e.g. getting a place at college or university. More recent work in psychology has emphasised the multi-faceted nature of motivation with several models being proposed.

Intrinsic and extrinsic motivation

Educational psychology has identified two basic classifications of motivation: intrinsic and extrinsic. **Intrinsic** motivation arises from a desire to learn a topic due to its inherent interest, for self-fulfilment, enjoyment and to achieve a mastery of the subject. One definition from the research literature claims that it refers to the spontaneous tendency "to seek out novelty and challenges, to extend and exercise one's capacity to explore, and to learn" (Ryan and Deci, 2000 p. 70). Intrinsic motivation can be likened to the concept of **flow** Csikszentmihalyi (1990). Flow refers to "states of total absorption, optimal challenge, and non-self-conscious enjoyment of an activity" (Di Domenico and Ryan, 2017 p. 4).

On the other hand, **extrinsic** motivation (essentially the same as instrumental motivation) is the impetus to perform and succeed for the sake of accomplishing a specific result or outcome. You might say, for example, that students who are very grade-oriented are extrinsically motivated, whereas those who seem to truly embrace their work and take a genuine interest in it are intrinsically motivated.

Most people (researchers too, by the way) would suggest that intrinsic motivation is the purer, higher-quality version, but it is not achievable in every situation. Capable teachers will normally do their best to develop intrinsic motivation in their students while making judicious use of extrinsic rewards. Researchers have arrived at three main conclusions about extrinsic rewards and their influence on intrinsic motivation.

1. **Praise can help increase intrinsic motivation**. Researchers (e.g. Cameron and Pierce, 1994) have found that offering positive praise and feedback when people do something better in comparison to others can improve intrinsic motivation.

2. **The 'over-justification effect'** (Deci, 1971). Intrinsic motivation decreases, when expected external rewards are given for completing a particular task or only doing minimal work, when the student perceives that the reward is not really justified. For example, if parents heap lavish

praise on their child every time they complete a simple task, they will become less intrinsically motivated to perform that task in future.

3. **Unexpected external rewards** do not usually decrease intrinsic motivation. For example, if a student gets a good grade on a test because they enjoy learning about the subject and we decide to reward them with, say, a certificate or merit points, the student's underlying motivation for learning about the subject will not be affected. However, we need to give such rewards with caution because they will sometimes come to expect them.

A framework for motivation

Williams and Burden (1997) produced this useful framework of factors influencing motivation in language learning (adapted slightly).

Internal factors

1. **Intrinsic interest of activity** - arousal of curiosity; optimal degree of challenge.
2. **Perceived value of activity** - personal relevance; anticipated value of outcomes; intrinsic value attributed to the activity.
3. **Sense of agency** - who makes things happen? who controls the process and outcomes?; ability to set appropriate goals for oneself.
4. **Mastery** - feelings of competence; awareness of developing skills and mastery in a chosen area; 'self-efficacy' (see below).
5. **Self-concept** - realistic awareness of personal strengths and weaknesses in skills required; personal definitions and judgements of success and failure; self-worth and learned helplessness (when a student gives up trying because of consistent failure).
6. **Attitudes to language learning in general** - to the L2; to L2 communities and cultures.
7. **Other emotional states** - confidence; anxiety and fear.
8. **Developmental age and stage.**
9. **Gender** - widespread evidence suggests that girls are more motivated to learn languages in school than boys (e.g. Carreira, 2011).

External factors

1. **Significant others and the nature of interaction with them** - mediated learning experiences e.g. type of interaction with teacher, peers, parents etc; the nature and amount of feedback; rewards; the nature and amount of appropriate praise; punishments, sanctions.
2. **The learning environment** - comfort; resources; time of day, week, year; size of class and school; class and school ethos.
3. **The broader context** - wider family networks; the local education system; conflicting interests; cultural norms; societal expectations and attitudes.

4. **Contact with L2 culture and people** – the nature and frequency of opportunities to engage with L2 speakers or experience the culture.

It is a dauntingly complex set of factors, but it should be possible to detect the ones over which we, as teachers, have some control. The key one, of course, is the nature of interaction with significant others. It is worth noting, however, that if you can get those interactions right, there will be an impact on some of the other internal factors. Put simply, there is a huge teacher effect at play when it comes to student motivation.

Motivation and classroom practices

We know the teacher's choice of activity can have an enormous effect on student motivation. Crookes and Schmidt (1991) refer to research on practices which work best. Summarised in Lightbown and Spada (2021), they include the following.

1. **Motivating students into the lesson.** At the start of lessons (and in transitions), positive remarks teachers make about forthcoming activities can lead to higher levels of interest. These include general goal setting or just putting an activity into some kind of interesting context. For example, if doing a lesson on Paris, preface it with a simple L1 or L2 question like "Has anyone been to Paris? What places have you heard of in Paris?"

2. **Varying the activities, tasks and materials.** Students are reassured by the existence of classroom routines they can depend on. Nevertheless too much use of the same routines can lead to boredom and a decrease in attention. Varying activities raises motivation.

3. **Using cooperative rather than competitive goals.** When students, including weaker ones, must collaborate on a task they gain in self-confidence because everyone has an important role to play. Knowing their peers are depending on them can raise motivation. This does not mean competitive activities have no role. Indeed competitive games can be extremely motivational.

4. **Duration of activities.** There are no hard-and-fast rules about these matters, but, in general, with younger students we should probably spend no longer than 10-15 minutes on a single activity before changing the focus. More able students, of course, have longer attention spans.

5. **Goal setting.** Setting a goal at the start of the lesson usually makes sense and some schools have specific policies on how this should be done. Some teachers like to make goals very explicit by differentiating objectives, writing up on the board, for example, what students must, should or could do. But goal setting can be more than a routine list of lesson outcomes which are referred to later. For example, to introduce a degree of curiosity, start a lesson by saying: "I want you to work out for yourself what the aim of the lesson is over the next five

minutes. Make sure you remind me to ask you in five minutes." Or: "At the end of the lesson I am going to ask you to write down what the main aim was." And remember a really useful question you can ask on frequent occasions: "Why do you think we are doing this particular activity?" That may be a good question to ask yourself!

Ten commandments for motivating language learners

Dörnyei and Csizér (1998) produced, from their studies, these 'ten commandments for motivating language learners'. They are of a general nature and make good sense; they are summarised here with our own observations.

1. **Set a personal example with our own behaviour.** This might suggest, for instance, that we will be organised, punctual, fair, consistent, caring, demanding and understanding of students' needs.

2. **Create a pleasant, relaxed atmosphere in the classroom.** Although this may not be achieved instantly, it is an excellent goal. We know students are more likely to learn when they are not too anxious, when they can take risks and are in a supportive classroom atmosphere. Some of the very best lessons we have observed over the years were not only methodologically competent, but took place in a warm, extremely supportive environment.

3. **Present the tasks properly.** This is open to a wide variety of interpretations! At the very least, there should be a logical order of presentation and practice, clarity, recycling of language and a range of presentational approaches. This is our consistent recommendation throughout this book.

4. **Develop a good relationship with the students.** Many teachers would say this is the number one factor. How this is done cannot easily be prescribed, but it is clearly tied up with all the other factors in the list. It is also a question of our own personality, self-belief, and confidence in our pedagogical approach, as well as cognitive and affective awareness of students' needs at every moment. It can take time to evolve. It can also depend on our reputation within school, so that when students arrive in the classroom there are certain expectations about how they will need to behave. Newly qualified and trainee/pre-service teachers are at a disadvantage in this regard, since a reputation takes time to be established.

5. **Increase the learners' linguistic self-confidence.** Sound pedagogical practice including clear presentation, the opportunity to do scaffolded, structured and repeated practice, a stepped progression in the scheme of work or curriculum plan, and effective formative assessment techniques and feedback all contribute to increasing students' linguistic self-confidence.

6. **Make the language classes interesting.** Stimulating language input and classroom activities are a must. According to Krashen's comprehension hypothesis (e.g. Krashen, 1982), all we need to do for students to progress is to provide 'compelling', meaningful input and acquisition will naturally occur. We do not agree it is this simple, but quite clearly, the more interesting we can make listening and reading resources and tasks, the better. This will mean, for instance, not doing every task in the textbook, performing a mental triage of possible activities to eliminate those which are likely to make classes switch off. It does not mean that every lesson has to be 'fun', but enjoyment and motivation can come from activities which are inherently interesting rather than simply fun. However, if we want to practise verb conjugations, this might be better achieved by chanting memorable songs with beginners, doing quick mini-whiteboard tasks, or playing a game of 'battleships' using a grid based on two axes of subject pronouns and infinitives, rather than just a traditional grammar worksheet.

7. **Promote student autonomy.** It is all too easy to 'spoon-feed' classes with the material they need for the next assessment, leaving them totally dependent on the teacher's input. We know our most successful students can work on their own if given the opportunity. This requires controlled practice and careful scaffolding in the early stages leading to greater skill and the capacity to work independently as time progresses. Appropriate pair work tasks, interesting homework, open-ended tasks which allow the fastest students to do more - all of these contribute to developing the autonomous learner.

8. **Personalise the learning process.** This could mean several things. We see it as involving effective, subtle differentiation during oral interactions in the classroom, individual feedback both orally and on paper, individual goal setting (either informally or through a school's established tracking systems) as well as allowing an element of task choice. Grouping by ability is also relevant in this context, as is providing prompt intervention when students are not meeting their expected goals.

9. **Increase the learners' 'goal-orientedness'.** Because language learning is a slow, cumulative process, it is useful to provide short term goals and reasons for doing tasks. Task-based activities can play a role, along with transactional tasks, activities involving native speakers and L2 country classes and, let us be frank, the assessment regime. Most students are motivated to work harder by the prospect of an upcoming test.

10. **Familiarise learners with L2 cultures.** It is likely that students, particularly younger ones, will be more motivated to acquire the second language if they understand its cultures better and, ideally, have opportunities to interact. We consider this in more detail in Chapter 15.

Ten theories of motivation and their implications

Here are some models of motivation from the field of psychology. We present them together with implications for the languages classroom.

1. Cognitive dissonance

Cognitive dissonance occurs when there is an unresolved conflict in our mind between two beliefs, thoughts or perceptions we hold about a given subject (Festinger, 1957). The level of tension resulting from such conflict depends on:

1. how strong the conflict is between the two dissonant thoughts;
2. how important is the issue they relate to;
3. how difficult it is for us to rationalise the dissonance.

Cognitive dissonance is a very powerful motivator which is often used in transformational change programmes both in the business and educational world. The reason it is so powerful is that, when used effectively, the clash of beliefs creates a sense of discomfort which results in one of two outcomes:

- The individual changes behaviour (possibly replacing the existing behaviour with the newly modelled one).
- The individual does not adopt the new behaviour and instead justifies his or her behaviour by changing the conflicting cognition created by the new information.

Teacher takeaways: If we want to change a student's attitude, we could first identify the beliefs at the heart of that attitude. When we have a clear picture, we can create cognitive dissonance by producing powerful arguments which counter those beliefs. To be effective, the degree of cognitive dissonance should be as high as possible for the attitudinal change we aim to bring about. For example, some students hold negative views about L2 cultures. If the goal is to change these attitudes, it helps first to identify the beliefs at the root of them (e.g. are they xenophobic stereotypes?). Then in a lesson or series of lessons objective and solid reasons can be given to counter those beliefs using supporting evidence which will resonate with students, thereby creating cognitive dissonance. This may lead to a change of attitude.

However, a word of caution: research suggests that trying to prove points by over-using statistics may be detrimental and that having a discussion on the issues after the new information has been provided, may increase the chances of a change in attitude.

2. Drive theory

This theory centres on the notion that we all have needs we attempt to satisfy. There are 'primary drives' which include basic innate needs (thirst, hunger, sleep etc.) and 'secondary drives' which relate to social identity and personal fulfilment. As we act on our needs, we become conditioned and acquire expectations, habits and subconscious responses (Hull, 1943). So, for example, when a child needs to feel good about him or herself, they may recite a poem, sing a song, perform a dance or other such feat to their parents, knowing they are going to get a positive response. Whenever they need recognition in other contexts, they may use the same tactics to get a similar response from a teacher or other figure of authority.

When an action does not satisfy a need or is frustrated, negative emotions (e.g. anxiety) arise. In the previous example: if the student is looking for a chance to show off their skills to an authority figure and they are not given the opportunity to do so, they may feel frustrated, angry or unappreciated.

Teacher takeaways: find out what drives the students, especially the difficult ones. Instead of approaching the problem by sanctioning them, have a one-on-one chat and try to discover what it is that they find fulfilling and see if opportunities can be found in lessons for them to satisfy their needs.

3. Attribution theory

When we make a mistake or fail at something, we tend to go through a two-step process. We first experience an automatic response involving internal attribution (i.e. the error is our fault); then a conscious, slower reaction which seeks to find an alternative external attribution (e.g. the error is due to an external factor). This is because we have a vested interest in 'looking good' in our own eyes – a sort of survival mechanism (Heider, 1958). This type of response, however, is unlikely to lead to improvement in the future, as the real internal cause of their poor performance is not addressed. Roesch and Amirkham (1997) found that more experienced and successful athletes made more self-focused attributions which lead to identifying and addressing the internal causes of their performance errors.

Teacher takeaways: when dealing with students who complain about not learning the vocabulary or grammar because it is too hard, show them – where applicable – that the reason they are not improving is not intrinsic to the nature of the language, but has to do with other factors under their control, e.g. study habits, including lack of systematic revision. This will also create cognitive dissonance and may have an impact on attitude, especially if they are shown strategies to improve.

4. Endowed progress effect

When people feel they have made some progress towards a goal, they feel more committed towards its achievement (Nunes and Drèze, 2006). Conversely, those making little or no progress are more likely to give up early in the process.

Teacher takeaways: Whatever the task, allow students to experience success in the initial stages. For example, with a comprehension or translation task, making earlier questions or sentences easier.

5. Cognitive Evaluation Theory

When faced with a task, we automatically assess it in terms of how well it meets our need to feel competent and in control. We tend to be intrinsically motivated by tasks we believe fall within our current level of competency and may be put off by those we deem too hard. This issue is more about self-perception of competency levels than objective truth.

Teacher takeaways: try to ensure that, before getting students to do challenging tasks which they may perceive to be beyond their levels of competence, they are adequately prepared, cognitively, linguistically and emotionally. For instance, before carrying out a difficult listening comprehension task, students could be exposed several times to any unfamiliar vocabulary or other language issue contained in the recording to make the task more approachable.

6. Self-determination theory

This assumes there are people for whom a feeling of being in control of their life and responsible for their actions is very important for personal fulfilment and, consequently, for their motivation. According to this theory, people need to feel the following to achieve psychological growth:

- **Autonomy**: People need to feel in control of their own behaviours and goals. This sense of being able to take direct action that will result in real change plays a major part in helping people feel self-determined.
- **Competence**: People need to gain mastery of tasks and learn different skills. Feeling they have the skills needed for success, means they are more likely to take actions that will help achieve their goals.
- **Connection or relatedness**: People need to experience a sense of belonging and attachment to other people.

In this theory the above three factors are claimed to lead to greater volition, motivation and engagement, which in turn foster greater persistence, achievement and creativity (Deci and Ryan, 2000). Fundamental to this theory is the notion of intrinsic motivation, referred to earlier.

Teacher takeaways: create a supportive classroom environment where positive relationships are the norm; include activities which allow students to use the L2 in creative ways, e.g. in the co-creation of stories; as with self-efficacy (see below) ensure students feel success by using comprehensible language. For much more on this, seek out the podcast *The Motivated Classroom* by teacher and consultant, Liam Printer.

7. Expectancy Theory

In this theory (Vroom, 1964), motivation relates to three factors.

1. **Valence**: what I expect to get out of a given action/behaviour (what's in it for me?).
2. **Instrumentality:** the belief that if I perform one course of action from a range of possibilities, I will be more likely to succeed.
3. **Expectancy:** the certain belief that I will be able to succeed (self-efficacy - see below).

Teacher takeaways: we can make clear to students why a specific outcome is desirable (e.g. getting a certain grade); provide them with a clear set of strategies to get there (e.g. independently seeking opportunities for practice) and support their self-belief that the outcome can be achieved (such as by mentioning examples of students of similar ability who did it).

8. Goal-related theory

To direct ourselves in our personal, educational and professional life we set ourselves goals. These should be:
1. clear (so we know what to do and what not to do);
2. challenging (so we get some stimulation);
3. achievable (so we do not fail).

If we set goals ourselves, rather than having them imposed, we are more likely to work harder to achieve them. Moreover, Locke and Kristof (1996) identified that specific and challenging goals are more likely to lead to higher achievement.

Teacher takeaways: instead of setting goals for students in a top-down fashion, we can involve them actively in the process of learning. Moreover, we can help them narrow goals and match these as accurately as possible to their existing level of competence. For example, instead of simply telling a student to check their next essay more accurately and giving them a lengthy error checklist, ask them to choose three challenging error categories that *they* would like to focus on and aim to achieve 100% accuracy in those categories the following week. Make sure the knowledge required to prevent or fix the errors is learnable and that the students are provided with learning strategies to assist them in achieving the set goals.

9. The Motivational Self System

Another influential (and language learning-specific) way of looking at motivation comes from psycholinguist Zoltan Dörnyei's **Motivational Self System**, e.g. Dörnyei (2009). This model suggests that motivation is based on three main considerations: the **ideal self**, the **ought-to self** and the **second language learning experience.** The ideal self (or possible self) is how we imagine we might be if we can speak another language. The ought-to self is about expected behaviours. The L2 learning experience is about the impact of the teacher, the curriculum, peer group or experience of success, but also many areas beyond the classroom. A good deal of Dörnyei's research was about how classroom pedagogy can influence motivation.

Teacher takeaways: obvious perhaps, but despite any extra-classroom factors which affect motivation, we have a lot of influence through the nature of the activities we design and the atmosphere we create in the classroom. Seek any opportunities for students to engage in enjoyable work outside class, including homework.

10. Self-efficacy theory

Williams and Burden's framework of internal and external factors (as described earlier) refers to the concept of **self-efficacy**. This concerns "the extent to which people develop behaviours that allow them to persist within potentially stressful situations" (Graham, 2022 p.187). It is partly about the expectancy of success, i.e. the extent to which we believe we shall succeed at a task. More precisely, it is the belief in our capabilities to organise and execute the courses of action required to produce given attainments (Bandura, 1997). In other words, self-efficacy is focused on personal agency. Success is brought about by the actions the individual undertakes (Graham, 2022).

By the way, as Graham (2022) points out, Bandura makes clear that self-efficacy mainly affects persistence, which in turn improves outcomes. With high self-efficacy learners choose more difficult tasks, work on them longer, attribute outcomes to their own efforts or strategies, and thus achieve more highly (Bandura, 1994).

Self-efficacy is sometimes likened to the notion of competence in Self-Determination Theory (see above).

Teacher takeaways: The development of self-efficacy and competence from the very early stages should be a priority. To coin a phrase, nothing breeds success like success. If students feel confident about tasks and experience a sense of mastery, their motivation is enhanced. Language input should always be comprehensible, tasks achievable and enjoyable. Methods and activities which create undue cognitive load should be avoided.

Strategies for increasing self-efficacy

- **At the early stages of learning emphasise 'horizontal' progression in lessons.**

This means not trying to progress too quickly within a lesson. It is better to recycle and consolidate knowledge and skills than move on too quickly in the mistaken belief that more progress has been made.

Progression is not only measured in terms of *easier* to *complex*; but also in terms of (a) the extent to which the vocabulary, grammar or pronunciation is being practised (what could be called 'horizontal' progression) and (b) depth of processing (how strongly the language is associated with pre-existing language stored in long-term memory). Consolidation through short-, medium- and long-term recycling is crucial for building up long-term memory. If students feel they have mastered an area, they will have raised their self-efficacy and expectation of future success.

- **Plan with self-efficacy in mind, especially at the early stages of teaching and with less able students.**

Planning for self-efficacy means scaffolding success, i.e. providing as many opportunities as possible for students to do well at tasks. This not only requires pitching the learning resources and activities to the right level, both of the class and individual students (through effective differentiation), but also gearing them up adequately before each task where the outcome is to be assessed. Before a reading comprehension activity, for example, ensure they are familiar with the words in a text (e.g. by playing vocabulary games or quizzes) until it is certain they will be able to identify the vast majority of the key words necessary to get the answers right.

Ultimately, the greatest challenge in planning for self-efficacy is to strike a balance between providing enough opportunities for success while not lowering expectations too much. The process requires great cognitive and affective empathy with the students, being strategic in our input and learning expectations and, finally, choosing the right summative tasks, not just the ones available in the textbook.

- **From the very early stages of instruction, model effective learning strategies.**

Equipping struggling learners with more effective learning strategies should enhance their perceived self-efficacy. The rationale is that if a student perceives memorising new words challenging, we need to train them in effective memory techniques and show them tangibly that the work will reduce their anxiety and raise their self-confidence (which will feed into their sense of self-efficacy).

In a study carried out in high schools in England, Macaro (2001) gave meta-cognitive and cognitive strategy training to intermediate students of French aimed at improving their writing accuracy. The results in terms of self-efficacy and engagement were positive.

Simple forms of strategic instruction, such as modelling basic memory strategies (e.g. using mnemonics, colour coding, spaced practice, saying out loud), do not require a lot of specialised knowledge and if the activities are stimulating, enjoyable and productive, they will have a positive impact on the students' sense of self-efficacy. Macaro's (2001) book describes a wide range of such strategies and activities, some of which have been successfully trialled in a range of high school settings. Some strategies can be imparted to the class as a whole, where the teacher feels that every student will benefit from adopting them; others can be taught to small groups or individuals where specific gaps in skills have been identified. For more on this, see Chapter 2 on listening and Chapter 8 on reading.

- **Give students a sense of ownership over the learning process through formative feedback.**

Students could have a say about the pace at which teachers are delivering the course. They do sometimes complain that teachers are going too fast. If they feel listened to, they should be able to ask the teacher to go over a specific point again, whether individually or for the benefit of small groups. A feeling of not having enough time to learn language creates anxiety, which in turn undermines self-efficacy.

By the same token we can, where possible and if there is one, ask students whether they are ready to take the traditional summative test at the end of a unit. Clearly, with a scheduled timetable for examinations or high-stakes assessment, we must ensure this is done in a timely fashion and with a touch of realism, as some would wish to put off the evil moment indefinitely.

- **Assess students using tasks they are familiar with.**

Essentially, try to ensure that, whatever the assessment, it involves tasks they are familiar with. This is particularly true for novices and less confident students. When we test them on unfamiliar tasks, we increase their risk of failing. This threat to self-efficacy can be controlled, e.g. by making sure students get prior practice with tasks like those they will get in an exam. It requires a little extra work on the part of the teacher, but it really pays off in the end.

- **Validity of assessments**

As we saw in Chapter 13, a test is valid when it measures what it purports to measure. The fact that a student knows most of the key vocabulary in a test, does not mean they have also learned how to use the reading comprehension strategies necessary to infer the meaning of words or expressions. Therefore a test requiring effective inference strategies is only fair when we have explicitly modelled and provided sufficient practice in those strategies prior to the test. In other words, we need to ensure we are testing students only on the skills and language they have been prepared for.

- **Attitude to error**

At early stages especially, consider choosing only to correct the most serious errors, i.e. those made in front of the whole class and that seriously impede meaning. At every level, correction needs to be done sensitively in order not to undermine the student's feeling of self-efficacy. Recasting (i.e. rephrasing the response correctly) is a commonly used approach. In tasks, where the focus is on general proficiency, we may choose to ignore error altogether (see Chapter 3).

- **Structured tasks versus unstructured tasks**

At early stages of language learning it is best to avoid unstructured tasks requiring students to work beyond their existing level of competence, as this usually leads to numerous grammatical and lexical problems. For less structured tasks, if we do not correct errors in output, there is no harm done. On the other hand, if we correct all or most of the errors, the student's self-efficacy will be reduced.

Language learning anxiety

For many years, researchers have specifically studied what is called **foreign language classroom anxiety** (e.g. Zheng and Cheng, 2018). There is research to suggest (Cortazzi and Jin, 2013) that this is a greater issue in some countries than others. For example, Chinese and Korean students, used to certain styles of learning, may find speaking in class particularly threatening.

Research also suggests that anxiety not only accompanies speaking, as we might expect, but also listening. Graham (2017) refers to studies (for example, Horwitz, Horwitz and Cope, 1986) which found that listening comprehension was a source of much anxiety. Students worry that they need to understand every word in order to comprehend. In addition, they often perceive listening activities as a test rather than a learning opportunity (see Chapter 2 and Conti and Smith, 2019).

Language learning anxiety has a variety of causes. Price (1991) writes that levels of difficulty in some lessons, students' perceptions of their own language aptitude, certain personality variables (e.g. perfectionism or fear of public speaking) and stressful classroom experiences were all possible causes of anxiety. Individual personality traits, such as introversion or extraversion, are associated with anxiety arousal (Brown *et al.*, 2001).

Young (1991) identified six possible sources of language anxiety from three origins: the learner, the teacher and the instructional practice. He claimed that language anxiety is caused by:

1. learners' personal and interpersonal anxiety;
2. learners' beliefs about language learning;
3. teachers' beliefs about language teaching;
4. teacher-student interactions;
5. classroom procedures;
6. testing.

Yan and Horwitz (2008) identified ten potential reasons for anxiety which included gender, aptitude, interest and motivation, class arrangements, teacher characteristics, language learning strategies, test types, comparisons with peers and achievement.

This all suggests that we need to reduce the threatening nature of speaking and listening by whatever means. This can mean accepting error, being sensitive about correction, avoiding setting tasks beyond the capability of students and creating a supportive classroom environment in which activities are enjoyable and feasible (Smith and Conti, 2021). As far as listening is concerned, it means reducing anxiety by providing highly comprehensible language perhaps supported by tasks which model the micro-skills of the listening process, to build in success rather than guesswork and failure. See Chapter 2 and Conti and Smith (2019).

Some researchers have investigated the idea that stress is not always a bad thing and that too much or too little stress are both undesirable. Crum *et al*. (2013) found that those study participants who had high levels of cortisol were able to lower it if they believed that stress can actually be good for you. Having a positive mindset about stress can help us feel better, perform better and make us more likely to seek out feedback. In essence, psychologists claim that a little bit of stress can help people learn and perform more effectively.

Concluding remarks

Motivation and aptitude are the key drivers of success in language learning. We cannot control aptitude, but we can influence motivation. This is a complex area and one which is closely related to the issue of behaviour management. Even defining motivation causes problems for theorists and researchers and we have seen the very different ways in which researchers approach it. Motivation is a phenomenon for which there is, as yet, no all-encompassing settled theory. Yet it is undoubtedly at the very heart of successful language learning and teaching. How do we get students to want to work for us and for themselves? How do we help them feel comfortable about the potentially daunting task of language learning? There are no magic solutions, but we have offered some pointers in the right direction and have dwelt on the concept of self-efficacy which needs to be a central concern in curriculum and lesson planning.

Many motivational factors are beyond our control as teachers and it is true that teaching other languages in an English-speaking context is a significant challenge. Not only is language learning time-consuming and difficult, but students also frequently fail to see its purpose. One could even argue that, for these reasons, language teachers in high schools have a tougher job than most others. Despite these provisos, language teaching offers unique opportunities for pleasurable interaction with students. If we succeed in motivating them, we will be remembered with great respect and affection.

17

Subject knowledge

Introduction

This chapter considers the question of subject knowledge in language teaching. What it is, its importance and what we can do to improve it. In languages, as with other subject areas, teachers arrive in the classroom with a wide range of knowledge and skills. Some readers may have been conscripted to teach a language they are less familiar with than they would like. If we are partly judged by our subject knowledge in the inspection or accountability system we work in, we may feel vulnerable about the issue. This is not unusual and applies to teachers in all subject areas. In languages, however, a lack of proficiency is hard to conceal, and it can undermine credibility, which, in turn, can affect the motivation and behaviour of classes. This need not be the case, as good teachers who are open and honest can turn perceived deficiencies to their advantage. This chapter considers:

Research evidence
✓ What is subject knowledge?
✓ How important is subject knowledge?
✓ Teacher cognition
✓ Developing teacher efficacy
✓ Developing teacher resilience

Classroom practice
✓ Improving subject knowledge

Research evidence

What is subject knowledge?

Subject knowledge is part of the wider area often called **teacher expertise**. This has been broken down by Shulman (1987) into several broad areas: knowledge of the purposes of education, principles of classroom management and organisation, knowledge of educational contexts (school, environment, community), understanding student needs, curriculum knowledge, pedagogical content knowledge (how to teach the subject) and specialist subject content knowledge. In addition, Calderhead (1988) defines **practical knowledge** as "the knowledge that is directly related to action ...that is readily accessible and applicable to coping with real-life situations and is largely derived from teachers' own classroom experience" (p. 54). Others use the term **craft knowledge** to refer to the same type of thing – knowledge which is not based on theory and can be very particular to each teacher (Brant, 2006).

Since the focus of this chapter is language teacher subject knowledge, let us break down more carefully what this means in our field. Most would agree it refers to competencies such as the following.

- Speed and fluency in speaking.
- The capacity to comprehend complex spoken and written language.
- Accuracy of pronunciation and intonation.
- The use of a range of grammatical structures and vocabulary available for spoken and written communication.
- Declarative knowledge, i.e. knowledge of how the grammar of the language works. The ability to explain it without necessarily being able to use it.
- Knowledge of L2 cultures.
- Knowledge of the syllabus and assessment regime.
- Knowledge of language teaching theory and pedagogy.

In terms of fluency, at one extreme of the spectrum is a teacher with native speaker proficiency and a complete knowledge of the language system (its syntax and morphology, its idiomatic usage and social functions). At the other end is one with little, if any, proficiency and poor knowledge of how the language works. All teachers fall somewhere between these extremes. Despite their advantage of competence in the language, without training, native speakers may not be capable of explaining the grammatical system, while some non-native speakers can do this with ease without being able to speak fluently.

In days gone by, when grammar-translation ruled the roost and the main goal was to help students develop the ability to read, translate and write the L2, declarative knowledge was the most important aspect from the above list. Procedural knowledge (the actual ability to use the language) was less important. In those days the teacher did not need to speak with any fluency but did have to know how to conjugate verbs and explain how tenses, case and inflections work. To put it another way, you could say knowledge counted for a good deal but skill relatively little. Non-specialist teachers with little proficiency were drafted in to take classes and kept 'one page ahead' by studying grammar summaries and word lists. They would communicate in L1 and do little oral practice beyond the simplest transactional exchanges.

While many teachers already broke that mould, the role of real language proficiency grew as the communicative movement took hold, perhaps even at the expense of meta-knowledge. Non-specialists still teach, but now it is probably harder for them because it takes far more practice to be proficient than simply to explain rules.

In addition, it is hard to completely divorce from subject knowledge a teacher's pedagogical knowledge, both in relation to generic teaching skills and an understanding of second language acquisition. The former refers to issues such as behaviour management, explaining concepts, managing classroom routines, building relationships with students and so on. The latter refers to how students learn languages and what we can do to facilitate the process.

How important is subject knowledge?

Wright (2002) puts forward three aspects of subject knowledge: the **user** domain, the **analyst** domain and the **teacher** domain. Essentially, the user domain refers to proficiency in the language, the analyst domain refers to knowledge of the language and the teacher domain refers to the awareness of how to create and exploit language learning opportunities (i.e. methodology). We focus here mainly on knowledge and proficiency.

Widdowson (2002) argues that teachers need to understand the various components of the L2 in such a way that they can determine what is most important for students to know, how to make this accessible and learnable, and how to make it useful and real for their own social and cultural context.

Coe *et al.* (2014), in their analysis of studies on 'what makes great teaching' (not specifically language teaching), place pedagogical **content knowledge** and **quality of instruction** as the two most powerful factors. They write: "The most effective teachers have deep knowledge of the subjects they teach, and when teachers' knowledge falls below a certain level it is a significant impediment to students' learning" (p. 2). They add that quality of instruction includes elements such as effective questioning and use of assessment by teachers. Specific practices, like reviewing previous learning, providing model responses, giving adequate time for practice to embed skills securely and progressively introducing new learning (scaffolding) are also aspects of high-quality instruction.

A study of New Zealand language teachers carried out by Richards *et al.* (2013) concluded that a lack of subject knowledge significantly affected teaching practice and emphasised the importance for teachers with limited levels of L2 proficiency of continuing to develop their subject knowledge to maximise the language learning experience of their students.

However, there has been little other research specifically in language teaching which correlates teacher knowledge (of any type) with student progress. It is easy to see why: it is impossible to define terms and measure subject knowledge precisely enough while distinguishing it from other factors in the classroom which promote student progress. These factors include the teacher's personality, behaviour management, the use of formative and summative assessment, and classroom pedagogy. Put simply, some teachers with excellent subject knowledge are not very good at their craft, whereas others with imperfect subject knowledge are excellent.

These days technology means that the teacher does not provide the only model of language students hear. Despite the availability of L2 audio and video, a teacher is at a disadvantage if their speaking proficiency is limited. It means that managing everyday oral work is laborious, students may hear poor models of pronunciation and examples of inaccurate language. Most may be blissfully unaware of errors in the teacher's grammar and vocabulary but are more likely to notice inaccurate pronunciation and a lack of fluency.

Lack of proficiency may be less important when teaching beginners, but with intermediate and especially advanced students it can place severe limits on what we attempt with classes. At advanced level we need to be able to converse confidently in L2 on a wide range of quite sophisticated topics, including issues of the day, film and literature. We also need to have the linguistic skills and knowledge to prepare students for higher levels of assessment, including essay writing and translation.

In general, however, generic teacher skills and classroom pedagogy trump subject knowledge when it comes to overall effectiveness. You do not need to be Albert Einstein to be a great physics teacher and we have all come across brilliant scholars who were terrible teachers. In our field native speakers can be poor teachers while teachers with weak proficiency can be effective. This fact may have even led us to somewhat undervalue subject knowledge in language teaching circles and goes a long way to explain why school leadership teams are often ready to allocate classes to teachers who lack subject expertise.

This may mean us having to teach a second language beyond our specialism or, as is frequently the case, primary (elementary) level teachers being required to teach a language without having been trained to do so. If a teacher is equipped with reasonable subject knowledge alongside the types of effective pedagogy laid out in this book, they can do extremely well.

Teacher cognition

Borg (2003) defines teacher cognition as "the unobservable cognitive dimension of teaching – what teachers know, believe, and think" (p. 81). Research has examined teachers' knowledge and views and how these might influence pedagogy.

There are many reasons why we teach the way we do. The most prominent refer to the way we were taught and learned languages ourselves. It is our language learning 'biographies', as researchers call our history as L2 learners, that shape our beliefs. Some of these are so strong and so deeply embedded that even years of pre-service and in-service teacher education will not alter them. Researchers refer to them as central or **core beliefs**. Others, the **peripheral beliefs**, are more amenable to change, but still require a good deal of conditioning to be modified.

So previous images of learning that we have acquired throughout our L2 acquisition experience seem to have a huge bearing on our beliefs about language teaching. Calderhead and Robson (1991) refer to images we hold about what teaching is like, how lessons should be run. These images may be based, for example, on memorised 'snapshots' of individual students or classroom incidents. They act as models of action, triggering automatic responses to the various contexts teachers face daily. Although teacher training courses only influence teacher cognition to a certain degree (Borg, 2003).

These courses, at best, enhance teachers' intellectual grasp of pedagogy along with their repertoire of techniques, i.e. their declarative knowledge about teaching (being able to describe practice). However, their 'automatic' teaching behaviour will be still determined by their previous images of learning for as long as it takes for the newly acquired pedagogy to be automatised – a process that may take several years and, in many cases, may never happen. Hence, **experienced teachers** are not necessarily **expert teachers**!

So, for example, a student teacher who has been trained in communicative language teaching (CLT), but previously taught in a grammar-translation setting throughout their history as an L2 learner, might have clear declarative knowledge of how a CLT teacher should teach and may be able to plan a lesson using the framework their trainers modelled; however, in their classroom practice when responding 'automatically' to a situation, especially if under stress, the images of learning embedded in their cognition will take over.

Developing teacher efficacy

When this concept emerged in research, it was defined as "the extent to which the teacher believes he or she has the capacity to affect student performance" (McLaughlin and Marsh, 1978, p. 84). Many studies subsequently confirmed the strong relationship between teachers' sense of efficacy and student performance at all levels of education. Most efforts to enhance teacher efficacy are based on the social learning theory of Bandura (1986), who proposed four major sources of how we perceive efficacy: mastery experiences, vicarious experiences (observing others), verbal and social persuasion, and emotional and physiological states. Among these, mastery experiences have proven the most powerful for teacher efficacy (Usher & Pajares, 2008). In other words, our personal experiences of success or lack of success strongly shape our efficacy beliefs. By contrast, efficacy beliefs are only modestly changed by watching others, logical persuasion, or emotional circumstances. Real change comes through teacher's encounters with students, some of whom may be hard to motivate.

How can teacher efficacy be developed? Research evidence shows that the focus should be on changing teachers' experience. Teachers benefit from support in using strategies that improve students' performance and help them gather evidence on those improvements (Guskey, 2021). Situations need to be created where teachers recognise their actions have a positive influence on student learning.

For this to occur, professional learning experiences are needed that focus on evidence-based practices in classroom contexts. In addition, procedures should exist where teachers can gain regular, specific feedback on how their actions are affecting students. Teachers must see explicit evidence from *their* students in *their* classrooms that the changes make a difference (Guskey, 2021). **Coaching** and **mentoring** are two ways of helping this process along. Coaching has a set duration and meetings are held in a more structured form, and on a regular basis. Coaching focuses on specific development areas, with the agenda aimed at achieving specific, immediate goals. Mentoring is an ongoing relationship that lasts for a longer period of time, taking a broader view of the teacher, and meetings are often informal. Teachers looking to improve their self-efficacy should always seek support if they want to improve.

Developing teacher resilience

Moving beyond subject knowledge for a moment, it is worth dwelling on how language teachers, and teachers in general, deal with the kind of challenges and setbacks often encountered during a career. These include tiredness, marking overload, chasing students over behaviour and work issues, lack of communication in a department, disappointing exam results, coping with new initiatives, lack of resources, and issues with leadership.

The term **resilience** has been used in various ways, depending on context. Descriptions of resilience include the ability to bounce back in the face of adversity, a process in which a person actively uses strategies to maintain their commitment and well-being in the face of challenges, and the ability to adapt to a tense context and maintain skill in a challenging social or cultural context (Wang, 2021).

Teacher resilience is of utmost importance in that it generates many positive outcomes. It produces job satisfaction, responsiveness, effectiveness, self-efficacy, sense of pride, sense of agency, interpersonal relationships, competency, autonomy, optimism, positive interpersonal emotions, empathy, and emotional intelligence (Wang, 2021).

Teacher resilience, perhaps more so than resilience for other professionals, is centred a good deal on relationships, with students, colleagues and parents/caregivers. Teaching is the "creation of caring connections and encounters between individuals" (Hiver, 2018 p. 7). One finding from research is that a degree of psychological invulnerability may be a key factor in teachers' effectiveness, the capacity to adapt and survive, and long-term commitment to the profession (Gibbs & Miller, 2014).

Hiver (2018) reports that research has identified several qualities resilient teachers possess. At a personal level, they have higher self-efficacy, draw on more coping strategies, have greater autonomy, altruism and sense of purpose in life, positive self-perception and greater optimism. At a collegial level they build positive relationships with competent and nurturing colleagues and leaders, seek out friends and partners who are supportive, and use the support and attachment of social networks in their professional lives. These qualities are not seen as innate or fixed traits – they can be developed over time with deliberate intent, along with coaching and mentoring. Hiver (2018) uses the term **language teacher immunity**, to describe the ability to cope psychologically with challenges. He describes it as: "…a robust armouring system that emerges in response to high-intensity threats and which allows teachers to maintain professional equilibrium and instructional effectiveness" (Hiver, 2018 p. 13).

In practical terms languages departments can work on developing resilience. Gordon (2016) suggests one approach which involves department members each noting down or sharing electronically a perceived challenge they are facing, collating these and establishing plans to address them. For instance, if a common challenge were excessive marking, ways to reduce marking could be set up, for example by using more whole-class feedback. If a common challenge were low level disruption to classes (excessive talking, answering out of turn), then ways to address this could be explored, e.g. using more cold-call questioning, having clearer lesson transition signals or shared sanctions and rewards for good behaviour.

Classroom practice

Improving subject knowledge

Some language teachers would like to improve their subject knowledge. Self-study is fine as far as declarative knowledge of vocabulary and grammar is concerned. It does not take too much time to learn the basic lexis and grammatical rules of the language for teaching beginners and low-intermediate students. There are numerous sources of support, ranging from grammar manuals, online videos, grammar explanations and word glossaries, to staff colleagues, colleagues online and native speaker language assistants.

Spoken fluency is a harder nut to crack because it takes time and practice to develop, but can be done in several ways, most of which do not require specific funding:

- Having regular conversation time with colleagues, especially native speakers. You could devote an hour a week formally at school or socially to conversation.

- Attending evening or vacation classes in the language, even to the point of taking formal qualifications. This could be a professional development target.

- Attending a study course in the L2 country. This has the added advantage of developing a more intimate intercultural understanding.

- Taking part in a school exchange. This may mean staying with a native speaker family for a week or two a year. One of the great sources of personal reward in language teaching for non-native speakers is the relationship built with colleagues abroad.

- Using online sources of practice: watching news programmes, listening to podcasts, watching films, listening to music, doing interactive grammar and comprehension tasks, using online dictionaries such as *wordreference.com* and *linguee.com* as well as apps such as Duolingo and Coffee Break.

- Making resources: the process of seeking out written or spoken texts and designing lessons around them broadens both subject knowledge and pedagogical skills.

- Doing extensive reading, fiction and non-fiction.

Many teachers have successfully developed their proficiency, gained significant self-fulfilment and made themselves more effective classroom practitioners as a result of one or more of the above approaches. In addition, teachers who already have a high degree of knowledge and skill can avoid these becoming stale by adopting similar strategies.

In terms of language teaching pedagogy it is possible to read books like this one, look at blogs, articles and videos online, attend professional development courses and, most importantly, take part in regular dialogue with colleagues online or in the staff room about what works best in the classroom. Facebook, Twitter and professional forums are well worth engaging with for advice and support. Professional associations can also be a useful source of help.

It is also possible to carry out our own classroom research, e.g. by comparing two approaches to vocabulary learning, trying a new method for a period, evaluating outcomes and student reactions. The idea of 'teacher as researcher' is advocated in some training institutions (see Christie and Conlon, 2016). Macaro (2003) gives examples of the types of small-scale research teachers can do. Below are two examples, the wording of which has been adapted:

1. Research question: At what point during an audio or video recording do students become most anxious or frustrated?

Background: Research suggests listening is one of the most anxiety-inducing skills. Anxiety can either be present before the text starts or build up as the complexity of the text becomes apparent to the listener and/or the listener cannot hold so much information in working memory. The teacher tries three ways to answer the research question:

Method 1: Observe their faces and actions as they listen and take notes.
Method 2: Ask them to provide written answers to a series of 'affective' questions after a listening session (questions about anger, anxiety, frustration, attitude to the L2). Or do this as a pre-feedback activity with the whole class.
Method 3: Combined with the above two methods, walk around and observe the relationship between the ongoing recorded text and the writing they are doing. A colleague can help by playing the recording during the task.

2. Research question: Which new language items (particularly syntax) do students notice when they are introduced via inductive methods such as oral interaction?

Method: Give students the opportunity to recall any changes to their mental models of the L2 rules at the end of the lesson. Do this systematically over a period of, say, six lessons. Test them on those language items.

Analysis: Are there common patterns of noticing for the whole class or is there a huge variation? Do the students notice only the simpler rules, or do they notice quite complex patterns (regardless of whether they understood the pattern correctly)?

Macaro (2003 p. 51) ends his paper on an optimistic note:

> *Knowing why you are doing something because research has provided evidence to support it is good. Having built on that research evidence with your own investigations is even better. Bonne chance et bonne recherche à tous!*

More recently Jones (2016) describes some small-scale teacher research projects carried out by trainees and recently qualified teachers in London schools. By doing these projects, as Jones puts it, "… students begin to understand how professional development is not separate from, but rather central to, effective teaching" (in Christie and Conlon, 2016 p. 6).

Effective teachers are constantly questioning and trying to improve their practice. They can evaluate activities for their potential usefulness and reject those which may be just fashionable but ineffective in promoting progress. While research shows that teachers make the most progress in their early years, skill is gradually refined over a long period and experience counts for a great deal.

Concluding remarks

Subject knowledge, in its various manifestations, counts for a good deal in the classroom. However, it is not necessarily the most crucial string to a teacher's bow. Ideallly, we would be happiest teaching the language we feel most confident with, but this is frequently not the case. More and more, language teachers are expected to be skilled in two or more languages, yet teachers who are highly proficient in more than one other language are rare. We have seen that there are ways to improve linguistic and pedagogical skills and that these need not just be seen as a professional duty or a burden, but as a source of personal and professional self-improvement.

In addition, a clearer awareness of cognition may also have a positive effect on teacher practice and the outcomes of students. If we are willing to examine critically our own language learning 'biography' and other beliefs, we may be able to further refine our practice. A great deal of self-reflection, observation, regular pedagogy-related professional development, keeping up with the latest research and experimentation are likely to make us better teachers over time.

18

Songs and drama

Introduction

In this chapter we consider the rationale for using songs and drama in language lessons. The chapter includes:
- ✓ The value of songs and singing
- ✓ Choosing the best songs
- ✓ What can we do with a song?
- ✓ The value of drama in language lessons
- ✓ Issues to be aware of when doing drama
- ✓ AIM language learning
- ✓ Three practical examples of drama use

Songs

The value of songs and singing

Some research confirms what most language teachers feel: the use of song and music can aid progress in second language acquisition. For example, setting language to memory with a tune helps with its subsequent retrieval from memory. Ludke *et al.* (2014) showed in a study that singing can improve short term phrase learning in an unfamiliar language (Hungarian). Sixty adults were randomly assigned to one of three 'listen-and-repeat' learning approaches: speaking, rhythmic speaking or singing. The adults who repeated and sang subsequently did better in tests when compared with those who spoke or spoke to a rhythm. The differences in performance were not explained by factors such as age, gender, mood, phonological working memory, or musical ability and training.

Added to this are the motivational factors associated with music and singing, along with the fact that, as explained in Chapter 5, retention of vocabulary is aided by having memorable associations with the words, it is not surprising that most teachers incorporate song in their teaching. We can sum up the advantages of using L2 song in the classroom as follows.

- Song lyrics are a good source of comprehensible input.
- Listening to songs can provide good listening-as-modelling tasks.
- Song is an enjoyable way to expose students to cultural aspects of L2 cultures.
- Singing can help memorise language.
- Singing is active and most students and teachers find it enjoyable.
- Singing can relax students, make them comfortable about using L2. It reduces their **affective filter**, as Krashen (1982) calls it.
- Singing has a calming effect and everyone is busy listening or interacting with the music.

Choosing the best songs

Some important principles to consider when selecting a song now follow.

- **Comprehensible input**: a song at the appropriate level of difficulty, with some support. The principle of going just a little beyond the current proficiency level is worth keeping in mind.
- **Linguistic relevance and value**: a song relevant to the linguistic goals of the students, i.e. that contains vocabulary and grammar related to the learning outcomes of the lesson or lesson sequence. Does it have vocabulary worth learning, i.e. with high transferable use? Consider how frequently used is the vocabulary.
- **Content and style**: songs with some serious content, perhaps linking with the topic you are covering at the time. There is nothing wrong with doing a 'one-off' song lesson with an interesting message in a style students enjoy. Equally, they benefit from being exposed to musical styles they are unfamiliar with - older songs too.
- **Cultural relevance and sensitivity**: 'cultural' here does not mean L2 country culture, but rather relevance to the cultures of students in the class. This is particularly so when working in an international school or other multicultural environment.
- **Clarity**: avoid songs with words which are hard to follow, too fast or unclear. It is easy to underestimate the difficulty of picking up words, especially against a musical background.
- **Availability of relevant multimedia resources**: songs with L1 translation and video available online and free. Internet lyrics should always be checked thoroughly as they sometimes contain spelling errors or small omissions. If captions are available (as with lyric videos), consider for each song whether there is value in using them.

What can we do with a song?

To recycle previous knowledge and the language related to the song's themes, it is possible to do a series of tasks which reuse vocabulary already covered and engage students in some kind of reflection. For French, Kenza Farah's song *Sans jamais se plaindre*, which deals with the theme of parents' daily sacrifices for their children, students could:

1. brainstorm in pairs, writing in French five sacrifices parents usually make for their children;
2. think about three people in their own families and list the sacrifices they have made in recent years to help the student;
3. list the qualities of an ideal father, mother and sibling and consider whether these and/or parental expectations are the same in different cultures.

Students can then be guided to understand the text through activities which involve working on the key vocabulary. This could involve semantic analysis of the lexis through split sentences activities, gapped sentences, odd-one-outs, matching exercises, etc.

Steve's tips for beginners and near beginners

With a little innovation and creativity many of our everyday classroom routines such as vocabulary and grammar reinforcement can be pepped up with various types of singing activity. If you play guitar or keyboard students may enjoy hearing you perform or join in with you.

- **Songs with actions**: give students something to do. Actions can serve as memory-joggers and can be used to reinforce vocabulary and structures.
- Using **simple verb chanting to familiar tunes**, accompanied by moving arms to indicate the personal pronoun, work well with beginners. Try the *Mission Impossible* theme with *aller* in French; YouTube has examples.
- **Singing numbers with clapping**: sing scales with numbers in various orders and ask students to clap or stay silent on certain numbers.
- **Singing lists to well-known tunes**, e.g. the days of the week to *The Flintstones* theme or *Camptown Races*; the alphabet to an American army marching tune.
- **Singing well-known tunes with made-up lyrics**: try a daily routine to the tune of *Uptown Girl*.
- **Singing rounds**: the classic example for French is *Frère Jacques*. Actions make these more memorable.
- **Introducing Christmas songs**: YouTube is a good source of these.

Gianfranco's tips for higher levels

- **Make a transcript** of the song, cut it up **and jumble the lines** so they are out of order. Students listen and tick the lines as they hear them or reassemble them in the correct order.

- **Use gap-fills** if we want students to listen out for particular vocabulary or grammatical features, e.g. tenses or inflections. Filling gaps is no doubt the most common activity undertaken with songs. It forces students to listen carefully for detail. They may be amused if short sections are replayed numerous times in quick succession.

- Give students a short **list of words** and ask them to note down how many times they hear each one.

- Give students a **set of lyrics with deliberate (plausible) errors**. They have to underline where the errors are and then, later, insert the correct words.

- Discuss the **themes** of the song, if appropriate.

- **Identify the different tenses or moods** in the text; categorise items by part of speech.

- Ask **questions in L1** about the language, e.g. in French or Spanish: "Why is an imperfect used here rather than a perfect tense?"

- As a plenary, **reflect on the value of using songs for language learning**, based on what you have just done, and ask for suggestions on how they could benefit by listening independently. Follow up by providing lists of singers and songs they might enjoy or asking them to find a band or artist they like, to share with the rest of the class in the next lesson, perhaps by means of a formal presentation.

Drama

The value of drama in language lessons

By one definition: "… drama is concerned with the world of 'let's pretend'; it asks the learner to project himself imaginatively into another situation, outside the classroom, or into the skin and persona of another person" (Holden, 1981). Many teachers like to introduce elements of drama into their language lessons. We would sum up its benefits as follows.

- For most students it makes language learning a stimulating and enjoyable experience.
- It can reduce the self-consciousness of using L2 by allowing students to have fun and to adopt different characters.
- Performing a mini-play or sketch is a task-based activity where language is used to achieve a specific goal.

- It provides opportunities for physical expression.

- It facilitates cooperation between students; it is a teamwork activity.

- It develops students' general communication and social interactivity skills.

- It is an opportunity to recycle language previously learned in a more structured way.

As teacher trainer Tom Godfrey (2010) puts it,

> *Drama liberates the student from the confines of the conventional classroom environment and gives the student the opportunity to draw on their own experiences and imagination, in creating the material on which part of the language class is based.*

Issues to be aware of when doing drama

Teachers who are inexperienced in this field may be wary of using drama techniques in the classroom. They may fear that classes will become over-excited and noisy, and they will lose control. However, if activities are well set up, clearly organised with abundant linguistic support and have a precise goal, groups can work collaboratively in a very productive way. We can then just monitor the activity, helping out and prodding where necessary. There are other issues to be aware of, however. Students may not use enough L2, not take part in a positive way, they may make lots of mistakes or some dominate at the expense of others.

Ways to avoid some of the pitfalls above include the following:

- **Explaining very clearly the rationale** behind the activity (an opportunity for them to try out their skills, develop fluency and not worry too much about making errors).

- **Preparing students thoroughly** by practising beforehand any relevant structures and vocabulary in a more traditional way.

- **Giving clear instructions** – the aim of the activity needs explaining, and any support materials supplied. Instructions can be checked by allowing students to ask questions.

- **Modelling the task** ourselves or asking volunteer students to do so.

- **Forming suitable groups**, with an eye on any problematic relationships.

- **Giving feedback** after the activity. Groups may volunteer to act out their performance or simply report back on how they got on - what was hard, what they got out of it and so on.

- **Relocating to a suitably sized room** where groups can work in a more uninhibited way.

Teachers who are reluctant to try out drama may like to bear in mind that lessons involving acting out are often very enjoyable and memorable for students. So even if you suspect the short term linguistic 'return on investment' is not as high as you would like, there are potential compensatory gains in terms of confidence and longer-term motivation.

AIM language learning

If you are interested in using drama techniques, you may like to consider an approach used by many teachers in Canada and other parts of the world. Pioneered by teacher Wendy Maxwell, it goes by the name of **Accelerated Integrated Methodology (AIM)**. This method has certain aspects in common with the TPR (Total Physical Response) approach devised by James Asher (2009) a 'natural', comprehension-based method centred around carrying out instructions, along with other types of comprehensible input approaches which focus less on traditional grammar.

AIM may appeal if you are a teacher who enjoys using lots of games, song, mime, drama, group and pair work. It is both a set of commercial resources and a methodology which gets youngsters very actively engaged in listening to and using L2 in all kinds of enjoyable ways. There is a strong emphasis on the use of mime and gesture, considerable use of music and acting out, all underpinned by an inductive approach to grammar. As with many methods, high frequency words are emphasised. The approach is not limited to young children. Stories are used rather than traditional textbook topics; these are designed to fire the imagination and can lead to more creative language use. Teachers who employ AIM sometimes become huge enthusiasts and report that their students make excellent progress.

For more detail about the AIM approach look at *aimlanguagelearning.com*. A YouTube search reveals filmed examples of teachers at work.

Three practical examples of drama use

1. Acting out sketches with near beginners.

This is a traditional and useful activity enjoyed by near-novice students. After working on the language needed to cope with ordering food and drink at the café, the class has read a model dialogue, learned, practised and recycled the language required. They then go into groups of about four to play out their own cafe sketches. One student takes the role of waiter, the other customers. Supply an adapted authentic (or genuine) cafe menu or display one on the board. Make sure the waiter takes a written note of any orders. The task can be spiced up by giving each student a specific identity, with their own likes and dislikes. You could insist that at least one must make a polite complaint (provide language support for this).

This type of contact situation is an easy one for students to extend with previously learned material: nationalities, asking someone to repeat, a waiter losing a pencil etc. Additionally we can request that particular characters perform in a certain way, e.g. impatiently or timidly.

2. Information-gap role-playing for intermediates.

These can come in many forms, but here is a pair work example where **Partner A** plays the role of a travel agent making holiday home reservations in (Spain/France/Germany etc) for a number of travellers. The student has a set of eight different client names, together with the dates they want and their requirements. **Partner B** has a sheet listing eight different homes with their facilities, location, cost and availability. Present students with a model dialogue showing the key language needed to carry out the task. The dialogue might go as follows:

A: *Hello. I'm phoning on behalf of a customer who wants to reserve a villa.*

B: *What dates do you prefer?*

A: *They would like to stay from the 15th to 30th of July.*

B: *What type of villa are they looking for?*

A: *They'd like two bedrooms with a total of four beds, a swimming pool, Wi-Fi and preferably a location near the sea.*

B: *Let me have a look (consults their list)… I can offer a house with three bedrooms, 4km from the sea, with Wi-Fi.*

A: *How much is that?*

B: *700 euros a week in July.*

A: *I'm afraid that is too expensive. Do you have anything smaller and less expensive?*

B: *Yes, we have a two-bedroom house at 500 euros a week, but it is 7km from the coast.*

A: *Let me have a word with my clients (pretends to consult clients)… Yes, that's fine. Can you reserve that for them?*

B: *Yes, no problem. I've reserved that house. Can you transfer a deposit within the next week?*

A: *Yes, certainly. Thank you. Goodbye.*

B: *Goodbye.*

Any number of information gap tasks like this can be devised: two friends planning a weekend together; talking about their imaginary schools; phoning a camp site to book a pitch; imaginary friends talking about what they did last weekend or during a recent holiday; complaining about hotel rooms, etc.

3. Simulation activity for advanced students – parent-child scenarios.

This task puts students in pairs, one playing the role of a parent, the other a teenage son or daughter. A series of scenarios can be presented which form the basis of a creative dialogue. Language support can be provided on the board to help things along. Here are some possible scenarios which should generate discussion:

- The parent has just received a phone call from the school principal explaining that the teenager has been missing lessons and not doing homework assignments. As a result they may fail their exams.
- The parent finds contraceptive pills in the drawer of the daughter's bedside table.
- The teenager explains that they are suffering from cyber-bullying. Another student is sending abusive texts and taking photos of them without permission.
- The teenager explains they have decided not to go to university but to go straight into a job. The parent has set their heart on their son or daughter following an academic path.

- The parent has detected the smell of cannabis in their son or daughter's bedroom. They decide to broach the subject.
- The parent returns from an evening out to discover the house in a total mess after their son or daughter's party.
- The teenager discusses whether to study sciences or languages at university.
- The teenager wants to tour the world before going to university or college. The parent disagrees.
- The teenager returns home in their car in a drunken state. This is the second time it has happened. A discussion ensues.

Students may like to write out their lines to reinforce learning, but this is not necessary. As with all acting out scenarios the important thing is the process, not any final performance.

Concluding remarks

Not all students enjoy singing and drama; this may reflect whether performing arts have a high priority in the school. They may be shy and reluctant to join in. Singing and drama may not be your cup of tea either but it may be that, once you have dipped your toe in the water, these activities become a regular part of your language teaching repertoire. There are numerous web sites to explore if you want to exploit song and drama further. Language teacher blogs often feature song videos with lyrics and exercises. For advanced students we recommend the site *lyricstraining.com* (available in 2023) where they can listen to songs and do gap-fills interactively at various levels.

Advanced classes can derive enjoyment and value from drama and role-playing tasks. The highest-achieving students can perform short plays (or indeed re-enact or adapt excerpts from films using the script). All students can engage in stimulating, creative and productive role-play tasks and imaginative storytelling.

19

Lesson planning for communication

Introduction

This chapter is about lesson planning. We begin by looking at a key priority for language teachers, planning individual lessons and lesson sequences. As Cheryl Mackay reminds us in her book *Learning to Plan Modern Language Lessons* (2019), alongside classroom management and the 'performance skills' a teacher needs, it is hard to think of anything more important than planning. Creating a lesson or sequence of lessons (since a lesson can hardly be viewed in isolation), involves thinking through how time can be best exploited to maximise learning. Decisions need to be made about the content of the lesson, the resources needed, the methods of delivery, the balance of teacher-led and student-student work, and how the four skills - listening, speaking, reading and writing – will be integrated.

This chapter considers:
- ✓ Guiding principles for planning
- ✓ How and when to plan
- ✓ A lesson structure
- ✓ Building a repertoire of procedures
- ✓ Lesson planning with TPRS
- ✓ Emphasising the communicative element
- ✓ Gamifying lessons
- ✓ Why do grammar lessons fail?
- ✓ Using technology and AI for lesson planning
- ✓ Homework
- ✓ Standby lessons

Guiding principles for planning

While planning is a key aspect of teacher expertise, we need to be clear that there is no single template for the ideal lesson, even if there are some useful guiding principles.

- Is the lesson based on sound principles of classroom language acquisition? Is there comprehensible input, interaction and repetition?
- Are students mentally active all the time? How can you tell?
- Is the lesson focused on communicating messages in L2?
- Is there a suitable balance of the four skills of listening, speaking, reading and writing? Do these skills support each other?
- Does the lesson include a variety of tasks?
- Is the lesson well-matched to the needs and knowledge of the class?
- Are the expected outcomes of the lesson clear? Does the class know them?
- Is the lesson part of a planned sequence, considering previous and future lessons?
- Does the lesson have a coherent structure – for example moving from receptive work to productive, or listening to speaking, or simpler tasks to harder?
- Does the lesson offer all the scaffolding needed for all students to succeed whatever their needs?
- Does the lesson offer opportunities for formative assessment, e.g. questioning, feedback, being able to monitor students' work?
- Is there a back-up plan if something goes wrong, for example if the computer does not work, the internet is down or the photocopier is broken (not an uncommon event in schools)?

How and when to plan?

Teachers learning their craft need to write down the content of their lesson in detail. More experienced practitioners find the process much quicker as they have built up a repertoire of procedures which work and they know from experience how to run a successful sequence of activities, with the main resource of the lesson becomes, in effect, the plan. The resource might be an aural or written text, sentence builder, dialogue, picture sequence, PowerPoint flashcards, narrow reading task – to name a few.

Planning can be a team activity, particularly when it comes to longer-term sequencing and goals. Teachers in the best departments work together to share planning as well as specific teaching ideas and resources.

In terms of when to plan, teachers take varying approaches. Naturally, there should be an overall curriculum guiding the sequence of content to be taught (see Chapter 20). But planning specific lessons too far ahead is problematic since you cannot be sure at what rate the class will work and what issues they will encounter. Many teachers, therefore, plan the details of specific lessons a week or less ahead of time, many the day before. As we shall see, planning can be fast once you have a good resource bank and repertoire of practised procedures.

A lesson structure

Because the length of lessons varies so much between schools, it is impossible to come up with a one-size-fits-all lesson structure. But broadly speaking, there will be a lesson **starter** (also known as a warmer), followed by a series of **interrelated activities**, then something to round off the lesson, often called a **plenary**. The role of a plenary can be to get students to reflect on what they have learned in the lesson (or previous lessons), to refer back to lesson objectives if you set them, to consolidate learning and encourage reflection. The lesson should form a coherent whole.

In some schools it is customary to state and display specific objectives in L1. There may be advantages to this and it is useful for students know what they are going to do and why. But if the posting of objectives becomes a mere ritual, there may be little point to it.

A good starter should ideally get them to retrieve previously used language, not just from the last lesson, but earlier ones. The term **retrieval starter** is used to describe tasks which require students to recall knowledge from long-term memory. The act of retrieval reinforces memory. A slight variation is the **do-now**, where the task is written on the board so that, as students enter, they can get on with something immediately.

The starter should ideally be a bridge between previous work and work to follow in the lesson. For workload reasons it is also useful if the starter demands little or no preparation. Because the start of a lesson is so important for setting the tone and getting students to pay attention, the starter needs to be very clear and involve everyone.

Below is a selection of low preparation starters and plenaries which could be used at various levels. For a longer list, see Steve's Language Teacher Toolkit blog, frenchteachernet.blogspot.com.

Low-preparation retrieval starters

Start the sentence. Display the end of a sentence. Students must come with as many ways as possible to start it. They can do this in pairs, with the loser being the first person who cannot give an example, or do so to a time limit. Otherwise the answers can be written down on paper or on a mini-whiteboard for you to see. Ends of sentences can be designed to produce a limited range of possibilities, e.g. if you want to force students to retrieve certain verb forms, or can be made more open-ended. They can be designed to elicit specific tenses. Note that the focus is on verb retrieval and that the input is minimal, so this is an **output** and **retrieval** task. The activity can be done orally, on paper, or both.

Change one thing. Display a set of sentences featuring known language, say three per slide. Students must change one element in the sentence, e.g. a time phrase, verb, noun or adjective. To do this, they must understand, then retrieve some language from memory. This can be done in pairs orally or on paper, or with mini-whiteboards to show you.

Sentence maker grids. These have something in common with sentence builders. Display the grid, as in the French example Table 19.1 below, then tell students in pairs or on paper to make up as many sentences as they can to a time limit. Design the grid to practise the chunks you wish to target (in the example below, the perfect tense of verbs with past participles ending in *u,* as well as past time phrases) Recall that adding a time limit encourages cognitive fluency. To add extra challenge and encourage retrieval of other language, students can add their own elements, or attempt to make the longest sentence they can.

Table 19.1 A sentence maker grid

j'ai vendu	au café	du coup	mes clefs
(I sold)	*(in the cafe)*	*(so ....)*	*(my keys)*
hier	dans la rue	le week-end dernier	non merci
(yesterday)	*(in the street)*	*(last weekend)*	*(no thank you)*
mon portable	j'ai répondu	ma voiture	à ma copine
(my mobile)	*(I replied)*	*(my car)*	*(to my friend)*
ma guitare éléctrique	très vite	sur Ebay	à la prof
(my electric guitar)	*(very quickly)*	*(on Ebay)*	*(to the teacher)*
la semaine dernière	à la question	j'ai perdu	au parking
(last week)	*(to the question)*	*(I lost)*	*(at the car park)*

Odd-one-out. Display four sentences where one is different, either semantically (focus on meaning) or grammatically (focus on form). Students identify the odd-one-out, either in pairs or on paper/mini-whiteboard. These can be the basis of a discussion about the language or as preparation for the focus of the lesson.

The yes/no game. In pairs, students ask each other questions you supply (or they supply). Answers must be given without saying *yes* or *no*. This is not for beginners, but it works well with some classes who have had at least a couple of years of experience as well as advanced learners.

Low-preparation plenaries

Complete my sentence. This can be made up on the spot and tailored closely to the class and the lesson. Just give the start of a sentence they have seen or heard during the lesson and students must supply the next word or words. They could jot down their choice on a mini-whiteboard or just respond hands up or hands down (cold calling).

What was easy? What was hard? This is a metacognitive activity to encourage reflection and could be a whole class discussion in L1 about aspects of the work they have been doing. It is a chance for students to get off their chest any issues they had, or to celebrate what they have successfully mastered. This could be done with hands up or cold-called, or else they can jot something down for discussion with you or a partner. Points written down could be handed in for your benefit. For you, of course, this can be very informative and help you plan future work. We often overestimate what students have understood!

One word at a time. Picking up the same topic as the lesson, explain that the class will make up a little story in five minutes, but using only one word each at a time. Students are allowed to say full stop if a sentence has reached a natural end. Model the task first. So, to do this in English, a sequence might go something like this:

> *Last - Saturday - my - friend - Eric - went - to - the - hospital - with - his - dog - full stop.*
> *The - dog - was - called - ....* and so on.

It is up to the class where the story goes. Stories can get silly, which is fine and fun. You cannot be certain that the language used will come from the lesson, but if you join in you can push the content in a certain direction. Or you can make sure a certain tense is used, for example. This should be cold called, but with the option to 'pass' if they cannot think of a next word, to take the pressure off. Insist that students do not plan their words ahead. In truth, this is hard to control, but it does encourage spontaneity and humour. To do this with some success they need a stock of language and some grammatical skill if you want a focus on accuracy. For example, if one student gives a feminine gendered article, the following word needs to be feminine.

Building a repertoire of procedures

For new teachers, planning can be daunting and they may be faced with a wide range of theories and advice on how to teach. In teacher education circles there is a debate around whether you should learn from a variety of methods, or be taught just one, to keep things simple, and from which you can build a more sophisticated approach with experience. We agree with Larsen-Freeman and Anderson (2011), Bauckham (2016) and Prabhu (1990) that there is no best method for every circumstance, but, as suggested in the introduction to this book, if you develop your own repertoire of procedures based on sound principles you will be off to a good start.

Having a set of familiar procedures, activities, plans and techniques saves time on preparation and keeps workload in check. Below are some teaching routines you could apply on a regular basis.

Working with a sentence builder

Remember that three great advantages of sentence builders are (1) their comprehensibility (everything is translated); (2) their clarity and transparency, i.e. it is clear to students exactly what they need to practise and (3) their adaptability, i.e. the many ways you can exploit them. A sentence builder can be the first part of a longer sequence of lessons involving narrow listening and reading texts, comprehension questions, translation, grammar exercises and less controlled productive tasks like free composition. In general, the principle, as we saw in Chapter 12, is about moving from receptive work to productive through careful steps, allowing much recycling of high-frequency language patterns. Even if you do not follow a strict MARS-EARS sequence as described in Chapter 12, there is still a wide range of ways a sentence builder can be exploited.

Working with a written text

At any level of proficiency the procedures described in Chapters 3, 4, 8 and 9 can be deployed. With a text at the right level (ideally, at least 95% of the words already known to students), we can work through a routine of interactions and other activities. With this toolkit of procedures, the text essentially becomes the lesson plan. Once again, lessons are built up with the early focus on comprehension, building the level of challenge gradually over a lesson or sequence of lessons. This takes practice and experience, of course, but over time a great deal of time is saved when planning.

   Here is a short, concocted novice text in English, followed by a sequence of possible activities. The text is short enough to be displayed on a screen, as well as printed off. Imagine how this would work in the language you teach.

> *Her name is Marie-Hélène. She is 9 years old. She lives in Toulouse in the south of France. She lives in a house with her two parents and her brother Alain. She has a cat called Raoul. He is black and he is very cute. She loves cats, snow and cartoons on TV. She also likes to play on the computer. In her room she has a bed, some books, a desk and a computer. She doesn't like mice; she prefers hamsters. She hates spiders. She thinks they're horrible!*

1. **Teacher reads aloud** the text.
2. **Choral repetition** of part of the text. Use the 'back-chaining' technique (see also p. 43). This means repeating a chunk, one syllable at a time, 'back-to-front', e.g. in the first sentence above: *ène, Hélène, is Hélène, name is Hélène, her name is Hélène*. Focus on awkward sounds and sound-spelling correspondences. (These could even be highlighted in the text, a technique known in the research literature as textual enhancement).
3. **Find the L2**. How do you say...?
4. **True/false**, e.g. *She lives in a house. She has a dog.*
5. **Correct false statements**, e.g. *She is 10 years old; she lives in New York.* Normally teacher-led, but in pairs with some classes.

6. **Question-answer** (using full range of question types and personalising the questions at times), e.g. *Is she ten years old? Does she live in Toulouse or Paris? Where does she live? How old are you? Where do you live?*

7. **Aural gap-fill** with the text not visible, e.g. *Her name is…. She is … She lives in… She lives with…*

8. **Students write answers** to questions previously practised orally.

9. **'Disappearing text'**, on successive slides remove more and more of the text for students to complete orally, starting with just a few words missing, then going as far as the class can manage. (See also p. 87).

10. **A gapped version of the text** to complete (with or without options). Gaps may be words, chunks or letters.

11. **Translation into L2** of chosen chunks from the text, either teacher-led or in pairs.

12. **Transcription** of chunks from the text, e.g. delayed dictation.

13. **Changing the perspective**. Students convert the text into the first person, orally and/or in writing.

14. **Free writing**. Students write their own narrative. With most classes this needs leaving very late, once you are sure the language has been recycled multiple times over more than one lesson. Students could record their writing on a phone.

Working with aural texts

Whether your text is from an audio or video source, or your own voice, a common sequence of activities can be used. The source text should, again, be highly comprehensible. Material which has too much unknown language will be off-putting to students and reduce their self-efficacy. It is often a good idea to use a transcript together with the spoken text. Here is a sequence that could be followed.

1. **A pre-listening task** such as working on some words and phrases students will hear in the text or some background information about the topic.

2. **Read aloud** the text twice as students follow.

3. **True-false statements** to judge, e.g. with mini-whiteboard responses.

4. **False sentences** to correct.

5. **A gap-fill task**, either with options provided or not.

6. **A 'faulty transcript' task**, where you give students a transcript which differs in a few ways from the original. They must find the discrepancies.

7. **A dictation task** based on bits of the text, e.g. running dictation, paired dictation or delayed dictation.

8. **Translation**.

Working from a picture or picture sequence

Refer to Chapter 10 for possible sequences for exploiting pictures. As with the above examples, the resource (picture or picture sequences) becomes the lesson plan. And the same picture(s) can be re-used in multiple ways, saving you time and effort. The same sort of techniques used in the previous sequences can be applied, with the same aim of recycling the language many times across the four skills.

Lesson planning with TPRS

We have already made clear that there is no single best way to teach a language. Many teachers choose to use approaches which might be considered outside the mainstream, breaking the current mould or orthodoxy. We include here an approach which many teachers find productive and inclusive in their setting, and which draws on certain research principles, notably the importance of comprehensible input and communication. The first is from the so-called natural, comprehension-based view of language acquisition. The second prioritises communicative, task-based principles. We should be clear, however, that there is often a large overlap between different general approaches and that teachers interpret these approaches in their own ways, adapting to the needs of the class and the syllabus, as they see fit.

Teaching Proficiency through Reading and Storytelling (TPRS)

This approach has been around since the 1990s, having originally been developed by American teacher Blaine Ray, and is an example of a natural approach (see Chapter 1). It is mainly to be found in the USA, but has been picked up by practitioners elsewhere, including in Europe. Its theoretical inspiration is to a large extent Krashen's **Monitor Theory**. Krashen has always argued that we acquire languages in one way – by understanding messages. This view has led to a methodology based on 'CI' (comprehensible input), with some teachers even calling themselves CI teachers. Printer (2019) concluded in his research study that TPRS was a motivating approach which developed the three elements of self-determination theory: competence, relatedness and autonomy.

In a nutshell, the starting point of TPRS is that students become proficient by being exposed to meaningful, 'compelling' listening and reading input. Grammar may be briefly taught, but only within the context of a story being told, re-enacted, or read. Lots of input is provided before significant amounts of output are expected. Key vocabulary ('core vocabulary') and structures are recycled, and a full range of aids are used to help students grasp meaning: pictures, gestures and objects. There are often elements of acting out involved, including having students come to the front and even dress up. The approach may not suit teachers who prefer a more formal approach to their lessons, since it helps a great deal if you are prepared to act out situations, use mime, props, humour and imagination.

Some elements which TPRS has in common with other approaches are the use of visual aids, using all four skills, question-answer sequences ('circling'), acting out, doing grammar pop-ups' (briefly explaining and modelling grammar structures and morphology) and using stories as a source of input. It is also common to apply the steps of a TPRS lesson to other content, such as describing, discussing, and reading about pictures, authentic resources, and short films or video clips.

Here is a typical lesson plan which Steve describes in his book *Becoming an Outstanding Languages Teacher* (2023) (with thanks to teacher and consultant, Martina Bex).

The heart of a TPRS lesson plan may be a story which is co-created by the teacher and students. A typical story outline looks like this:

- A character has a problem.
- The character tries to solve the problem and fails.
- The character tries to solve the problem in a new way and fails again.
- The character tries to solve the problem in a new way and finally succeeds.

While some teachers prefer to co-create stories on the spot and with no outline in mind, others prefer to do so using 'scripts', or basic story outlines, that guide the story and/or intentionally expose students to specific vocabulary (words or phrases). A basic story script might look like this:

- (Character) wants (thing). (Character) doesn't have (thing).
- (Character) goes to (place 1) to find (thing). There are no (things) at (place 1), only (thing 2).
- (Character) goes to (place 2) to find (thing). There are no (things) at (place 2), only (thing 3).
- (Character) goes to (place 3) to find (thing). There are (things) at (place 3). (Character) (decides that s/he no longer wants it, it's too expensive, or buys it and is happy, etc.)

How does a story turn into a lesson?

1. **Establish meaning** for the core vocabulary, or the key words that will be used many times in the story. A typical TPRS lesson might feature three key words or phrases that are repeated throughout the story outline. Translation is the preferred method for this, although you might establish meaning with visual links such as images or gestures (e.g. when students do not have a shared first language).

2. **Write the core vocabulary** on the board in L2 and L1. Typically, students are not encouraged to repeat the word as the teacher writes and says it out loud, while they just listen. Then, the teacher demonstrates a gesture for the word. Students mimic the gesture as the teacher repeats

the word aloud in L2 several times. Meaning is typically confirmed once or twice by asking a student in English, "What does [L2 structure] mean in English?" This ensures that students are creating an accurate link between the new word/phrase and its meaning. This is also more efficient than waiting for them to guess the meaning of an image or gesture.

3. **Ask personalised questions** that feature the core vocabulary structures. If the structure is 'goes to sleep', you might ask *When do you go to sleep? What do you need to go to sleep?, When is it difficult to go to sleep?,* etc. These questions are discussed with students.

4. '**Ask a story**' (i.e.co-create a story) using the story script or by coming up with a story out of the personalised conversation. TPRS teachers often bring students to the front and have them use props to make the story come to life. The story evolves through question and answer with occasional checks for meaning in English. If the teacher is using a script, they tell some aspects of the story and ask students to contribute original details, thereby personalising the story as well.

5. **Read the class story.** You may write up the story after the lesson so that it can be read out next time, or you might use a strategy known as 'write and discuss' to re-tell and write the story together with students. The story is displayed for all to see so that it can be read together. During this step of a TPRS lesson, the teacher combines elements such as choral reading with conversational and instructional elements, such as question-answer, comprehension checks, and asking personalised questions to help students create real-life connections to the story.

6. **Complete several story activities.** These can include familiar tasks such as hiding the story then retelling from memory, answering questions from memory, doing a true-false task or matching starts and ends of sentences.

The use of stories which are memorable and can relate to students' lives is one merit of TPRS. (Psychologists have understood for a long time the link between memory and stories, e.g. Bower and Clark (1969).) The personalisation element is strong in TPRS. For examples of this style of teaching search TPRS on YouTube, and Liam Printer's *Motivated Classroom* podcast referred to in Chapter 16, where there are many practical classroom activities used not just in TPRS lessons, but across other methodologies.

Emphasising the communicative element

In their book *Common Ground: Second Language Acquisition Theory Goes to the Classroom* (2021), Florencia Henshaw and Maris Hawkins draw on aspects of the research literature which can be marshalled to support a strong emphasis on communicative tasks in the classroom.

The authors start from the assumption that acquisition is the "mostly implicit process of building a linguistic system through the interpretation of meaning" (p. 20). Their departure point is a definition of communication from VanPatten (2017) as the expression, interpretation, and negotiation of meaning with a purpose in a given context. In this view, communication cannot mean learning some vocabulary, then learning some grammar, then finding something to talk about using the language learned. The communicative goal should come first.

The authors ask whether a range of classroom activities are really communicative. In other words, is there information being conveyed and what can the audience do with the information? Compare these two tasks from Henshaw and Hawkins (2021):

1. Students write a list of ingredients of their favourite dish then the class or their partner has to guess which dish it is.
2. Students make sentences based on word prompts, such as 'Mary/walk/park/yesterday'.

The first is communicative, the second is not. (The second activity may well be useful, but if the lesson is being planned around the idea of communication, it is not optimal.)

In light of this, a communicative lesson plan would prioritise the genuine communication of information or ideas *with a purpose*. Activities do not necessarily need to be based on real-life scenarios, but there does need to be an information gap between students, or students and teacher. A first key point to make here is that communicative activities have the potential to be more motivational because there is a purpose involved. This applies to many purposeful games too. A second point is that if you want students to focus on the *form* of the language, it needs to be done in a meaningful way so that form-meaning relationships are clear.

What does this mean in practice? The authors provide an example of how a mundane drill can be turned into a communicative activity. So if your topic is talking about the past using past tense verbs, you could practise as follows:

Did you go to the store yesterday? (Yes, I went to the store yesterday.)
Did you watch TV yesterday? (No, I didn't watch TV yesterday) etc

Alternatively (and better!), you could make the work more communicative as follows:

Step 1: On this (L2) handout, tick the activities you took part in last weekend:

Last weekend, I…
> *…watched a TV show*
> *…revised for a test*
> *…read a book*
> *…went to a friend's house*
> And so on.

Step 2: Now, compare answers with a classmate and summarise the information you learn here:
- Activities my partner and I have in common

- Activities neither of us did
- Number of places I went to
- Number of places my partner went to

Step 3: Based on the information, who had the busier weekend? Who likes to go out? Who prefers to stay at home?

If we keep in mind this principle of communication, it may help us choose activities which are likely to be more motivational than others. Key to their success is whether the students have the linguistic means to carry them out successfully. This is why some argue that students need to go through a sequence of less communicative tasks before they can handle communicative ones. With some creativity, however, tasks can be designed which provide structured repetition within the context of a communicative goal. Information-gap tasks and guessing games often fulfil this purpose.

Gamifying lessons

Most language teachers enjoy exploiting the advantages of games or game-like activities in lessons. Games provide a goal for an activity, may be competitive and fun, and can be designed to further our objectives of promoting communication through comprehensible input and interaction. Teachers often feel that games are a way to 'sweeten the pill' of learning and there is nothing wrong with this, providing the game is worthwhile. But how do we know a game is worthwhile? Below are some factors to bear in mind when evaluating a game. If the game scores well on most or all of these factors, it is worth including in a lesson plan.

- **Fun factor**. Will the game be enjoyable?
- **Input**. Will it provide comprehensible input?
- **Output**. Will it elicit feasible output, i.e. language students can easily manage?
- **Communication**. Will it promote oral or written communication between learners or between learners and teacher?
- **Surrender value**. Will the impact of the game justify the time spent on it?
- **Inclusivity**. Will the game involve all students?
- **Management**. Will the game be easy to set up and manage? Will it lead to disruption?
- **Formative assessment**. Will it provide opportunities for this? (see Chapter 13).

There is too little space in this book to describe many games, but examples are easy to find online. Here are two locations where recommended games can be found:

Steve's website. https://www.frenchteacher.net/teachers-guide/games-that-work/

Gianfranco's blog. https://gianfrancoconti.com/2017/05/01/10-minimal-preparation-games-to-enhance-phonological-awareness-and-decoding-skills/

Steve's favourite communicative game: Alibi

This is a whole class game lasting around 30 minutes for students who have done at least four years of the language. Tell the class that a crime was committed the evening before, e.g. the theft of a mobile phone at 8 p.m. from an elderly man on the street. Explain that the police are seeking two suspects, aged around 15-17. Add that the police think the suspects come from this school and may even be in this classroom!

At this stage some students will still believe the crime is real. Others have cottoned on to the fact that this is all made up.

Seek two volunteer suspects who must leave the room for about five minutes. During this time they must establish an alibi – something they did together the previous evening which makes their involvement in the crime impossible. Stress that the suspects must prepare in detail what they did so their stories are identical when they come back into the room, one by one, to answer questions from the class. The classroom becomes, therefore, a sort of court room.

While the suspects are outside, prepare questions with the rest of the class, anticipating what each suspect might say: where they were, how they got there, what they were wearing, what they spoke about, what they ate, and so on. Display some of these questions on the board as helpful prompts.

When each suspect returns, ask them to swear an oath of truth (e.g. on the text book), then students ask questions, while someone notes the answers down. Help the class along with this if they run out of ideas. After both suspects have answered, the class must decide democratically if the two stories are close enough to be a valid alibi.

Using technology and AI for lesson planning

Digital tech is a fast-evolving area. Apps, learning platforms and websites come and go. But it is fair to say that many teachers make successful use of tech to enhance lessons and to further language learning. At the time of writing (2023) a range of apps and websites are popular with language teachers and can be recommended. These include *The Language Gym, Textivate, SentenceBuilders, Languagenut, ThisIsLanguage, Quizlet, Blooket,* not to mention the many digital resources which accompany textbook courses. Cost is a significant factor in the choice of digital resources. Departmental budgets are often tight, so decisions need to be made based on some principles. Here are several items to consider.

- Does the tech support sound principles of acquisition? (Meaningful input, interaction, repetition.)
- Does it enhance delivery compared with other methods? For example, how does a digital formative assessment tool compare with the humble mini-whiteboard?
- Does it raise the motivation of students? In itself, the 'fun factor' may promote other forms of learning.
- Does it help make learning accessible, e.g. enabling effective remote learning or supporting students with alternative needs?
- Is it time-effective? How much time is spent on activities which promote language learning?
- Does the tech represent value for money?

Points to be wary of include the three below.

1. **The bandwagon effect** – is the tech a 'shiny new toy' which looks appealing, but which may not help with learning.
2. **Training**. Are teachers fully trained in the use of the new tech, e.g. if there is access to an interactive or smart board, do staff know how to get the best from it?
3. **Distraction**. If students are using notebooks, phones or tablets, are these always being used appropriately?

Language departments should have clear guidance for tech use so that teachers do not either overuse or underuse it. Underlying this would be a recognition that language learning is above all a social activity, so tech use may be overdone. The social nature of language learning implies an emphasis on listening and speaking, so if tech does not support these skills, it needs to be questioned at the very least.

It cannot be assumed that all students will take to tech activities. Like teachers, some will lack technical skills, others will just prefer to learn in other ways. This means that we need to support such students with extra help and by explaining the merits of the tech being used. This includes training them in the use of web-tools and apps so they can use them independently, e.g. how to use verb conjugation trainers and AI tools as well as *YouTube, Google Translate, Wordreference, Deepl, Linguee* etc. Incidentally, any new resources can be piloted with some students before purchase.

Finally, regarding the 'Google Translate/AI issue' (and plagiarism in general, for that matter), it may be worth explaining precisely from the outset what plagiarism is and asking students to promise never to commit it. They can be reminded of their pledge and sanctions made clear for any flouting of the rules. In our experience this works well.

Using AI for lesson planning

At the time of writing (mid 2023), ChatGPT is making a lot of waves in educational circles, and by the time you read this, there will already be a more mature understanding of how it can be used to support language teaching Below is a selection of ways in which AI could help.

- Writing texts at various levels of comprehensibility and in various formats, including narrow reading/listening tasks, parallel translations and stories.
- Producing comprehension exercises to accompany texts.
- Writing planning documents.
- Correcting student work for feedback purposes.
- Generating vocabulary lists, including definitions and/or translations.
- Creating gap-fill activities, multi-choice questions and matching tasks.
- Generating conversation questions on selected topics.
- Producing ready-made lesson plans.

We should be clear that when using AI to generate plans and resources, care is needed to ensure that the material is right for the class. Experience suggests that a degree of editing is needed to match resources precisely to the level and prior knowledge of the class.

Homework

Homework is often an essential part of lesson planning and it is clear from experience and research (Hattie (2011) that well-conceived homework at high school level allows students to progress faster.

Homework has several functions. For example, it can add to what goes on in the classroom. It allows students to further develop the use of study skills, such as grammar and dictionary reference. It is a source of differentiated activities, for example open-ended free writing. Homework also provides evidence for assessment. Furthermore, it shows parents/caregivers what students are doing in the classroom and can involve them in the process (bearing in mind that some can help more than others). Importantly, homework gives the chance to intersperse between lessons, extra opportunities for language input and practice.

In most instances we recommend the traditional model of homework being used to reinforce work done in the classroom on the same day, or very soon after. The 'flipped' model is another option. This means that work is done prior to the lesson so that class time can be used to discuss or practise what has been studied at home. There is no doubt a role for the flipped model in language learning, e.g. pre-learning vocabulary for a test or for use in discussion work, or studying a grammar presentation on YouTube before revisiting it in the classroom. At advanced level flipping is common when studying, for example, a work of literature when students are expected to read a section of text, perhaps with guided comprehension questions, before discussing it during the next lesson. Experience shows that the required preparation does not always happen, which can jeopardise the success of the subsequent lesson. However, it is worth trying out the approach to see how a class responds.

Most of the time homework is an integral part of the lesson plan, following on logically from the classroom teaching sequence. Many teachers feel that reading and writing tasks are well suited to homework, enabling more time to be spent in the classroom on listening and speaking. There is certainly room, however, for listening and speaking at home provided that every student can access the material if technology is required. Time-filling tasks which are set purely because the school says homework must be set are not advised; homework needs to provide useful further input and output.

Commonly used homework tasks include:

- completing **grammatical exercises** such as meaningful pattern drills;
- **cloze tasks and questioning** (the more meaningful, the better);
- **compositional writing** (from sentences, to paragraphs and longer written compositions);
- **writing dialogues**;
- doing **reading comprehension** tasks (passages accompanied by exercises);
- **oral presentation** tasks (either rehearsed out loud for presentation to the class or a partner, or recorded and submitted to the teacher);
- **vocabulary learning** (e.g. from a sentence builder);
- **designing** tasks (e.g. posters and brochures);
- **online research**;
- **extensive reading** (advanced level);
- **self-selected online reading and listening** (e.g. one task a week);
- **watching online videos**, for example songs, with the aid of a worksheet;
- **memorising a poem**;
- **learning a mnemonic** for a grammar point (e.g. the perfect tense in French, or prepositions taking the accusative case in German);
- **completing an information grid**.

Some teachers like to give students a choice of activity, perhaps differentiated. Others have experimented with 'takeaway' menus for homework. Where it is not obvious how to match a piece of homework to a specific lesson, students can choose from a menu of tasks over a school term. These might be of a generic type, not related to any specific area of grammar or vocabulary. Students can pick and choose as they wish. Here are some examples.

- Make a poster showing how to say five different pastimes in the present and the past explaining the difference between the two.
- Record on your phone a 90-second presentation about yourself or a family member.
- Find a famous French recipe online and write down in French ten ingredients used to make it.
- Find 15 food or drink items in your kitchen and translate them into Spanish.
- Interview a family member and write down in German twenty sentences about them.
- Write a diary of what you did during the previous week.
- Research a Spanish-speaking tourist destination and create a poster with the aim of persuading people to visit.
- Create a fact file sheet about francophone countries around the world.
- With your phone, do a guided tour of your house or apartment.

Standby lessons

Things can sometimes go wrong at school. The computer breaks down, we have to teach a lesson we were not expecting, or we did not get time to plan that lesson we intended. This is when we need standby lessons which can be adapted to various levels. So here are four we can recommend which can be part of your repertoire. With these you will never be short of a lesson!

Simon Says. This is a hit at all levels. It can be used to teach body parts from scratch or to revise them at any time. The pace can be adjusted to suit the class, it encourages careful listening, and is good fun. The Simon Says idea can be used to get students to mime activities, rather than just touching a part of the body.

Mental math(s) bingo. Instead of reading out a number, give classes a simple mental sum to solve which leads to the number on their card. Simple terms like *plus, minus, multiplied by* and *divided by* need to be taught. The advantage of this variation is that it provides more mental challenge. The downside is that students do not make the immediate link between the numbers being read out and the number they see in front of them.

My holiday in…. Good for low-intermediate and above. Tell the class what you did during a holiday in some detail. Students may take notes in L2 or in English. Then give them true/false or not mentioned statements. Keep a careful mental note of what you have said. Next, tell them to report back to you, or a partner, what you did. This is a good comprehensible input task. Other topics could include *last weekend, my pastimes, when I was young* etc.

Concluding remarks

Several key points have been made in this chapter. First, although there is no single template for an effective language lesson, lesson plans should be based on sound evidence-informed principles. Second, although planning is time-consuming for pre-service and inexperienced teachers, it becomes more efficient with experience, once successful procedures have been developed.

Some points also worth keeping in mind are the following.

- Do plans generate self-efficacy in students (Chapter 16)?
- Does planning ensure success?
- To what extent is the notion of 'opportunity cost' taken into account? In other words, was the time spent planning and doing an activity in class worthwhile?
- Could the same or better learning gains have been made more efficiently?
- Could an existing resource be used or adapted effectively, rather than creating one from scratch?
- Could the same resource be re-used in different ways with the same class, or a different class?

Finally, since planning is one of the more enjoyable and creative tasks a teacher does, we need to try to make sure we do not overload ourselves with correcting students' work, at the expense of time spent planning enjoyable lessons.

For detailed descriptions of lesson plans, see Steve's book, *50 Lesson Plans for French Teachers* (Smith, 2020).

Planning a communicative curriculum

20

Introduction

In this chapter we move away from lesson planning to more general issues concerning the curriculum. Although curriculum planning may fall under the responsibility of a Head of Department, it is important that all language teachers be aware of some key principles. As Richards (2001) explains, being an effective teacher means more than being a skillful classroom practitioner. It is also about learning how to adapt resources, plan and evaluate courses, adapt teaching to students' needs and work within a particular institutional setting. In short, we need to understand our practice within the context of factors and processes that are often referred to as curriculum development. This enables us to evaluate critically our curriculum as well as proposed changes to it.

This chapter considers:

✓ Curriculum design principles
✓ Three types of curriculum design
✓ Key questions about curriculum
✓ Curriculum planning with a textbook
✓ Why does a grammatical syllabus fail for most students?
✓ Planning for exam success
✓ A communicative curriculum

Curriculum design principles

The terms curriculum and syllabus have been used in various ways over the years. Here the terms are used interchangeably. One definition of curriculum is:

...the overall plan or design for a course and how the content for a course is transformed into a blueprint for teaching and learning which enables the desired learning outcomes to be achieved. (Richards, 2013 p. 6)

An initial point to make clear is that a curriculum is more than a list of vocabulary, grammar, topics and communicative functions to be covered. It encompasses a department's philosophy, including general principles of language acquisition. This section outlines an overview of curriculum design based on Nation and Macalister (2010). It may provide food for thought when evaluating an existing curriculum or setting up a new course. These are general curriculum planning issues, not the detailed planning of, say, a unit of work. Their overall model of curriculum design is founded on three principles: **Environment**, **Needs** and **Principles**.

Environment

Several factors can be taken into account with respect to what Nation and Macalister refer to as 'environment'. They mention the following:

- Students' interest in the subject.
- Students' future intentions, e.g. going to university.
- Time available for the course.
- Class size.
- The proficiency range of classes.
- The immediate survival needs of students.
- Availability of teaching materials.
- Teachers' experience and training.
- The learners' use of their first language.
- The need for learner autonomy.

Needs

Student needs depend to a great extent on the context of learning. For example, they may be immigrants who need to acquire the language of their new country for employment or for educational needs (e.g. examinations or proceeding to a further stage of education). In a school setting, the immediate needs are less obvious, but could include the requirement to pass exams or learn a language for future study or use on holiday or in employment.

Principles

Research on second language acquisition and learning in general should be used to guide discussion on curriculum design. Principles from second language acquisition include the importance of input and interaction. General principles include the importance of repetition, thorough processing of material, individual differences, including student attitudes and motivation.

What specific principles do Nation and Macalister put forward? Here is an abbreviated summary. They are essential to curriculum planning.

a) Content and sequencing

1. **Frequency**: teach high frequency language which provides the best return on learning effort.
2. **Strategies and autonomy**: train learners in how to be more aware of how they are learning and to become more independent.
3. **Spaced retrieval**: provide spaced, repeated opportunities to engage with language in varying contexts.
4. **Language system**: put the focus on generalisable features of the language.
5. **Keep moving forward**: include progression in the curriculum.
6. **Teachability**: sequence items appropriately, bearing in mind when learners are ready to learn new items.
7. **Learning burden**: help learners make good use of previous learning.
8. **Interference**: sequence items so they have the best effect on each other for learning.

b) Format and presentation

1. **Motivation**: make the learning interesting, exciting and of value.
2. **Four strands**: include a roughly even balance of meaning-focused input, language-focused learning, meaning-focused output and fluency tasks.
3. **Comprehensible input**: provide lots of comprehensible, interesting listening and reading.
4. **Fluency**: provide activities which build fluency of comprehension and production of already known language.
5. **Output**: include pushed output activities (making students speak and write).
6. **Deliberate learning**: include learning about the sound system, spelling, vocabulary and grammar.
7. **Time on task**: maximise the time spent using the L2.
8. **Depth of processing**: input should be processed as thoroughly as possible.
9. **Integrative motivation**: encourage positive attitudes towards L2 cultures.

10. **Learning style**: students should have chances to work with material in the way they prefer. (This is now considered controversial at best. Research does not support the idea that matching activities to a preferred learning style increases progress (e.g. Riener and Willingham, 2010), but it is common sense to suggest that a range of learning activities should be provided. Students may have learning preferences.)

c) Monitoring and assessment

1. **Ongoing needs and environmental analysis**: selection, ordering, presentation and so on should match the needs of students. This includes the syllabus requirements.
2. **Feedback**: students should receive feedback which can help them improve. Short term achievement tests are an important part of the plan. These provide feedback for the teacher and motivation for the student. Larger summative tests check if the curriculum is working (e.g. end of course or end of year exams).
3. **Baseline or proficiency tests**: may be useful for placing students in the right class. Diagnostic tests can reveal what gaps in knowledge need to be filled.
4. **Monitoring**. There are other ways of monitoring if the curriculum is functioning as it should, e.g. observing and monitoring using checklists, homework, collecting samples of student work and getting learners to talk about their learning (e.g. in focus groups). Best curriculum design needs to include opportunities for all the above.

Three types of curriculum design

Richards (2013) proposes that curriculum consists of **input** (the language content, e.g. vocabulary, communicative functions, grammar), **process** (how the input is taught) and **output** (what learners are able to do as a result of the teaching). He sets out three types of curriculum design: **forward design**, **central design**, and **backward design**. Here is how he defines these:

1. **Forward design**: developing a curriculum through moving from input, to process, and to output. In this case, the main driving force of the curriculum is the language content and this is what many of us would consider a traditional view. We decide what needs teaching and then design appropriate activities and procedures to deliver that content.

2. **Central design**: starting with process and deriving input and output from classroom methodology. In this view, the starting point is the activities, procedures and general methodology to be used, e.g. in task-based language teaching, the idea of the communicative 'task' takes priority, ahead of any language input or expected output. Language is brought in as appropriate to the task. Unlike the other two designs, the focus here is on the *process* of acquisition, not the language itself.

3. **Backward design**: starting from output and then dealing with issues relating to process and input. In this case, we decide what we want to students to be able to do with the language, then choose the language and methodology to achieve those goals. A variety of teaching strategies can be employed to achieve the goals but teaching methods cannot be chosen until the outcomes have been described. The output depends on an analysis of the students' needs, e.g. do they need to acquire basic conversational skill or the ability to read texts. Alternatively, the output may be written into a set of 'can do' standards such as those in the Common European Framework (CoE, 2001) or ACTFL Standards (see Chapter 13).

Richards (2013) argues that none of these three approaches to curriculum design is inherently better than the others, but that the forward design option may be suitable where a compulsory curriculum is in place and teachers have little choice over what and how to teach. This would be the case, for example, in England where the vocabulary and grammar are laid out explicitly in the GCSE examination, taken by many students at the age of 15-16 years old. Teachers have little choice in what language elements should be taught. Proponents of backward design argue that we should prioritise what students need to do with language, as it corresponds to their needs, not the requirements of a prescribed syllabus. In the USA, the ACTFL (2012) recommends backward design as one of its core principles (actfl.org).

As we saw in Chapter 13, whether the curriculum is designed backwards or forwards, it is important that the teaching and assessment are aligned and that the assessment regime avoids creating negative washback.

Key questions about curriculum

Based on sound principles of curriculum design, several key questions can be asked.

- Why and how are we teaching the language(s)?
- Is our curriculum structure suitable, e.g. number of languages, when they are introduced and how they are timetabled?
- What are pupils achieving as a result of the teaching?

In more detail, here are three general areas which, to an extent, pull together many areas we have considered in this book.

1. Why and how are we teaching the language(s)?

- To what extent are we focused on developing practical skill rather than just knowledge of the language(s)? How does knowledge become skill? (How can declarative knowledge become procedural?)

- What do we want students to be able to do? (And what would they like to be able to do?) Hold simple conversations? Be able to read and listen to a basic level? To know more about L2 countries and cultures? To prepare for later study of a language in adult life? To be 'global citizens'?

- Do we have clear goals for all students, whatever their needs and abilities? Is the goal for some to achieve a degree of comprehension and conversational skill after two or three years? Is the goal for others to prepare for more advanced study?

- How does our chosen methodology meet the above goals? What is our focus? If we want students to hold simple conversations, are we focusing enough on listening and speaking? Is our approach in line we what we know about how languages are acquired? Do we have the expertise in the teaching team (e.g. a 'research lead') to be sure why we are employing a certain methodology? Should the same methodology be used with all classes and by all teachers?

- Do we group students by ability/prior attainment? If so, why?

- Do we have resources, both human and material, to achieve our goals? Do we have the right textbooks (if we have them)? Do we have the basic equipment which can further our aims, e.g. visualisers, computers, mini-whiteboards?

- Are we giving appropriate attention to each of the four skills, ensuring these skills are use in an integrated way?

- Do we prioritise spaced repetition, interleaving, a spiral curriculum and thorough processing of language?

- Do we have a default position on L2 use with principled guidelines about when we would expect to use L1?

- Are we firmly focused on the idea of maximum 'surrender value' for all activities? Do we use games for learning or just to have fun? Do we use technology efficiently?

- Do we pay adequate attention to metacognitive strategies (thinking about learning)? Do we have enough knowledge about assessment and a planned approach to exam preparation?

- Are we clear that the best input is highly comprehensible to reduce anxiety and increase self-efficacy? What other practices do we employ to maximise motivation, e.g. rewards, 'student of the week', etc?

- Are we too focused on isolated word learning, at the expense of using language in chunks and sentences?

- Does our classroom organisation maximise learning, e.g. seating arrangements and displays?

- Are we clear on issues surrounding formative assessment?

- Is our teaching always 'responsive' to students' behaviour at all times?

- How are our cognitive and affective empathy skills?

- Do we have the knowledge of effective questioning and drilling to help all students do well?

- Do we all have at least a basic understanding of cognition - how learning and memory works, for example? Are we aware of cognitive load theory?

- Do we organise overseas trips, study visits or exchanges? Do we invite visitors to talk to students, e.g. local L2 speakers, university students or former students?

2. Is our curriculum structure suitable?

- Do we wish to strive for excellence in one language from novice level? Do we want to give students a taste of more than one L2 to the possible detriment of excellence? Are we providing equal opportunity to all students?

- Is the amount of time available appropriate? Are lessons of an appropriate length and intelligently spaced to best effect for memory retention? What can be done within the school's timetable framework to make learning more successful?

- Does our structure allow for adequate uptake at the point where the L2 may become an optional (elective) subject?

- Is there enough homework being set within this framework, efficiently monitored? Do all teachers stick to the agreed policy?

3. What are students achieving?

- How successful are we in terms of student retention, attitudes and results?

- What is behaviour like? If poor behaviour is holding back achievement, what steps can be taken to improve it? Do teachers receive the necessary professional development support? Are rewards and sanctions by staff consistently applied?

- Do we measure success by what students can actually do with the L2?

- How do students achieve in the four skills? Do they perform better in listening, speaking, reading or writing? Does a bias in our teaching affect their scores?

- Do we contribute to the whole school ethos with enough focus on literacy, e.g. attention to phonics, spelling, grammatical terminology, plenty of reading (including reading aloud)?

- Do we use tracking data sensibly to check if our students are broadly achieving in line with expectations? Do we have processes in place to help them get on track?
- How popular is the subject in whole school surveys?

Curriculum planning with a textbook

Many language departments work with textbooks, often accompanied by ancillary digital resources. But few teachers follow books to the letter. Instead, they opt to adapt them to the needs of classes and their own preferences. But is there a proper rationale for how to adapt textbooks to best effect?

Nation and Macalister (2010) look specifically at this issue of adapting course books. Below are several key points they make.

When teachers depend heavily on the textbook

There may be good reasons for sticking quite closely to the course book. Nation and Macalister mention the following points:

- The school or Ministry of Education requires the book to be followed closely. Reasons may be to standardise the quantity and quality of education or a lack of trust in teacher skill.
- Teachers may be inexperienced or untrained, so the book offers some security and teachers may not have the skill to adapt it.
- The teacher may believe in the high quality of the course book.
- Students may want to cover every part of the book.

We would add that inertia can play a role in the case of departments where there is reluctance to change or the current approach may already be yielding good results. In other departments, where in-house resources are not shared, this may lead to greater dependence on the textbook.

Nation and Macalister point out that even when teachers follow a book closely, they may vary in the way they present and practise material, as well as how they monitor and assess achievement. Ways to vary the presentation of textbook material include varying the speed of recordings, increasing the number of repetitions of audio or video material and adapting exercises, including some as homework.

Where there are existing unit tests, these can either be omitted or adapted to suit the needs of the class. For example, audio texts can be read aloud, exercises shortened or extended. In particular, time-consuming oral assessments can be omitted.

Adapting a textbook

Some teachers prefer to adapt their course book in major ways. Reasons for doing this, according to Nation and Macalister, include:

- The book does not include tasks teachers have used successfully before.
- It does not fit with the time available for the course.
- The book contains material unsuitable for the age or proficiency of the class.
- It lacks the language items, skills, ideas or strategies the students need.
- The book does not apply principles the teacher believes in.
- It does not allow for any student input into the course.

It is also true that in some cases the book may align poorly with the requirements of a specific examination. For example, in the UK, and in schools following an English exam board syllabus such as GCSE, the book may not match sufficiently well with the specific requirements of the high-stakes exam for which students are preparing. Conversely, some books may follow the examination syllabus so slavishly that they lack the interest and variety some teachers would like to see. For example, they may lack communicative tasks, enough practice examples, or interesting aural and written texts. A common criticism we come across is that the subject content is not sufficiently cognitively challenging or of intrinsic interest. Other criticisms would be the apparent lack of a principled approach to spacing, retrieval and comprehensible input, i.e. including texts beyond the comprehension level of students.

Where the above points make a book undesirable for teachers they have a choice: abandon it, or adapt it substantially. Many teachers find themselves in this position, and choose to adapt the course book, partly because it contains useful audio material which may seem hard to source elsewhere. How can the textbook be adapted? Nation and Macalister suggest the following:

1. **Add or omit content**. (A common approach whereby you skip over the bits you do not like or add your own materials, e.g. more grammar practice examples, sentence builders or texts.)
2. **Change the sequencing of the content**. This can be done for all sorts of reasons. For example, if a self-created text containing new grammatical structures is used, material from further ahead in the book may be used. Or we may just feel dissatisfied with the way grammar is selected and sequenced, and so introduce more complex structures sooner.
3. **Change the format**. A particular unit may be re-sequenced, starting with an activity occurring a little later in the unit. Keep in mind that good books sequence their content carefully, but often in a predictable sequence, so one reason for reordering would be to simply provide some variation. This might even depend on the mood of the class that day (and the teacher's!).
4. **Change the presentation**. Use different techniques for teaching the content to those suggested in the book or Teacher's Book. Usually, lack of space means that texts are exploited

superficially, so a range of tasks should be created to enable a text to be understood and processed.

5. **Add or omit monitoring**. For example, students can test each other to check progress.
6. **Add or omit assessment**. Extra quizzes or tests can be added to supplement the published end of unit test.

The same authors go on to suggest that one significant way to adapt a book is by adding a programme of reading, or supplying extra listening material. This would be to respect three core principles listed below.

- **Comprehensible input**. There needs to be a substantial amount of interesting written and spoken input.
- **Fluency**. The course should provide opportunities to increase fluency by using language they already know repeatedly.
- **Time on task**. As much time as possible needs to be spent on focusing on language use (as opposed to descriptions of the language – 'talking about the language').

In sum, we may already adapt our course book in an instinctive way, without thinking through our rationale. We have a gut feeling that an exercise will work, a text is dull or a task too hard. Some teachers, often those who are less experienced or trainees, may need more help refining the skill of evaluating and adapting the course book. For us, the key thing is whether the book applies sensible, research-informed principles of language learning and teaching, such as the primacy of interesting comprehensible input, repetition, spacing, retrieval, interaction and practice?

Why does a grammatical syllabus fail for most students?

In this chapter we suggest that, in designing a curriculum, the focus in typical high school settings should be kept on communication as far as possible. Let us examine this further. For many language teachers who were successful classroom learners brought up on a diet of grammar and word learning, it can be hard to put ourselves in the shoes of a young student of average aptitude who may not be motivated by a grammatical approach. In Chapter 6 we outlined many of the issues involved in grammar acquisition.

The value of learning and practising grammar rules in language learning has been debated for centuries, but we still debate it. We know for sure that the grammar-translation approach (see Chapter 1) only worked for a minority of motivated students in selective schools, and even for them, it was more about developing skills in reading comprehension and translation. We know that twentieth century offshoots of the direct method (see Chapter 1) which stuck to a grammatical syllabus also only worked with the minority, even though there was a laudable emphasis on teaching grammar orally and aurally. The audiolingual approach of the 1950s through to 60s/70s, focused primarily on drilling through speech and listening, but also grammar, at the expense of vocabulary and communication. It was seen to be a failure and is now widely discredited as an over-arching method.

All the above approaches assumed that grammar patterns could be explained, practised, then put into use, allowing learners to become creative language users as they slotted in the vocabulary to the system of rules. This is sometimes called a **dictionary plus grammar** or **words plus grammar** approach. It does not seem to work for most learners.

Why does the grammar-based approach fail for most students? Let us rehearse the common arguments put forward against the grammar syllabus.

1. Teachers are often optimistic about the extent to which we can 'teach a rule' and for it to become internalised (proceduralised, automatised, acquired - depending on your preferred learning paradigm - see Chapter 6 concerning the interface question). Students do not easily acquire what we teach. They must be developmentally ready and be exposed to structures that are learnable and probably not too different from the structures of their first language(s). Because they also tend to acquire structures in a certain order, at least somewhat immune to the teaching, many structures just do not stick. Recall how frustrating it can be when, despite repeated practice, students do not seem able to use a structure. This may reflect a misunderstanding about the nature of declarative and procedural knowledge. It is hard to create the second from the first.

2. Teachers may believe that a language can be broken down into bits and built back up again like a lego model. It is a tempting analogy. We have phonemes, morphemes, words, phrases, sentences. We just need to be able to put these bits together for the language to be used. But language is too large and complex for that. And even if we cut right back on the number of words and rules, students still find it hard to piece together the bits, during conversation, under time pressure, in what researchers call real operating conditions. By the way, this is not to say that useful work cannot be done at each level, whether it be phonemic, lexical or syntactic, but the 'put together' (synthetic) view of language learning has few fans in the research community (e.g. Long and Robinson, 1998; Jordan and Gray, 2019).

3. A motivational issue. Most students are not excited by grammar, however much we sweeten the pill through stimulating activities and games. What is more likely to interest them is compelling content in language they understand - having conversations, carrying out purposeful tasks, playing games and engaging with intercultural input. They would like feasible activities which allow them to succeed at a level they can manage. They might also be interested in aspects of language awareness or linguistics, such as social aspects of language use, dialects and accents, child language acquisition and etymology.

Now, you might ask... but surely all approaches fail for most students, given the time available in school settings? The answer to that question has a lot to do with goals we set for classroom language learning. If we know that many, if not most, will stop learning a language in school after two or three years, then we must question whether the focus on rich vocabulary, along with accurate use of a large number of morphological and syntactic rules, is the right objective. Alternative, quite reasonable goals might be:

- Hold and understand simple conversations on topics of interest using a limited range of vocabulary.
- Learn about the cultures of target language countries and speakers, so developing intercultural competence and making more rounded, tolerant, independent persons.
- Deal with a range of 'survival' situations, e.g coping in shops, on holiday, meeting a stranger, talking about oneself, asking questions of another person.
- Become more aware of how language works, out of general interest and to prepare for future learning and better writing in L1.
- Develop an interest in and affection for language learning.
- Explore the language experience of bilinguals in a diverse classroom.

If these were our goals, would we spend much time learning the rules of grammar? What would we do instead?

Now of course there are many students who will continue to learn a language up to the age of 15/16, and beyond. In non-anglophone countries, most or all will learn English up to the age of 18. Because their needs must be catered for, we tend to look at language learning as a long-term goal, where quick wins may not be the priority. We choose, therefore, to teach grammar in the belief that this is what will enable learners to use the language creatively.

Because of what we know from research about grammar acquisition, the needs of our longer-term learners can still be met by a more communicative curriculum. Such a curriculum does not mean a lack of seriousness or challenge. If a so-called rigorous grammar syllabus fails, there is not much point in that type of rigour. Another way of looking at challenge would be through the prism of successful communication. The general learning principles of cognitive load, working memory limitations, spaced repetition, the retrieval practice effect and Transfer-Appropriate Processing can still be applied within a communicative paradigm, where listening, speaking, reading and writing are effectively practised.

With a sound, enjoyable foundation, our keener students (maybe more of them?), can begin to develop more sophisticated language use later. At that point they may be more 'focused on form' as well as meaning. There is support in the research literature for the idea that an early diet of constantly recycled chunks (multi-word units) can be the basis for later rule-based competence (see Chapter 12). We may be able to reconceive curriculum design for the needs of the majority of our students, not the few who will study languages in higher education.

Planning for exam success

Since this book is not written for teachers from a particular country or working with a certain assessment regime, we cannot go into the detail of preparing for specific exams. But some general points are worth bearing in mind, especially for teachers who are new to the profession.

We have a responsibility to prepare students thoroughly for exams which may affect their future curriculum choices and university entrance. Exam success is important not just for students, but for teachers who are held accountable for their outcomes. In some countries, the accountability measures may even affect a teacher's career advancement and salary.

With teaching based on sound principles and effective practice, students will stand a better chance of success, but exam success requires quite specific planning. Here are some points to keep in mind.

- Teachers need to be thoroughly versed in the formal requirements of the syllabus, sometimes called a specification. Key information from the syllabus should be shared, including how answers are graded. Students benefit from seeing mark schemes, otherwise known as rubrics. We should model how these are applied to exemplar pieces of work and have students assess work themselves. They need to hear and read examples of successful performance. It may also be useful to share examples of less successful work.

- The TAP (transfer-appropriate processing) effect suggests strongly that students remember more and achieve more highly when they have practised the type of questions they will encounter in the exam. Therefore, a planned programme of practice questions and past papers is important. This does not mean, however, that exam-style questions need to be practised from the beginning of a course.

- Students need to do practice exams to the specified time limit and be taught how to manage their time. For example, how to prepare before starting to write a composition or essay and how much time to leave for checking work. By the time they arrive in an exam hall, they should already be thoroughly prepared for the experience. Some may even relish the prospect!

- When it comes to the nitty-gritty of producing successful answers, classes benefit from having pre-prepared lists of useful phrases and structures which will help attract higher grades. Train students in what hoops to jump through to achieve high marks, e.g. by including statements of opinion, different time frames, rich vocabulary and idioms. Tell them how to check their writing for accuracy, e.g. by re-reading with the aim of finding specific errors: gender, verb endings, adjectival agreement, common spelling errors. Exercises can be set up in advance to practise this skill.

- Speaking tests are a particular source of stress, for students of all abilities. To help them cope with last-minute panic, it is possible to arrange for a test to be carried out by someone else just prior to the real test. In advance of orals, have them practise at length with partners, the teacher or other helpers, such as parents/caregivers and, in some cases, tutors.

In sum, exam preparation is a valuable part of our planning. One challenge is to get the balance right between focusing on the needs of an exam, and doing other work which may be more interesting. Even though the exam is a powerful source of extrinsic motivation, it would be a mistake to tip the balance too much towards exam preparation.

A communicative curriculum

In general, teachers' own experience of language learning may bias them towards a curriculum based on a list of topics, grammar and vocabulary (see Chapter 17 about teacher cognition). Given the potential limitations of a tradition grammatical syllabus, it is possible to design a curriculum in which communication takes priority. Such a curriculum would look quite different from a traditional one. Yalden (1987) puts forward a list of components which would make up a communicative curriculum designed to meet the needs of students. (See Table 20.1). Note how the order reflects the fact that grammar and vocabulary are there to serve communication rather than being the main drivers of the curriculum.

Table 20.1 The components of a communicative curriculum

Component	Explanation and examples
Purposes	The purposes for which learners need to acquire the L2, e.g. to converse in a business setting, to acquire technical language, to pass an exam
Setting	Where and how learners will need to use the L2, e.g. on holiday, in a work setting, in an oral assessment
Role of learners	The socially defined role of the learners and their interlocutors, e.g. will the learners be part of a work team or will they be holidaymakers?
Communicative events	The interactions learners will be involved in, e.g. everyday situations, vocational/professional settings, academic contexts
Language functions	What the learner will need to do with or through the language, e.g. request information, write correspondence, communicate online
Notions	What the learner will need to talk about, e.g. topics such as the environment, holidays, personal identity, family
Skills	The abilities required to 'knit together' oral and written discourse, e.g. rhetorical skills, being coherent, turn-taking conventions
Varieties of L2	The type(s) of L2 that learners need to acquire and the levels of oral and written L2 learners are expected to reach
Grammar	The traditional list of grammatical content needed for the above communicative components
Vocabulary	The traditional set of vocabulary needed for the above communicative components

Concluding remarks

Time would be well spent in language departments focusing regularly on the intent and impact of curriculum, since it is what ultimately drives our practice as language teachers. The curriculum is not just a list of items to be covered, but includes a department's language learning goals and beliefs. Not surprisingly, therefore, this chapter has referred back to some fundamental methodological principles. Above all, these include the need to develop self-efficacy in our students through interaction with comprehensible language. How the fine detail of this is organised depends on our own educational settings and these vary enormously. The earlier chapters in the book have been largely concerned with this detail.

The point has been clearly made in this chapter that some traditional views of curriculum are problematic. But with knowledge of second language acquisition research it is possible to design and critically evaluate a curriculum for the benefit of students. A key point is that curriculum design needs to take account of *all* students, whatever their aptitude or background. Supporting the most able and motivated is important, but the bigger, more difficult challenge has always been to motivate weaker learners. Sound curriculum design is a prerequisite for that task.

Final reflections

If you read our blogs and use our resources, you will know that we are interested in both ends of the second language acquisition spectrum: conscious learning (explanation and skill acquisition through practice) and unconscious (natural and with the focus on meaningful input). The longer we have taught and examined the theory and research over the years, the more we think that there is merit in both these perspectives and, indeed, that the two should work together. Research into additional language learning, cognitive science and neuroscience is still relatively young. Although a lot has been learned, we cannot yet be sure what is happening in the 'black box' of the brain, or to what extent learning is a cognitive or socio-cultural phenomenon. But if we make sure we provide meaningful, repetitive, structured exposure to connected language, with explanation, practice and communicative interaction, learning will occur. It is also important to strike the right balance between our experience of the classes in front of us and interpreting the outcomes of research. This may guard us against following the latest fashion.

Now, the rate at which learning occurs depends on a range of factors, including, crucially, motivation and student aptitude for language learning. Others such as teacher quality, the number and frequency of lessons, amount of homework, spacing of lessons and quality of input all play a role. Anything which can be done to optimise these factors will improve the pace of acquisition.

Given that we cannot yet be certain to what extent second language learning is like first language learning (it seems very unlikely they are identical), then the sensible course is to exploit a mixture of principled approaches based on what we know about both language learning and learning in general. There is no need to defend one approach against all the others. If it provides the elements above - input, output, repetition and reinforcement, interesting material, explanation and so on, it should work.

It is also probable that this kind of eclectic approach makes sense given the variation we see in our students. Some seem to thrive on more highly natural or communicative methods, whereas others enjoy a degree of formal explanation to supplement the input. Some like to listen a lot, others like to read; some prefer talking, others writing; some want to become fluent speakers, the majority may just want to get by with some simple situational or conversational language.

Not only do students vary, so do teachers. Whatever approach, or combination of approaches, is adopted, you need to believe in it, understand its rationale and execute it efficiently. We believe an excellent all-round teacher will get better results with what might seem a dubious approach (such as grammar-translation), than a less skilled teacher trying to use an allegedly superior method. We know that in our craft so much is about classroom relationships, being able to adapt to the moment, having a feel for what students enjoy and, of course, behaviour management.

We began our book by referring to the idea of principled eclecticism. Why not exploit a range of principled approaches? See how they work with your classes, adjust them, listen to students and let your practice evolve. Naturalist, meaningful, implicit learning can co-exist with explicit, form-focused work. An approach with elements of each is likely to be a firm foundation on which to build as a language teacher.

Steve and Gianfranco

Steve Smith

@spsmith45
frenchteacher.net
frenchteachernet.blogspot.com
YouTube: Steve Smith Languages

Gianfranco Conti

@gianfrancocont9
language-gym.com
gianfrancoconti.com
YouTube: The Language Gym

Bibliography

Sources available online in 2023 are indicated.

ACTFL (American Council on the Teaching of Foreign Languages) Proficiency Guidelines (2012). Available at : https://www.actfl.org/educator-resources/actfl-proficiency-guidelines

Agar, M. (1994). The intercultural frame. *International Journal of Intercultural Relations, 18 (2)*, 221-237.

Anderson, J. (2016). Why practice makes perfect sense: the past, present and potential future of the PPP paradigm in language teacher education. *English language teacher education and development* 19, 14-22.

Anderson, J. (2017). A potted history of PPP with the help of ELT Journal. *ELT Journal, 71*.

Anderson, J.R. (1982). Acquisition of a Cognitive Skill. *Psychological Review*, 89, no. 4 p.369-406.

Anderson, N. J. (2003). Metacognitive reading strategies increase L2 performance. *The Language Teacher*, 27, 20-22.

Andrä, C., Mathias, B., Schwager, A., Macedonia, M. & von Kriekstein, K (2020), Learning Foreign Language Vocabulary with Gestures and Pictures Enhances Vocabulary Memory for Several Months Post-Learning in Eight-Year-Old School Children. *Educ Psychol Rev* **32**, 815–850.

Andrews, S.J. (2007). *Teacher Language Awareness*. Cambridge: Cambridge University Press.

Andringa, S. & Rebuschat, P. (2015).New directions in the study of implicit and explicit learning: an introduction. *Studies in Second Language Acquisition, 37*, 185–196.

Asher, J.J. (2009). *Learning Another language through Actions* (7th edition). Sky Oaks Productions.

Bachman, L.F. & Palmer, A.S. (1996). *Language testing in practice*. Oxford: Oxford University Press.

Baddeley, A., & Hitch, G. J. (1974). Working memory. In G. A. Bower (Ed.), *Recent Advances in Learning and Motivation* (Vol. 8, pp. 47-90). Academic Press.

Bahrick, H.P., Bahrick, L.E., Bahrick, A.S., & Bahrick, P.E. (1993). Maintenance of Foreign Language Vocabulary and the Spacing Effect. *Psychological Science 4/5*. http://www.psych.utoronto.ca/users/shkim/Bahrick%20et%20al.%20(1993)%20spacing%20effect.pdf

Bandura, A. (& National Inst of Mental Health) (1986). *Social foundations of thought and action: A social cognitive theory*. Prentice-Hall, Inc.

Bandura, A. (1994). Self-efficacy. In *Encyclopedia of Human Behavior*, vol. 4, ed. V.S. Ramachaudran, 71–81. New York: Academic Press.

Bandura, A. (1997). *Self-efficacy: The exercise of control*. New York: Freeman.

Barcomb, M. & Cardoso, W. (2020). Rock or lock? Gamifying an online course management system for pronunciation instruction: focus on English /r/ and /l/. *CALICO Journal, 37(2)*, 127-147.

Barcroft, J. (2004). Second language vocabulary acquisition: A lexical input processing approach. *Foreign Language Annals, 37, 2*, 200-208.

Bauckham, I. (2016). The Teaching Schools Council Review of MFL Pedagogy. Available at: https://pure-research.york.ac.uk/ws/portalfiles/portal/54043904/MFL_Pedagogy_Review_Report_TSC_PUBLISHED_VERSION_Nov_2016_1_.pdf

Bialystok. E. (1997). The structure of age: in search of barriers to second language acquisition. *Second Language Research*, 13.

Biedroń, A. (2011). Personality factors as predictors of foreign language aptitude. Studies in *Second Language Learning and Teaching*. 1. Available at: https://www.researchgate.net/publication/277106948_Personality_factors_as_predictors_of_foreign_language_aptitude

Bjork, E. L., & Bjork, R. A. (2011). Making things hard on yourself, but in a good way: Creating desirable difficulties to enhance learning. In M. A. Gernsbacher, R.W. Pew, L. M. Hough, J. R. Pomerantz (Eds.) & FABBS Foundation, *Psychology and the real world: Essays illustrating fundamental contributions to society* (pp. 56–64). Worth Publishers.

Black, P. J., Harrison, C. Lee, C. Marshall, B. & Wiliam, D. (2002). *Working inside the black box: Assessment for learning in the classroom.* London, UK: nferNelson.

Bock, J.K. (1986) Syntactic persistence in language production. *Cognitive Psychology, 18*, 355–87.

Boers, F. (2021). *Evaluating Second Language Vocabulary and Grammar Instruction: A Synthesis of the Research on Teaching Words, Phrases, and Patterns (1st ed.).* Routledge.

Borg, S. (2003). Teacher cognition in language teaching: A review of research into what teachers think, know, believe, and do. *Language Teaching, 36/2.* http://eprints.whiterose.ac.uk/1652/1/borgs1_Language_Teaching_36-2.pdf

Bower, G. H., & Clark, M. C. (1969). Narrative stories as mediators for serial learning. *Psychonomic Science, 14*(4), 181–182.

Brant, J; (2006). Subject knowledge and pedagogic knowledge: ingredients for good teaching? An English perspective. Edukacja , 94 (2) pp. 60-77. Available at : https://core.ac.uk/download/pdf/82407.pdf

Brown, D., Liu, Q., & Norouzian, R. (2023). Effectiveness of written corrective feedback in developing L2 accuracy: A Bayesian meta-analysis. *Language Teaching Research, 0*(0).

Brown, H. D., & **Abeywickrama, P.** (2010) *Language assessment: principles and practices.* White Plains, New York: Pearson.

Brown, J. D. & **Hudson, T**. (1998). The alternatives in language assessment. *TESOL Quarterly*, 32 (4), 653-675.

Brown, J. D., Robson, G., & Rosenkjar, P. R. (2001). Personality, motivation, anxiety, strategies, and language proficiency of Japanese students. In Z. Dornyei & R. W. Schmidt (Eds.), *Motivation and second language acquisition* (pp. 361-398). Honolulu: University of Hawaii, Second Language Teaching and Curriculum Center.

Brown, R. (1973). *A first language.* Cambridge, MA: Harvard University Press

Brumfit, C. (1984). *Communicative Methodology in Language Teaching: The roles of fluency and accuracy.* Cambridge University Press.

Brysbaert, M. (2019). How many words do we read per minute? A review and meta-analysis of reading rate. *Journal of Memory and Language*, 109. Available at: https://www.researchgate.net/publication/335174808_How_many_words_do_we_read_per_minute_A_review_and_meta-analysis_of_reading_rate

Butzkamm, W. & **Caldwell, J.** (2009). *The Bilingual Reform. A Paradigm shift in Foreign Language Teaching.* Available at: https://www.researchgate.net/publication/304579219_The_Bilingual_Reform_A_Paradigm_shift_in_Foreign_Language_Teaching

Bygate, M. (2018). *Learning Language through Task Repetition.* John Benjamins Publishing Company.

Byram, M. (2021). *Teaching and assessing intercultural communicative competence: Revisited* (2nd ed.). Multilingual Matters.

Calderhead, J. (1988). *The development of knowledge structures in learning to teach. In Teachers' professional learning*, ed. J. Calderhead. London: The Falmer Press

Calderhead, J. & **Robson, M.** (1991). Images of teaching: Student teachers' early conceptions of classroom practice. *Teaching and Teacher Education*, 7/1.

Cameron, J. & **Pierce, W.** (1994). Reinforcement, reward and intrinsic motivation: Protests and accusations do not alter the results. *Review of Educational Research, 66*, 39-52.

Carpenter, S. (2017). Spacing Effects on Learning and Memory. *Chapter in Reference Module in Neuroscience and Biobehavioral Psychology.*

Carpenter, S.K. & Olson, K.M. (2012). Are pictures good for learning new vocabulary in a foreign language? Only if you think they are not. *Journal of experimental psychology. Learning, memory, and cognition, 38 1*, 92-101.

Carreira, J.M. (2011). Relationship between motivation for learning EFL and intrinsic motivation for learning in general among Japanese elementary school students. *System, 39 (1)*, 90-102.

Carroll, J. B. & Sapon, S. M. (1959). *Modern Language Aptitude Test.* Bethesda, MD: Second Language Testing.

Chase, A. (2015). *Target Language Toolkit.* CreateSpace Independent Publishing Platform.

Christie, C.M. & Conlon, C. (eds.) (2016). *Success Stories from Secondary Foreign Languages Classrooms.* Trentham Books. Available at: https://discovery.ucl.ac.uk/id/eprint/1503647/

Coe, R., Aloisi, C., Higgins, S. & Elliot Major. L (2014). What makes great teaching? Review of the underpinning research. Sutton Trust/University of Durham. Available at: https://www.suttontrust.com/wp-content/uploads/2014/10/What-Makes-Great-Teaching-REPORT.pdf

CoE (Council of Europe) (2001) Common European Framework of Reference for Languages: Learning, teaching, assessment. Cambridge University Press.

CoE (Council of Europe) (2016). Guide for the development and implementation of curricula for plurilingual and intercultural education. Available at: https://rm.coe.int/CoERMPublicCommonSearchServices/DisplayDCTMContent?documentId=090000 16806ae621

CoE (Council of Europe) (2018) Reference Framework of Competences for Democratic Culture. Volume 1: Context, concepts and model. Strasbourg.

Conklin, K. & Schmitt, N. (2012). The Processing of Formulaic Language. *Annual Review of Applied Linguistics, 32*, 45 - 61.

Conlon, C. (2016). Making the most of the mixed experience Y7 classroom. In Christie, C.M. & Conlon, C. (eds.) (2016). *Success Stories from Secondary Foreign Languages Classrooms.* Trentham Books.

Conti, G. (2001). E possibile migliorare l'efficacia della correzione attraverso l'istruzione strategica? *Tuttitalia, 25*, 4—14.

Conti G. (2004). *Metacognitive enhancement and error correction.* Unpublished doctoral dissertation, University of Reading, Reading, UK.

Conti G. & Smith S.P. (2019) *Breaking the Sound Barrier: Teaching Language Learners How to Listen.* Independently published.

Cortazzi, M. & Jin, L. (2013). Introduction: Researching Cultures of Learning. In: Cortazzi, M. & Jin, L. (eds) *Researching Cultures of Learning.* Palgrave Macmillan, London.

Costa, P. T. Jr., & McCrae, R. R. (1992). Revised NEO Personality Inventory (NEO-PI-R) and NEO Five-Factor Inventory (NEO-FFI) professional manual. Odessa, FL: Psychological Assessment Resources.

Coyle, D., Hood, H. & Marsh, D. (2010). *Content and Language Integrated Learning.* Cambridge: Cambridge University Press.

Craik, F. I. M. & Lockhart, R. S. (1972). Levels of processing: a framework for memory research. *J. Verb. Learn. Verb. Behav.* 11, 671–684.

Crichton, H. (2009) 'Value added' modern languages teaching in the classroom: an investigation into how teachers' use of classroom target language can aid pupils' communication skills. *The Language Learning Journal, 37 (1)*, 19-34.

Crookes, G., & Schmidt, R.W. (1991). Motivation: Reopening the Research Agenda. *Language Learning, 41*, 469-512.

Crum, A.J., Salovey, P. & Achor, S. (2013). Rethinking Stress: The Role of Mindsets in Determining the Stress Response. *Journal of personality and social psychology, 104*.

Csikszentmihalyi, M. (1990). *Flow: The Psychology of Optimal Experience.* New York: Harper and Row.

Dagilienė, I. (2012). Translation as a Learning Method in English Language Teaching. *Studies about Languages, 21.*

De Bot, K. (1992). A Bilingual Production Model: Levelt's 'Speaking' Model Adapted. *Applied Linguistics*, 13, 1-24.

Deci, E. (1971). Effects of externally mediated rewards of intrinsic motivation. *Journal of Personality and Social Psychology, 18(1),*105-115.

Deci, E.L. & R.M. Ryan. (2000). The 'what' and 'why' of goal pursuits: human needs and the self-determination of behaviour. *Psychological Inquiry* 11, no. 4: 227–268.

Dehaene, S. (2009). *Reading in the Brain: The New Science of How We Read.* New York: Penguin.

DeKeyser, R. M. (1997). Beyond explicit rule learning. *Studies in Second Language Acquisition*, 19(2), 195–221.

DeKeyser, R. (2003). Explicit and Implicit Learning. In C. Doughty, & M. H. Long (Eds.), *The Handbook of Second Language Acquisition* (pp. 313-348). Oxford: Blackwell.

DeKeyser, R.M. (2007). *Practice in a Second Language: Perspectives from Applied Linguistics and Cognitive Psychology.* New York: Cambridge University Press.

DeKeyser, R.M. (2010). Cognitive-psychological processes in second language learning. In Long and Doughty (eds). *The Handbook of Language Teaching.* Oxford: Wiley-Blackwell.

DeKeyser, R. (2012), Interactions Between Individual Differences, Treatments, and Structures in SLA. *Language Learning, 62*, 189-200.

DeKeyser, R. (2017). Knowledge and skill in ISLA. In S Loewen and M. Sato (eds.) *The Routledge Handbook of Instructed Second Language Learning.* New York: Routledge.

DeKeyser, R.M. & Sokalski, K.J. (1996). The differential role of comprehension and production practice. *Language Learning, 46*, 81-112.

Derwing, T.M. (2017). L2 fluency development. In Loewen S., Sato M. (Eds.), *The Routledge handbook of instructed second language acquisition* (pp. 246–259). Routledge.

Derwing, T., Munro, M., Thomson, R. & Rossiter, M. (2009). The relationship between L1 fluency and L2 fluency development. *Studies in Second Language Acquisition, 31*, 533 – 557.

Derwing, T., Rossiter, M., Munro, M. & Thomson, R. (2004). Second Language Fluency: Judgments on Different Tasks. *Language Learning, (54)* 655 - 679.

Dewaele, J.-M. (2009). Individual differences in Second Language Acquisition. In W. C. Ritchie & T. K. Bhatia (Eds.), The new handbook of second language acquisition (pp. 623–646). Bingley: Emerald.

Dewaele, J.-M. & Furnham, A. (2000). Personality and speech production: A pilot study of second language learners. *Personality and Individual Differences,* 28, 355-365.

Dewaele, J., Botes, E., & Greiff, S. (2022). Sources and effects of foreign language enjoyment, anxiety, and boredom: A structural equation modeling approach. *Studies in Second Language Acquisition,* 1-19.

DfE (Department for Education) (2015). SEND Code of Practice 0-25 Years. Available at: https://assets.publishing.service.gov.uk/government/uploads/system/uploads/attachment_data/file/398815/SEND_Code_of_Practice_January_2015.pdf

Di Domenico, S. I., & Ryan, R. M. (2017). The emerging neuroscience of intrinsic motivation: A new frontier in self-determination research. *Frontiers in Human Neuroscience, 11,* Article 145, 1-14.

Dörnyei, Z. & Csizér, K. (1998). Ten Commandments for Language Teaching. *Language Teaching Research* 2/3.http://www.zoltandornyei.co.uk/uploads/1998-dornyei-csizer-ltr.pdf.

Dörnyei, Z. (2009). The L2 motivational self system. In Dörnyei, Zoltán & Ushioda, Ema (eds.), *Motivation, language identity and the L2 self,* 9–42. Bristol: Multilingual Matters.

Doughty, C. & Mackey, A. (2021). Language aptitude: Multiple perspectives. *Annual Review of Applied Linguistics, 41*, 1-5.

Duff, A. (1994). *Translation.* Oxford: Oxford University Press.

Dulay, H. C., & Burt, M. K. (1974). Natural sequences in child second language acquisition. *Language Learning,* 24, 37-53.

Dweck, C.S. (2012). *Mindset: How You Can Fulfil Your Potential.* New York: Ballantine Books.

Ebbinghaus, H. (1885). *Über das Gedächtnis. Untersuchungen zur experimentellen Psychologie.* (*Memory: A Contribution to Experimental Psychology.* Martino Fine Books, 2011.)

Education Endowment Foundation (accessed 2023). Setting and streaming. Available at: https://educationendowmentfoundation.org.uk/education-evidence/teaching-learning-toolkit/setting-and-streaming

Ellis, N. C. (2005). At the interface: Dynamic interactions of explicit and implicit language knowledge. *Studies in Second Language Acquisition*, 27(2), 305–352.

Ellis, N.C. (2007). The Weak-Interface, Consciousness, and Form-focused instruction: Mind the Doors. Available at: https://sites.lsa.umich.edu/nickellis/wp-content/uploads/sites/933/2021/07/Weak-Interface.pdf

Ellis, N.C (2012). Learned attention and blocking. In P. Robinson (Ed.) *The Routledge Encyclopedia of SLA* (pp. 370-372). New York: Routledge.

Ellis, N. C. (2015). Implicit and explicit learning: Their dynamic interface and complexity. In P. Rebuschat (Ed.), *Implicit and explicit learning of languages* (pp. 3-23). Amsterdam: John Benjamins.

Ellis, R. (1990). *Instructed second language acquisition.* Oxford: Blackwell.

Ellis, R. (1994). *The Study of Second Language Acquisition.* Oxford: Oxford University Press.

Ellis, R. (2005). Principles of instructed language learning. *Asian EFL Journal.* Available at: http://asian-efl-journal.com/sept_05_re.pdf.

Ellis, R. (2006). Current issues in the teaching of grammar: an SLA perspective. *TESOL Quarterly, 40 (1),* 83-107.

Ellis, R. (2008). *The Study of Second Language Acquisition (2nd ed.).* Oxford: Oxford University Press.

Ellis, R. (2009). Corrective Feedback and Teacher Development. *L2 Journal, 1(1).* Available at: https://escholarship.org/uc/item/2504d6w3#main

Ellis, R. & Shintani, N. (2013). *Exploring Language Pedagogy Through Second Language Acquisition Research.* New York, NY and London, UK: Routledge.

Ellis, R., & Yuan, F. (2004). The effects of planning on fluency, complexity, and accuracy in second language narrative writing, *Studies in Second Language Acquisition*, 26, 59-84.

Erler, L. (2003). Reading in a foreign language--- near-beginner adolescents' experience of French in English secondary schools. Ph.D thesis. University of Oxford.

Erler, L. & Macaro, E. (2011). Decoding Ability in French as a Foreign Language and Language Learning Motivation. *The Modern Language Journal.* 95. 496-518.

Ferris, D.R. (1999). The case for grammar correction in L2 writing classes. A response to Truscott (1996). *Journal of Second Language Writing, 8(1),* 1-11.

Festinger, L. (1957). *A theory of cognitive dissonance.* Stanford University Press.

Field, J. (2009). *Listening in the Language Classroom.* Cambridge: CUP.

Finocchiaro, M. & Brumfit, C. (1983). *The Functional-Notional Approach: from Theory to Practice.* New York : Oxford University Press.

Fitzpatrick, T. (2012) Tracking the changes: vocabulary acquisition in the study abroad context. *The Language Learning Journal*, 40:1, 81-98.

Flieischmann, M., Hübner, N., Nagengast, B. & Trautwein, U. (2023). The dark side of detracking: Mixed-ability classrooms negatively affect the academic self-concept of students with low academic achievement. Learning and Instruction, 86. Available at: https://www.sciencedirect.com/science/article/pii/S0959475223000221?dgcid=rss_sd_all

Fletcher-Wood, H. (2018). *Responsive Teaching: Cognitive Science and Formative Assessment in Practice.* London: Routledge.

Forrin, N. D. & MacLeod, C. M. (2018). This time it's personal: the memory benefit of hearing oneself. *Memory, 26 (4),* 574-579. Available at: https://uwaterloo.ca/memory-attention-cognition-lab/sites/ca.memory-attention-cognition-7591lab/files/uploads/files/forrinmacleodmem18.pdf

Foster, P. & Skehan, P. (1996). The Influence of Planning and Task Type on Second Language Performance. *Studies in Second Language Acquisition, 18*(3), 299-323.

Freeman, D. (2016). *Educating second language teachers.* Oxford: Oxford University Press.

Fulcher, G. (2000). The 'communicative' legacy in language testing. *System*, 28 (4), 483- 497.

García, O. (2009). Education, multilingualism and translanguaging in the 21st century.A. In: A. Mohanty, M. Panda, R. Phillipson & T. Skutnabb-Kangas (eds). *Multilingual Education for Social Justice: Globalising the local*. New Delhi: Orient Blackswan, pp. 128-145.

Gardner, H. (1983). *Frames of mind: The theory of multiple intelligences*. New York: Basic Books.

Gardner, R. C. & Lambert, W. E. (1972). *Attitudes and motivation in second language learning*. Newbury House: Rowley, MA.

Garrett-Rucks, P. (2016). *Intercultural Competence in Instructed Language Learning: Bridging Theory and Practice*. Information Age Publishing.

Gatbonton, E. & Segalowitz, N. (1989), Creative Automatization: Principles for Promoting Fluency Within a Communicative Framework. *TESOL Quarterly*, 22: 473-492.

Gatbonton, E. & Segalowitz, N. (2005). Rethinking Communicative Language Teaching: A Focus on Access to Fluency. *Canadian Modern Language Review*, 61. 325-353. Available at: https://www.researchgate.net/publication/253545034_Rethinking_Communicative_Language_Teaching_A_Focus_on_Access_to_Fluency

Geary, D.C. (2008). An Evolutionarily Informed Education Science. *Educational Psychologist,* 43(4), 179-195.

Gibbs, S., & Miller, A. (2014). Teachers' resilience and well-being: A role for educational psychology. *Teachers and Teaching: Theory and Practice, 20*(5), 609–621.

Gibson, S. (2008). Reading aloud: a useful learning tool?, *ELT Journal*, 62(1),, 29–36.

Godfrey, T. (2010). Drama in English language Teaching: a Whole-Person Learning Approach. *tomgodfrey.wordpress.com.*

Goh, C. (2008). Metacognitive Instruction for Second Language Listening Development: Theory, Practice and Research Implications. *RELC Journal*. 39.

González Fernández, B. & Schmitt, N. (2017). Vocabulary Acquisition. In S. Loewen, & M. Sato (Eds.), *The Routledge Handbook of Instructed Second Language Acquisition* (pp. 280-298), New York, NY: Routledge.

Goo, J., Granena, G., Yilmaz, Y. & Novella, M. (2015). Chapter in Implicit *and explicit instruction in L2 learning* (p. 443-482).

Gordon, A-L. (2016). Creating and nurturing resilient MFL teams. In C.Christie & C.Conlon (eds). Success Stories from Secondary Foreign Languages Classrooms. Trentham Books.

Grabe, W. (2009). *Reading in a Second Language: Moving from Theory to Practice* (Cambridge Applied Linguistics). Cambridge: Cambridge University Press.

Grabe, W. (2011). Teaching and testing reading. In Long, M.J. and Doughty. C.J. (eds) (2011). *The Handbook of Language Teaching,* Wiley-Blackwell.

Grabe, W. (2013). Key Issues in L2 Reading Development. CELC Symposium. Available at : http://www.nus.edu.sg/celc/research/books/4th%20Symposium%20proceedings/2).%20William%20Grabe.pdf

Grabe, W., & Stoller, F.L. (2019). *Teaching and Researching Reading* (3rd ed.). Routledge.

Graham, S. (2017). Research into practice: Listening strategies in an instructed classroom setting. *Language Teaching, 50 (1),* 107-119.

Graham, S. (2022) Self-efficacy and language learning – what it is and what it isn't. *The Language Learning Journal*, 50(2), 186-207. Available at: https://www.tandfonline.com/doi/full/10.1080/09571736.2022.2045679

Guichon, N. & Mclornan, S. (2008). The effects of multimodality on L2 learners: Implications for CALL resource design. *System*, 36/1). Available at: https://hal.archives-ouvertes.fr/hal-00356243/document.

Guskey, T. R. (2019). Grades versus comments: Research on student feedback. *Phi Delta Kappan, 101(3)*, 42–47.

Hakuta, K. (1974). Prefabricated patterns and the emergence of structure in second language acquisition. *Language Learning, 24* (2), 287-297.

Harris, V. (1997). *Teaching Learners How to Learn: Training in the MFL Classroom.* London: CILT.

Hattie, J. (2011). *Visible Learning for Teachers.* Oxford: Routledge.

Hazell, C. (2020). *Independent Thinking on MFL.* Independent Thinking Press. Crown House Publishing.

Heider, F. (1958). *The psychology of interpersonal relations.* New York: Wiley.

Henriksen, B. (1999). Three dimensions of vocabulary development. *Studies in Second Language Acquisition, 21*(2), 303-317.

Henshaw, F. & Hawkins, M. (2021). *Common Ground: Second Language Acquisition Theory Goes to the Classroom.* Hackett Publishing.

Henry, A. (2021). Motivational connections in language classrooms: A research agenda. *Language Teaching, 54*(2), 221-235.

Hiver, P. (2018). Teachstrong: The Power of Teacher Resilience for L2 Practitioners. In *Language Teacher Psychology* (Eds. S. Mercer & A.Kostoulos) (pp.231-246). Multilingual Matters.

Hodges, S. & Myers, M.W. (2007). *Encyclopedia of social psychology.* Empathy. 296-298.

Hoeft, F., McCardle, P. & Pugh, K. (2015). The Myths and Truths of Dyslexia in Different Writing Systems. International Dyslexia Association. Available at: https://dyslexiaida.org/the-myths-and-truths-of-dyslexia/

Hoey, M. (2005). *Lexical priming: A new theory of words and language.* Abingdon, England: Routledge.

Holden, S. (1981). *Drama in Language Teaching.* London: Longman.

Horwitz, E.K. (1988). The beliefs about language learning of beginning university foreign language students. *The Modern Language Journal, 72.*

Horwitz, E.K. Horwitz, M.B. & Cope, J. (1986), Foreign Language Classroom Anxiety. *The Modern Language Journal, 70,* 125-132.

Hosenfeld, C. (1977). A preliminary investigation of the reading strategies of successful and non-successful second language learners. *System, 5.*

Hsieh, L. T. (2000). The effects of translation on English vocabulary and reading learning. Paper presented at the Ninth International Symposium on English Teaching, Taipei, Taiwan.

Hughes, A. (2003). *Testing for language teachers.* Cambridge, MA: Cambridge University Press.

Hull, C. L. (1943). *Principles of behavior: An introduction to behavior theory.* New York: Appleton-Century-Crofts.

Hunt, A. & Beglar, D. (1998). Current research and Practice in Teaching Vocabulary. In *The Language Teacher,* 22/1. http://www.jalt-publications.org/old_tlt/articles/1998/01/hunt

Hutz, M. (2018). Focus on Form: The Lexico-Grammar Approach. In *Teaching English as a Foreign Language* (pp. 133-158). Stuttgart: J.B. Metzler.

Iwashita, N. (2001). The effect of learner proficiency on interactional moves and modified output in non-native-non-native interaction in Japanese as a foreign language. *System,* 29.

Jazuli, A.J.M., Din, F.F. M., & Yunus, M.M. (2019). Using Pictures in Vocabulary Teaching for Low Proficiency Primary Pupils via PI-VOC. *International Journal of Academic Research in Business and Social Sciences, 9 (1),* 311–319.

Jones, J. (2016). Teachers as emergentTrentham Books. critical researchers of practice. In C. Christie & C.Conlon (eds.). Success Stories from Secondary Foreign Language Classrooms. Available at: https://discovery.ucl.ac.uk/id/eprint/1503647/

Jones, J. & Wiliam, D. (2007). Modern foreign languages inside the black box: assessment for learning in the modern foreign languages classroom. Granada.

Jordan, G. & Gray, H. (2019). We need to talk about coursebooks, *ELT Journal, 73 (4),* 438–446.

Kang, E.Y. (2015). Promoting L2 Vocabulary Learning through Narrow Reading. Available at: http://rel.sagepub.com/content/46/2/165.abstract

Kang, E.Y, Sok, S. & Han, Z. (2018). Thirty-five years of ISLA on form-focused instruction: A meta-analysis. *Language Teaching Research,* 23.

Karimah, A. (2020). Revisiting translation as a foreign language learning tool: contrasting beliefs of diversely proficient students. *SAGA: Journal of English Language Teaching and Applied Linguistics, 1 (1)*, 9-16. Available at: https://media.neliti.com/media/publications/318883-revisiting-translation-as-a-foreign-lang-20918433.pdf

Karpicke, J. D., & Roediger, H. L., III (2008). The critical importance of retrieval for learning. *Science*, 319, 966–968.

Kato, S. (2012). Bridging Theory and Practice: Developing Lower-Level Processing Skills in L2 Reading. *The Language Learning Journal*, 40, 193-206.

Kato, S. & Tanaka, K. (2015). Reading Aloud Performance and Listening Ability in an L2: The Case of College-Level Japanese EFL Users. *Open Journal of Modern Linguistics*, 5, 187-206.

Kavanagh, B. & Upton, L. (1994). *Creative use of Texts*. London: CILT.

Kellogg, R. T. (1996). A model of working memory in writing. In C. M. Levy & S. Ransdell (Eds.), *The science of writing: Theories, methods, individual differences, and applications* (pp. 57–71). Lawrence Erlbaum Associates, Inc.

Kelly, M. (2014). Second language teacher education. Chapter in J.Jackson (ed.) *The Routledge Handbook of Language and Intercultural Education*. London: Routledge.

Kern, R.G. (1994). The Role of Mental Translation in Second Language Reading. *Studies in Second Language Acquisition, 16/4.*

Kerr, P. (2019). The use of L1 in English language teaching. Part of the Cambridge Papers in ELT series. [pdf] Cambridge: Cambridge University Press. Available at: https://languageresearch.cambridge.org/images/CambridgePapersInELT_UseOfL1_2019_ONLINE.pdf

Koller, H. (2012). Visual processing and learning disorders. *Current Opinion in Opthalmology, 23* (5), 377-383.

Kormos, J. (2013) New conceptualizations of language aptitude in second language attainment. in G. Granena & M.H. Long (eds), *Sensitive periods, language aptitude, and ultimate L2 attainment. Language Learning and Language Teaching*, 35, John Benjamins, Amsterdam, pp. 131-152.

Kormos, J. (2017). *The Second Language Learning Processes of Students with Specific Learning Difficulties.* London: Routledge.

Kowialiewski, B., Krasnoff, J., Mizrak, E. & Oberauer, K. (2022). The semantic relatedness effect in serial recall: Deconfounding encoding and recall order. *Journal of Memory and Language, 127.*

Krashen, S.D. (1982). *Principles and Practice in Second Language Acquisition.* Prentice-Hall (also available free online at *sdkrashen.com*).

Krashen, S.D. (1996). The case for Narrow Listening. *System, 24 (1).* http://sdkrashen.com/content/articles/the_case_for_narrow_listening.pdf

Krashen, S.D. (2004). The Case for Narrow Reading. *Language Magazine, 3 (5).* http://www.sdkrashen.com/content/articles/narrow.pdf

Krashen, S.D. & Terrell, T.D. (1983). *The Natural Approach: Language acquisition in the classroom.* Oxford: Pergamon.

Kumaravadivelu, B. (1994). The postmethod condition: (E)merging strategies for second/foreign language teaching. *TESOL Quarterly*, 28, 27– 48.

Kwon, E-Y. (2005). The "Natural Order" of Morpheme Acquisition: A Historical Survey and Discussion of Three Putative Determinants. Teachers College, *Columbia University Working Papers in TESOL & Applied Linguistics, 5,* (1).

Ladson-Billings, G. (1995). Toward a Theory of Culturally Relevant Pedagogy. *American Educational Research Journal, 32.* 465-491.

Lafleur A, & Boucher V.J. (2015). The ecology of self-monitoring effects on memory of verbal productions: Does speaking to someone make a difference? Conscious Cogn., 36, 139-46.

Lalande, J.F. (1982). Reducing composition errors: An experiment. *Modern Language Journal*, 66.

Larsen-Freeman, D. (1997). Grammar and its Teaching: Challenging the Myths. Available at: https://www.researchgate.net/publication/254407193_Grammar_and_Its_Teaching_Challenging_the_Myths_Grammar_and_Its_Teaching_Challenging_the_Myths_Grammar_and_Its_Teaching_Challenging_the_Myths_Grammar_and_Its_Teaching_Challenging_the_Myths

Larsen-Freeman, D. & **Anderson, M.** (2011). *Techniques and Principles in Language Teaching.* Oxford: Oxford University Press.

Larsen-Freeman, D. & **Long, M.H.** (1991). *An Introduction to Second Language Acquisition Research* (1st ed.). Routledge.

Laufer, B. & **Rozovski-Roitblat, B.** (2011). Incidental vocabulary acquisition: the effects of task type, word occurrence and their combination. *Language Teaching Research, 15 (4),* 391–411.

Lemov, D. (2015). *Teach Like a Champion 2.0: 62 Techniques That Put Students on the Path to College.* Jossey Bass; Pap/DVD edition.

Levelt, W. J. M. (1989). *Speaking: From intention to articulation.* The MIT Press.

Levine, G. S. (2014). Principles for code choice in the foreign language classroom: A focus on grammaring. *Language Teaching,* 47(3): pp. 332–348.

Lewandowski, N. & **Jilka, M.** (2019). Phonetic Convergence, Language Talent, Personality and Attention. Frontiers. Commun., Sec. Language Sciences. Available at: https://www.frontiersin.org/articles/10.3389/fcomm.2019.00018/full

Lewis, M. (1993). *The Lexical Approach.* Hove: Language Teaching Publications.

Li, S. (2015). The Associations Between Language Aptitude and Second Language Grammar Acquisition: A Meta-Analytic Review of Five Decades of Research, *Applied Linguistics, 36 (3),* 385–408. Available at: https://academic.oup.com/applij/article/36/3/385/2422456

Libben, G., & **Lindner, O.** (1996). Second Culture Acquisition and Second Language Acquisition: Faux amis? *Zeitschrift für Interkulturellen Fremdsprachenunterricht, 1.*

Lichtman, K. & **VanPatten, B.** (2021). Was Krashen right? Forty years later. *Foreign Language Annals.* 54. 1-23.

Lightbown, P.M. & **Spada, N.** (2021). *How Languages are Learned (fifth edition).* Oxford: Oxford University Press.

Locke, E.A. & **Kristof, A.L.** (1996). Volitional choices in the goal achievement process. In P.M. Gollwitzer and J.A. Bargh Eds) *The psychology of action: linking cognition and motivation to behaviour,* New York: Guilford.

Loewen, S. & **Sato, M.** (Eds.). (2017). *The Routledge Handbook of Instructed Second Language Acquisition (1st ed.).* Routledge.

Loewen, S. & **Sato, M.** (2018). Interaction and instructed second language acquisition. *Language Teaching, 51*(3), 285-329. Available at: https://www.cambridge.org/core/journals/language-teaching/article/interaction-and-instructed-second-language-acquisition/78A156EE200F744F5978F99BFB073DBE

Long, M. H. (1981). Input, interaction, and second language acquisition. *Annals of the New York Academy of Sciences, 379,* 259–278.

Long, M. H. (1983). Does second language instruction make a difference? A review of the research. *TESOL Quarterly, 17,* 359–382.

Long, M. H. (1991)' Focus on form: A design feature in language teaching methodology. rn K. de Bot, R. Ginsberg, &c. Kramsch (Eds.), *Foreign language research in cross-cultural perspective.* Amsterdam: John Benjamin.

Long, M.H. (1996). The role of linguistic environment in second language acquisition. In W. C. Ritchie, & T. K. Bhatia (Eds). Handbook of second language acquisition (pp. 413-468). San Diego: Academic Press.

Long, M.J. & **Doughty. C.J.** (eds) (2011). *The Handbook of Language Teaching,* Wiley-Blackwell.

Long, M. & **Robinson, P.** (1998). Focus on form: Theory, research and practice. In Doughty, C., & Williams, J. (eds.) *Focus on form in classroom language acquisition.* Cambridge: CUP

Lotto, L. & de Groot, A.M.B. (1998), Effects of Learning Method and Word Type on Acquiring Vocabulary in an Unfamiliar Language. *Language Learning, 48*, 31-69.

Lu, X. & Li, C. (2023). Task Repetition in Second Language Writing: The Role of Written Corrective Feedback, Working Memory, and Language Aptitude. Preprint available May 2023 at: https://papers.ssrn.com/sol3/papers.cfm?abstract_id=4419797

Ludke, K.M., Ferreira, F. & Overy, K. (2014). Singing can facilitate foreign language learning. *Memory and Cognition*, 42/1.

Lyster, R . & Ranta, L. (1997). Corrective feedback and learner uptake. Studies in Second Language Acquisition. *Studies in Second Language Acquisition*, 19. Available at: https://www.researchgate.net/publication/252160472_Corrective_feedback_and_learner_uptake

Macaro, E. (1997). *Target Language, Collaborative Learning and Autonomy*. Clevedon: Multilingual Matters.

Macaro, E. (2000). lssues in target language teaching. In: Field, K. (ed.) *Issues in Modern Foreign Languages Teaching*. London: Routledge/Falmer, pp.l71-189

Macaro, E. (2001). *Learning Strategies in Foreign and Second Language Classrooms*. London: Continuum.

Macaro, E. (2003). Second language teachers as second language classroom researchers. *Language Teaching Journal, 27*, 43-51. Available at: https://www.ittmfl.org.uk/modules/effective/6d/paper6d2.pdf

Macaro, E. (2010). The Target Language in the Classroom: Where are we now? Available at : http://www.education.ox.ac.uk/wordpress/wpcontent/uploads/2010/08/Macaro2010.pdf.

Macaro, E. & Woore, R. (2021). *Debates in Second Language Education*. London: Routledge.

Macedonia, M. (2014). Bringing back the body into the mind: gestures enhance word learning in foreign language. *Frontiers in Psychology, 5*. Available at: https://www.ncbi.nlm.nih.gov/pmc/articles/PMC4260465/

Mackay, C. (2019). *Learning to Plan Modern Language Lessons*. London: Routledge.

Mackey, A. & Goo, J. (2007). Interaction research in SLA: A meta-analysis and research synthesis. In Mackey, A. (ed.), *Conversational interaction in second language acquisition: a series of empirical studies*. Oxford applied linguistics, Oxford University Press, p. 407-453.

Maurice, K. (1983). The fluency workshop. TESOL Newsletter, 17(4), 29.

Mayer, R.E. (2001). *Multimedia learning*. Cambridge: Cambridge University Press.

McLaughlin, B. (1978). The monitor model: Some methodological considerat*ions. Language Learning*, 28, 309-332.

McLaughlin, M. W. & Marsh, D. D. (1978). Staff Development and School Change. *Teachers College Record, 80(1),* 1–18.

Meara, P. (1996). The Vocabulary Knowledge Framework. Vocabulary Acquisition Research Group Virtual Library. Swansea: Swansea University.

Meara, P. & Wolter, B. (2004). V_Links, beyond vocabulary depth. *Angles on the English Speaking World*, 4, 85-96.

Meisel, J.M, Clahsen, H. & Pienemann, M. (1981). On determining developmental stages in natural second language acquisition. *Studies in Second Language Acquisition, 3* (2), 109-135.

Moghadam, A. S., Karami, M. & Dehbozorgi, Z. (2015). Second language learning in autistic children compared with typically developing children: "Procedures and Difficulties". *Ανακτήθηκε στις, 30* (1).

Molway, L., Arcos, M., & Macaro, E. (2022). Language teachers' reported first and second language use: A comparative contextualized study of England and Spain. *Language Teaching Research, 26*(4), 642–670.

Na, D. & Nguyen, T. (2022). The Effects of using Pictures on EFL Learners' Vocabulary Retention. *International Journal of Emerging Trends in Social Sciences*, (13), 1-13.

Nakanishi, T. (2015), A Meta-Analysis of Extensive Reading Research. *Tesol Quarterly, 49*: 6-37.

Nassaji, H. (2017). Grammar acquisition. In Loewen and sat (2017) *The Routledge Handbook of Instructed Second Language Acquisition*. New York and London: Routledge.

Nassaji, H. & Fotos, S. (2004). Current Developments in Research on the Teaching of Grammar. *Annual Review of Applied Linguistics.* 24. 126-145.

Nassaji, H. & Fotos, S. (2011). *Teaching grammar in second language classrooms.* New York and London: Routledge.

Nation, I.S.P. (1989). Improving speaking fluency. *System, 17(3),* 377–384.

Nation, I.S.P. (2006). *Learning Vocabulary in Another Language* (1ˢᵗ ed.) Cambridge: Cambridge University Press.

Nation, I.S.P. (2007). The Four Strands. *Innovation in Language Learning and Teaching, 1 (1),* 2-13.

Nation, I.S.P. (2014). Developing fluency. In T. Muller, J. Adamson, P. S. Brown, & S. Herder (Eds.), *Exploring EFL Fluency in Asia* (pp. 11–25). Basingstoke: Palgrave.

Nation, I.S.P. (2022). *Learning Vocabulary in Another Language* (3ʳᵈ ed.) Cambridge: Cambridge University Press.

Nation, I.S.P. & Macalister, J. (2010). *Language Curriculum Design.* New York & London: Routledge.

Nation, I.S.P. & Newton, J. (2009) *Teaching ESL/EFL Listening and Speaking.* New York: Routledge.

Nation, I.S.P. & Yamamoto, A. (2012). Applying the Four Strands to Language Learning. *International Journal of Innovation in English Language Teaching,* 1 (2).
Available at: https://www.victoria.ac.nz/__data/assets/pdf_file/0003/1626123/2012-Yamamoto-Four-strands.pdf

Nemati, A. (2010). Active and passive vocabulary knowledge: The effect of years of instruction. *Asian EFL Journal, 12,* 30-46.

Norris, J. & Ortega, L. (2000). Effectiveness of L2 Instruction: A Research Synthesis and Quantitative Meta-Analysis. *Language Learning,* 50, 417-528.

NSW Curriculum K-10 Syllabus (accessed 2023). Available at:
https://curriculum.nsw.edu.au/syllabuses/modern-languages-k-10-2022

Nunes, J. C. & Drèze, X. (2006). The endowed progress effect: How artificial advancement increases effort. *Journal of Consumer Research, 32*(4), 504–512.

Ofsted Research Review Series: Languages (2022). Available at:
https://www.gov.uk/government/publications/curriculum-research-review-series-languages/curriculum-research-review-series-languages

O'Brien, M. G. (2019). Targeting pronunciation (and perception) with technology. In N. Arnold & L. Ducate (Eds.), Engaging language learners through CALL (pp. 309–352). Sheffield, UK, and Bristol, CT: Equinox Publishing Ltd.

O'Brien, M.G. (2021). Ease and Difficulty in L2 Pronunciation Teaching: A Mini-Review. *Frontiers in Communication.* L2 Phonology Meets L2 Pronunciation. Available at:
https://www.frontiersin.org/articles/10.3389/fcomm.2020.626985/full

Pachler, N, Evans, M., Redondo, A. & Fisher, L. (2014). *Learning to Teach Foreign Languages in the Secondary School.* London: Routledge.

Paivio, A. (1971). *Imagery and verbal processes.* New York: Holt, Rinehart and Winston.

Papachristou, E., Flouri, E., Joshi, H., Midouhas, E., & Lewis, G. (2022). Ability-grouping and problem behavior trajectories in childhood and adolescence: Results from a U.K. population-based sample. *Child Development,* 1, 341– 358. Available at :
https://srcd.onlinelibrary.wiley.com/doi/full/10.1111/cdev.13674

Parsons, S., & Hallam, S. (2014). The impact of streaming on attainment at age sevenEvidence from the Millennium Cohort Study. *Oxford Review of Education,* 40(5), 567– 589.

Pawlak, M. (2021). Explicit versus implicit grammar learning and teaching. Chapter in Macaro, E. and Woore, R. (eds.) *Debates in Second Language Education.* London: Routledge.

Pawley, A. & Syder, F.H. (1983).Two puzzles for linguistic theory: Nativelike selection and nativelike fluency. In: J. C. Richards & R. W. Schmidt (eds.), *Language and Communication.* pp.191-225.

Peters, H. (2020). Gender-inclusivity and gender-neutrality in foreign language teaching: the case of French. *Australian Journal of Applied Linguistics, 3 (3),* 183-195. Available at:
https://files.eric.ed.gov/fulltext/EJ1287702.pdf

Pica, T. (1996). Second Language Learning Through Interaction: Multiple perspectives. *Working Papers in Educational Linguistics,* 12/1.

Pienemann, M. (1998). *Language processing and second language development: Processability theory.* Amsterdam/Philadelphia: John Benjamins.

Pimsleur, P. (1966). *The Pimsleur Language Aptitude Battery.* New York: Harcourt.

Polat, N. (2016). *L2 Learning, Teaching and Assessment. A Comprehensible Input Perspective.* Multilingual Matters.

Potter, H., Marsden, E. & Hawkes, R. (2023). Rationales for supporting writing production in a foreign language. NCELP. Available at: https://resources.ncelp.org/

Prabhu, N.S. (1987). *Second Language Pedagogy.* New York, Toronto: Oxford University Press

Prabhu, N. S. (1990). There is no best method – why? *TESOL Quarterly, 24 (2),* 161-176.

Prabhu, N. S. (1992). The Dynamics of the Language Lesson. *TESOL Quarterly,* 26, 225-241.

Price, M.L. (1991). The subjective experience of foreign language anxiety: interviews with highly anxious students. In E.K. Horwitz, D.J. Young (Eds.), *Language anxiety: From theory and research to classroom implications,* (pp. 101–108). Englewood Cliff: Prentice Hall.

Prince, P. (1996). Second Language Vocabulary Learning: The Role of Context versus Translations as a Function of Proficiency. *The Modern Language Journal,* 80/4.

Printer, L. (2019). Student perceptions on the motivational pull of Teaching Proficiency through Reading and Storytelling (TPRS): a self-determination theory perspective. *Language Learning Journal, 49(3).* Available at: https://www.researchgate.net/publication/330601652_Student_perceptions_on_the_motivational_pull_of_Teaching_Proficiency_through_Reading_and_Storytelling_TPRS_a_self-determination_theory_perspective

Qian, D. D. (2002). Investigating the Relationship Between Vocabulary Knowledge and Academic Reading Performance: An Assessment Perspective. *Language Learning,* 52 (3), 513-536.

Raithby, K. & Taylor, A. (2020) *Teaching Literature in the A Level Modern Languages Classroom.* London: Routledge.

Ramage, G. (2012). *The Modern Language Teacher's Handbook.* London: Continuum.

Richards, H., Conway, C., Roskvist, A. & Harvey, S. (2013). Foreign language teachers' language proficiency and their language teaching practice. *The Language Learning Journal,* 41/2.

Richards, J. C. (1990). *The Language Teaching Matrix.* Cambridge: Cambridge University Press.

Richards, J. C. (2001). *Curriculum Development in Language Teaching.* Cambridge: CUP.

Richards, J. C. (2013). Curriculum Approaches in Language Teaching: Forward, Central, and Backward Design. RECL Journal, *44 (1),* 5-33. Available at: https://www.professorjackrichards.com

Richards, J. C. & Rodgers, T.S. (2014). *Approaches and Methods in Language Teaching.* Cambridge: Cambridge University Press.

Repetto C, Pedroli E, & Macedonia M. (2017). Enrichment Effects of Gestures and Pictures on Abstract Words in a Second Language. *Frontiers in Psychology, 8.* Article 2136.

Riener, C. & Willingham, D. (2010). The Myth of Learning Styles. *Change: The Magazine of Higher Learning.* 42, 32-35.

Robinson, P. (2005). Aptitude and second language acquisition. *Annual Review of Applied Linguistics, 25,* 46-73.

Roehr-Brackin, K. (2022). Explicit and implicit knowledge and learning of an additional language: A research agenda. *Language Teaching,* 1-19.

Rogers, J. & Cheung, A. (2018). Input spacing and the learning of L2 vocabulary in a classroom context. *Language Teaching Research.* 24.

Roesch, S.C. & Amirkhan, J. H. (1997). Boundary conditions for self-serving attributions: Another look at the sports pages. *Journal of Applied Social Psychology,* 27.

Rossiter, M., Derwing, T., Manimtim, L. & Thomson, R. (2010). Oral Fluency: The Neglected Component in the Communicative Language Classroom. *Canadian Modern Language Review*, 66: 94, 583-606. Available at :
https://www.researchgate.net/publication/228648705_Oral_Fluency_The_Neglected_Component_in_t he_Communicative_Language_Classroom

Rost, M. (2002). *Teaching and researching listening*. Harlow: Longman.

Ryan, R. M. & Deci, E. L. (2000). Self-determination theory and the facilitation of intrinsic motivation, social development, and well-being. *American Psychologist, 55*(1), 68–78.

Sánchez-Gutiérrez, C.H., Serrano, M.P. & García, P.R. (2019) The effects of word frequency and typographical enhancement on incidental vocabulary learning in reading, *Journal of Spanish Language Teaching,* 6:1, 14-31,

Schmidt, R. (1990). The role of consciousness in second language learning. *Applied Linguistics*, 11, 129–158.

Schmidt, R. (2010). Attention, awareness, and individual differences in language learning. In W. M. Chan, et. al *Proceedings of CLaSIC 2010*, Singapore, December 2-4 (pp. 721-737). Singapore: National University of Singapore, Centre for Language Studies.

Schmitt, N. (1998). Tracking the Incremental Acquisition of Second Language Vocabulary: A Longitudinal Study. *Language Learning*, 48: 281-317.

Schumann, J.H. (1986). Research on the acculturation model for second language acquisition. Journal of Multilingual & Multicultural Development, 7(5), 379-392.

Segalowitz, N. (2010). *Cognitive Bases of Second Language Fluency (1st ed.).* London; Routledge.

Selinker, L. (1972). Interlanguage. *International Review of Applied Linguistics*, 10.

Seo, S. (2014) Does Reading Aloud Improve Foreign Language Learners' Speaking Ability? GSTF Journal of Education, 2.

Sherrington, T. (2014). Dealing with Day-to-Day Differentiation. From the blog *teacherhead.com.* Available at: https://teacherhead.com/2014/02/01/dealing-with-day-to-day-differentiation/

Shinozuka, K., Shibata, S., & Mizusawa, Y. (2017). Effectiveness of Read-aloudInstruction on Motivation and Learning Strategy among Japanese College EFLStudents. *English Language Teaching 10*(4), 1-14.

Shintani, N. (2013). The Effect of Focus on Form and Focus on Forms Instruction on the Acquisition of Productive Knowledge of L2 Vocabulary by Young Beginning-Level Learners. *Tesol Quarterly*, 47: 36-62.

Shulman, L. (1987). Knowledge and teaching: foundations of the new reform in Harvard *Educational Review*. (57) 1, 1-22.

Singleton, D. (2017). Language aptitude: Desirable trait or acquirable attribute? *Studies in Second Language Learning and Teaching.* 7 (1), 89-103. Available at: https://files.eric.ed.gov/fulltext/EJ1137943.pdf

Skehan, P. (1989). *Individual Differences in Second-Language Learning.* London: Edward Arnold.

Skehan, P. (1998). *A cognitive approach to language learning.* Oxford: Oxford University Press.

Smith, S.P. (2023). *Becoming an Outstanding Languages Teacher* (2ⁿᵈ Edition). London: Routledge.

Smith, S.P. (2020). *50 Lesson Plans for French Teachers.* Independently published.

Smith, S.P & Conti, G. (2016). *The Language Teacher Toolkit* (1ˢᵗ Edition). Independently published.

Smith, S.P & Conti, G. (2021). *Memory: What Every Language Teacher Should Know.* Independently published.

Smoker, T. J., Murphy, C. E., & Rockwell, A. K. (2009). Comparing Memory for Handwriting versus Typing. *Proceedings of the Human Factors and Ergonomics Society Annual Meeting*, *53*(22), 1744–1747.

Spada, N. & Tomita, Y. (2010), Interactions Between Type of Instruction and Type of Language Feature: A Meta-Analysis. *Language Learning*, 60: 263-308.

Storch, N. (2002). Patterns of interaction in ESL Pair Work. *Language Learning, 52*, 119 - 158.

Strelau, J. (2000). Osobowo jako zespócech. In J. Strelau (Ed.), Psychologia. Podrncznik akademicki: Vol. 2. Psychologia ogólna (pp. 525-560). Gdansk: Gdanskie Wydawnictwo Psychologiczne.

Suk, N. (2017). The Effects of Extensive Reading on Reading Comprehension, Reading Rate, and Vocabulary Acquisition. *Reading Research Quarterly, 52(1),* 73-89

Sun, X. (2021). Revisiting postmethod pedagogy: Adopting and adapting Socratic circle to secondary EFL teaching. *TESOL Journal, 12.* Available at: https://onlinelibrary.wiley.com/action/showCitFormats?doi=10.1002%2Ftesj.601

Suzuki, J. (1998). A Reprisal of Reading Aloud: An Empirical Study on the Effectiveness of Reading Aloud (pp. 13-28). LET Kansai Chapter Collected Papers 7, Kobe, Hyogo: Rokko-Shuppan.

Suzuki, Y. & DeKeyser, R. (2017). The interface of explicit and implicit knowledge in a second language: Insights from individual differences in cognitive aptitudes. *Language Learning,* 67, 747-790.

Swain, M. (1993). The output hypothesis: Just speaking and writing aren't enough. *Canadian Modern Language Review,* 50.

Swan, M. (2006). Teaching grammar – does grammar teaching work? *Modern English Teacher 15(2).* http://www.mikeswan.co.uk/elt-applied-linguistics/teaching-grammar.htm

Sweller, J. (1988). Cognitive Load During Problem Solving: Effects on Learning. *Cognitive Science, 12,* 257-285.

Taguchi, N. (2009). Corpus-informed assessment of L2 comprehension of conversational implicatures. *TESOL Quarterly, 43,* 738-749. Available at : https://www.researchgate.net/publication/229784031_Building_Language_Blocks_in_L2_Japanese_Chunk_Learning_and_the_Development_of_Complexity_and_Fluency_in_Spoken_Production

Thomson, R. I. & Derwing, T. (2015). The Effectiveness of L2 Pronunciation Instruction: A Narrative Review. *Applied Linguistics, 36(3),* 326-344.

Tian, L. & Jiang, Y. (2021). L2 Proficiency Pairing, Task Type and L1 Use: A Mixed-Methods Study on Optimal Pairing in Dyadic Task-Based Peer Interaction. *Frontiers in Psychology.* Available at: https://www.frontiersin.org/articles/10.3389/fpsyg.2021.699774/full

Towell, R., Hawkins, R. & Bazergui, N. (1996). The development of fluency in advanced learners of French. *Applied Linguistics,* 17 (1) 84–119.

Treffers-Daller, J. & Milton, J. (2013) Vocabulary size revisited: the link between vocabulary size and academic achievement. *Applied Linguistics Review, 4 (1),* 151-172.

Tribushinina, E., Dubinkina-Elgart, E. & Mak, P. (2022). Effects of early foreign language instruction and L1 transfer on vocabulary skills of EFL learners with DLD. *Clinical Linguistics & Phonetics.* 1-18.

Truscott, J. (1996), The Case Against Grammar Correction in L2 Writing Classes. *Language Learning, 46,* 327-369.

Turnbull, M. & Arnett, K. (2002). Teachers' uses of the target and first languages in second and foreign language classrooms. *Annual Review of Applied Linguistics, 22,* 204–218.

Ullman, M. (2006). The declarative/procedural model and the shallow structure hypothesis. *Applied Psycholinguistics,* 27, 97-105.

Uludag, P., McDonough, K., & Payant, C. (2021). Does Prewriting Planning Positively Impact English L2 Students' Integrated Writing Performance? *Canadian Journal of Applied Linguistics, 24 (3).* Available at: https://www.erudit.org/en/journals/cjal/2021-v24-n3-cjal06641/1084815ar.pdf

Ur, P. (1981). *Discussions that Work.* Cambridge: Cambridge University Press.

Ur, P. (1988). *Grammar Practice Activities.* Cambridge: Cambridge University Press

Ur, P. (1996). *A Course in Language Teaching: Practice and Theory.* Cambridge: Cambridge University Press.

Usher, E. L. & Pajares, F. (2008). Sources of self-efficacy in school: Critical review of the literature and future directions. *Review of Educational Research,* 78(4), 751–796.

Vafaee, P. (2016). The relative significance of syntactic knowledge and vocabulary knowledge in second language listening comprehension. Unpublished doctoral thesis. Available at: https://drum.lib.umd.edu/bitstream/handle/1903/18320/Vafaee_umd_0117E_17069.pdf?sequence=1&isAllowed=y

Vandergrift, L. (2002). It was nice to see that our predictions were right: Developing metacognition in L2 listening comprehension. *The Canadian Modern Language Review, 58*, 555-575.

VanPatten, B. (2015). Foundations of processing instruction. *International Review of Applied Linguistics in Language Teaching*, 53 (2), 91-109.

VanPatten, B. (2017). *While We're on the Topic*. American Council on the Teaching of Foreign Languages.

Van Zeeland, H. & Schmitt, N. (2013). Incidental vocabulary acquisition through L2 listening: A dimensions approach. *System*, 41, 609–624.

Vold, E.T. & Brkan, A. (2020). Classroom discourse in lower secondary French-as-a-foreign-language classes in Norway: Amounts and contexts of first and target language use. *System, 93*. Available at: https://www.duo.uio.no/bitstream/handle/10852/78389/Classroom%2Bdiscourse%2Bin%2Blower%2Bsecondary%2BFrench-as-a-foreign-language%2Bclasses%2Bin%2BNorway_%2BAmounts%2Band%2Bcontexts%2Bof%2Bfirst%2Band%2Btarget%2Blanguage%2Buse.pdf?sequence=2

Vroom, V.H. (1964). *Work and motivation.* Wiley.

Walter, C. (2008). Phonology in second language reading: not an optional extra. Tesol Quarterly, 42 93), p. 455-474.

Wang, Y. (2021). Building Teachers' Resilience: Practical Applications for Teacher Education of China. *Frontiers in Psychology, 12*. Available at: https://www.frontiersin.org/articles/10.3389/fpsyg.2021.738606/full

Webb, S. (2007). The Effects of Repetition on Vocabulary Knowledge. *Applied Linguistics, 28 (1),* 46-65.

Wen, Z. (2016). *Working memory and second language learning: Towards an integrated approach.* Bristol: Multilingual Matters.

Widdowson, H. (2002). Language teaching: Defining the subject. In H. Trappes-Lomax (ed.), *Language in Language Teacher Education.* Amsterdam: John Benjamins.

Widdowson, H. (2003). *Defining Issues in English Language Teaching.* Oxford: OUP.

Wilkins, D. A. (1972). *Linguistics in Language Teaching.* Cambridge: MFT Press.

Wiliam, D. (2011.) What assessment can – and cannot – do. Originally published in Swedish translation as *Bryggan mellan undervisning och lärande* (The bridge between teaching and learning) in the September 16, 2011 issue of *Pedagogiska Magasinet*, a Swedish education journal.

Wiliam, D. (2021). Formative assessment in 2050: Possibilities and challenges. Online article for European Schoolnet. Available at: https://www.assessforlearning.eu/news/article?id=230170

Wiliam, D. (2023). Mind the Gap podcast with Tom Sherrington and Emma Turner. John Catt. Available at: https://www.youtube.com/watch?v=7ynsMwzsCsg

Williams, M. & Burden, R. (1997). *Psychology for Language Teachers.* Cambridge: Cambridge University Press.

Willis, D. (2003). *Rules, patterns, and words. Grammar and lexis in English language teaching.* Cambridge: Cambridge University Press.

Wilson, J.J. (2008). *How to Teach Listening.* Pearson Education Limited.

Winstanley, C. (2005) Investigating the notion of children with multiple exceptionalities' Occasional Paper No. 6, Warwick: NAGTY. Available at: http://www.nagty.ac.uk/research/occasional_papers/documents/occasional_paper6.pdf

Wood, D. (2006). Uses and Functions of Formulaic Sequences in Second Language Speech: An Exploration of the Foundations of Fluency. *The Canadian Modern Language Review*, 63 (1), 13-33.

Wood, D. (2010). D. *Formulaic language and second language speech fluency: Background, evidence, and classroom applications*. London/New York: Continuum.

Woore, R. (2022). What can second language acquisition research tell us about the phonics 'pillar'? *The Language Learning Journal, 50(2),* 172-185.

Woore R., Graham, S., Courtney, L., Porter, A., & Savory, C. (2018). Foreign Language Education: Unlocking Reading (FLEUR) A study into the teaching of reading to beginner learners of French in secondary school. Available at: https://ora.ox.ac.uk/objects/uuid:4b0cb239-72f0-49e4-8f32-3672625884f0/download_file?file_format=pdf&safe_filename=Woore_et_al_Foreign_Language_Education_Unlocking%2BReading-FLEUR_.pdf&type_of_work=Report

Wright, T. (2002). Doing language awareness: issues for language study in teacher education. In H. Trappes-Lomax (ed.), *Language in Language Teacher Education.* Amsterdam: John Benjamins.

Xu, X., Kauer, S. & Tupy, S. (2016). Multiple-choice questions: Tips for optimizing assessment in-seat and online. *Scholarship of Teaching and Learning in Psychology, 2,* 147-158. Available at: https://www.researchgate.net/publication/303957288_Multiple-choice_questions_Tips_for_optimizing_assessment_in-seat_and_online

Yalden, J. (1987). *Principles of course design for language teaching.* New York: Cambridge University Press

Yan, J.X. & Horwitz, E.K. (2008), Learners' Perceptions of How Anxiety Interacts With Personal and Instructional Factors to Influence Their Achievement in English: A Qualitative Analysis of EFL Learners in China. *Language Learning,* 58: 151-183.

Young, D.J. (1991). Creating a low-anxiety classroom environment: what does language anxiety research suggest? *The Modern Language Journal,* 75, 426–439.

Zheng, Y. & Cheng, L. (2018) How does anxiety influence language performance? From the perspectives of foreign language classroom anxiety and cognitive test anxiety. *Language Testing in Asia, 8,* 13.

INDEX

Made in United States
Orlando, FL
28 June 2023

34607141R00198